Homeopathy for Diseases

Vital Remedies for Epidemics, Trauma and Chronic Diseases

Homeopathy *for* Diseases

Vital Remedies for Epidemics, Trauma and Chronic Diseases

Peter Chappell, Hon FS Hom
Harry van der Zee, MD

Homeolinks Publishers

Important notice: Medicine, like every other science, is subject to continuous development. Research and clinical experience broaden our knowledge, particularly as far as treatment and medical therapy are concerned. Whenever there are dosages or applications mentioned in this manual, the reader may rest assured that the author, editor and publishers have taken great care to ensure that the information given represents the standard of knowledge at the time of completion of this book.

However, the publishers cannot assume responsibility as far as the information on dosage and form of application of the remedies is concerned. Each user of this manual is asked to please check, by carefully studying the patient information data and where necessary consulting a specialist, whether the indicated recommendation for dosage or possible contraindications in this book harmonise with the information given in the patient information data or by the specialist. This kind of verification is particularly important in cases of rarely used medicines or in the case of newly introduced items. Every dosage or application is made at the user's own risk. The authors and the publishers appeal to each user to please pass on possible inaccuracies that come to his or her notice.

Protected trade names (trademarks) are not marked in any special way. Therefore, it should not be assumed from the lack of such a mark that the trade name is free.

Title:	**Homeopathy for Diseases**
Subtitle:	**Vital Remedies for Epidemics, Trauma and Chronic Diseases**
Authors:	**Peter Chappell, Hon FS Hom & Harry van der Zee, MD**
Correctors:	**Candace Charlton, Corrie Hiwat & Jenni Tree**
ISBN/EAN	**ISBN/EAN: 978-94-90453-07-7**
Cover design:	**Maurits Peerbolte, Xsample mediavormgeving**
Lay–out:	**Maurits Peerbolte, Xsample mediavormgeving**
Publisher:	**Homeolinks Publishers**
	P.O. Box 68
	9750 AB Haren
	Netherlands
	Fax: +31 (0)50 5341252
	E-mail: office@homeolinks.nl
	Website: www.homeolinks.nl
Printer:	**Drukkerij Scholma BV**
	Bedum, Netherlands

Table of Contents

Foreword

If you haven't read this book you might well wonder if a disease specific approach is homeopathic. It seems like a contradiction in terms, the juxtaposition of homeopathy and diseases. It sounds like clinical homeopathy, which is often regarded as violating the fundamental homeopathic laws or at least as an inferior form of homeopathy.
Classical homeopathy in which each and every case is individualized is the true and only form of homeopathy. And we agree individualized homeopathy is the highest expression of the art and science of homeopathy ... for individual problems and diseases.

However, for clearly collective conditions like epidemic diseases, Hahnemann himself already showed that it is necessary to individualise for the disease itself. This we know as the Genus epidemicus. Here we are still individualizing but now for a disease that affects a much larger totality than that of a single individual.

Working with epidemics in Africa we found that individualizing for a disease is indeed extremely effective.

To increase the efficacy and to make the treatment modality available to health professionals who have little or no skills in homeopathy we found a way to narrow the number of resonances for a specific condition to one. This, of course, is in common with conventional medicine, with one big difference; whereas conventional medicine attacks symptoms and vectors etc., homeopathy aids natural recovery by stimulating the immune system.
This was often more a great theory than reality within the homeopathic Materia Medica, given that a number of remedies may be needed to cover a disease totality, from which a prescriber would have to select the right one for the patient. (Using Mercury for syphilis might be one exception to this.) By using a new method of creating disease specific remedies – PC Resonances – we have made it possible to use one remedy for an epidemic disease. This represents a breakthrough for Africa, where epidemics are rampant and homeopaths scarce.

Later we found this also works extremely well as a collective approach to trauma. This is especially so for collective trauma as in wars and natural catastrophes, again, a great advantage for places like Africa where medical help is scarce, let alone homeopathic treatment, and also a great advantage in situations where thousands or even millions of people are traumatised.

An even more challenging step in the process we have experienced in the past decade is the discovery that a disease specific approach is also viable for chronic diseases. We came to understand that chronic diseases are in part long running epidemic diseases transmitted by the epigenetic process (which explains the homeopathic miasm concept in scientific terms.) Thus epidemic principles apply to chronic diseases.

The fact that this approach will almost always be used in combination with individualized treatment, the one complementing the other, and where homeopathic skills are essential to reach a cure, is what makes this approach viable.

Some of the PC Resonances have been proven by conventional homeopathic proving methods, and the proving symptoms had significant correspondences to the disease for which they were designed.

PC Resonances are provided as core stocks to homeopathic pharmacies and then produced by potentisation for dispensing.

In this book you can read how we argue cogently that the principles and practice of using PC Resonances correspond to the principles and practices already outlined by the founder of homeopathy in his Organon. They also require identical methods of case management and in reality only homeopaths know how to use PC Resonances for chronic diseases intelligently without additional training.

We call them PC Resonances to differentiate them from remedies made from material substances. But remedies made from material substances are not the only source of homeopathic resonances. For example some of Hahnemann's remedies, those connected to magnetism come from nonmaterial sources.

For all these reasons we conclude that PC Resonances come within the spectrum of homeopathy. The theory that we extensively discuss makes *Homeopathy for Diseases* legitimate homeopathy. The number of case examples of a wide variety of epidemic diseases, forms of trauma and chronic diseases treated with PC Resonances provides the required confirmation in everyday practice.

For those who have been asking us to explain how PC Resonances are being made this book offers the long awaited answer. We trust we have taken the right decision by revealing the process, as we trust that PC Resonances will reach those who are meant to receive them.

Peter Chappell & Harry van der Zee
April 2012

Introduction

This book is about advances within homeopathic medicine that on the one hand build on two centuries of homeopathic philosophy and practice and on the other hand incorporate modern views and techniques to further improve the success of homeopathy.

The reason for writing this book is that both the level and the collective nature of suffering on the planet demand that homeopathy looks at the larger picture. This means in practice that the classical individual approach alone is often insufficient. To render consistent and lasting results, collective derangements of the vital force need also to be recognised and addressed.

In Part I of this book we present the basic theory of how this can effectively be done and as simply as possible. In each following Part we present case studies to show the practicalities of this new system, which has been tested in over 20,000 cases on a variety of continents for a wide range of indications.

We have concentrated most of the theory in Parts II-V.
In Part II we provide the theory of treating infectious and epidemic diseases.
In Part III we provide the theory of treating trauma.
In Part IV we provide the theory of treating intoxication including vaccination damage.
In Part V we provide the theory of treating chronic diseases.
In Part VI you find a summary of all the new theory plus practical instructions on how to use PC Resonances.

In the following Parts VII – X we provide the practice of treating the conditions whose theory has been discussed in the previous four parts.
In Part VII we provide the practice of treating infectious and epidemic diseases.
In Part VIII we provide the practice of treating trauma.
In Part IX we provide the practice of treating intoxication including vaccination damage.
In Part X we provide the practice of treating chronic diseases.

In the remaining Parts XI and XII we present provings and discuss sound as carrier for healing information.

In Part XIII we present a hypothesis of how, based on the unified field of science, homeopathy and PC Resonances in particular could be used to create coherence in the collective.

Part XIV discusses future advances of PC Technology and Part XV is the conclusion.

Those who only wish to read the general theory may omit the chapters on specific diseases and case presentations – Parts VI-IX. In these Parts however, theoretical discussions are included where we feel we have meaningful information to share.

Those wishing to learn how to treat a specific condition can read the simple general instructions in Part I and then directly go to the chapter discussing the specific disease or condition.

We hope that the way we have organised this book makes it easy for each reader to derive from it what is sought.

To shorten the still extensive chapter on AIDS we have moved a part of the information we wish to share to Appendix 1. In Appendix 2 you find information on Amma Resonance Healing Foundation and in Appendix 3 shamanic journeys to microbes by Eileen Nauman. Appendix 4 is on the inner workings of survival instincts.
In Appendix 5 all available PC Resonances are listed.

We have written this book with a wide audience and homeopaths in mind. It was unavoidable that for some areas homeopathic expertise is assumed as the theory and practice discussed there requires homeopathic skills.

Although in most homeopathic practices the treatment of chronic diseases is the main area of focus, it comes last in this book. The main reason is that this book is mainly concerned with a Genus epidemicus approach for epidemic diseases and trauma. The preparation and use of disease specific remedies for chronic diseases was and still is not the main focus of the authors, but nevertheless an outcome of our process that has given results we don't want to withhold from the reader.

Most homeopaths that have used PC Resonances will have done so for chronic diseases. The disease specific approach on which PC Resonances are based is actually far from as consistently reliable in chronic diseases as it is in epidemics and trauma. The simple explanation is that individualizing the case is far more important in the treatment of chronic diseases, and even essential in the vast majority of cases. This means that a successful use of a disease specific approach for chronic diseases is highly dependent on the skills of the homeopath to prescribe individually as well, and to manage the case properly.

There are web sites describing the new technology:

- www.vitalremedies.com
- www.healingdownloads.com
- www.arhf.nl
- www.trauma-healing.org
- www.aidshealing.org

The Human Story

Peter's story

The methodology and resonances described in this book are revolutionary but were never intended to be that. They were born out of a heartfelt desire by Peter Chappell to help the millions of people in Africa who suffer from AIDS, and because the available homeopathic Materia Medica at that time lacked a suitable simillimum for HIV/AIDS. It was not renewal and extension of homeopathy that was sought but healing for patients who often were lacking any kind of medical care. It was again not the desire for a new development in homeopathy that inspired this to come into existence but compassion for a neglected continent and its people. The development of trauma resonances was also not intended but simply called for when in Rwanda in 2005 it appeared that AIDS patients were still heavily traumatised from the genocide in 1994 and would only be able to completely heal from their AIDS-related symptoms if their Post-Traumatic Stress Disorder would also be treated.

The discovery that making a disease specific resonance for a so-called chronic disease is possible is another accidental result of working with diseases in Africa (where there are few resources, many language barriers, and little time) while yet having the technology to create resonances for a cause. Whereas in the West, chronic disease remedies need to be used within a comprehensive treatment plan starting with the individualized remedy, this works often in a stand-alone way in Africa, because for generations people in the West have stored toxic emotional pain memories deep inside.

Another revolutionary option of using music or images as the carrier of healing information homeopathic to a disease was not born of a desire to create something new, but of the necessity to find a way to spread healing resonances in situations like a pandemic, where due to the predictable panic and failure of normal distribution systems, usual pills and potions would not reach the millions needing them. Although this book also discusses transmitters other than water for carrying healing information, the main focus is on using granules and dropper bottles, as homeopaths have successfully done for over two hundred years.

Harry's story

As editor of *Homoeopathic Links* Harry van der Zee was in close contact with Peter Chappell since 2001. This started with a letter to the editor in which Peter called for help to find a simillimum for HIV/AIDS in Africa. It was at a homeopathic congress in 2003 where Peter was one of the speakers presenting his results with PC1, as he had called the resonance he had developed, that Harry really became inspired by realizing the potential of Peter's project. A case 'accidentally' presented at the same congress showed how a deeply depressed homosexual man dramatically transcended his depression after being prescribed PC1 for being HIV-positive. Where all other homeopathic remedies had failed to relieve his depression, PC1 triumphed. Before PC1 the patient could not imagine that anybody could ever love him, and the only purpose he could find in his life was to kill himself. After PC1 he was radiant and in tears told how he now loved anyone, anything. This case showed that PC1 was not only able to treat the symptoms of AIDS, as Peter had shown in his presentation, but apparently also touched what could be considered to be the core of the epidemic – a lack of love, care and responsibility for oneself and others that causes the epidemic to continue. A subsequent journey to Malawi, where Peter had treated a large number of patients, convinced Harry of the long-term effects of PC1 after which he offered his help to promote the treatment.

Our story

Considering the above one could say that this book came into existence by accident. In a perfect universe though there are no accidents, so we gladly believe that we were and are at the right place and at the right time and that all we ever did before led up to who and where we are now and to what we are presently doing.

Our belief is that the development and experience of using resonances (of which homeopathic remedies are one example), for epidemic diseases, trauma and chronic diseases, justifies the writing of this book. Although in many ways this is all still at grassroots level, evidence in the form of successful cases is quantitatively and qualitatively such that the validity of the method and the efficacy of the resonances used are now beyond reasonable doubt for those with open minds. Having said that, we realise that nevertheless a lot of research is still needed, especially if we want to make resonances for epidemics and collective trauma available at a global level, as well as develop practical, evidence based, treatment protocols for chronic diseases.

We realise that the contents of this book could never have been written without the work of *Samuel Hahnemann*. This gifted founder of homeopathy and thousands of homeopaths after him, as also many others, served as inspiration. Although we as authors have written this book we realise that calling it 'our' book does not do justice to history, to all the patients and homeopaths who were open and willing to try out PC Resonances in practice, to the source from which we receive these resonances or to the true nature of a creative process in which inspiration is anything but personal. From Hahnemann to you the reader and all others instrumental in providing homeopathy for humanity, we wish to express our gratitude. We hope this book will be an inspiration for many and will serve the noble goal of healing the sick and transforming suffering on this planet into healthy and successful lifestyles and lives.

Without the rich history of homeopathy in the West and our experience in Africa the developments written down in these pages could not have evolved. Although especially in the West homeopaths can benefit enormously from the tools handed to them by the philosophy and practice of this book, this book is mainly written for Africa and other developing countries and for the people in those countries who are studying and applying homeopathy to reduce suffering and induce health. For them this book follows the Amma4Africa Manual and the Amma4Trauma Manual, which give concise overviews of homeopathy and provide tools to use PC Resonances for some of the major epidemics and trauma present in Africa. This book does not replace a homeopathic training for how to treat chronic conditions but offers the theory and practice of how a disease specific approach can complement the usual homeopathic approach in those cases.

The authors of this book started collaborating over the treatment of AIDS with a new type of homeopathic remedy in Africa, which was successfully demonstrated in its use in many countries. We called the new technology PC Technology and the created resonances PC Resonances. Peter wrote a book about the first years of this new development titled *The Second Simillimum*, which was published by Homeolinks Publishers in 2005. At that stage we talked to presidents, prime ministers, ministers of health and several other officials in various countries, to discuss the ways forward. Disappointingly, we never managed to make any significant inroads into the medical and political powers that be, and we never had the resources to mount a campaign that the breakthrough justified. In 2007 we formed a foundation called the Amma Resonance Healing Foundation (www.arhf.nl) to persevere with this work.

The next step in PC Technology development process was the treatment of collective trauma such as genocide in Rwanda and rape in Africa and the effects of earthquake induced trauma in Haiti, where we were able to demonstrate highly effective treatments. Another development was to use PC Technology as a complement to the classical (individualized) homeopathic approach for treating chronic diseases and there are examples of successful results here in this book.

Then came research into sports people and what limited their performance, which connected up with the study of genius and human potential research and epigenetics and the connection to the conscious mind. This allowed us to develop the technology further and to understand it better.

The journey of exploration continues.

Acknowledgements

The authors wish to honour Samuel Hahnemann. Homeopathy was his life's work, the magnitude of which still needs to penetrate the hearts and minds of many that can't believe that anything subtle, mild, safe, cheap and non-material can bring about cure. With a history of two centuries of homeopathy we are thankful to our teachers and those before them that have passed on the tradition and kept the philosophy and practice of homeopathy alive.

We are most grateful to the many patients who have put their trust in us and the remedies we provide for them. And also to the many colleagues that tried this new approach out in their practices.

We thank all those who have allowed us to include their case in this book. Their testimonies give substance to it and illustrate the philosophy behind it.

Our gratitude also goes to those that have made donations to our projects in developing countries. These individuals and foundations have made it possible for thousands of sick and traumatized people to receive help.

We wish to mention John Morgan of Helios pharmacy (UK), Martin Dicke of Hahnemann Apotheek (Netherlands) and Ulrike Breyha of Apotheke zum heiligen Florian (Austria). These pharmacies and their staff make PC Resonances available throughout the world and have supported us in many ways. They donate any profits from PC Resonances to support our work and have made remedies available at cost price for Amma Resonance Healing Foundation, so patients and health providers in developing countries can receive them for the lowest possible price, which often means for free.

Chetna Shukla (India), Katka Lucka (Czech Republic), Dana Stechow (Germany) and Priti Shah (India) have done blind provings of PC Resonances and through this have shown the similarity of PC Resonances and the conditions they are designed to treat.

Des Mervin has throughout the years developed and maintained several websites in support of our work without asking for any payment.

Rainer Steiner and Harald Walach have as researchers been very helpful in developing research protocols to study the efficacy of PC1 for HIV/AIDS.

In the heart of Africa Klaus Schustereder has tested many PC Resonances under difficult conditions as well as proved to be a valuable intellectual sparring partner. Nico Beentjes has undertaken several trips to Africa and Haiti to promote the solutions for epidemics and trauma that form the core of this book. Corrie Hiwat has joined Harry on trips to Malawi and South Africa and has been helpful in keeping our purposes and intentions clear. As Africa is where many PC Resonances were first used we are grateful to the many other homeopaths who had the courage to work and live in Africa and the openness of mind to use PC Resonances for their patients, as we are grateful to the many Africans that developed the skills to work with them for the benefit of their people. Thank you Joseph, Mary, Estnat, Rachael, Davis, Marie, Flory, Alain, Jules, Richard, Abel, Mariane, Gordon and the dozens of students, doctors and nurses we have trained. You truly are the ones carrying the torch that was lit in Ethiopia in 2002.

Anne Vervarcke was amongst the first to test the new concepts in this book in Europe and Wolfgang Brysch and Irene Schlingensiepen offered their hospitality and sharp minds in support of our projects. Monika Grühn has given stimulating feedback and suggestions, as have many others. Corrie Hiwat, Candace Charlton and Jenni Tree have made corrections to the manuscript and have given suggestions as to the content.

Hana Chappell and Bodhana Kabatova are thanked with gratitude for their continuing support. Craig Riddell is thanked fot his contribution to the section on survival instincts.

Margreet van der Zee is thanked for her support by accepting a regularly absent husband and the consequences of his exchanging a successful practice in the Netherlands for voluntary work in Africa.

All these wonderful people and many more not mentioned here we wish to thank from the bottom of our heart.

Part I
New Advances in Homeopathy

A Bird's Eye View of this Book

The authors of this book have decades of experience in individualised homeopathic treatment and are strong propagators of classical homeopathy. They have practised and taught it in dozens of countries. Through their work in developing countries – especially Africa – they have experienced that in many conditions there are collective roots that need to be considered and addressed with specifics. 'Specifics' is used in its homeopathic meaning as 'specific remedies for particular diseases, situations or recognized sets of symptoms'. This book discusses in detail the theory of using specifics in epidemics, trauma, intoxication and chronic diseases. It explains how to integrate specifics in daily homeopathic practice and thus improve the success of homeopathy.

Awaiting basic research that can explain the fundamental principles underlying homeopathy – the similia principle and especially the ability of water to memorise information - full acceptance of homeopathy and the many positive studies as to its efficacy are met with scepticism and disbelief. Owing to this the potential of homeopathy to relieve suffering at this time is only scarcely implemented and researched.

The new advances presented here were not developed to that purpose but might very well help to cross the bridge between the current western medical paradigm and the homeopathic paradigm. This is because, especially in the case of epidemics and collective trauma, this new development allows the use of homeopathic remedies within an allopathic treatment model. It combines the advances of homeopathy (safe, no side-effects, low costs, no therapy resistance) with those of allopathy (diagnosis).

Epidemics

For the treatment of epidemics Hahnemann had already developed the Genus epidemicus approach. Theoretically the treatment of an epidemic disease requires one homeopathic remedy specific to that disease because it's the same situation for everybody. The disease is not rooted in an individual derangement of the vital force as in the case of many chronic diseases, but has an external cause as it were and affects the collective. Although in principal one remedy would be sufficient, the homeopathic approach to epidemic diseases was generally not that simple because the remedies for each disease had not been found. Thus, in the approach of an epidemic usually a group of remedies fitting the totality of the symptoms was defined from which a homeopath would select the one mostly fitting an individual case.

The work from which this book is the result started in Africa with the successful treatment of AIDS in early 2002.

After thorough analysis of a number of AIDS-cases in Ethiopia we were not able to identify a homeopathic remedy in the extant Materia Medica that would cover the syndrome. In Africa we therefore created a new technology, which we call PC Technology, which allows the making of specific remedies for specific diseases. This development makes it possible to treat epidemic diseases with consistent results with PC Resonances. As only few skills and funds are needed this new method can easily be implemented worldwide.

It's important to see the simplicity here. Diagnosis = Remedy. The case taking process has been done by medical science by identifying diseases accurately, and all that is needed is the specific remedy.

This allowed us to treat AIDS with a high degree of success. After almost a decade we still think this is the best treatment available for AIDS. Thousands of people with AIDS have been successfully treated this way, including many five-year plus survival cases.

We extended this technology to treat other epidemic diseases and have shown it to be effective in the main epidemic diseases of Africa, such as malaria, tuberculosis and gonorrhoea.

Trauma

Trauma is universal and different forms of trauma can easily be identified. For the treatment of trauma homeopaths usually use a limited set of remedies, which is actually similar to the way epidemic diseases are approached. Typical traumas come from sudden events and mimic epidemics in many significant ways. This means that the Genus epidemicus approach can theoretically be used for different forms of trauma, and that also in trauma one single PC Resonance can be designed and prescribed to all suffering from a similar traumatic event. We have demonstrated that in situations like genocide, war and rape traumas it is possible to easily treat people with specific remedies for these traumas that otherwise would last a lifetime. The great advantage is that it is possible to treat thousands of people in a short amount of time. In 2010 for instance 10,000 people were successfully treated in Haiti for the trauma of natural catastrophe. In 2011 we treated 5,000 refugees for the trauma of war.

Intoxication

Toxins increasingly lower the vitality of the world population while vaccination programmes take the immune system out of balance resulting in a wide variety of conditions. To restore health to the world population, detoxification (detox from here) programmes are essential. It is possible to prepare a homeopathic detox remedy from any toxin or vaccine and apply these (without antidoting the beneficial effects of vaccination). Another option is to create general detox remedies as has been done with PC Technology. As an alternative to vaccination homeoprophylaxis deserves serious consideration and PC Resonances can prove to be a reliable tool, as in the treatment of diseases they have been shown to give more consistent results than the corresponding nosodes (E.g. *Tuberculinum* is not known to consistently cure tuberculosis, whereas the PC Resonance for TB in our experience does).

Chronic diseases

We then extended the ideas and principles of treatment to the treatment of chronic diseases, because we reasoned that chronic diseases are really the result of epidemic diseases, epigenetic effects and transgenerational trauma effects combined with toxins, which together become pathology. From this position we produced remedies for chronic diseases. When included in a proper homeopathic treatment plan, and used according to homeopathic case management, they are able to make a serious contribution to treating chronic diseases. This means in practice that besides the simillimum for the patient also a simillimum for the diseases can be prescribed, the one complementing the other. This new development we feel can improve the success rate in homeopathic practice significantly.

There has been an ongoing conflict between classical homeopathy (one remedy fitting the totality of the case) and clinical homeopathy (usually combinations of remedies to address specific tissues or conditions). Being the results of suppressed or unresolved infectious diseases and/or trauma we can consider chronic diseases as slow moving epidemics (what once started with an acute epidemic/infectious disease continues its action in chronic diseases). The theoretical consideration that a disease specific remedy (second simillimum) can complement the patient's specific remedy (first simillimum) is confirmed for a variety of diseases for which disease specific PC Resonances have been designed.

Hahnemann's theory of miasms underlying chronic diseases is one of the aspects that make it hard for contemporary medicine to take homeopathy serious. Modern science in the meantime though has moved ahead in the field of epigenetics, which provides a new foundation for explaining the transmission of trauma, diseases and much more, and redefines Hahnemann's concept of miasms in modern terminology. We will discuss epigenetics and its consequences for homeopathic treatment further on in this book.

Sound as carrier

We also made another leap of technology by impregnating these new resonant remedies into sound waves rather than homeopathic-like pills and have demonstrated that they have similar effects. This has many advantages, especially if the world were to face another serious epidemic disease as it did with the Spanish flu, which killed many tens of millions of people in a twelve week period. These resonances could be supplied via the internet worldwide in a matter of days to billions of people.

This in a nutshell is what we have to offer in this book. While building on the foundations of Hahnemann's legacy we will provide a lot of food for thought, use new scientific insights to support new advances in homeopathy, and present a good number of cases of a wide variety of conditions to serve as living proof of the validity of the theoretical discourses.

Resonance

Resonance is a critical part of the theory and practice of how PC Resonances work.

Without resonance we wouldn't have:

- voices
- mobile/cell phones
- television
- music
- atomic clocks
- pendulum clocks
- playground swings

- MRI scanners
- homeopathy

Mechanical resonance

Resonance is a common thread, and runs through almost every branch of ...

- engineering
- science
- our bodies

... and yet a lot of people have never studied it or know anything about it.
It is a bit like gravity: always there and taken for granted. However, gravity is a lot more tangible.
Resonance occasionally causes a bridge to collapse: the new Millennium Bridge in London was affected by unintended resonance from a thousand feet tramping across it at once on its first day in use. The collapse of the Old Tacoma Narrows Bridge, nicknamed Galloping Gertie, in 1940 is an example of resonance still regularly broadcast by TV-stations around the world until today. The catastrophic vibrations that destroyed the bridge were not due to simple mechanical resonance, but to a more complicated oscillation between the bridge and winds passing through it.

The physicist and inventor Nikola Tesla carried out resonance experiments at Colorado Springs, USA, which produced such powerful electrical tensions that they resulted in the creation of artificial lightning.

Due to their extremely low frequency, these waves could penetrate the earth without resistance, allowing Tesla to discover the resonance frequency of the earth.

This was later connected to brain alpha rhythms by Herbert König at Munich University.

Emotional resonance

On an emotional level, when Princess Diana died, there was a massive grief resonance in the UK especially, but also around the world. It is said she touched a million hearts. Likewise, 9/11 had a worldwide resonance, as did the recent Tsunami in Asia, the earthquake in Haiti and the demonstrating masses in Tunisia followed by Egypt and other Arab countries.

These are more subtle forms of resonance than physical resonance and perhaps much more powerful.
Being inspired by and copying the movements of great athletes is also a form of resonance.
Issues between children and parents are resonance in action.
What is difficult for us to deal with in a relationship with another person is that we hit the same resonance issue in them as we have. If, for example, we are irritated by their issue/attitude, it is resonating with a similar issue/attitude in us. If we deal with these issues in ourselves, they will stop bothering and resonating in us. The whole issue of projection as Jung called it works through resonance.

Resonance as a healing method works like this. It amplifies the problem briefly for a few seconds in a safe and specific way. It causes the traumatic memory – for example food, the idea of starving to death, which is probably the root of all eating disorders and all overeating – to increase.
By amplifying it briefly, our consciousness sees that the response is unrealistic and does not correspond to reality.

The natural processing then goes to work and files away anything that the resonance shows to be useful, resolving, dissolving and discarding the rest.
It is all done within seconds. It sees the food situation is OK, not urgent, and not likely to be a problem – there is no shortage, the shops are still full – and effectively jettisons this idea by resolving it internally.
This is how resonance works.

Homeopathy and resonance

Hippocrates, the Greek physician born in 460 BC on the island of Cos, became known as the founder of medicine and was regarded as the greatest physician of his time. Many doctors in the world today when receiving their licence take the Hippocratic oath, based on the original text that is included in the Declaration of Geneva.

Not all doctors taking the Hippocratic oath know that Hippocrates had already mentioned that there are two principles that can be used to cure symptoms. Substances can be used that create opposite symptoms – *Contraria Contraribus Curentur* – and substances can be used that can cause similar symptoms – *Similia Similibus Curentur*. The contraria principle is what underlies regular medicine that is based on suppressing symptoms and killing microbes that cause diseases. The similia principle is the one used in homeopathy. This principle is based on resonance, and it is this healing principle of resonance that according to Hippocrates is the superior one.

Samuel Hahnemann (1755 - 1843), for the first time in history systematically applied the similia rule as the underlying principle of homeopathy. *Similia Similibus Curentur* is also known as the *Law of Similars, Like Cures Like* or *Resonance.*

The nature and action of PC Resonances is similar in many ways to the homeopathic process. If we analyse a single homeopathic remedy, for example the famous *Arnica*, we know that the plant Arnica montana has its own conscious intelligence, which exists independent of any individual plant, but every individual plant is connected to it, in fact is a total expression of all the intelligence of the plant. It is the intelligence that keeps the plant regenerating from generation to generation. It is encapsulated within the seed.

When we make a homeopathic remedy from the plant we extract the conscious intelligence resonance of the plant by the potentisation process. When a person takes this resonance it creates a conscious response within the person and if the response corresponds to the message they need to hear, they will get better.

The selection of the homeopathic remedy is based on the totality of symptoms which if correctly and fully perceived reflects the message the person is externalizing and not able to 'internally hear'. A well-chosen resonance multiplies the strength of the message the person is resisting hearing, or is unable to hear. Then they may hear it and understand they are cured to the extent that the message is relevant.
It releases the energetic knot in them, and the energy can flow properly again, and depending on the depth of the message, the cure happens naturally.

PC Technology: Creating Intelligent Resonances

Critical to the development of PC Resonances was the development of a new technology of creating resonances, which we have called PC Technology.
Resonance is relatively well understood on the physical level, as we've discussed above. The way that homeopaths use resonances, with diseases and trauma, goes beyond the physical realm. Homeopathy uses the principle and practice of amplifying a derangement of the vital energy – a diseased state – to bring it to our attention. The amplification makes it stand out and the natural healing forces within us then pay attention to its implications and construct a natural solution. This is something our complex immune system – in the widest sense of the meaning – is extremely good at.

With the exception of the imponderables, homeopathic remedies are prepared using a method of potentisation of substances. In the preparation of PC Resonances we use a different source.

Homeopathy acknowledges the existence of an immaterial world that underlies the material world and all forms manifesting in it. Hahnemann chose the term *vital force* to point to this all pervading intelligence or life-giving principle. Homeopaths have used provings to contact the intelligence present in a wide variety of forms. Other traditions like shamanism have used similar or different techniques and contacted many dimensions of existence to find information that is meaningful on the human dimension. Together, all these traditions point to the existence of intelligence and consciousness on any possible level. Even modern physics suggests conscious intelligence as the fabric of the universe.
So, not only humans possess consciousness. Similar to visible light representing only a small part of a wide range of light frequencies, we can say there is a whole band of levels of consciousness, some of which we can easily perceive, while others are normally beyond our daily perception. As with provings they can be contacted provided we make the effort.

Not only do humans seek contact with other levels of intelligence, the opposite is also true. All cultures and religions narrate stories of how people have been able to be in contact with other forms of intelligence, and they all have their own names for them, like angels, devas, et cetera. Many traditions share the knowledge of what we could call beings of light that support planet earth and life on it.

The PC Resonances we have been working with are directly created from accessing what we may call an advanced intelligence source. We access an intelligence from a level of consciousness far in advance to that which has yet been generally achieved. Humans can access this level of consciousness but as it is beyond our daily consciousness we call this a source of advanced intelligence. What we, with our limited understanding, can share is that this intelligence is available to support evolution on planet earth and the human quest for enlightenment. We contact this intelligent source to create the resonance that we need to work with, for instance an epidemic disease, a form of trauma or a chronic disease. We do not make the resonances nor do we channel them by an altered state of consciousness. We access this intelligence by the procedure described below (see The Resonance Making Procedure).

We do this for two core reasons:

1. We want a resonance that covers the totality of a specific disease. This is not reliably found by homeopathic potentisation methods and homeopathic remedy sources, as it is very rare to find one substance in the current Materia Medica that has a complete

enough similarity to a disease. A simple glance at a repertory rubric for malaria for instance makes that clear. Jan Scholten has proposed one remedy for HIV/AIDS in Africa, but it is not clear whether it is a single substance remedy or a complex remedy. Jeremy Sherr who currently focuses on the Genus epidemicus for AIDS has narrowed it down to some fifteen remedies, a much more common outcome in the history of applying Genus epidemicus.

2 Besides covering the signs and symptoms of the disease, we want the resonance to also cover the intelligence of the disease so it can bring about an effect that fulfils the purpose of the disease. This deeper insight into the disease we can't provide ourselves, as we simply are not that intelligent. This core aspect of a disease is known at a super intelligent level and is included in the resonance made.

In this way a resonance is created with the highest possible similitude to the disease on all levels. In effect, based on our request an intelligent resonance is created to stimulate in the diseased person an intelligent response by the vital force.

Back tracking

Initially I (Peter) took decades to make the connection to what has been called super intelligence in myself and to develop it as a systematic process. It was a process that started off in the intelligences found in the shamanic journeying world and gradually I developed very specific affinities. From many specific experiences I gradually understood how the process worked. I carried out experiments in myself to locate all sorts of different levels of intelligence above and below my reality. I did this originally only to know it was possible.

In this period I at some point contacted the intelligence that now helps us by creating PC Resonances as a cooperative exercise. Now, who or what is this intelligence? Identity as we know it as humans is a concept based on our limited understanding of ourselves and the oneness of life. I tend to believe the thought that I'm Peter and that I'm separate from you, but I know this is not true. Peter is just a name, not who I am. So, I can't give you a name, an identity, for the intelligence that has teamed up with us. Only for the ease of discussion let's call this intelligence PCR. The actual contact and cooperation is based upon a way of identification that cannot easily be described in words. This is not an uncommon situation, as for example the taste of a strawberry cannot be easily communicated in words either. We can only know the taste of strawberries from the experience. This in a similar way is also true of working with PCR, which makes this connection a hard concept to explain. The true nature of the connection is more like a knowing awareness. A sort of awareness of a benign nature with infinite patience and kindness, a love that is likewise infinite and unfathomable. Although it seems to me that the gap between me as the human and PCR as a holder of consciousness is vast, to meet sort of half way has proved to be possible for me and for those I have trained.

It took me a long time, a decade or so, before I started to use this process deliberately because I didn't have an application. Actually I think while I was receptive I was at the same time stubbornly sceptical and disbelieving. It was only when I was faced with AIDS in Africa, and the seeming impossibility of finding an intelligent resonance (simillimum) for it, that I took a step into the unknown and began actively working with the intelligence PCR to help me make a first intelligent resonance. The fact that it worked absolutely beyond my imagination and was amazingly effective was for me an indication that I was definitely on the right track. Even though, at the same time I still found it completely unbelievable. Only reliable and consistent cures finally punctured my scepticism.

The starting point to use this principle to create the resonances for AIDS was reached in early January 2002 in Addis Ababa, where I ran an official AIDS clinic. I had already established it was possible using conventional homeopathy to obtain good improvements in AIDS cases, but it was labour-intensive and the results were not consistent.
The massive numbers of people suffering and dying and the very limited amount of available homeopaths in Africa demanded a simple and consistently reliable approach. So, my intention was to find a solution that could have wide application and could also be used by low skilled health professionals lacking any knowledge of homeopathy. My approach was similar to the traditional homeopathic approach, already established in the early days of homeopathy: a Genus epidemicus (ideally one remedy) for each epidemic (which of course is the same approach therapeutically as conventional medicine but with opposite intentions and effects). I extensively searched the homeopathic Materia Medica to find such a remedy and, despite the latest software and the help of many others, was not able to find it.

So I made a resonance for HIV/AIDS with the help of this specific advanced intelligent source of resonances.

This all came to fruition when AIDS patients returned from the realm of the 'almost dead' and very consistently recovered within two or three weeks. This showed clearly that intelligent resonance was possible and effective. Like all homeopathic remedies it was observed to be completely safe and free of side effects.

When I first established the way this could be done, it was an amazing experience. But I was also quite clueless about how to proceed further. It took me two years to really believe the consequences of what had been achieved.

PCR could be called a Preserver of a specific level of consciousness that has teamed up with us as we share similar goals for decreasing suffering and increasing awareness on planet earth.

The next important step was that my colleagues and I found this new technology to work more generally in epidemic diseases and that it could be further developed and applied to a whole range of human diseases and conditions. This extension took years to formulate theoretically and then to apply it practically.

Also, step-by-step over a decade, I learned to connect this source of intelligent resonances not only to substances like liquids, but to sounds and video.

I had to break through many barriers of my own personal disbelief to make these steps: some of them took years.

In this period I doubted whether or not to reveal the way these resonances are made. Homeopathy is unorthodox by itself and this new development is even further removed from mainstream physical medicine. Would revealing my method serve the purpose of making PC1 available to as many AIDS-patients as possible? Would it be beneficial to the acceptance and use of all other PC Resonances? Because of these doubts I have previously been deliberately vague and deceptively obscure about the PC Technology.

Incidentally, as the rights of the technology of making PC Resonances for epidemics and trauma have been donated to the Amma Resonance Healing Foundation, it is not commercial considerations that made us hold on to the usual concept of IP (intellectual property).

We've come to understand that it is not our business whether others accept the existence of intelligence beyond the normal human condition and this new development that is based on it. We realize this is up to any person that hears or reads about it to decide for him- or herself. We've always known that keeping secrets is not the way in which we wish to relate to others. But even though we felt unhappy with it we, for a long time, saw no other way.
As we see it now, these remedies are available to us for the benefit of humanity and there is no way in which we own them in the conventional materialistic way of thinking. Super intelligence works beyond the concepts of material reality like money, greed or IP.

As said earlier, it has taken a long process for me (Peter) to reach the moment in time where I felt inspired and was able to facilitate the making of these intelligent resonances. Having come to this point though, it has proved possible to teach others to do the same, so the possibility to renew stock or create new remedies no longer depends on the availability of one person. There is now a secure team in place to ensure continuity.

We will now explain as much as we can the process of preparing a PC Resonance, which doesn't mean that this is a manual to make them. You would need to be introduced to the PCR source, the source of consciousness. You need to receive a key to PCR, as it were, from the key keeper, which is Peter.

The resonance making procedure

A PC Resonance is created by

- Connecting to the source of advanced intelligent resonances (for which you need training)
- Requesting an intelligent resonance.
- For a specific disease or state (typically a well-known medical diagnosis)
- Including the deeper meaning and purpose of it.
- Providing a sample in which the resonance is made. The sample stock/substance can be a liquid, an MP3-like sound file, or a video file, et cetera.

After having followed these steps the intelligence resonance precipitates in the correct form into the substance.

For the preparation of granules and dropper bottles the master tinctures are sent to the pharmacies that provide PC Resonances. Following an agreed special standardised potentisation-like protocol they prepare fresh tubes of granules or fresh dropper bottles on demand.

Homeopathic remedies over 200 years old are reported to still be active and we have no indication that PC Resonances lose their action with time either. This includes the pharmacy core stocks and the stocks dispensed to homeopaths. Even though pharmacies have to follow the regulations and therefore work with it, the conventional concept of expiry date does not apply for PC Resonances and homeopathic remedies in general. An important practical prerequisite of course is that they should be kept under reasonable conditions. Unfortunately, homeopathy has yet to develop the equipment to measure the activity of remedies and to show that conventional expiry dates do not apply.

Practical instructions on how to effectively use PC Resonances are found in Part VI.

Part II

Infectious and Epidemic Diseases

History of Homeopathy and Epidemics

The efficacy of homeopathic treatment remains a hot item in many medical journals and also in the general press. If there is one field of medicine where homeopathy more than deserves acknowledgement it is that of epidemics.

Long before antibiotics and improved hygiene started to change the impact of epidemics in the western world, homeopathy was used with great success in several epidemics like cholera and the Spanish flu.

In the American Homeopath (1998 – 'As If One Patient') *Greg Bedayn* describes how Hahnemann discovered how to treat epidemic diseases:

> "In 1799 Hahnemann first applied the genus epidemicus; the single homeopathic remedy to treat a similarly affected population, during a scarlet fever epidemic he treated in Königslutter, Germany. The story of how he accidentally discovered the genus epidemicus is interesting: There was a large family that had members with scarlet fever.
> Hahnemann noticed that one of the children who had been taking Belladonna for another reason did not have symptoms of scarlet fever. He discovered that by giving the other members of the family Belladonna, as a prophylactic, they did not get scarlet fever. Hahnemann concluded that a remedy that rapidly cures at the onset of an illness would be the best preventative.
> This serendipitous discovery led Hahnemann into developing the principle of genus epidemicus – where if one takes the symptom-totality from each person in a epidemic population and then puts those features together into one case, as if one person, and gives the indicated simillimum to the entire affected population – that it will cure."

This approach, as Hahnemann found out, worked well. Bedayn continues:

> "The curative results of the genus epidemicus were so positive during the epidemics in the ensuing decades that they not only cured the majority of those affected where nothing else had worked, but they also drew international acclaim towards homeopathy, the new, the rational, medicine. There is something intrinsically powerful about the success of homeopathy in curing large populations that is undeniably attractive to anyone gifted with the power of observation, and it was through these early cures with epidemics that Hahnemann was able to quickly and widely spread the word: Homeopathy.

It was from his discovery of the genus epidemicus that Hahnemann later developed his theory of miasms; the taints that colour and shape all family trees, as representing the basis of chronic disease."

Hahnemann later writes about the Genus epidemicus principle in his *Organon §101*:

> "It is possible that a physician meeting with the first case of a certain epidemic should fail to perceive at once its perfect image, because every collective disease of this kind will not manifest the totality of its symptoms and character until several cases have been carefully observed. But after having observed one or two cases of this kind a physician may approach the true condition of the epidemic that he is enabled to construe a true characteristic image of the same and to discover the true homoeopathic remedy." [Hahnemann, Samuel, Organon of the medical art, sixth edition 1842, edited and annotated by Wendy Brewster O'Reilly, Birdcage Books, Redmond 1996]

Hahnemann broadens this general principle in §102, when he says the complete knowledge is only to be obtained in a perfect manner by observations of the affections of several patients of different bodily constitutions. [ibid.]

In several sources we can find proof of the success of the 'as if one person' approach in epidemic diseases:

> In epidemics the mortality per 100 patients is 'one in two' to 'one in eight' in homeopathic hospitals, compared to allopathic hospitals. [Bradford, 1900]

> In the Russian provinces Saratoff, Tambtoff and Twer, in the years 1830 and 1831, 1270 patients suffering from cholera were treated with homeopathy: 1162 of these were cured, 108 died ... Similar results with homeopathic treatment in cholera were reported in Hungary, Mähren and Vienna. [Gebhardt, 1929]

> When in the year 1854 cholera came to Palermo, 1,513 soldiers fell ill ... Of these 902 were treated with allopathy of which 386 died, a bit more than 42%; 611 were treated with homeopathy, of which only 25, so almost 4%, died. [ibid.]

> In the abovementioned years cholera also visited the Caribbean, and on the 'pearl' of these islands, Barbados, 2113 people fell ill. Of the 346 treated with allopathy 154 died, but of the 1767 treated with homeopathy only 370. [ibid.]

> 3% of the cholera patients under homeopathic treatment died (Cincinnati 1849). The mortality rate of cholera patients under allopathic treatment was 40 - 70%. [Humphreys 1849]

> "Homeopathy had become very popular in North America during its early years due to its amazing successes obtained by the 'old guard' during the epidemics – epidemics of diphtheria, scarlet fever, cholera, malaria, yellow fever – especially yellow fever; the death rate for that was 55% when allopathic treatment was used, but less than 5% in cases with homeopathic treatment; and it was the same for cholera. It is here with the 'old guard' that homeopathy obtained its golden letters." [Saine, 1994]

> The success of the homeopathic treatment of yellow fever was so great that the report of the United States Government's Board of Experts mentioned several homeopathic remedies, despite the aversion to homeopathy of some of its members. [Coulter, 1982]

> Homeopathic treatment of the Spanish influenza during the pandemic of 1914-1918 was effective. [Golden, 2004]

> "Dean W.A. Pearson of Philadelphia collected 26,795 cases of influenza treated by homeopathic physicians with a mortality of 1.05%, while the average old school mortality was 30%. Explanation: conventional treatment of folks with flu caused at least 8,038 deaths while the homeopaths lost only 281 patients. That is a statistically significant difference."

> "Thirty physicians in Connecticut responded to my request for data. They reported 6,602 cases with 55 deaths, which is less than 1%. In the transport service (during WWI) I had 81 cases on the way over. All recovered and were landed. Every man received homeopathic treatment. One ship (using conventional therapy) lost 31 on the way. H.A. Roberts, MD, Derby, Connecticut." (Explanation: a number of homeopathic physicians served in the Armed Forces during WWI and made use of their homeopathic training.) [Dearborn, 1923; Dewey, 1921]

> Ever since Samuel Hahnemann homeopathy has time and again been able to successfully treat epidemics/pandemics with a small number of remedies. [Stahl, Hadulla, Richter, 2006]

It should be mentioned that conventional treatment at that time often did patients more harm than good. Nonetheless the overwhelming evidence shows that homeopathy is highly effective in epidemics and doubtless has many great advantages. For example if bird flu were to break out in the world at the moment the most effective, safest and cheapest treatment that could be manufactured and supplied worldwide within days would be homeopathic treatment.

Considering the many disadvantages of suppressive treatment with antibiotics or antiviral treatment, among which side-effects, costs and the increase of therapy resistance, the WHO [www.who.int/drugresistance/en/] and other institutions should seriously consider alternative treatments for the many epidemics that still take millions of lives every year. Among these, homeopathy has proven to be highly effective, extremely cheap, free of side-effects and without the risk of inducing therapy resistance and more virulent (malignant) strains of the respective bacteria and viruses.

As we will discuss in the chapter on vaccination (See Part IV) the WHO should not only consider homeopathy and PC TECHNOLOGY for treating epidemics, but also and perhaps even more so as prophylaxis. The prophylactic use of resonances that include the role and purpose of diseases does not simply prevent disease and death but also supports humanity to make the very transitions in consciousness these diseases are aimed to bring about.

Homeopathy and Epidemics Today

With the decline of homeopathy in the beginning of the 20th century, reports of successful homeopathic treatment of epidemics have become scarce. However in the past few decades homeopathy has again flourished and the Materia Medica has been both extended and explored in much more depth, and individual treatment has reached an unequalled level: the time has come to again live up to the great possibilities homeopathy has to offer in epidemic diseases. It is beautiful that we can give good individualized treatment to thousands of people, but why ignore the possibility of treating millions of people suffering from epidemics like AIDS, malaria and TB? Why spend a lot of effort and resources on proving that homeopathy works for constitutional diseases if we can treat much larger numbers of patients suffering from epidemics with a higher probability of success, and know that the current suppression of epidemics by conventional medicine underlies many of the chronic diseases we treat?

This book is mainly the result of an attempt to treat a major epidemic of our times, AIDS. The health and well-being of millions of people in Africa is the main focus of the authors and the AMMA RESONANCE HEALING FOUNDATION they established together with Corrie Hiwat in 2007. The impact of the work in Africa and other developing countries on the further development and use of resonance homeopathy for healing is potentially huge. The result is a new approach for addressing epidemics in a simple and successful way, and as a derivative of that, an effective complementary treatment for chronic diseases.

References

- Bedayn, Greg, As If One Patient, *The American Homeopath* 1998
- Dearborn, Frederick M. MD, American Homeopathy in the World War; 1923
- Dewey, W.A., Homeopathy in Influenza - A Chorus of Fifty in Harmony, *Journal of the American Institute of Homeopathy* in 1921
- Bradford, T. Logic of Figures, Homeopathic Education USA June 1984
- Gebhardt, A. v., *Handbuch der Homöopathie*, Leipzig, Germany 1929
- Golden, Isaac, The Safety of Long-term Homeoprophylaxis - Research findings, Homœopathic Links Vol 17/4, p261, Haren, Netherlands 2004
- Hahnemann, Samuel, *Organon of the Medical Art*, sixth edition 1842, edited and an notated by Wendy Brewster O'Reilly, Birdcage Books, Redmond, USA 1996
- Humphreys, F., Cholera and its homoeopathic treatment, New York: William Radde Publisher, 1849
- Saine, André. From its Roots Upwards, Interview with André Saine, N.D., D.H.A.N.P., Vienna January 1994
- Stahl E., Hadulla M.M., Richter E., Homöopatische Behandlung der Influenza – Vogelgrippe, Algemeine Homöopatische Zeitung, 2006
- Winston, J., Some history of the treatment of epidemics with Homeopathy by Julian Winston, 2006, www.whale.to/v/winston.html

Experiences of AIDS and Malaria

Peter Chappell first started working on epidemic diseases in Ethiopia with AIDS in 2001. This is fully documented in the book *The Second Simillimum*. Here is a summary with excerpts from chapters 8 and 9 of that book so that you can understand the process.

> "In October 2001, around my sixtieth birthday, I travelled to Ethiopia to see what I could do with homeopathy for people with AIDS. Initially I prescribed individually with what I now term the First Simillimum, and I had good results with that. But I did not come to treat dozens or even hundreds of people, I came to see whether there would be a homeopathic solution for the millions of people in Africa infected with HIV/AIDS. I was aware that AIDS is a pandemic and that defining the Genus epidemicus should render a picture on which a
> homeopathic remedy could be prescribed for all patients suffering from AIDS. This is where my investigation, which has resulted in a whole new method of designing homeopathic remedies for diseases, started.

The first fundamental step in curing any disease is to understand its totality. In the case of HIV/AIDS this means understanding the totality of the epidemic.
One of the aspects belonging to the totality of AIDS is chronicity. Every acute symptom becomes a very chronic set of symptoms that are persistent since there are no recovery powers. This is because the micro-immunity is damaged. Opportunistic infections occur due to a weakened immunity. This is a confusing issue, because it relates to the exposure to infections in the past or present. They have nothing to do with HIV/AIDS itself, but nevertheless complicate the recovery and the management protocol. For example a childhood primary infection of tuberculosis, and the subsequent calcification, will frequently unravel due to the immune weakness and become the first sign of having HIV/AIDS. Likewise an earlier herpes infection will recur, or even manifest itself for the first time. Likewise, an external amoebic contamination can become chronic, hourly, diarrhoea, failing to elicit an immune response. These opportunistic infections have to be separated from the symptoms of the presenting case, otherwise the picture is unclear. They can aggravate the disease, but are not symptoms of the disease. They relate primarily to past and present disease exposure and weakness of the immune system. Likewise other severe or chronic pre-existing diseases such as asthma, leprosy, gonorrhoea, syphilis etc, can be aggravated in the absence of sufficient immunity."

"The main core symptoms, for example, of AIDS in Ethiopia and everywhere in Africa in the non-white-skinned population (based on my research) are:

- Weakness, loss of strength, can't walk far, can't work much
- Loss of appetite
- Loss of breathing capacity
- Loss of weight, independent of appetite
- Reduced recovery powers
- Chronicity

The more consequential symptoms are:

- Old infections resurface – TB, Herpes, (depending on the country)
- New diseases are easily acquired
- Permanence/chronicity is the modality of every symptom

Apparent mental symptoms after the diagnosis are:

- Deep panic
- Hopelessness
- Fear of dying
- Great concern about their children; who will look after them?

In other words these are personal responses to a life-threatening crisis according to individual remedy type, and would occur in any other life-threatening crisis. They are not related to HIV/AIDS. These are consequences and not the mental symptoms of the disease.
The HIV disease bigger picture could also include:

- Five to ten year stealth infection
- Entrance via sex, one of our greatest pleasures, and a dominant survival instinct
- Destruction of our defences systematically over time
- Protection of itself through its stigma and the need to remain secret, even to the point of the patient's death from starvation rather than risk admitting the disease and being supported
- Denial/Secrecy must be the foremost AIDS emotion
- We can deduce that HIV wants us to fight it so it can mutate and become a hydra-headed genetic defect pattern – a miasm in homeopathic language

- It is very abundant, creating 10,000,000,000 viruses daily per person and infecting 10,000 more people daily
- It has learnt to destroy our immunity, instead of just overwhelming it by sheer numbers
- It is becoming immortal as it becomes a chronic, everlasting pandemic
- This disease wakes us up to our sexual reality, revealing what is under the surface in sexual terms within humanity. Supposedly puritanical and moral societies prove to be otherwise
- It points to the need to change behaviour in personal relationships, to the need to bring honesty, trust, commitment and better communications into relationships
- It is breaking down religious taboos by exposing them to clear-sighted scrutiny and the hard facts of reality. Roman Catholic teaching is in direct contradiction to the needs of safe sex. Churchmen are still preaching against AIDS-infected people and throwing them out of churches
- It is probably creating evolutionary consciousness, a unique level of consciousness, on a different level from our present one
- It is all part of the divine plan in action
- Obviously it does not want to wipe us out; it seeks coexistence in us any way it can
- It is highlighting human society's inequalities, as with the malnutrition of Africa

I am not saying this is a complete description of the total picture, but more an illustration of the idea ...
Diseases have individual messages to individuals and a global message to the human race. AIDS is saying very clearly that unprotected sexual contact is not risk-free. It is not a moral lesson but it is a hygiene message. It is also a message about honesty, commitment and trust. We did not learn this from gonorrhoea or syphilis, now we must learn it from AIDS.

Some of the more detailed symptoms of AIDS in Ethiopia (and these are mostly universal) are:

- Internal burning sensation everywhere, systemically, and localised anywhere. The digestive system is a common site.
- Itching, and the sensation of something crawling under the skin, causing irresistible scratching and leaving abundant and very noticeable surface wounds, lesions. The face, arms, lower legs, body are prominent sites. It can be disfiguring.
- The weakness can be systemic and can focus in the knees, especially, and in the joints generally.
- There can be peculiar localised paralytic effects, which affect any single part and seemingly have no medical logic to them (for example the inability to raise the arms or to move the legs. I presume there might be local lymph swelling, pressing on a nerve).
- Dimness of vision and a feeling of a film over the eyes.
- Fungus affections of the tongue and vagina are common (The tongue can have the most amazing coatings, going deep into the throat and chest, and every known and conceivable disfiguration. This is very typical, and I wonder whether a vaccination (such as diphtheria) or chronic disease (such as Candida and fungal diseases) might be responsible for it.
- Initially there is often herpes, which is very indicative of HIV/AIDS.
- Diarrhoea is frequently an opportunistic infection.
- Headache is very common, again, as are all the above, and permanence is its main modality. This is also associated with fever and sweating or digestive burning, suggesting smallpox or smallpox vaccination, to which it is almost identical in its effects.
- Fever and sweating can exist independently or together.
- Silking and loss of hair is very common as the disease progresses (poor absorption of nutrients maybe partly responsible for this).
- There is frequently widespread and hard lymphatic congestion.

- Loss of weight.
- A wide variety of individual symptoms of any form that are intense, strong, damaging, limiting and often unusual in expression.

In the population there is great fear and ignorance, and rejection of the diseased individual, a deep stigma, a profound survival-based fear of contagion (which is characteristic of uncured syphilis, and has much to do with AIDS), and consequential rejection of the individual. It is a primitive instinct, survival of the fittest, primal, deep, overwhelming, unconscious fear that provokes crude, unthinking survival reactions. Typical examples of this are to prohibit the diseased individual from cooking or use of the kitchen; to reserve special plates and cups, etc. Maids lose their job – often they are also too weak to work. Likewise there is rejection/ejection from the home. This is common for any new plague – witness the reaction to SARS and the history of isolation hospitals, and isolation communities for those with leprosy – and it is not hard to understand that this is a common aspect of all such disease psychology.
Street living, dire poverty and starvation are the natural consequence and the latter precipitates rapid death once AIDS is established.
In the face of all this, secrecy becomes the individual's habitual reaction, the core mode of survival and very necessary. However this cuts sufferers off from the social services that are there to provide for them, and compounds the problem, especially in the terminal stages.
This is perhaps sufficient information to get an idea of the totality of the disease pattern. From my understanding of this I decided to design a remedy for this state."

After making this analysis based on taking 70 cases in great detail I (Peter) looked in the homeopathic Materia Medica for a remedy that would fit the totality of signs and symptoms belonging to AIDS. I had a laptop with state-of-the-art software including all relevant homeopathic sources and failed to find a remedy that sufficiently matched the Genus epidemicus of AIDS. I had contact with several colleagues around the world and received no realistic suggestion from them either. It was at that moment that I decided to try out something I had never done before, namely to create a remedy without using any substance to make it from. I took the concept that 'Like creates Like' as the remedy design principle and created a remedy by directly imprinting water with the simillimum for AIDS. I formed on a metaphysical level the likeness concept of HIV, from all the information above, its consciousness, its love, its purpose, its psychology, its action in the body; a likeness of HIV in its simillimum/totality as expressed above. The synthesis of all this formed the thought with which I approach the higher form of consciousness (See earlier chapter on PC Technology) to create a resonance for HIV/AIDS.

Now of course the great question was whether this new remedy would have any effect at all. At some level I was confident it would, but to be honest I also had my doubts and actually each time I returned to Africa I needed be convinced by clear results again. I have found that it works reliably in cases of AIDS and so have many others (See the chapter on AIDS).

The first point about understanding epidemic diseases is to understand that like everything else they are in our opinion living entities with a form of intelligence. They may not look like a super organism as is the case with a beehive or an anthill or a swarm of locusts, but there are billions of whatever the causative agent is, they exist on or in many different living creatures, and they have a communal mindset unknown to us, just as a swarm of ants or bees.

Because we were dealing with serious epidemic diseases that were killing millions of people we decided to try and understand the intelligence of the epidemic diseases we were looking at.

We found a way to do this by using shamanic journeys conducted by *Eileen Nauman*, a skilled shaman homeopath (See Appendix 3 for all journeys she performed). For some people this may be a step too far, but in our experience investigating by whatever way is possible is better than sticking our heads in the sand and ignoring the issue. And once you've had experience of shamanic journeys, you know they work, and provide a consciousness experience different to anything you can do on the practical, materialistic plane. They are a quite straightforward method of journeying to other types of consciousness. With training and skilled guidance anybody interested can learn how to do it.

In studying the signs and symptoms of epidemic diseases and through such shamanic journeys with these intelligences we discovered some pretty important things. For example the purpose and role of the intelligence that is an epidemic disease, is to help maintain the human race as a whole, healthy and well functioning.

None of the diseases we investigated recognized individuality within the human race. The idea of individuality within the mind-body construct is in fact a fallacy, even if it is widely believed. Basically, we see a human being as an awareness manifesting through a mind-body. The awareness exists before the mind-body is created and it continues after the mind-body is let go.

If you examine the language we humans speak you will find that it's almost impossible to talk without being framed in the idea of having an identity. Everything about every western culture emphasizes the idea of individuality and identity. So it's a hard habit to break and a hard idea to break out of. We could say that individuality is one of the fundamental delusions of the human race!

We, the authors, now have no problem with this lack of individuality and the fact that the consciousnesses of the epidemic diseases didn't see it either, just confirmed our experiences. But when we first carried out these journeys, we didn't understand it that way, and it caused us some confusion, as you will see in the journey details given.

The second point about epidemic diseases as we've come to understand them is that they are in fact a level of instruction and education. They are trying to inform and wake up the human race and to make it more conscious, to make us aware that we are consciousness itself. So the diseases are working on evolving our conscious mind!

Taking these two points together, in making a PC Resonance for an epidemic disease we had to consider achieving the same form of teaching as the epidemic disease delivers or better. If a PC Resonance would not help fulfil the real purpose of the epidemic disease and only treat its superficial symptoms we would prevent it from keeping the human race healthy on a deeper level.

When it comes to AIDS for example, we can see that one purpose of AIDS is to force a more explicit contract between sexual partners with a mutual respect for each other. In the West this especially involved gay relationships whereas in Africa AIDS is a heterosexual epidemic. Currently in many parts of Africa, the richer a man is, the more wives he has, and this is typified by the current president of South Africa and also the King of Swaziland who both have many wives and are still collecting more. It's also a situation we have seen in lorry owners in Malawi; owning a lorry is to be rich, so one had six wives.

The problem comes down to this at a practical level. The lorry owner had AIDS and was highly infectious because his AIDS was well advanced. One of his wives had the beginning of AIDS. The lorry owner, the husband, had told her that if she told any of his other wives about his situation or her own, he would subject her to some significant violence. And there was no way he was going to have protected sex with her. I (Peter) explained to her that if she wanted to stay alive and to mother her children and to become a grandmother she needed a solution to this situation. I explained to her that infective sex, sex without condoms, would be fatal to her, or else she could easily be restored to good health using PC1, the PC Technology remedy for AIDS. She sat there for a minute or so thinking before deciding what to do. She decided that she would wait until the tobacco harvest was in, and the cash situation therefore improved, and plead headaches up to that point in refusing sex. There were five other wives after all! Then she would take some cash and her particular children and go to another part of the country and live with her parents. This would be a huge step for her, taking responsibility for herself instead of letting herself be a victim to circumstance and the customary role pattern between men and women. This shows the sort of practical conscious shift engendered by AIDS.

Another observation was made by one of our close colleagues in the Central African Republic, amongst a group of nomadic people where the tribal instincts are tremendously strong. Individuality in terms of how many cows you personally owned was actively discouraged. The very idea of anybody in the tribe doing something for themselves was a fairly strong anathema. Just the idea of using a condom was to make somebody stand out as they were making a change outside of tradition. They were making a statement outside of the tribe awareness. They were in fact waking up to some sense of who they were on a different level than before. You could imagine a tribe where individual 'I'-dentity virtually didn't exist.

This is not so different to what we find in the West. Family structures are often so tightly controlling that individuals succumb to the pressure of their parents and extended family all their lives. When healing is attempted, the family cracks that open up are felt to be so threatening, that they stop the therapy, be it yoga, homeopathy etc. It's just too hard for their extended social structure to take.

Returning to the concepts of the intelligence of epidemic diseases, these things are both incredibly subtle and incredibly profound.

What we found is that the conscious intelligence of a specific epidemic disease is something like a profound silence yet with immense timeless wisdom on the level of awareness outside of normal experience. The consciousness is completely oblivious to individual humanity and transcends our perception of time and space, and exists in a whole different realm to which we have very little connection.

Nonetheless it became very clear to us that unless we built in a superior intelligence that reproduced everything that the original intelligence was trying to do and creating the same beneficial effects of the epidemic disease in a new way or the shorter timescale, we weren't doing anything helpful.

For example, in treating malaria, which most people in Africa tend to get at least once or twice a year, the homeopathic approach must generate the intelligent shifts in human consciousness that malaria has to bring, in a permanent way, so that there is no further need to have the disease. Then its purpose has been fully accomplished if the cure is to remain.

Incidentally, we think malaria may be Africa's main problem. Malaria induces a sort of helplessness; a way of thinking that whatever you do you cannot succeed. That is the homeopathically understood psychology of malaria and we have seen it on many subtle levels undermining whole lives.

A part of the teaching of malaria is that success is possible. And if the homeopathic approach to malaria is to work profoundly and properly and to replace the disease, it has then to bring out in the person the feeling that they can succeed. Thinking about Africa, the one idea that anybody having any contact with the continent has is that nothing will succeed. We have come across many projects in Africa requiring outside support which, when withdrawn leads to project collapse. In contrast our experience in educated countries in the West is that a new idea, once rooted, takes off and is sustained indefinitely locally. We think this is why malaria is so critical to Africa. It undermines the continent's success. Our understanding is that its role and purpose is to awaken individual abilities. African tribal culture frustrates individual initiative. Malaria, seen as an intelligent evolutionary force, has already taken thousands of years to bring about this change, involving a lot of suffering. Any truly effective treatment has to bring out the success that is inherent in every African, as world leaders like Nelson Mandela, Martin Luther King, and Barrack Obama clearly show. In our idea, if malaria were effectively treated across Africa, and this is incredibly easy to do technically with PC Technology, Africa would more than happily look after itself and become a thriving part of the world community. Incidentally we are not criticising tribal life. It seems a highly desirable ideal, but we presume it has now to incorporate some aspects of individuality.

Including the conscious intelligence of a specific epidemic disease in the appropriate PC Resonance is luckily not dependent on our limited understanding of it, but is provided by the same advanced intelligence that at our request creates the resonance.

A Shamanic Journey to HIV

Here is the story of one Virus Journey to illustrate how an insight into the role and purpose of an epidemic disease can be gained. Eileen Nauman, a skilled colleague and Native American shaman made this journey for us on request. (See appendix 3 for an explanation of shamanic journeying.)

Shamanic journey to HIV
Eileen Nauman, 2005

> "I got permission to go to the virus. My spiritual teacher came with me. He took me deep down inside Mother Earth. I saw the magma core glowing red hot and orange. I was seeing it two-dimensionally with the circle and a vertical core of magma in the centre of it from South Pole to North Pole.
>
> We entered a cave near the magma chamber. The tunnel was long and narrow and of black basalt (lava). It was rough and sharp. We entered a round cave and I was reminded of a vagina (tunnel) and chamber (womb). There was a regal, aristocratic woman in mediaeval red dress wearing a tall, red hat on her head. I wondered why she was dressed from the Middle Ages. She granted us permission to visit the HIV virus. We left the chamber and we went into darkness.
>
> I saw red, billowing clouds like thunderclouds building higher and higher. And then I saw a pair of women's bare breasts, rounded, full and beautiful. Next the scene returned to the billowy clouds. I questioned my judgement. Why would I see a pair of woman's breasts? The rounded globes were many and reminded me of a huge cauliflower floating out in the dark of space (I saw no stars). It was huge; continually shifting and changing. The movement was slow but discernible. The rounded globules were like bunched circles, lumpy, rounded and glowing red and orange.
>
> We introduced ourselves. The answering voice was that of a woman. Her voice was low, like the wind softly talking to us. This was a feminine virus. She created a gold doorway for us. Entering the virus, the door shut and then disappeared. My teacher told me to go on; he would be with me in spirit. Walking through the rounded areas there were no sharp corners; everything seemed soft and rounded. It all moved; it was never still – but it was slow, like watching slow motion in a movie. I looked under my feet ... and saw nothing; I was just walking in the red-orange surface.
>
> As I looked up, I felt I was looking up many stories into a skyscraper. I saw a foetus in a womb floating by. And then I saw a woman's pregnant belly. I saw more women's breasts. What was going on? I couldn't figure this out. Why was I being shown these things?
>
> I asked her where she came from. She showed me the centre of Mother Earth. I asked her why had she come above ground to harm humans. I felt her rankle; not anger, but DISTURBANCE. She showed me women being burned at the stake and I realized this was the Dark Ages. The virus did not speak; rather, our communication was telepathic and I could feel her 'voice' vibrating through me. She said men did not respect women. She showed me women being raped, beaten and dying in a hundred different ways. It was brutal. I groped to understand. Anger, I asked. You were created out of anger? I felt her patient smile as if I were some young child completely unable to grasp the wholeness she was showing me.
>
> She said through the ages the rage of women congealed. And that was when she was created. So, I asked: then you are a virus of revenge? Again, I felt that patient smile and a shaking of her head that I could ask such a stupid question. She had a higher purpose.
>
> So you were not created out of women's rage?

'I came to heed the call of women who are still seen as so little even now.'
But, you KILL women, too!
I got nothing but silence from the virus.
I don't understand your mission. Can you explain it to me?
'The imbalance must be rebalanced.'
I struggled with this. Yes, women are still considered second-class citizens to this day. They don't get a fair share from the patriarchal world. Women are still subjugated by men around the world. She was right: the world IS imbalanced because the only energy in it is MALE and in order to achieve balance, there must be a RESPECT of male AND female energies. I could sense the virus following my thoughts. I felt her smile benignly as if to agree with my logic.
Then why do you kill so many in Africa?
'Your race began there. You will die there.'
Again, I struggled to understand. She showed me black women from Africa, the Cradle of our Civilization, as we know it. I felt the virus was harming the very gender she was supposed to be helping. I didn't understand.
But you infect men AND women. If you're trying to rebalance this situation, why are you harming women, too?
'If men cannot love women, then they will both die. If there is respect between them, they will not. There must be love to create the bond between man and woman. If more men would love the women they take, then I would not affect them.'
So, you are saying that if a man loves a woman, then sex is safe?

I got no answer. Just silence. The virus had shared as much as she was going to. I felt as if this virus was very, very complex; far more so than the Ebola virus. She had many facets to her. I now understood why she was showing me women's breasts, the foetus in the womb, and a woman's pregnant belly. These are things that matter to her. I felt a sacredness of the virus toward these pictures or symbols. That didn't answer my question or aid my understanding that if she were here to help women ... why was she killing them, too?
'It is time for you to leave. Visit me again.'
I said I would, and left. I was aware of incredible depth to this virus and simultaneously the detachment incumbent upon doing a job on behalf of our population. I felt no anger from her, no vengeance, nothing. She was just repeating 'facts' about who and what she was."

(End of first journey)

Later Eileen made a second journey to HIV:

"We went to the Red Queen first and I asked her what lessons we were to learn, as man and woman regarding the HIV virus. She waved me off, as if frustrated with me. On asking what her 'job' entailed she replied there were many facets to it and told me I should put my questions to the virus. I was trying to understand her connection to all of this. She did say '*Men created this virus.*' She again showed me the transgressions against women down through the millennia. She said: '*You cannot suppress anything, human or otherwise, including Mother Earth, or there will be an EQUAL response in return to it.*' She inferred that all diseases were due to this maligning of energy and that is how she saw it: we are all made of energy. When our energy is repressed or suppressed by another, this creates a reverse reaction within us. If there is enough that this suppression occurs to, then, she said a bacteria or virus would manifest.

The HIV virus welcomed me back. As I walked in, I saw a man's penis hanging limply and then, suddenly, it burned up and was charred and dissolved into nothingness. I wondered what that was about but didn't want to get distracted. I did not see anything else other than her voluminous, cumulus cloud-like billowing self of red and orange colours. She is beautiful.

I asked the virus what lessons we were to learn from her. I asked first about men, but she said the following:

'*We are either born here in a woman's body or a man's.*' I asked if this was in keeping with my teaching that within us we had either the male or female energy that we must integrate. She said no, that when we are born into a physical body, we have a gender. It is in that body that we learn what it is like to be a man or woman. The key, she said, was that a man was to learn how to become a woman in a male body. Just as a woman was to learn to become a man in a woman's body. I understood this to mean that each could learn from the other (through observation, living with them, one assumes).

Our job was to 'integrate the MISSING energy'. In this case, man was to learn to integrate woman's energy. Woman was to learn to integrate man's energy. It was very complicated and different, in some respects from what I was taught – but essentially, the same. I felt as if the virus wanted people to observe one another and 'trade' or 'share' what they were, with one another. For example, if a woman cried openly, the man was to learn that. If a man were to set strong boundaries about something and maintain them, a woman was to observe this and take that experience into her and then make it her own. There was this 'trading' that was going on.

She also brought up dualism. She said we were not whole as human beings. We were one, or the other. That, '*the natural state of being is Oneness*'. That was why it was important for us to learn about the opposite gender energy, absorb it, take lessons from it and what was positive or healthy about it, integrate it into ourselves. What was not healthy, we were to avoid.

I asked about the pattern of her disease and she said to me: That although you (Peter) had the disease pattern of her, you did not have the pattern beneath it. She showed me two circular templates with black drawings of some kind on each one. To me, they looked like a petri dish with rectangular, black bits of material in them. Each looked a little different, yet similar. She showed me the 'base plate' of the person and then her pattern or template, above it. I got it.

She said she would not be here if the inequality between men and women were not present. You might be able to destroy her pattern in humans who were infected with her, but she said they would turn around and go out and commit the same pattern of offences as they did before and get re-infected. She stressed it was the foundational pattern where man suppresses woman, that needs to be addressed, too. She said she wouldn't be here in the first place if that pattern of gender equality had not been out of balance in the first place.

I told her I didn't understand why she was killing off so many women. She said that women who were unable to integrate their masculine traits, create strong boundaries and say NO, were the ones who were dying. And those men who continued to want to suppress women, who didn't respect or love them, contracted her disease.

I told her that with so many people dying, what would be left? So many children were already orphaned. She smiled patiently and said that by contracting her (the virus), when she brought their fever high (104 - 105F) she created a linkage between the person who was in an hallucinogenic state and forged a link to the Creator so that they might understand what real love was; and that was one way of learning. The high fever was to bring the dying person to an hallucinogenic experience with the Creator. In that, there was learning, education and awareness about love, and being loved.

I said: "Still, they died." She smiled again. She said that when these people died, they had gone through the experience and that on the other side in spirit, they were then beginning to understand *why* it had happened to them and what they had to do in the next incarnation to practise what they had just learned – to, in essence, do it all over again, but with this awareness and teaching and understanding within them of what sexual gratification without love, without respect of the partner, leads to (disease/death from HIV/AIDS). And if they came back to practise love associated with sex, their lesson had been learned. So, she told me, their dying wasn't a bad thing; rather, it was simply another way to be educated at a soul level. In this way women are being treated better than before. How did it get this way in the world? By dying and being reborn to learn such lessons. She said souls learned this lesson in many ways, not just through contracting a sexually transmitted virus. There have been other diseases over the ages.

She pointed out the Black Plague and said it had arisen to address the murder of millions of women in Europe by religion – the direct response to these murders manifested the Plague that killed so many in Europe. Each of those who died needed this SAME lesson about respect of women as equals, as people do today. It was simply a different disease that came in to address this imbalance.

The virus was very matter-of-fact about all this. There was no emotion, no connection about what she did or how she did it. She knows her job and goes about doing it; understanding that it is a path through which a person can learn about sexuality and love.

I thanked her, my head spinning with so much information. I hadn't ever thought of the high fever inducing a state of consciousness that could be linked to the Creator. Nor did I realize another pattern beneath the disease pattern that also had to be addressed. It made sense to me. Further, the eruption of a disease – well – this makes me want to go back and look at the 'state of mind' of humans when each of these diseases manifested. What was going on at the time? What was being repressed? Or suppressed? What human actions were questionable and not spiritually or ethically correct that created these bacteria or viruses to manifest?

She invited me to come back again. I think she enjoys this repartee. My sense is that few humans visit her. And I must say she was *not* in the least trying to influence my knowledge and knowing. She was simply centred and detached."

(End of second journey)

This and other journeys helped us in understanding epidemics better. We leave you to make of them what you will.

Intelligent Diseases

Epidemic diseases have an intelligent organism behind them, a virus, bacteria, parasite or fungus.

We know scientifically that bacteria for example are intelligent because when we oppose them with antibiotics they automatically evolve to overcome what must appear to them to be an increasingly hostile environment and thrive, rendering many antibiotics useless. This is standard medical knowledge and a huge problem for regular medicine as increasing therapy resistance (adaptive intelligence as the diseasing agents are trying to help humanity, not dull it down) makes regular medicine powerless.

We have been brought up in a culture where diseases are the bad guys and drugs are the good guys. To even begin to understand epidemics and germs, we have to reframe our consciousness and our beliefs. We have to understand that diseases are forms of love, a wise and loving consciousness helping to look after the human race.

As we learned from Eileen Nauman's shamanic journeys disease agents see humanity as a whole, as one entity, and that with the infection of an individual nothing personal is either involved, or intended. We discovered some of the innate intelligence of such diseases.

Childhood epidemics and 'winter acutes'

In childhood we have a range of endemic diseases (measles, whooping cough etc.), which in theory every child could have and recover from. It seems obvious that one benefit of this process is that the immune system faces challenges that strengthen and develop it just as exercise develops the physical body. This lack of opportunity to have high fever diseases is the key downside of vaccinations, not their toxic complications. Serious as they are, toxic complications can be avoided by using different preservatives or homeopathic techniques of vaccination. Fevers, as well as enhancing the immune system, allow a new conscious understanding to arise.

Suppressing disease intelligence

Acutes are commonly treated with drugs, fevers being quashed by antipyretics, antibiotics and the like, inflammations by steroids. We know the common consequences: pathology follows as a substitute diagnosis and as a rule affects the organism on a deeper level. Research shows that the use of antibiotics increases allergies and causes immature immune systems. Vaccinations very likely do the same. Yes, on an individual level vaccinations or antibiotics can save lives, and ... on a collective level the massive use of them, which we may call abuse, deteriorates the health of humanity as a race.

We can call this suppression, although the conscious intelligence cannot be suppressed and will find expression one way or another. It is like a spring, and once the water flows, it must find a way. You can dam it, create a lake, you can divert it, leak it, but you cannot stop it. Likewise if you use drugs the conscious intelligence may find alternative expressions or substitute pathologies but there are no possibilities of it being suppressed.

What homeopaths mean by suppression is a form of expression which has a lower level than the original natural expression like a fever and which if suppressed mutates into poorer outcomes, for example a recurring sore throat in adulthood or later a thyroid dysfunction.
Not uncommonly in the course of homeopathic treatment we find we have an adult with a

typical childhood complaint like tonsillitis or an earache. The reason for this can be that drugs were used to suppress the acute, which was in all probability the result of an epidemic disease some time in the past. For this we give the very same remedy we would probably have used 20 to 30 years before had we had the opportunity, and commonly this works.

When the suppression is lifted, something new appears. When we give an individualised remedy to an adult for a problem that we normally associated with childhood, the patient not only gets better but also grows up and wakes up with a raised consciousness.

The same is seen to happen in a detox from the suppression that may have caused the original problem, be that a drug or vaccination. For example an athletic, healthy adult received a detox for the repeated use of penicillin he was given as a young child for throat infections. After the detox, which laid him low for a while, he found a new level of self-expression in speech.

The above suggests that our immune system development and our conscious awakening are intimately connected. When our immune system doesn't develop properly and fully, we don't develop properly either. This is a very important point that is not often acknowledged and is not researched; yet we homeopaths know it to be true from our clinical experience.

We also know that when there is a lack of personal development and poor self-esteem this finds its outlets in violence, alcoholism, social unrest, unemployment, resorting to street drugs, personal dysfunction and obviously more chronic diseases. We know this because when we treat such conditions successfully we reverse them into more natural and confident behaviour.

Dysfunction can also be expressed by ego amplification, like excessive ambition, or the drive to be best.

The following statistic makes this stark reality clear. Self-confident people live 35 years longer than those subject to feelings of chronic helplessness. [Dawson Church, 2007]

All this seems to point to one conclusion. When we don't understand the fundamental intelligence of epidemic diseases and base our medical approach on considering infectious agents as enemies, we are causing more trouble than we are apparently 'curing' with antibiotics and other drugs and vaccinations. This not only means weaker immunity, more chronic disease and early death, but also serious levels of dysfunction in society.

George Vithoulkas, a world authority within homeopathy and winner of the Alternative Nobel Price, has written extensively and often about this. He believes that "conventional medicine, instead of curing diseases, is actually the cause of the degeneration of the human race. Vithoulkas believes that conventional modern medicine will soon be recognized as a dead end, and that it should be taken apart and restructured according to the guidance of homeopaths". [http://en.wikipedia.org/wiki/George_Vithoulkas] This puts it in a nutshell!

This does not mean we should not use some vaccinations or antibiotics, but to attempt to stop all childhood diseases, common influenzas and acute illnesses with antibiotics and vaccinations et cetera. seems foolhardy.

We know that fighting germs causes them to adapt and there is a massive fifty years of evidence to support that, according to the WHO:

"Respiratory infections, HIV/AIDS, diarrhoeal diseases, tuberculosis and malaria are the leading killers among the infectious diseases. Resistance to first-line drugs has been observed in all these diseases. In some cases, the level of resistance has forced a change to more expensive second or third-line agents. When resistance against these drugs also emerges, the world will run out of treatment options. Drug resistance can be considered as a natural response to the selective pressure of the drug." [www.who.int/drugresistance/en/]

Bacteria learning how to survive in a more hostile climate have already rendered many antibiotics useless. From the bacteria's point of view this may be an essential survival strategy for the benefit of humanity, and proof of high intelligence. We have yet to learn that fighting epidemic diseases is in the end a no-win situation as they will and do evolve and return with increased virulence. The very information that tells us this is staring us in the face, from the WHO quote above.

Right now they are plastering mud huts in Africa with insecticides and impregnating the mosquito nets likewise and this is temporarily saving lives from malaria. [The Guardian Weekly (UK) 04-01-08] This life-saving measure means that eventually the mosquitoes that carry malaria will become immune to these insecticides, as the malaria parasite has done to quinine and DDT in the past. As the climate warms up, African diseases are spreading north. This has been widely reported; for example, a typically African disease, chikungunya fever, occurred in Italy in the summer of 2007. We can predict with some confidence that due to the intelligence of mosquitoes and the malaria parasite, when malaria returns to Europe, having been (partially) eradicated by pesticides and the draining of swamps, it will be more virulent, less stoppable and more deadly than ever before.

The reduction of the world population is an important effect of epidemic diseases as happened with the plague or Black Death.

With a greatly increased population already, living on a highly polluted planet whose people have seriously compromised immunity after half a century of blanket vaccination and overuse of antibiotics etc. (not to mention depleted foods, grown on exhausted soil, and irreparably over-processed in their production), it's only too easy to see that humanity faces a potential epidemic wipe-out. Epidemic diseases will perform their intelligent role. They will naturally arrive, and given the vulnerability, could cause inordinate mortality.

Some epidemics are not dependent on a weakened immune system and have their highest mortality amongst the fit and young as their immune system overreacts. Conventional homeopathic concepts of susceptibility can be reversed in epidemics. Nonetheless, the basic possibility of population reduction by epidemic diseases seems increasingly likely to happen. Modern transportation guarantees that viruses will be spread over the whole planet in no time.

Whether you attack the germs with drugs to kill them in the regular way of medicine or if you boost immunity by Genus-epidemicus-based homeopathy so that the immune system focuses intensely upon the germ to kill it, the consequences are essentially the same. You are trying in both cases to stop the epidemic and keep everybody healthy and alive.

We know from individualised homeopathy that it is no use just treating the symptoms; we have to address the cause, which at some level means the person has to shift their conscious awareness and their consequential actions so that they stop making themselves sick. Otherwise the illness or disease is destined to return. And it's the same process when we are treating humanity as a whole for epidemic diseases.

The meaning of the disease and its purpose has to be addressed, by a process involving a change of consciousness with actions that coherently follow so that the cause of the disease has been removed. Humanity thus remains healthy and by extension the whole planet is also kept healthy. If the population of the world is becoming a serious and debilitating stress upon the planet [UN on population] then the role of an epidemic disease is either to reduce the population or to wake it up to the need for a new consciousness and a new action, or both of these as part of an on-going process.

In the light of a possible role of epidemics in population control a Genus epidemicus approach is fine provided it accompanies another intelligent option, which would be to reduce the human race's impact upon the planet. The Nobel Prize awarded to *Al Gore* for his documentary 'An inconvenient truth' is surely evidence that this impact is becoming more widely accepted.

The other possibility is to include in Genus epidemicus the bigger picture and to choose a remedy that has the bigger totality. This approach is possible by choosing substances that include both the symptoms as well as the bigger picture, the context of an epidemic disease, and by consciously creating remedies/resonances using new technology as described in this book.

A very important point here is that while the build-up of civilizations, and for that matter share prices and house prices, goes on over a long period of time, adjustments downward are much more rapid and collapse happens very fast and unexpectedly, confounding all the experts, as happened in the banking crisis of 2008. This is the rule according to long–term human civilisation studies. [Jared Diamond, *Collapse* 2005]

For an example of such a series of events that could easily happen right now, imagine a deadly bird flu that creates 5% mortality. This will undermine house prices which will precipitate a further banking crisis and an economic collapse which in turn could precipitate famine, shortages, survival instincts, street riots (Arabia, Africa, India 2011), looting, and soon wars over resources (which is already happening in Iraq and many African countries), and inflames religious fanatics etc. The world is far more fragile than it looks and once it moves outside well-controlled norms, multiple factors can create a catastrophe and a general meltdown of civilisation, as we know it.

Because of the likelihood of too little happening too late and a lack of consciousness generally, a painful process of adjustment can be expected this century. This is quite normal and is something humanity is familiar with. Typically we individual human beings prefer to have a disease rather than to raise our consciousness, and we don't expect humanity as a whole to be any different. Judging from today's politics there is no reason to hope that suddenly the world naturally, in a velvet revolution, will become ecological, sustainable and eco-medical.

This scenario points to the direction for homeopathy to take this century: a major role for homeopathy in this 21st century (as in the 19th century) may prove to be the rapid treatment by single Genus epidemicus remedies, of deadly pandemics which may sweep across the world. Bird flu and the new strain of Ebola could do this in days [Medical News Today]. Regular medicine will be seen to have insufficient answers and logistics. ['Doubts cast over whether anti-flu drug Tamiflu works' – recent headline from NHS UK - http://www.nhs.uk/news/2012/01January/Pages/tamiflu-ineffective-claim.aspx]. Increasingly drug-resistant diseases making a comeback such as tuberculosis, as well as endemic 'African' diseases now migrating northwards into Europe, also need homeopathic attention.

At the same time the treatment has to go hand in hand with eco-realism and changing behaviour. Saving lives without changing behaviour is a doomed endeavour; 'The primrose path to the everlasting bonfire.' (Shakespeare, *Macbeth*.)

Recognition is needed of the wisdom of George Vithoulkas, as quoted above, and then a fundamental shift of our current medical paradigm to an holistic one. To achieve this, conventional medicine must be recognised as the 'naked emperor' whilst simultaneously homeopathy becomes acclaimed for its rapid effective treatment of epidemics and pandemics. It may take a major epidemic catastrophe to effect such an upheaval and bring about change.

So it's up to us homeopaths to get our act together and develop our epidemic credentials and put in place something like a Homeopathic Centre for Disease Control with the necessary facilities. This will be one of the many facilities that need to be put in place to move towards an ecologically sustainable world.

References

- Amma in Judith Cornell Piatkus. *Amma: A living Saint*, 2001 UK p.164
- Church, Dawson. *The Genie in Your Genes*, Elite Books, Fulton, 2007
- Diamond, Jared. Collapse: *How Societies Choose to Fail or Succeed*, Viking Penguin USA, 2005
- Ebola. Medical News Today, www.medicalnewstoday.com/articles/90364.php and www.newsweek.com/id/74101
- Gore, Al. www.algore.org/ - An Inconvenient Truth - the film also on www.climatecrisis.net/ (Also on film's accuracy - www.sfgate.com/cgi bin/article.cgi?file=/news/archive/2006/06/27/national/a105014D57.DTL)
- Working with US soldiers after Iraq.
- UN on world population - http://www.un.org/esa/population/publications/ longrange2/WorldPop2300final.pdf
- Vithoulkas, George. http://en.wikipedia.org/wiki/George_Vithoulkas

Nosodes and the Treatment of Epidemic Diseases

Nosodes are homeopathic remedies made by taking the bodily secretions or infected tissues of well-diagnosed and diseased persons, and potentising them in the normal way. They form one category of remedies that can be considered to prevent and treat epidemics. Nosodes have earned their place in homeopathic practice as remedies

- that can fit as a simillimum for an individual
- that complement the simillimum by treating the epigenetic (miasmatic) background of chronic diseases
- as prophylaxis against epidemic diseases
- for the treatment of epidemic disease

In a study recently completed in Cuba millions of people were successfully protected for two following years against the yearly epidemic of leptospirosis[1] using homeoprophylaxis – the nosode prepared of the diseasing agents was given orally before the usual outbreak in the rainy season. [Bracho 2009]

Nosodes are under threat of being banned by health authorities, as they are considered unsafe in conventional medicine. There is no logic to this as they are diluted and succussed above Avogadro's constant; however conventional science still insists that although 'they have nothing in them and therefore no effect', they may simultaneously be unsafe! A possible explanation is that homeopathic nosodes and regular vaccinations (which clearly are unsafe) are similar technologies and thus the (much cheaper) use of nosodes to prevent and cure infectious diseases may be seen as a threat to the prosperity of the health industry.

However, nosodes deserve to be critically re-examined. In the acute or chronic stage of an infectious disease the efficacy of nosodes is limited. Even in epidemics the appropriate nosode will not consistently cure each and every case.

When the nosode is made of the disease (tissue, excretions) we would expect it to cover the large totality. Reality is that a nosode is usually a mix of the disease agent and the infected individual. *Arsenicum album* in potency can be routinely given in the acute phase of arsenic poisoning (there is scientific research with rats and humans to prove this), but it is clear that a remedy made from the vomit, diarrhoea or sweat of a poisoned individual may not have the same reliable effect, containing as it does a lot more information than that of the diseasing substance itself. The same is true for nosodes prepared from secretions.
Logically, if the nosode treated the totality of the disease it would do the job of curing the disease and all its after-effects, as well as being an effective prophylactic and a vaccine substitute.

Therefore this failure of nosodes to reveal the full potential of the source has something to do with the remedy source or the process of potentisation, or both.
With exceptions (i.e. when indicated) the nosode *Medorrhinum* does not cure gonorrhoea, *Tuberculinum* does not cure acute tuberculosis and likewise *Syphilinum* does not cure syphilis, the HIV/AIDS nosode does not cure AIDS, *Carcinosinum* does not cure cancer.

Both the nosode and the complementary remedies used are compromises to try to get over the fact that *we do not have a single remedy to counteract the original disease in its entirety*. The consequence is that the cure of diseases is partial and incomplete by such methods.

The Genus epidemicus for any infectious disease may not even include the nosode, as it doesn't cover a substantial part of the signs and symptoms. A homeopath will usually have to select one remedy from a group of Genus epidemicus remedies that will have great results. The problem with epidemics and certainly with pandemics is that thousands to millions of people require treatment in a short period of time. True killer epidemics sweep across the world in 8-12 weeks killing tens of thousands or more. No country has enough sufficiently skilled homeopaths to successfully treat all patients by a hit or miss or individualising method.

1 Leptospirosis - bacterial disease that affects animals and humans; infection occurs through contact with water, food, or soil contaminated by animal urine; symptoms include high fever, severe headache, vomiting, jaundice, and diarrhoea; untreated, the disease can result in kidney damage, liver failure, meningitis, or respiratory distress; fatality rates are low but left untreated recovery can take months.
http://www.indexmundi.com/cuba/major_infectious_diseases.html

This is even truer for many developing countries, especially in Africa. There only a low-skilled, safe and cheap approach would work, and it is our experience with a variety of infectious diseases that PC RESONANCES do cover the totality of the disease and can thus be reliably prescribed based on nothing other than the medical diagnosis. Here the best of homeopathy (like cures like – non-toxic) meets the best of conventional medicine (diagnosis), a win-win situation that, to the benefit of millions, may bridge the borders between homeopathy and allopathy (conventional medicine).

That PC TECHNOLOGY makes it possible to create a disease specific remedy without using substance has another advantage, in that some of the nosodes are no longer available or are prohibited because of concerns about their supposed safety and for other reasons cited above. Pharmacies now prepare nosodes from old stock that soon passes the shelf-life dates formulated in legal rules and regulations. The fact that disease specific remedies can now be made that are more effective (cover the disease totality) and are safe (can never contain active diseasing agents) is something we hope the homeopathic community will come to realize and make use of. Several case examples in later chapters in this book will illustrate the method and the results. Case collection is only a first level of research and we would welcome and support any homeopath or institute interested in seriously studying the use of PC RESONANCES to prevent or treat an epidemic disease.

References

- Bracho, G. and Golden, I. (2009) The Adaptability of Homeoprophylaxis in Endemic, Epidemic and Stable Background Conditions. *Homœopathic Links*. Winter 2009: Vol 22: p.211-213.

The Role and Purpose of Miasms

The concept of a 'miasm' (from Greek 'miasma', taint, stain, pollution) does not originate from *Hahnemann*, (for example see *Lamarck*[2]) but probably no (contemporary) physician elaborated on the concept as he did. In Hahnemann's time, and before the germ theory (connecting microorganisms to diseases) was accepted, miasma was a commonly used term for the cause of diseases we now call infectious. With miasma a dangerous influence or atmosphere was indicted as responsible for contamination or pollution causing sickness, death or decomposition. In his *Organon of the Medical Art* Hahnemann explains what his understanding of the concept entails. Hahnemann clearly describes miasms as negative forces that seemingly served no purpose other than to guarantee humans a miserable life and an untimely death. Miasmatic thinking is based on the limitations of homeopathic cure, proposed by Hahnemann to explain patient relapse, despite what were considered correct prescriptions. "Their beginning was promising, the continuation less favourable, the outcome hopeless." [Hahnemann, 1839] Hahnemann postulated that inherited influences as remnants of infectious diseases of an "unknown primitive malady" act as obstacles to cure.

2 http://www.pbs.org/wgbh/evolution/library/02/3/l_023_01.html

Organon §78:

> "The true, natural, chronic diseases are those that arise from a chronic miasm. When left alone (without the use of remedies that are specific against them) these diseases go on increasing. Even with the best mental and bodily dietetic conduct, they mount until the end of life, tormenting the person with greater and greater sufferings. Besides those diseases that are engendered by medical malpractice (§74), these are the most numerous and greatest tormentors of human race, in that the most robust bodily anlage (rudimentary basis of an organism), the best regulated lifestyle, and the most vigorous energy of the life force are not in a position to eradicate them." [Hahnemann, 1842]

With the example of the venereal diseases we get the idea of contamination, after which a miasm starts its destructive influence on our health.

Organon §80:

> "The internal monstrous chronic miasm of Psora is immeasurably more widespread, and consequently more significant, than the two chronic miasms just named. While Syphilis marks its specific internal wasting sickness with the venereal chancre and Sycosis does so with cauliflower-like growths, Psora documents itself (only after the complete internal infection of the whole organism) by means of a peculiar skin eruption, sometimes consisting of only a few vesicles, accompanied by an unbearable tickling voluptuous itch and a specific odour. Psora is the true fundamental cause and engenderer of almost all the other remaining forms of disease which are numerous, indeed countless ... " [ibid.]

Kent stated in his *Lectures* "the human race ... is little more than a moral leper" and further established the moral stigma that miasms symbolize as the infectious diseases connected to Psora, Sycosis and Syphilis are all sexually transmitted. "Psora is the evolution of the state of man's will, the ultimate of sin." Therefore, miasms were understood to be a source of suffering tormenting the human condition as a result of original sin (psora), a vision based on Christian doctrine (Kent was a disciple of the Christian mystic *Swedenborg*). Although not stated as such the underlying belief is obvious: miasms originate from sin and thus come from the devil, and as the devil is considered to be all bad (as opposite of God representing all good forces) fighting miasms is the logical result.

"If we overlook the moral tone, we can see that Kent was ahead of his time in recognising *the state of human consciousness* as being fundamental to understanding what the miasmatic energies are really about." [Watson, 2009]

Although Hahnemann is less moralistic in his expressions about miasms, the way he speaks about them is actually very un-homeopathic. He uses allopathic vocabulary with terms like: 'that thousand-headed monster' (Psora); 'drives the enemy out'; 'these hostile powers which produce disease and against which the vital force alone is no match'; 'invading morbific enemy'; 'parasitic'; 'infection'.

Hahnemann's allopathic language on miasms was actually completely in line with the germ theory of disease as developed by one of his contemporaries – *Jenner* (1749 - 1823).

Watson summarises Hahnemann's context for understanding the miasms as follows:

- miasms are invisible malevolent forces, each of which creates a range of suffering of a particular kind

- miasms are wholly negative influences which need to be eradicated
- transmitted by inheritance, sexual contact or (in the case of psora) merely by proximity or touch (lodging places, towels, wearing gloves someone else wore previously etc.)
- the innate self-healing capacity of the human organism is unable of its own accord to overcome the negative morbific influence of the miasms
- anti-miasmatic homeopathic treatment is necessary in order to 'drive out the enemy' of miasm-induced disease

It is amazing to see how with the introduction of the miasms by Hahnemann, allopathic thinking entered homeopathic practice, and even more so that for almost 200 years it went unremarked, and that only at the beginning of this century a broader vision was presented. [e.g. van der Zee, 2000]

Hahnemann himself however, lifted the concept beyond the diseases connected to the miasms he recognised per se. He considers psora as 'immeasurably more widespread' (§80) than the other miasms and says about it – Organon §81:

> "It is, to some extent, understandable how psora could now unfold itself in so many countless disease forms in all the human race since this age - old infectious tinder has gone, little by little, through many millions of human organisms over the course of hundreds of generations, thus attaining an incredible proliferation. This is all the more understandable when we consider the multitude of circumstances that have tended to contribute to the formation of this great diversity of chronic diseases ... "
> [Hahnemann, 1842]

In his later work *Die chronische Krankheiten* (The Chronic Diseases) Hahnemann further explains how the suppression of the psoric eruption leads to a great diversity of chronic diseases as secondary symptoms of psora.

If we, in the spirit of Hahnemann, keep investigating and improving our philosophy and method, we can see a clear and logical next step regarding the nature of the miasms.

In §11 Hahnemann states that only the life force, and not the morbific agent, can create symptoms. A **symptom** is an expression of the vital force trying to restore health, and from this derives the homeopathic notion that the suppression of symptoms is as a consequence a suppression of the vital force resulting in a weakened rather than strengthened organism.

A **disease** is a combination of symptoms, and it is therefore a logical next step to state that suppressing a disease is likewise counterproductive. Research in recent decades has also made clear that diseases can induce a process of change and development in the individual. Diseases are teachers that can help the individual to grow in awareness.

Miasms, being the long-term effects of (suppressed) infectious diseases (and, within a broader concept, other life-force-deranging influences like various forms of trauma or intoxication), express themselves in chronic diseases, and therefore as a logical consequence, just like the individual symptom or the individual disease, also serve the purpose of restoring health.

In §2 we can read: "The highest ideal of cure is the rapid, gentle and permanent restoration of health ...". In the context of the above, the expression 'restoration of health' needs to be defined clearly. As Hahnemann writes it in the paragraph quoted, it implies going back to a previous healthy state. But as part of a process of individuation which each human goes through in life, the phrase 'restoration of health' takes on a different meaning. Since diseases can function as teachers, suppressing diseases prevents the individual from learning the lessons diseases have to offer.

A disease is then both the problem and the solution. It is not something that never should have been, but rather exactly what should be: an opportunity for the individual, or in epidemics the group, to pass through a dearly needed experience. It is a form of communication from our consciousness to our attention. Homeopathy can then be used to induce the awareness that underlies the disease, which is the cure, in a more rapid and less painful way. In that sense the restoration of health means the attainment of a new equilibrium that includes a new awareness and brings the individual, or humanity as a whole, closer to fulfilling the higher purpose of his/its existence. Life is dynamic thus once the new equilibrium is reached something else is likely to threaten its stability, for there is so much more potential in humanity to be unfolded.

Organon §9:

> "In the healthy human state, the spirit-like force (autocracy) that enlivens the material organism as dynamis (vital force), governs without restriction and keeps all parts of the organism in admirable, harmonious, vital operation, as regards both feelings and functions, so that our indwelling, rational spirit can freely avail itself of this living, healthy instrument for the higher purposes of our existence." [ibid.]

Within this vision of growth and development, disease plays a role and is instrumental in fulfilling the higher purposes of our existence, as much on an individual level as a collective level. Where this process of manifesting our true self gets blocked, symptoms, diseases, epidemics and miasms occur as a sign of the vital force inducing the change needed, and by reading these and by selecting a simillimum, homeopathy can induce the required awareness, again on both individual and collective levels.

Miasms are part of the evolutionary impulse of the human condition requiring the ability to adapt and change. Repression or suppression does not stop the intelligence and forming force behind the infectious disease from fulfilling its role and purpose. On the one hand miasmatic diseases can be seen as limitations based on inherited dispositions, and on the other hand as continued stimulant for change and progress. Out of suffering comes transformation. Change however requires the ability to adapt, and failure to do so creates suffering and disease on the individual level and the collective level. Both individual and collective levels interact and reflect one another. On both levels disease should be seen to include more than purely medical conditions, but also social and spiritual expressions of imbalance.

A conclusion we can arrive at is that the totality of a disease besides consisting of its signs and symptoms should also include an understanding of its role and purpose for the individual, or, in the case of epidemics, for a certain group, population, race or even humanity as a whole. This understanding is important during the epidemic as well as later when homeopaths will have to contend with the after-effects – the corresponding miasm.
We may expect that the largest possible meaningful totality will have the highest ability to cure a disease; a prerequisite for inclusion will be the very reason for the existence of the disease is a prerequisite. Contrary to epidemic diseases, in the treatment of an acute or chronic disease the role and purpose of the disease is often indirectly present in the causal history, and thus is often already included in the homeopathic case taking as also the prescription.

In constituting the Genus epidemicus for epidemic diseases or collective trauma, awareness of its context makes it possible to also include the role and purpose of the disease or trauma and results in a higher similitude with higher efficacy, both in the acute situation as well as in the long-term miasmatic effects. To understand the role and purpose may not always be easy, but realizing the possible importance of it, should not prevent homeopaths from making a serious attempt. We could start by learning from history.

Analysing the changes inside a society during and after an epidemic shows us the impact of the epidemic, which in accordance with the postulating of an intelligent purpose should contain the purpose amid all the symptoms and suffering.

Slower moving epidemics like AIDS in Africa give us the opportunity to observe the changes and come to a deeper understanding of the role and purpose of AIDS while dealing with it. If we look beyond all the death and suffering that AIDS causes in Africa a pattern of development becomes visible:

- For instance the chance of survival is higher in people that are able to let go of tribal taboos, and decide to go to a doctor to be tested and treated.
- A woman who, against tribal customs, refuses men who want to have sex with her, or who insists her husband uses condoms, is more likely to live long enough to bring up her children. Her children will not become orphans, and may not have to prostitute themselves for food and thus contract AIDS as well.
- A man who decides to lead a monogamous life despite that he can afford more wives or to visit prostitutes has a much lower chance of becoming HIV-positive.
- In South Africa for instance many white people do wonderful work of love in AIDS clinics and hospices thus beginning to heal the wounds of apartheid and colonialism.

Many more observations like this can be made that show the possible impact of AIDS on African society, on the relationship between men and women etc. All these issues can then also be expected to be part of the AIDS miasm, that with or without AIDS still being present, will stay with humanity for the coming century at least; or, considering the universal nature of the connected issues, for ever.

After a Genus epidemicus remedy has acted well for an epidemic, an insight can be found into the changes the disease has to offer for the society involved. From many experiences we have come to understand some of the deeper themes and if a remedy is indicated during an epidemic we may expect its major themes to be connected to the epidemic. By observing changes in society during and after an epidemic in the light of the general theme of the Genus epidemicus remedy, this shift of consciousness can be understood as having been the real cause and the very reason why the society needed the disease. After an epidemic the corresponding miasm will still express itself in the population as its message keeps echoing in those individuals with a susceptibility to it. Similar to the understanding gained by a patient after an effective simillimum, this is a very powerful way of understanding the real journey of the disease and healing, and the exact nature of the pre-existing problem. The same holds true for an epidemic.
Miasms are nothing but the shadow side of phases in a healthy process of developing awareness. Their role and purpose is to bring the subconscious dark part into the light in order to fulfil and complete the corresponding phase, individually and collectively.

Different societies are in different phases of development and different epidemic diseases and their miasmatic consequences are fitting to each. Of some epidemic diseases and miasms we have some understanding; of many homeopathy still needs to discover their meaning, role and purpose.

No doubt many miasms need to be added and better understood to the few that homeopaths recognise today. It is clear that diseases like Polio, Pestilence, Chlamydia, Herpes zoster, Smallpox [Scheiwiller - Muralt, 2002] and many others influence the miasmatic heritage of mankind. Despite the fact that Hahnemann had already done groundbreaking work on the miasms, this is an area homeopaths are only beginning to discover, and rarely successfully use in practice.

By treating chronic diseases, the result of persistent miasms, which again have been caused by epidemic diseases, homeopaths are downstream trying to save drowning people from the miasmatic river. By moving upriver we could be much more effective, because either people have only just stepped into the water and are still in a relatively healthy condition, or we may even be in time to prevent people from falling into the miasmatic river.

Analysing the evolutionary impulse of epidemic diseases and the role and purpose of the associated miasms is one way to move upriver, and deserves to be placed high on the agenda of homeopathy's future. Since evolution follows a path and specific epidemic diseases can occur during specific stages we may conclude that epidemic diseases and miasms fit within a process and are like pearls on a necklace, one leading to the other. Since evolution and the individuation process of mankind is much more complex than a linear process, there are of course many strands that together weave the cloth of human destiny, and diseases and miasms can have their meaning at several places in time and in changing combinations.

For a more detailed description of how the homeopathically well-described miasms fit into the human individuation process the reader is recommended to read *Miasms in Labour* and *Homeopathy for Birth Trauma.* [van der Zee, 2000, 2007]

Evolution of the Concept of Miasms in Homeopathy

Hahnemann described three main miasms:

- Psora – "the most universal mother of chronic diseases" as the result of the suppression of leprosy ("… in ancient times … psora mostly confined itself to its dreadful cutaneous system, leprosy."). As an example of the confusion concerning miasms we find psora is connected with scabies in most texts and homeopaths extending the number of miasms have added leprosy as a separate miasm. "The symptoms of *psora* … are generally assumed to be scabies. … This assumption originated in Hahnemann's use of the German word *Krätze*, meaning *itch*, but which is used specifically to mean scabies ad was translated as such by Hempel." [Klein, 2009]
- Sycosis – resulting from suppressed gonorrhoea
- Syphilis – resulting from suppressed syphilis

Hahnemann concluded that all chronic diseases stem from any of these three miasms (mainly psora) or a combination of two or three of them.

> "... at least seven-eighths of all the chronic maladies spring from it (psora) as their only source, while the remaining eighth springs from syphilis and sycosis or from a complication of two or three of these chronic diseases, or (which is rare) from a complication of all three of them."

Hahnemann himself started to extend the number of miasms and used pseudo-psora as a remedy, which is thought most likely to have been a nosode of tuberculosis.

> "In this sense, Hahnemann evidently accepted that there were more than three miasms ..." [Klein, 2009]

Boenninghausen stated it as follows:

> " ... there may perhaps, besides the three above mentioned anamnesis indications, and besides the medicinal diseases, be one or another additional miasm to which may be ascribed a similar influence upon health." [Boenninghausen, 1908]

With the introduction of a remedy made from breast cancer *Burnett* indirectly introduced another miasm – the cancer miasm. An interesting development as the direct connection to microorganism was now dropped.

In the second half of the 20th century Latin American homeopaths like *Ortega* and *Paschero* published new theories on miasms that were less moralistic and more holistic. The direct connection to infectious diseases was released.

- Psora was related to inflammation and excitation [Paschero], or deficiency, inhibition, lack [Ortega]
- Sycosis was related to proliferation and inhibition [Paschero], or excess, escape, exudation [Ortega]
- Syphilis was related to destruction and loss of function [Paschero], or destruction, degeneration, perversion [Ortega]

Also miasms were now placed in a sequence, each showing a different level of a state or disease. From psora through sycosis to syphilis pictured three phases leading from life to death.

Later *Praful Vijaykar* connected the three miasms to cellular functions. He describes the survival mechanisms of the body as

- Homeostasis (Psora)
- Growth / Repair (Sycosis)
- Defence / Destruction (Syphilis)

The miasms in his model represent disturbances in cellular and body function. Disrupted homeostasis leads to inflammation and functional abnormalities, disturbance in growth and repair leads to overproduction of cells, and a disturbance in the defence mechanism of cells leads to loss of tissue.
Based on the embryonic tissue involved in pathology he developed what he called 'predictive homeopathy' as now the direction of cure could be predicted, following the laws of Hering, from mesothelium to endothelium to epithelium. [Vijaykar, 2005] These three pathological pathways of the human organism point in our opinion to a much larger concept than the three diseases Hahnemann connected them to. Scabies, Gonorrhoea and Syphilis as single diseases are connected to them but do not fully cover the totality of the corresponding miasms – psora, sycosis and syphilis. They are representatives of these miasms among many other diseases.

To many contemporary homeopaths it is now a feasible idea that in principle every infectious disease can be the basis of a miasm that is transmissible from generation to generation and can be treated by the appropriate nosode and specific anti-miasmatic remedies.

Rajan Sankaran created a system of ten miasms, which he placed within a flow chart. *Jan Scholten* placed these miasms within the periodic table of elements and connected them with the stages he described in *Homeopathy and the Elements*. [Scholten, 1996] There are clearly more miasms and we can consider the theory of miasms a work in process. *Louis Klein* has started a thorough research of nosodes and miasms and, if more homeopaths will by using his book prescribe a broader variety of nosodes and discover signs of symptoms of more miasms in their cases, we may expect that gradually a much more detailed map of the landscape of miasms will emerge.

Sankaran sees miasms as an expression of the depth of a state. "The miasm is therefore, in my understanding, a measure of *how much* or *how intensely* or *how acutely or chronically* or *how deeply* or *desperately* the situation is perceived to be." [Sankaran, 2004] A diseased state is based on a false perception of reality (delusion), which on a deeper level is experienced as a sensation, which calls forward a response that shows the miasm. Sankaran sees sensation and miasm as inseparable: "One should keep in mind that *the disease state could be described as being at the crossing point of the sensation and the miasm*." [ibid.]

The expression of such a state in a human being Sankaran calls the 'other song' as opposed to the natural 'human song'. At the danger of this becoming a play of words it is important to analyse whether indeed a diseased state should be considered as an expression of something not belonging to the natural state of man.

The fact that Sankaran was able to connect the variety of experience of a state with the miasms and so design a matrix of sensations (pointing to a family of remedies) and miasms (pointing to specific members of that family) and that this appears to function in homeopathic practice asks for an explanation of what these miasms then entail. Homeopathic remedies belonging to a specific miasm (e.g. sycosis) indicate that these remedies have similarity to the disease of that miasm (e.g. gonorrhoea). As discussed earlier in this book infectious diseases are actually teachers of mankind, and each miasm has a particular gift or lesson to convey. They are logical, natural and inevitable consequences of human acts, deeds or neglects – similar in nature to the Vedic term karma. If a person is not experiencing wholeness (which these days is the norm ... but neither normal nor natural!) those parts that are not experienced as self are projected on the outside world and the person is confronted with them in the outside world.

One way for nature to bring disowned parts home is through disease. On the level of DNA/RNA one could say that parts of our biological library that are missing or 'switched off' are being offered or triggered from outside through microorganisms that carry that particular part of information. They seem to carry and express something that we experience as not belonging to us (the other song). Only when the message has been incorporated and brought in harmony with the rest of us, can suffering end and our natural human song be heard again, be it now enriched by a part that was lacking before. It is important to realize here that at least 95% of our genetic material originally stems from microorganisms. Milestones signifying the building in of new information offered to us by the microorganisms with which we make this cosmic dance, mark our whole evolution. Or, said in another way, a human being is the amazing outcome of many different microorganism that together have built the DNA for a multi-cellular organism that makes new expressions of the flow of consciousness possible – like science, the arts, spirituality and love.

The kind of miasm expressed in response to a sensation shows the level of desperation [Sankaran] but it does more than that. It also shows how close the person is to getting the message home, as the more intense the situation becomes and the stronger the sensation is experienced the closer the individual comes to acceptance. In a bad dream one can run away from some frightening image and when there is no more escape and the monster is looked into the eye it turns into a helpless sad being, the opposite of what was feared. If we can look our monsters (other songs) into the eyes at an early stage (psora) we will be spared a lot of suffering. If we only look them in the eyes after having gone through many phases (walking away from them, denying them, etc – in fact all other miasms and their patterns of behaviour) and ultimately see no other option but to try to kill them with all the power that is in us (syphilis), it is at the moment that we feel we've lost it and give up in exhaustion, that suffering ends and instead of dying we are reborn into a better version of ourselves.

In *Miasms in Labour* [van der Zee, 2000] the stages of the birth process were analysed and compared with *Hahnemann*'s main three miasms – Psora, Sycosis and Syphilis – and the Acute miasm. Also, the stages of birth were compared with the different steps in *Jung*'s description of the individuation process. The conclusion, illustrated by several cases, was that the birth process is an analogy as well as an expression of the journey of mankind, and that in this journey miasms play a more far-reaching role than just creating pathology. Miasms are elemental in helping mankind to make the required steps in its development, just like an individual disease can become meaningful if it initiates growth and awareness in a person. Each individual is expressing or working on a specific element of the individuation process in a lifetime, and the birth experience is a first expression of this.

Here are some of the conclusions reached based on the analysis of the birth process in a large number of cases [van der Zee, 2007]:

- The birth process shows in a nutshell the journey of mankind on this planet.
- An individual birth history shows in a nutshell the main themes of the individual.
- The nature and pace of a delivery is similar to the nature and pace of the individual born.
- The same state is often already visible during pregnancy and conception.
- Rather than being causal, birth is therefore synchronous with and similar to the state of an individual.
- Following the tenets of reincarnation, it is clear that a person enters life in a state determined by earlier experiences – conception, pregnancy, birth and the life situation after birth fit to this state.
- An individual person enters life with a purpose – conception, pregnancy and the birth experience already serve to fulfil this purpose.
- Birth can be seen as the moment where the back up of the past software is installed on the new hardware – astrology is the science confirming this.
- A thorough analysis of the birth history in children as well as adults can help to understand and solve a case.
- There is a clear analogy between the phases of birth and the miasms.
- There is a clear analogy between the phases of birth and steps in the individuation process.
- Analysing the birth process deepens the understanding of the miasms.
- Miasms play a role and serve a purpose in the development of the human race.

- Each miasm is connected to a phase in or aspect of human development.
- Miasms are connected not only to pathology but also to qualities they invoke.
- Each miasmatic layer in an individual plays a role in unfolding qualities connected to it in the individual.
- Individual diseases and traumata are teachers at an individual level.
- Epidemics, collective traumata and miasms are teachers at a collective level.

In such a wider scope miasms are nothing but thc shadow side of phases in a healthy process of developing awareness. Their role and purpose is to bring the subconscious dark part into the light in order to fulfil and complete the corresponding phase, both on an individual level as well as in the collective.

Earlier in this book we have already discussed that comparable to infectious diseases traumatic events and intoxications can also be held responsible for transgenerational effects, and that the term miasm therefore deserves to be broadened to include any form of stress that can induce long-term effects that transcend generations, and consequently that there are, on an individual and collective level, more ways in which evolution is supported besides through infectious diseases.

As we see in the above the term miasm has different meanings with different authors partly because of an evolution of the concept, but the term has also become an umbrella for all kinds of ideas and theories. Within a bigger picture discrepancies seemingly disappear. Essential for this more encompassing view is the realization that infectious diseases and miasms not only create pathology but also fuel our individuation process and are instrumental in our evolution.

To avoid misunderstanding it would be helpful to bring clarity in the terminology. We therefore propose to use the term META-MIASMS for what Hahnemann meant by psora, sycosis and syphilis and to use terms like scabies miasm, gonorrhoea miasm and syphilis miasm and many others to point to specific miasms connected to specific diseases.

META-MIASMS: there are three meta-miasms – *psora*, *sycosis*, and *syphilis* - that have their basis in the nature of pathology (*inflammation, proliferation, destruction*) and the tissues involved (*epithelium, endothelium, mesothelium*). Their domains are not limited by being only related to and the direct result of a specific infectious disease (respectively leprosy/scabies, gonorrhoea or syphilis) but represent larger concepts.

A closer analysis will very likely show great similarities of the three miasms with other triple systems of classification like the Tridosha concept in Ayur Veda – *vata* (ether/air – anabolism), *pitta* (fire – catabolism), *kapha* (water/earth – metabolism). In homeopathic practice this classification is especially helpful in a proper understanding of the healing process (Hering's Laws).
In the part on trauma we will extensively discuss the survival instincts. The three main survival instincts are called *freeze, flight* and *fight.*

Hahnemann's three basic miasms are roughly summarized as underperformance, excessive performance and destructive performance. He identified three core traits within the human race very intelligently and did the best he could in the circumstances of his time.

If we look at the survival instincts in connection to the miasms there is a correspondence between:

- underperformance = freeze
- excessive performance = flight
- destructive performance = fight

These three primitive miasms we earlier suggested calling META-MIASMS we hypothesise are not then related to diseases but to our survival instincts. To us this makes much more sense and grounds Hahnemann's ideas in a primitive hard-wired reality that we all share. Everybody has virtually the same survival instincts because these were finished and encapsulated in a hard-wired primitive brain that we have all inherited.

We can then understand that some epidemic diseases are effectively the materialisation of these survival instincts, which date back to the time life, as we know it, began. They have precipitated out of consciousness as a materialisation of a survival instinct.

To carry the understanding Hahnemann's core miasms a step further we first need to discuss a new field of science – epigenetics.

References

- Boenninghausen, C.M.F. von. *Lesser Writings of Boenninghausen*, Ed. T.L. Bradford, Tr. L.H. Tafel. Republished: B. Jain Publishers, New Delhi 1994
- Hahnemann, Samuel. *Organon of the Medical Art*, sixth edition 1842, edited and annotated by Wendy Brewster O'Reilly, Birdcage Books, Redmond 1996
- Hahnemann, S. *The Chronic Diseases – Their Peculiar Nature and Their Homeo pathic Cure*, Tr. L.H. Tafel 1839, republished: Homeopathic Book Service, Sittingbourne, Kent, 1998
- Klein, Louis. *Miasms and Nosodes*, Narayana Publishers, Kandern 2009
- Sankaran Rajan. *The Sensation in Homoeopathy*, Homoeopathic Medical Publishers, Mumbai 2004
- Scheiwiller-Muralt, Erika. Variolinum, Vaccininum and Malandrinum - The powerful smallpox nosodes and their therapeutic use, *Homœopathic Links* Vol 15/4, Haren, Netherlands 2002
- Scholten, Jan. *Homeopathy and the Elements*, Stichting Alonnissos, Utrecht, 1996
- Watson, Ian. *The Homeopathic Miasms* - A Modern View, Cutting Edge Publications, Devon 2009
- Vijaykar, Praful. *Predictive Homoeopathy* (Part 3) – The end of Myasmtion, Mumbai 2005
- Zee, Harry van der. *Miasms in Labour*, Stichting Alonnissos, Utrecht 2000, reprint Homeolinks Publishers, Haren 2009
- Zee, Harry van der. *Homeopathy for Birth Trauma*, Homeolinks Publishers, Haren 2007

Epigenetics and Miasms

Science has now come up with a new mechanism for understanding miasms, which completely rewrites the old ideas and also makes sense of all the previous ideas. It's called epigenetics and it allows us to have a new and scientifically verifiable and acceptable way of understanding and explaining the miasms. Also, because it fits in so much better with what we homeopaths know, it seems epigenetics is the key that opens up a whole new dimension that embraces prior homeopathic and human evolution and unites homeopathy with modern science again.

Epigenetics describes a mechanism by which genetics modify from one generation to another. We will try to describe this in very elementary terms.

- *DNA methylation* is a process by which certain DNA bases repress gene activity.
- *Histone modification* is a process by which combinations of different molecules attach themselves to the tails of proteins called histones. These alter the activity of the DNA wrapped around them.

The rest is quite straightforward. The modified DNA makes the chromosomes that make up the nucleus of the cell. Divide and multiply this to ten trillion cells and you have a human being. Every cell is obviously a specialized version of the first genetic cell we start with at conception.

An interesting author to read along with many others, including *Bruce Lipton*, is *David Schenck* and his book *The Genius in All of Us.*

We propose to call those formative genetic information patterns SPECIFIC MIASMS. They are related to a specific disease, trauma or other condition, and are being passed on in a modified, deranged way from one generation to another. We also propose a new concept to explain Hahnemann's core META-MIASMS based upon our research.

Although trauma is a subject by itself and is discussed in detail in Part III of this book, we need to discuss trauma here in relationship to the forming forces of diseases.
The forming forces of SPECIFIC MIASMS can be summarized like this:

- Trauma in the form of
  - physical trauma
  - emotional trauma
  - sexual trauma
  - spiritual trauma
  - nutritional and food trauma
  - disease trauma (the old miasms)
  - drug and toxicity trauma (including vaccinations)
  - environmental trauma
  - etc.
- Nurturing which exacerbates or ameliorates the above effects.

Each of these items will now be discussed in detail.

Trauma

We all experience trauma. And there is a natural way of processing it. If this happens fully there is nothing left and there is no epigenetic trauma.

What happens though is that, because of the hyperactive survival instincts and other pre-existing trauma that get in the way of processing new trauma, we accumulate trauma increasingly with time. It tends to accumulate around already existing foci of trauma and in the process of living the accumulated trauma becomes stronger and stronger. The psychiatrist *Stanislav Grof* in his analysis called these COEX-systems – systems of condensed experience. We would argue that the reason we get old is that we accumulate trauma, which stiffens us up, and increases the levels of toxins and finally terminates our existence in a body.

While there are many obvious categories of trauma, like poisoning, it is also possible that traumas occur that have many different aspects to them. For reasons of understanding and treating them, isolation of the different aspects creates potentially great possibilities for treatment.

For example if a person is poisoned by arsenic, homeopathic arsenic will usually be the first rational treatment of choice, and could be more effective than individual treatment. This so-called isopathic approach especially seems to be very effective in the early stages after the poisoning and might be all that is required. The longer ago the trauma took place the harder it is to detect the cause and the more individualised prescribing is required. But without identifying the cause and prescribing for it, a cure may never be reached. The same might apply to rape, specific epidemic disease trauma etc.

Epidemic trauma

Perhaps with the exception of syphilis, which is relatively new in the west and of which hereditary conditions have been described, we have not seen yet from contemporary medicine the evidence that any one epidemic disease makes an epigenetic imprint. This is nevertheless expected to happen soon because homeopaths have recognized this for two centuries and used it to great effect therapeutically. The obvious hypothesis is that every epidemic disease can and will impact epigenetically.

It has been shown that the homeopathic remedies made from disease products (nosodes) can be used therapeutically as prophylactics against the disease.

The only difference between vaccinations and homeopathic nosodes for an epidemic disease, seems that the one makes profit and is toxic while the other is very easy to make, can be mass-produced in a matter of days in terms of billions of doses, is safe and free of side-effects, non-toxic and non-profitable. It is not common sense but profit and the materialistic paradigm tends to ignore or ridicule anything non-material like homeopathy and determines which one is used.

When it comes to a worldwide epidemic, on the same scale as the 1918 epidemic, there may be no better solution than the homeopathic one, which could save hundreds of millions of lives. Because of the level of prejudice and lack of research homeopathy is indeed not likely to be used at this point in time. As a result many lives may be sacrificed needlessly, or a successful suppression of the epidemic may result in the disease going underground to be expressed in other ways, specifically in chronic diseases.

In practice the homeopathic nosodes have not however been shown to be universally successful in the treatment of epidemic diseases, which is one of the reasons why PC Technology was developed. Why nosodes do not effectively treat the diseases they are related to is something we discussed earlier in this book.

Nosodes have their place in the treatment of chronic diseases based on a miasmatic history, but cannot be consistently used to treat the infectious disease itself in the acute or chronic state. PC RESONANCES in our experience are both prophylactic and curative. Hahnemann's original findings about scarlet fever and *Belladonna*, that it is in principle possible to select one remedy for an infectious disease, are confirmed by our experience with PC RESONANCES.

When epidemic diseases are recognized to have epigenetic effects scientifically, then we can expect the gap between homeopathy and conventional medicine to get closer.

Spiritual trauma

Consider this case. A young woman is found to have a very low CD4 count, which is commonly indicative of AIDS, and the HIV test is positive.

However her case history does not follow any normal pattern. What in fact happened is that she was brought up in a strictly religious family, and chose to break away from her religion. In breaking away from her religion, she loses her religion and all its dogma and restrictions, the rules and regulations so strictly followed by its adherents. She also loses her family that is completely committed to this religion. In Africa in situations where you are a member of a tribe, it is a death sentence to become excommunicated from the tribe. Life loses its structure and collapses and people often die in such situations.

So it is not surprising that this event in her young life is extremely damaging. This is a spiritual crisis and a trauma of the highest order, worse because it's neither as visible as the effects of genocide et cetera nor so easily understood by society or by herself.

On a larger scale we could say this is a problem of Africa. When you study African traditional spiritual practices – and there are some great books on the subject, for example books by *Maldoma* – we would say that Africans have suffered from a terrible spiritual crisis brought about by colonialism, missionaries, slavery, and rape of their natural resources and the total non-recognition of their culture. In retrospect one could regard the attitude of missionaries in the era of colonialism as arrogant and ignorant. There was no need to destroy the native religions. There was every possibility for helping them understand the teaching of Jesus and adding that into their practices, if it was missing. But the idea of teaching love at the point of a gun is a contradiction and could not be understood by the African cultures. Catholics and others had investigated the previous African cultural practices and they chose to eradicate the old methods. The idea of forcing upon them Islam or Christianity lock stock and barrel without any consideration or respect for their native religion and culture and its values is in hindsight unbelievable. This is not to say all was well with Traditional African Medicine, but a closer look at the history of Christianity or Islam should allow for more modesty.

Toxic trauma

The long-term trans-generational effects of toxins is actually already an important part of Hahnemann's definition of miasms, as in his opinion miasms are the results of the suppression of symptoms. Syphilis, for example, was treated with high doses of mercury, known to be poisonous, and this suppression had an energetic aspect to it in terms of the suppression of the life force by a toxic component. The fact that mercury is the main remedy to treat the syphilitic miasm shows the clear link to toxicity, as mercury was used in high dosages to suppress syphilis.

Hahnemann was a pioneer also in this field and it is only recently that science is more focused on investigating the long-term effects of toxins.

There is another big example of this recently. In the beginning of the use of anti-retroviral drugs for AIDS, specifically AZT was used in massive doses before it was properly researched, and it is now considered by some that the first generation of AIDS cases who hoped to receive extra life by the drugs were killed by the side-effects. Crazy as it sounds, but as we might expect homeopathically, AZT causes AIDS-like symptoms, and the painful reality is that tens of thousands of gay people have died from these. In Africa and other countries AZT is still being used, be it in lower doses, as it is relatively cheap.

On a larger scale, when experts have analyzed the death statistics in the United States they have reached the conclusion that the number one major cause of death in the United States is death by the side-effects of drugs. In other words the drugs used to treat people are killing them. The golden standard in medical research, randomised controlled trials, has a paradoxical effect. "... the more supporting the frame conditions [of a treatment] are, the less a specific therapy will perform better than a placebo. **The more damaging the context of a treatment, the more effective a specific therapy will appear in the context of a randomised trial.** The conclusion is as simple as it is frightening: That is, the better we treat our patients, the more we come up to their singularity, the more we support their self-healing process, the more a therapy will seem to be a placebo-therapy. This can be formulated even more strictly: If the activation of a self-healing mechanisms is defined as a placebo effect and only the interference with inner regulation is defined as 'specific therapy', then every regulative therapy cannot be something else than a placebo therapy." [Ivanovas, 2012]

Homeopaths fortunately don't have to suffer the problem of side-effects because in homeopathy these are essentially not possible. There are no toxic quantities of substances used in homeopathy. Homeopathy does suffer from the paradox mentioned above in that it doesn't damage and therefore may seem ineffective.

In one epigenetic study fruit flies exposed to a drug called geldanamycin showed unusual outgrowths on their eyes that could last through at least thirteen generations of offspring even though no change in DNA has occurred (and generations two through thirteen were not directly exposed to the drug). [Time Magazine]

A new analysis of U.S. health data links children's attention-deficit disorder with exposure to common pesticides used on fruits and vegetables. [Huffington Post]

According to the Center for Disease Control in the United States there are 212 toxic chemicals in our blood stream that should not be there. [World Press] Every one of these chemicals has the possibility of creating serious abnormalities in a human body. The abnormalities that two or more of these chemicals acting together can cause is hard to predict and in most cases probably unknown. The combinations of these chemicals working together offer limitless possibilities for epigenetic modification. This would seem like a very important discovery and should ring alarm bells everywhere. It is an emerging medical opinion both conventionally and alternative that infants are particularly susceptible to this process and that the accumulation of toxins possibly has epigenetic effects passed on for generations and is a reason for current behavioural problems of epidemic proportions like autism and ADHD.

This list does not include those toxic substances that are used as drugs to treat diseases which, as we've pointed out before, are being considered as a major cause of death, but which in the light of epigenetics may also cause trans-generational effects of a magnitude that can only be imagined.

We are seeing, generation after generation, a more toxic human race. It is certainly our experience of Africa and other 'grow your own food populations', that they are more vital and much more easily treated with homeopathy than Westerners. One simple explanation for this is the level and variety of toxins in tissues and the bloodstream.

We were once incredibly vitalized, healthy dynamic, invulnerable to cold, strong and able to work all day in the fields. We have systematically degraded our physical health generation upon generation without recognizing it, but now, three generations after this started in earnest, we have serious percentages of people with depleted energy as well as toxic kids. If smoke from cigarettes and coal fires was the outer toxic problem of the first half of the 20th century, then inner smog in our bloodstream that is far more toxic, is the problem of the 21st-century.

Psychological trauma

Research has shown that traumatized chickens pass the trauma on to their chicks. [Time Magazine] So we can see that trauma patterns can be passed down the generations. This corresponds to the homeopathic experience of *Staphysagria* for rape. Women whose mothers have been raped often respond well to *Staphysagria*, which fits the picture of rape as a trauma. It's probable that every woman would benefit from a dose of Staphysagria at least once in her life to address this particular Specific Miasm. Current studies show that one out of three women on this planet have suffered from sexual abuse one way or the other, meaning on average in a genetic line either grandmother, mother or daughter has been or will be sexually abused. In other words sexual abuse or rape is within the constellation of practically each and every family.

Nutritional trauma

Food has already been scientifically demonstrated to have an epigenetic effect. [David Shenk and Time magazine] Studies have shown that when one generation suffers nutritional deficiencies due to the failure of the harvest, subsequent generations suffer from serious life-shortening conditions.

On top of this:

- There is depleted food - we grow a lot of food in soil that is insufficiently nurtured and maintained. We use fertilizers to force the food out of the ground, but the nutritional content has sunk over the generations so we tend to eat food which is depleted and therefore is neither vital nor energy providing. Junk food is what it says: junk.
- We also eat traumatized food in the form of farmed animals and farmed fish. These creatures are kept in unsavoury conditions of huge overcrowding, fed hormones to fatten them, and often antibiotics to keep them from the infections rife in such overcrowded situations. We end up eating meat full of the sorrows of abject animal life, secreted by the endocrine glands into their flesh: we eat their misery which adds to our own and includes the antibiotics they receive. All the drugs excreted in urine and insufficiently filtered out when the water is recycled for human benefit pollute the water. We end up with infants overfed on hormones in the womb having exaggerated breasts as infants.

- And there is of course the immunity to antibiotics that might be necessary later on to save our life. Because of the enormous amounts of antibiotics given to animals, therapy-resistant bacteria are on the rise and are consumed by humans as well. For instance, 88% of all chicken meat in Dutch shops is contaminated with therapy resistant ESBL bacteria, and people getting sick from them can in turn infect others, so even vegetarians aren't safe. [http://badnewsfromthenetherlands.blogspot.com/2010/04]

Other unnamed trauma

The limit to which epigenetics may be affected is not known. Unless proven differently it seems wise to assume that every kind of trauma has an effect to some extent or other. In the above we are defining some of the obvious and major events that can have an influence.

Nurturing

Nurturing is what happens from conception onwards, in the womb, at birth, and in upbringing. Depending on the circumstances and the awareness of parents and others, nurturing exacerbates or ameliorates the epigenetic variations caused by unstable survival instincts and unresolved trauma.

The nurturing itself is of course disturbed by survival instincts that overrule awareness because the survival instincts then dominate everything including nurturing, feeling and thinking.

The simple formula is that nurturing multiplies epigenetic changes. It's not a question of nurturing or nature. It's nurturing multiplying nature that creates who we are. The problem is that good nurturing brings out the best of us and bad nurturing brings out the worst of us. And generally speaking we get a good dose of both, but unfortunately the majority of nurturing leads to huge underperformance in comparison with our potential.

This is because most people are greatly underperforming so in turn they can only mirror this to their children however well intentioned they are. It is the situation of the human race at the present time – great underperformance everywhere (the psoric lack in another disguise).

Nurturing starts with conception and continues during pregnancy and birth. The choices made by parents in this period already influence the child. A birth process either or not induced, either or not under the influence of analgesics or other drugs, either or not replaced by a caesarean, either or not followed by breastfeeding, either or not followed by vaccinations on day one, these are all fundamental choices that already set the tone for the quality of nurturing. It is a strong sign of our times that nowadays many babies do not receive breastfeeding or only for a very short time. We know from the homeopathic remedies made from substances like the placenta, the umbilical cord, colostrum (first breast discharge) and from mother's milk that any disturbance in the early nurturing process on a physical and/or psychological level can have profound and lifelong psychological influences.

We also know from sports people like the Williams sisters, Monica Seles and Tiger Woods and from the study of geniuses like Mozart, that early nurturing of talent, if it proves to be there (parents often try nurturing talent that isn't there, and the child gives up, and sensible parents give up too), can result in the very early development to extraordinary talent. Nurturing talent can at the same time be traumatic. E.g. Yehudi Menuhin told how this was traumatic for him and at the same time we see where it got him.

We also know there is an approximate figure for how many hours of practice it takes to develop a talent. Something like 10,000 hours of deliberate practice is required to nurture talent to a high level in any field of human endeavour. Deliberate means practising the hard bits as well as the easy parts. This is in music, aircraft engine design, sports and as far as I can see every field of human endeavour including homeopathy. It is no surprise that Rajan Sankaran's father was a significant homeopath. What is interesting is how George Vithoulkas came to be a great homeopath without this beneficial start to life, but both for sure invested their 10,000 hours plus to get where they are. Starting at a young age though has great advantage as the earlier the neurological pathways are nurtured the easier and more naturally skills are acquired.

We could also say the opposite. With 10,000 hours worth of training, called parenting, we can drill into our children all the worst habits we have.

In one particular case we studied, the mother was very overprotective of her son. She herself had been a gymnast and had been completely unable to perform in public, in spite of eleven years of training and many, many injuries, because she was too nervous. The sports training did not address her psychology at all. When her toddler son started to run away in the countryside where there was no traffic and no real danger, she grabbed him back quickly, with scolding and punishment, as if he could come to terminal harm. His grandmother and his great-aunt did likewise. What was obvious to us was that she was training him to expect there to be danger at every corner and in every situation. In virtually every situation every minute and hour of the day, they were teaching him the extreme nervousness that was in the family. This type of negative nurturing can be found in every family that we have observed including our own. It takes a high degree of awareness not to transmit to our children the hyperactive survival instincts and unresolved trauma in the specific forms that we have inside us. For example if we have a high degree of guilt, it's pretty certain our children will too. It may be there genetically as a possibility; with nurturing it becomes a certainty.

The whole system of schooling, which enforces children to sit at desks and learn by rote or some other method, is in itself a form of indoctrination and brainwashing and rather kills creativity and originality than nurtures them. While there are many attempts to get away from this idea, it's still endemic in many countries and continents. It's brainwashing by the 10,000 hours method. It's fine when it comes to the good parts, but given that the teachers themselves are generally living well below their potential, that's the key message they teach the children.

We think this understanding gives a rational to broaden the homeopathic approach and to radically update the core therapeutic methods to better address what is happening in the real world. It opens up the possibilities of understanding how humans fail and how we can use homeopathy to help people develop into the geniuses that we all potentially are.

In the above Hahnemann's original miasms, being caused by three infectious diseases, have been stretched out over many more different causes. By only extending the number of miasms the thinking and attitude behind them though is still largely the same. All sorts of events happen and damage genetic material and homeopaths are well equipped to clean up the mess. As discussed before, homeopaths have actually considered miasms in an allopathic way. While in the treatment of patients it is generally understood that symptoms are a healthy sign of the dynamis in action, the diseases themselves and the miasms underlying them are being considered in a very similar way to an allopath's treatment of a pathogen. Only the method of getting rid of the pathogen, disease or miasm is different. In the next chapter we intend to further lift the whole understanding of miasms and their role and purpose to a higher level.

References

- Schenk, David. *The Genius in All of Us - Why Everything You've Been Told About Genetics, Talent, and IQ Is Wrong*. Doubleday, New York 2010
- Grof, Stanislav. *Realms of the Human Unconscious*. Viking, New York 1975
- http://www.time.com/time/health/article/0,8599,1951968-3,00.html
- Ivanovas, George. Individualisation and the Practitioner's Paradox - Homeopathy and Evidence Based Medicine part 2, *Homoeopathic Links* 2012 (publication planned June 2012)
- http://www.huffingtonpost.com/2010/05/17/adhd-pesticides-in-fruits_n_578366.html
- http://greeningourchildren.wordpress.com/2010/04/06/the-perils-of-plastic-time-magazine-april-1-2010/

Part III

Theory of Treating Trauma

Trauma and Epigenetics

In the chapter Epigenetics and Miasms (Part II) we have already discussed the importance of trauma for the formative forces of diseases. We proposed to call those formative genetic information patterns that are being passed on in a modified, deranged way from one generation to the other SPECIFIC MIASMS. Many different forms of trauma can be identified, e.g.:

- physical trauma
- emotional trauma
- sexual trauma
- spiritual trauma
- nutritional and diet trauma
- epidemic disease trauma (the old Hahnemannian miasms)
- medical and street drug, alcohol and cigarette and other chemical toxicity trauma including vaccinations
- environmental trauma

The realisation of the importance of trauma in relation to diseases – be they acute, infectious, epidemic, endemic or chronic – justifies a thorough discussion of it. An important starting point in our opinion is the topic of the survival instincts.

Trauma and Survival Instincts

All traumas can be seen as being rooted in our survival instincts and all physical pain as unexpressed emotional pain/trauma.

Also, on a deeper level all diseases can be seen as manifestations of chronic trauma patterns. As this is not a common understanding we describe this process in depth.

The survival instincts (see figure 1) that live in our reptilian brain largely determine our behaviour, especially at critical times.

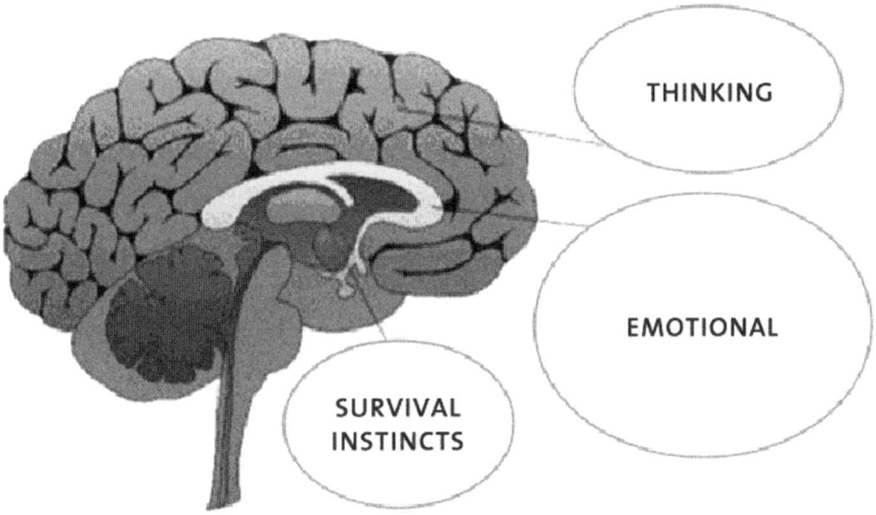

Figure 1: Survival instincts (© 2011 Jiří Vokáč Čmolík, Prague)

The reptilian brain, also called the amygdala, was roughly half a billion years or so in the making and our human brain by comparison is just a few hundred thousand years old. The reptilian brain is fast; it works in about one-hundredth of a second, whereas our human brain is two to three times slower. The reptilian brain is also instinctive, crude, thoughtless, and pre-verbal as it was developed before speech existed. It seems as if it is hardwired and impervious to thinking. The human brain has very little influence upon the reptilian brain whereas the reptilian brain has a fast and overwhelming influence upon the human brain. The reptilian brain messages tend to dominate us at critical moments, which occur many times daily.

It seems that the reptilian brain cannot be adapted and does not respond to new programming, as does the thinking brain.

The above may not seem very obvious. It's a very hard point to get across in words. Unless you can reflect upon the experiences when you have been shocked, and the adrenaline rush happens, you will not fully appreciate the importance of the survival instincts. You will think that two hundredths of a second is not very much. It's the gap between the reptilian brain's response and the thinking brain's response. But in our experience it has s tremendous importance, because from our research we understand that the reptilian brain dominates human behaviour at all times. Not just in times of shock but in any periods of disharmony or incongruity in conversation, as well as in action.

It is important to understand this idea clearly, as it is a very important part of human behaviour. What happens is that sensory input, especially sight and hearing is relayed simultaneously to both the reptilian brain and the human brain. By the human brain we mean the neo-cortex, the brain we have developed since we were animals, and which manages thinking and thoughtful responses. While the information is relayed simultaneously to both brains, the reptilian brain is about three times faster in response and a lot more powerful in its biochemical effects. The reptilian brain is the alarm system of the body and fulfils the necessity for a powerful instantaneous instinctive and hardwired response. It causes us to experience immediate fear as a way to protect us from imminent danger, and because it is so powerful, it primes the whole body for action. This is why it is so hard to control. We can all know this from personal observation and from observation of others. When we sense danger while driving, our foot is on the brake even before we have evaluated the problem or even thought about it consciously. The reptilian has the stronger pathway to action.

More importantly even, when the danger has ceased the reptilian brain takes a long time to calm down because the signal from our thinking human brain is much weaker and has less influence upon the reptilian brain. The problem is that when we are, or just think we are, in acute danger the survival reaction starts a cascade of biochemical responses and activates the reptilian brain; the body's adrenaline is secreted to activate fast responses. We go to top level alert.

Animals, in running to escape, use up the adrenaline, and don't stay on alert unnecessarily. We don't have this advantage because many of the situations that trigger the response do not involve a physical threat but are more experienced on a psychological level. Many times we stay, either from need or social convention, in situations we would actually prefer to run away from. We have the instinct but not the natural way to recover and wind back down to zero.

Unless the immune system is told to 'stand down' or to go back to a non-crisis situation, it will continue to generate and maintain a 'high alert status' in the body. Imagined threats can also keep us in the over-alert state for decades after serious trauma.

There is an important consequence to this high alert state.

We have a hardwired hierarchy and a prioritising system within us against different levels of threat.
When survival is a threat all other functions are given a lower priority: so food is not important and appetite is suppressed, heat and cold are not important, sleep is not important, recovering from illness is not important so the immune system is inactivated; only survival is important.
During an acute illness rest and sleep become of priority; mental and physical action are not a priority; and drinking but not eating is a priority; immune action is a top priority as often shown by fever.
When normal living is the priority, then we eat, sleep and live naturally, not on alert, and with the immune system at rest.

The problem comes when we don't use up the adrenalin, when we don't wind down, keeping the body in a state of chronic alert. The immune system is then chronically suppressed, because it is natural to be so in this state of survival alert. This alert can last a lifetime since time does not exist in terms of body memories (see later chapters); it is as if it happened yesterday. This is common after catastrophic events like genocide and earthquakes; even after fifteen years survivors say it's as if it happened yesterday.

The next step to understand this process is that this chronic alert state can be passed down from one generation to the next by the epigenetic and nurturing process. As a result the next generation, having a residual chronic alert without knowing why, becomes hyper-reactive to all sorts of emotions – without knowing why – and is permanently running on adrenaline, whilst the immune system under-functions as a consequence. It also has the effect of undermining our personal life because we become over-reactive to everything and from this we often shrink and underperform in every aspect of life. It also leads to simple things like high blood pressure without any apparent reason.

The suppressed immune system makes us vulnerable to opportunistic diseases and can trigger illnesses. On a deeper level it can mean that inherited tendencies get a hold. We all have in us the seeds of many illnesses and our immune system normally keeps them at bay, destroying any rogue cells that try to express themselves and weaken our health.
Over-reactive survival instincts not only put us into a chronic alert state, which undermines our personal life and our success in life, but they also undermine our health.

A key point is that survival instincts are not commonly recognised as a problem. They are not commonly recognised in coaching, sports training, education, parenting, legal matters, therapies of any description, yet they dominate many areas of life. Outside most boxes, they affect everybody, like one huge blind spot. This shows up in research in top performers like surgeons who feel routinely overstressed, and it contributes to high blood pressure and hyperactivity in children, but it is neither well recognised nor understood.

What is also clear is that we need effective tools to deal with these hyperactive survival instincts.

Our Violent History Over-stimulates Our Survival Instincts

The history of the last hundred years and more shows an impressive amount and variety of traumatic events.

There has been enormous violence against individuals over the last hundred years involving the deaths of hundreds of millions of people. The successful intention was often to intimidate the billions of survivors.

People have been killed, tortured, intimidated, disappeared, raped, violated and scared to death, which in turn has a deep effect on billions of other people.
See www.amnesty.org for current events in this area.

The violence against people and groups have included up to eleven million people in each of the following categories and tens and hundreds of millions more people terrorised in some way by each incident:

- Mass starvation – in the Ukraine alone, under Stalin between seven and eleven million people starved to death – www.ukemonde.com/news/rferl.html (we can only try to imagine how the survivors felt and remembered).
- Much mass extermination often involved tens of thousands of people.
- Firestorms in Dresden, Tokyo, Yokohama, Hamburg, Darmstadt, Pforzheim, Hiroshima, London etc. resulted in 10,000 to 120,000 dead overnight in some cities and millions more traumatised by the fire – en.wikipedia.org/wiki/Firestorm
- Widespread ethnic cleansing/genocide (not just the Holocaust) against whole nations and groups of people, religions and castes:
  - There were about 50 such major events last century.
  - There have already been about fifteen so far this century.
  - Many of these involved groups of 100,000 to eleven million people.
  - They took place on every continent.
  - Russians, Serbians, Albanians, Sikhs, Palestinians, Indonesians, Greeks, Turks, Congolese, Kurds, Burmese, Vietnamese, Italians, Hondurans, Bangladeshi, Cambodians, Bulgarians, Armenians, Sri Lankans, Indians, Kalimantanese, etc. – See en.wikipedia.org/wiki/Ethnic_cleansing.
- Wars of unimaginable proportions glibly called World War I and World War II involved a full range of terrifying events.
- More and more powerful weapons of mass destruction (atomic bombs on Japan) were created.

www.thereader-movie.com is just one of these stories, told in a very compelling award winning way.

There was also a range of sudden catastrophic natural events such as:

- Tsunamis
- Erupting volcanoes
- Earthquakes
- Floods

... involving in some cases 200,000 deaths as well as terrible memories for the millions of survivors.

There are also deadly epidemics, like the bird flu of 1918 which killed 20-40 millions in a short span of time and implanted fear and grief in many millions more.

There are also currently potentially dangerous events such as childbirth, which if not handled properly can be hospital-made catastrophes as any number of seemingly life-threatening situations can arise at childbirth. There are numerous books on this, for example Stanislav Grof's *Psychology of the Future: Lessons from Modern Consciousness Research* and www.stanislavgrof.com, which lists a lot more books on this and other subjects.

Such violent events now affect hundreds of millions if not billions of people.

There can also be serious long lasting consequences from:

- Accidents
- Operations
- Anaesthetics
- Incubation
- Adoption
- Terrible parenting
- Incest
- Violent punishments/beatings (e.g. to a young child for innocently showing and comparing its genitalia to another child or a fourteen-year-old for the crime of falling in love with someone of the wrong sex, caste, age, race, colour or belief)
- Abuse

These can leave strong impressions lasting a lifetime if not resolved.

The result is that, in most parts of the world there have been massive threats to survival to every human being in previous generations. These threats have now been transferred to the current generations as an over-activated reptilian brain through parenting, epigenetics and simply growing up with people living in this nightmare. We are now living out the unresolved effects of these events.

Here is one simple Western example to show the process of trauma transmission.

In Eastern Europe under the Nazis and later Stalin:

- Dozens of people disappeared every day
- They were taken into police custody and shot
- There were firing squads operating daily often within earshot of others
- This method was used for two decades to intimidate the population
- Complete peoples were forced to leave their home country, and by foot or cattle train driven to remote areas.

If you fast-forward this to current generations, from a study of people in one such area, it is not uncommon for people to feel

- That if they in any way stand out they could be shot
- That it is dangerous to speak up, or that it is somehow difficult
- That they are never settled or never really belong to the population.

Such common situations, such as difficulty in raising your hand in classroom or speaking to an official, can come from such a history that goes back 50, 100 or 200 years.

This leads to great underperformance and personal suffering.

The transmission of trauma, a 200-year example

A brilliant brain scientist who has made a career from identifying a killer profile gives this fantastic example of how this transmission process down the generations works in his family. (http://blog.ted.com/2009/07/psychopathic_ki.php)

His great great great great great (maybe more) grandfather was *Ezra Cornell* (January 11, 1807 – December 9, 1874) an American businessman and, with Andrew Dickson White, the founder of Cornell University.

Also, in his family line on his father's side is Lizzie Borden (July 19, 1860 – June 1, 1927), a New England spinster who was the central figure in the now famous hatchet murders of her father and stepmother on August 4, 1892 in Fall River, Massachusetts in the United States.

On top of this, seven more men on his father's side were all murderers.

Here is the first one.

> "What was strange about Widow Cornell's death? In the evening, Rebecca's body was found badly burned, lying some distance away from the hearth in the downstairs room she inhabited in the Cornell family's large, clapboard homestead. Her married son Thomas, his wife, teenage sons, and boarders had been eating supper in an adjacent room, on the other side of a closed door, apparently oblivious to the catastrophe.
> After watching two physicians conduct an autopsy and discover near Rebecca's heart a hole that might have been made with a long, narrow, iron spindle, the inquest jurors concluded that the widow had died not just from fire but also from a "Suspicious wound." This turn of events, along with now-circulating rumours that Rebecca had recently complained of ill treatment by her son Thomas, and with the fact that Thomas had been "the last man in her company" spending more than an hour alone with his mother before supper on the evening she died, led to Thomas Cornell's arrest and indictment for murder."

On top of this case there were six other murderers in the family history.

And then his father and his father's brothers were conscientious objectors – which means people who are really against violence. You can understand this differently. A well-known concept in psychology is that what you deny you also have. For example if someone came to you and said "I'm absolutely against violence and I really dislike violence and do everything to avoid violence and I'm a pacifist" then you know they have suppressed violence. Denial means the opposite as well. It is a basic rule of psychology.

So the fact that his uncles and father were against violence still says violence is a strong issue in the family.

And then of course there is this scientist's career, which has culminated in the study of killers and the idea of identifying the ultimate killer profile. His whole career revolves around violence in the form of killing other people. Violence is still shaping his life.

And there's another thread running down his family line, which is called Cornell. Obviously a highly intelligent man who created a leading university and now many generations later this trait continues in this brilliant scientist.

This is a great example of how epigenetics multiplied by family nurturing and conditioning directs the life for good and bad.

There are maybe seven generations here and his life is a combination of the effects of violence and the effects of educated intelligent minds. It looks as if Cornell, the great mind, and Thomas Borden, the killer, wrote the book of his life seven generations ago.

We think we have freedom in the way our lives work but, here we have an example where we could argue that his life story was written in the 1800s and he's living it in the 2000s.

This does not mean it is a wasted life, or without purpose, completely the contrary. But it lets us understand how lives are shaped, for every one of us.

In our understanding, we are not the life shaped by the past, but the awareness living through this shaped-by-the past mind-body, and the historic story acts as a focus for life. Like a telescope or microscope, it gives our body-mind a useful focus for our true nature to operate through. Just look what a useful life this scientist has led!

Rwanda Genocide

As an example of many of the above let's look at the Rwanda genocide. We discuss this specific traumatic event in more detail because just as AIDS was the condition that inspired a new approach in dealing with epidemics, so the Rwandan genocide trauma was what launched a Genus epidemicus approach to trauma.

There are many residual traumas within humanity as we have already mentioned. We want now to highlight just one in greater depth to illustrate the far-reaching, widespread effects and complexities involved in trauma. Instead of genocide you could choose any other trauma like terrorising, torture, parental verbal abuse and see it also transition into a multifaceted world-wide trauma that no one escapes.

Genocide is traumatic, even to read about. To show real footage is rarely done except in very special situations as it's just too traumatic to watch. People who do, typically journalists, who go to war zones, become traumatised and anaesthetised. This can also happen by watching the news daily.

Before leaving England for Rwanda in 2005, I (Peter) met a survivor in London, a 21-years-old Tutsi living in UK, a genocide victim. This was her simplified version as she put it.

Hutus were the aggressors. Tutsis were the victims. Those that survived hid themselves well, under beds, on roofs, anywhere or ran like hell away like she did. Those that were not well hidden, men, women and children were simply killed. All of the aggressors were Hutus, except many of them naturally rebelled at the idea and were killed, or worse, forced to kill their families, their wives and children, if their family were mixed marriages. Many deeply regret what they did and feel unimaginable remorse. Others are still in denial and still, to this day in 2005, eleven years later, killing the witnesses of what they did personally. The killing bloodbath went on for months so that every day was another opportunity to be killed while life also continued in some way, shopping for food supplies etc.

I asked my informant how she felt now about it and she said '*it's as if it happened yesterday.*'

This exact story, *as if it happened yesterday*, we have heard from many teenage survivors of her generation in Rwanda, DRC Congo and Burundi. We imagine they all feel thus, if they have the strength of mind to push it into the subconscious.
She said there is great sadness amongst the remaining living Tutsi people. We cannot even begin to imagine the states people are still in.

Rwanda's 1994 genocide, which claimed an estimated 850,000 lives over the course of 100 days, left permanent scars on Rwanda, its culture, and its children. In what Philip Gourevitch – author of the critically acclaimed book on the Rwandan genocide, *We Wish to Inform You that Tomorrow We Will Be Killed with Our Families* – called the fastest, most concentrated murder spree of the 20th century. Hutu militiamen, soldiers, and men and women citizens, hacked men, women, and children from Rwanda's Tutsi minority to death with machetes.

If you watched the documentary *Hotel Rwanda* you will have some idea of what happened. Obviously they could only show the briefest of glimpses of real video shot at the time, as these were too horrific to show. Just to watch even now would be severely traumatic, and so the film can only convey the impression of what happened, but while we were not there at the time of the genocide, we think the film corresponds closely to reality. If you multiply the killing shown by thousands of times you get some idea of what happened. What the film does not show are the consequences many years later. It does not show the hearts and minds – the mental and emotional states – of the survivors or the perpetrators. This would be worth another film in its own right. What happened in those ten or so weeks was etched into the hearts and minds of all those involved, and for many quite simply, their hearts and minds were broken forever. Not hurting, not just traumatised, but utterly broken beyond the imagination of anyone who has not experienced it. We will describe the effects later, but this still does not allow us inside their horror of horrors.

Here is another version of genocide in Rwanda

Most of the dead were Tutsis – and most of those who perpetrated the violence were Hutus. Even for a country with such a turbulent history as Rwanda, the scale and speed of the slaughter left its people reeling. The genocide was sparked by the death of the Rwandan president Juvenal Habyarimana, a Hutu, when his plane was shot down above Kigali airport on 6 April 1994. Within hours of the attack, an orchestrated and planned campaign of violence (they had the hatchets already imported) spread from the capital throughout the country, and did not subside until three months later. But the death of the president was by no means the only cause of Africa's largest genocide in modern times.

Ethnic tension in Rwanda was nothing new. There have always been disagreements between the majority Hutus and minority Tutsis, but the animosity between them has grown substantially since the colonial period.
The two ethnic groups are actually very similar – they speak the same language, inhabit the same areas, intermarry and follow the same traditions.

But when the Belgian colonists arrived in 1916, they saw the two groups as distinct entities, and even produced identity cards classifying people according to their ethnicity. This was a crude divide-and-rule strategy. The Belgians decided the Tutsis were superior to the Hutus. Not surprisingly, for the next twenty years, the Tutsis enjoyed better jobs and educational opportunities than their neighbours. Resentment among the Hutus gradually built up, culminating in a series of riots in 1959. More than 20,000 Tutsis were killed, and many more fled to the neighbouring countries of Burundi, Tanzania and Uganda. When Belgium relinquished power and granted Rwanda independence in 1962, the Hutus took their place in power. Over subsequent decades, the Tutsis were portrayed as the scapegoats for every crisis.

Building up to genocide

This was still the case in the years before the genocide. The economic situation worsened and the incumbent president, Juvenal Habyarimana, began losing popularity. At the same time, Tutsi refugees in Uganda – supported by some moderate Hutus – were forming the Rwandan Patriotic Front (RPF). Their aim was to overthrow Habyarimana and secure their right to return to their homeland. Habyarimana chose to exploit this threat as a way to bring dissident Hutus back to his side, and Tutsis inside Rwanda were accused of being RPF collaborators. In August 1993, after several attacks and months of negotiation, a peace accord was signed between Habyarimana and the RPF, but it did little to stop the continued unrest. When Habyarimana's plane was shot down at the beginning of April 1994, it was the final nail in the coffin.

Exactly who killed the president – and with him the president of Burundi and many chief members of staff – has not been established. Whoever was behind the killing, its effect was both instantaneous and catastrophic.

Mass murder

In Kigali, the presidential guard immediately initiated a campaign of retribution. Leaders of the political opposition were murdered, and almost immediately, the slaughter of Tutsis and moderate Hutus began. Within hours, recruits were dispatched all over the country to carry out a wave of slaughter. The early organisers included military officials, politicians and businessmen, but soon many others joined in the mayhem. Encouraged by the presidential guard and obscenely provocative radio propaganda, an unofficial militia group called the Interahamwe (meaning those who attack together) was mobilised. At its peak, this group was 30,000 strong. Soldiers and police officers encouraged ordinary citizens to take part. In some cases, Hutu civilians were forced by military personnel to murder their Tutsi neighbours or wives. Participants were often given incentives, such as money or food, and some were even told they could appropriate the land of the Tutsis they killed. On the ground at least, the international community largely left the Rwandans alone. The UN troops withdrew after the murder of just ten soldiers. The day after Habyarimana's death, the RPF renewed their assault on government forces, and numerous attempts by the UN to negotiate a ceasefire came to nothing.

Aftermath

Finally, in July, the RPF captured Kigali. The government collapsed and the RPF declared a ceasefire. As soon as it became apparent that the RPF was victorious, an estimated two million Hutus fled to Zaire (now the Democratic Republic of Congo) and other countries. These refugees include many who have since been implicated in the massacres. These refugees were fed and supported by the UN and international NGO charities, humanitarian agencies and created army bases of the genocidaires, the name given to the Hutus involved in the genocide, who then continued the genocide which resulted in more years of killings of Tutsis. France even supplied them with arms and the French President Mitterrand said "In such countries genocide is not too important". (Peter: Eleven years later I could not find people suffering in any way differently than I would expect had it happened in France or the UK. The emotional illiteracy or sheer racism of this remark I find astounding).

Back in Rwanda, UN troops and aid workers then arrived to help maintain order and restore basic services. But the traumatised Hutus and Tutsis of Rwanda were relatively neglected by the UN and even made to appear as the persecutors. On 19 July a new multi-ethnic government was formed, promising all refugees a safe return to Rwanda. Pasteur Bizimungu, a Hutu, was inaugurated as president, while the majority of cabinet posts were assigned to RPF members. But although the massacres were over, the legacy of the genocide continued, and the search for justice has been a long and arduous one. About 500 people have been sentenced to death, and many thousands are still in prison, including innocent, falsely accused people (by the perpetrators), which serves to protect the killers. Some of the ringleaders have managed to evade capture by residing in western countries, and many who lost their loved ones are still waiting for justice. The UN created a court to try the ringleaders in another country; then did little to persecute anyone, giving the impression that the western complicity was leading to an attempt to sabotage peace-making efforts.

A USA ambassador said this:

> "The failure of the international community to respond adequately to both the genocide and the subsequent mixing of the genocidal killer with the legitimate refugee population in the former Eastern Zaire only served to prolong the conflict. The climate of impunity was further exacerbated by ethnic cleansing and conflict in the northern region – and also by President Mubutu's policies of allowing these genocide forces to operate, recruit and re-supply on his territory. Tragically, this chapter is not yet closed. Reports of widespread killings continue. All of us, the new government in the Congo, its neighbours and the international community, have a responsibility to stop the killing of innocent civilians. We must also protect legitimate refugees, continue repatriation efforts and work to bring the genocidal killers to justice."

US President Bill Clinton realized the grave mistakes that had been made (genocide denial at the UN) and went personally to Rwanda to apologise.

A typical case

Tragically, Claire M's case could well be called typical. In 1994, she watched as Hutu extremists murdered her two children. She was gang-raped and left for dead after her left arm was hacked off by a machete. After the genocide, she adopted an orphaned boy, Emmanuel. Then she discovered she was HIV-positive. Claire doesn't know what will happen to Emmanuel should anything happen to her. "Thinking of the future weakens us so much," she says.

In the last decade one organization [http://www.warchild.org/] says ten million children have been traumatized by wars like this, so multiply this case above by ten million.

In his book *The State of Africa* Martin Meredith describes the many conflicts Africa has suffered from in the past 50 years. The sum total of victims includes millions of dead and many more survivors. In the East of DRC Congo alone it is estimated that three to five million people have been killed in ethnic conflicts and the attempt to control the wealth of the mines. The very children who witnessed the atrocities in Rwanda are living out and repeating their trauma as members of rebel groups that kill and rape and spread AIDS in East Congo. This continues. Recently (2011) we intended to visit a school in Eastern DRC Congo where we had treated traumatised children in 2008 and 2009. Our contact told us that owing to rebels in the area it would not be safe to go there now. Possibly the same children and women we had treated for the effects of violence and rape are again witnessing or experiencing the same.

"There is a lot of potential for violence in grief and trauma," says Dr. Magne Raundalen, a Norwegian psychologist with long experience in Africa who visited Rwanda on behalf of UNICEF. "The basic emotion in a child is sadness," he explains, "but long-term it can turn to hate and violence."

Many of Rwanda's orphans have seen their entire families slaughtered before their eyes. All have nightmares; many experience hallucinations. Others have possibly more complicated memories. These are the Hutus, children of the majority Hutu ethnic group that carried out the genocide. Many of these children have witnessed their own fathers, uncles and brothers participate in mass murder. Not a few, including some as young as ten-years-old, were lured into participating themselves.

So Rwanda could well be at war for many years. It is in this fluid and ethnically polarized environment that the orphans themselves provide a revealing – and troubling – window on their country's predicament. Like all children, Rwanda's orphans have absorbed the prejudices and stereotypes of their parents. These were compounded in Rwanda's case by a bitter four-year civil war, and by the long campaign of racist propaganda, broadcast primarily on two government-backed radio stations that relentlessly demonized the Tutsis. For many orphans, Tutsi and Hutu alike, what they have witnessed this year has confirmed their worst suspicions about each other.

Rwanda and thirty genocide cases

I (Peter) was invited to Rwanda to treat AIDS and I could not see how I could treat AIDS, which was commonly the outcome of being raped during the genocide, without treating the genocide. My early research showed that after eleven years nothing had really helped the post-traumatic stress, and that these stresses were still very active amongst the population of Rwanda.

The keynote symptom I found from my research was the tormenting memories after a sudden but premeditated, planned, savage attack of short duration.

For the survivors there are detailed flashbacks of extremely frightening, horrific moments during war (as the local people called it) or genocide, that were life threatening, deeply painful, humiliating or remorseful. These flashbacks are occurring daily, even hourly, even every minute of every day, and have lasted many years already.

As a consequence of these images, thoughts and responses, the sufferers:

- Cannot get to sleep or remain asleep, without tormenting images
- Can only get light and partial sleep over many years and are not fully rested or refreshed after sleep
- Cannot focus on daily problems as these are linked immediately to genocide

images, which they normally try to blank out; any inner thinking goes directly to their mind's 'TV' and the genocide images flash up and overwhelm their mental capacity
- Cannot respond to the needs of others – typically their large family – and instead neglect them because they are unable to feel and think.

They are also:
- Afraid that they could be killed at any moment and frightened to death day and night by any sound
- Very frightened because the killers are still at large, and may even be living next door
- They cannot accept apologies if they are offered
- Deeply disturbed by not having been able to bury their relatives. This lack of closure is a very common and serious trauma in its own right.

Also, as a consequence of their internalised fearful and deeply frightened state:
- They fear the neighbours in the community to which the killers belong, and don't socialise, don't go to church, don't engage in conversation, never laugh and joke, and instead stay at home, isolated from society. They can even become speechless for long periods
- They do not allow themselves to be helped by others
- They feel it is impossible that anyone could even want to help them
- They feel completely unable to even think about reconciliation and forgiveness.

They become dependent victims, having to beg for food, unable to think of work and instead are living in dire poverty, starving (eating a small meal every few days), homeless, rootless yet often having to support large families of orphans, not having buried their relatives, and are completely unable to think their way out of this.

Children drop out of school due to the memories and the consequent inability to study.

While I am sure this is not the full picture, I am sure it is an accurate picture of the inner world for the many women and men I interviewed, and I believe it must be replicated millions of times across the world.

As a result I made a PC Resonance for War and Genocide focused upon this chronic alarm state.

All thirty of the people in Rwanda who took this genocide resonance had dramatic improvements *without exception*.

The tormenting memories of genocide with which they had lived, and which had lasted eleven years, virtually disappeared overnight and they had many benefits from this. This is a summary of the results of these thirty cases.
- They could get to sleep without tormenting thoughts.
- They slept deeply, possibly the first time in eleven years.
- They could focus on daily problems without these being linked to genocide thoughts and could then make rational decisions rather than stay buried in these overwhelming thoughts.

- They stopped fearing the neighbours in the community, and started socialising, chatting, going to church, laughing and joking.
- They stopped feeling they could be killed any moment, and that any sound would frighten them to death day and night, and instead could socialise.
- They now believed that they could be helped and allowed others to help them.
- They felt able to begin the process of forgiveness.
- They could respond to the needs of others – typically their large orphan extended family.
- They decided to stop being dependent and having to beg, and started thinking about setting up a business and becoming independent.
- One child that had dropped out of school due to the memories wanted to return.
- A businessman who took it, because of high blood pressure and heart palpitations that occurred around the anniversary of the genocide, found it resolved his symptoms, which is not surprising. This is just one example of symptoms due to unresolved PTSD and I suggest that this is the answer for millions of others. When medical textbooks say that the cause of a chronic disease is unknown, and there is no cure, it is probably unresolved trauma.

Comments derived from this experience

I observed that there were three levels to post traumatic stress in Rwanda:

- There was the reaction of the uneducated who had permanent flashbacks in the 'now'.
- There was the reaction of the educated young people who could suppress the flashbacks because they had been educated and had stronger thinking minds. But even they, if asked how it was for them in the eleven years after the event, would say, "It was as if it happened yesterday," and their faces clouded over. So they were barely able to suppress the genocide flashbacks, but functioned a lot better because they had stronger minds.
- The third category was the older educated person who could suppress the thoughts of genocide into pathology, as in the case above into angina, showing very clearly how post traumatic stress becomes pathology.

People in all three categories have had babies before recovering from the trauma. Those children have internalised their mothers' states without experiencing that situation, which could have helped them to make sense of it, and this is how the problem becomes systemic rather than a problem specific to the people to whom it happened. We think this explains why people in the West have such a lot of buried trauma as was mentioned earlier. Generations before us have been educated and so we have the mental equipment to suppress trauma into the unconscious. For the uneducated person it's like a shark that's taken the place of their mind. In the educated younger people it is like a shark living just below their consciousness. In the older adults it is like a shark buried in their unconscious and eating away at them and producing pathology.

We have one further observation to make about this. In Africa it is still traditional to wail at funerals, which can take up to ten days as they wait for the extended family, of anything up to 300 people to arrive, and every one of them has the opportunity to wail. It seems that we in the West have lost this ability, and may even have developed positive resistance to allowing people to weep openly, or to be angry or to 'freak out,' or even to be excited.

To understand the extent of the recent violent history in the human race, you can read recent history books such as:

- *A People's Tragedy - the Russian Revolution 1891 to 1924*, by Orlando Figes, http://www.penguin.co.uk/nf/Author/AuthorPage/0,,1000010920,00.html
- *Post War A History of Europe since 1945* by Tony Judt, http://en.wikipedia.org/wiki/Tony_Judt

Or you can go back a bit further to the effects of slavery:

- *The Black Jacobeans* by C L R James, http://en.wikipedia.org/wiki/C._L._R._James
- *William Wilberforce* by William Hague, http://search.barnesandnoble.com/book-search/isbnInquiry.asp?r=1&ISBN=9780151012671&ourl=William - Wilberforce%2FWilliam - Hague

Or if you prefer fiction based on historical research try:

- *Shogun*, *King Rat* etc. by James Clavell, http://en.wikipedia.org/wiki/James_Clavell
- *The Journeys of Socrates* by Dan Millman, www.danmillman.com
- *Disillusion* by C J Sansom http://en.wikipedia.org/wiki/C._J._Sansom
- *A Thousand Splendid Suns* and *Kite Runner* by Khaled Hosseini, www.khaledhosseini.com, for Afghanistan.

An Inner Look at the Psychology of Trauma in Former Yugoslavia

We know that orphans often suffer terrible isolation. When war caused their situation, an extremely dangerous psychology can grow out of this that is nihilistic and can lead to killing in cold blood. There is a freezing of emotions from a very difficult experience like being an orphan, having no parents or extended family at all, and being unsupported and feeling deeply alone in the world. This leads to a permanent state of feeling deeply to be alone in the world and also to wanting to kill everyone in it, and to return to the world that existed before humankind. The idea is that everyone else is so unkind, cruel and full of aggression that it's best to kill them all and to give the world back to nature. Such people obviously find it extremely difficult to maintain a healthy loving relationship and could become the opposite, a real killer. The typical occupation could be the sniper in Sarajevo, Bosnia during the attempted genocide who every day attempted and often succeeded in killing people walking in the streets.

> I (Peter) treated the two daughters of such a man, employed by a dictator and then hired to kill all the remaining opposition to the dictator's rule in the country. Even when peace was established he continued in this job, executing any seriously divisive people within the country so that there was no effective opposition for the rest of this dictator's long life. After this the man retired to the country and lived in nature. His daughters grew up with him and took on his psychology and tried to live normal lives, which was difficult. They found marriage impossible to sustain and had boys who put swastikas on their bedroom doors. One of the sisters went to therapy for ten years and by the age of 50 years was functioning quite well, running a business. But when I gave her homeopathic Camphora she was deeply transformed, and the result was way beyond the effects of the therapy and released her soul to breathe a different tune. The other sister had not undergone therapy, so the effect, while deeply dramatic, was not so deep and all-embracing, but Camphora was deeply impressive nevertheless, and more so with repetitions. (This was all long before PC Resonances for trauma were created).

These two cases illustrate a few points. Depth psychology does determine people's lives. Intensive therapy is effective but with really deep psychology, it often takes decades to get to the bottom of things. And in places like Bosnia, the subject of rape is taboo, so psychotherapy is not possible. Homeopathy by comparison gets there in days or weeks, and can transform lives quickly and more deeply than any other simple method we know of. And we are very open to other methods of healing, from prayer, acupuncture, shiatsu, chi gong to yoga and many, many more besides. I (Peter) have in my time directed three clinics where up to sixty different therapies were on offer.

And the final point, dictators, secret police and assassins do come with perverted and hardened psychologies and once established they can rule and kill for decades. It seems that unless a country has deeply democratic institutions, people with disturbed, inflated and dangerous egos often come to power. It has happened in the United Kingdom in our lifetime, and it has happened widely throughout the world. The world needs a new way of evaluating in depth the psychology of potential leaders, to prevent offensive and vicious people from achieving power. Such people will do anything and everything possible to get into power and they do get there because other people are psychologically much less violent and self-seeking. People with really cruel psychologies can be very intelligent and stop at nothing to achieve power. This doesn't just happen in politics, you see these people at the top of all types of institutions. It's clear to us that one of the major shifts the world needs is to have people in power who instead of living out their trauma really serve the electorate and not themselves. This needs a special educational process.

Denial

A question you might ask yourself is "Why don't I know about my family trauma from my personal family history?"

We don't know because there are so few stories told in families:

- Firstly the dead don't talk
- Commonly, those who suffered terribly yet survived never talk about it.
- One reason they don't talk about it is because they do/did not have the words and the mechanisms of communication to talk about it.
- Another reason is they tried to talk about it initially, but the close ones they talked to don't/didn't have the ability to listen.
- Another common reason is that they become battle-hardened; shutting it deep inside and never talking about it again. They become hardened members of society, functional cripples.
- One British WWI veteran waited until he was over 100 years old before telling his story from 80+ years before. He wept while telling his story even then. This shows that stored grief has no time association; it's as if it happened yesterday.
- It requires uncommon listening ability, which few people have – to understand listening try www.rc.org.
- Most people don't realise that high-quality listening takes a lot of training.
- So, in effect, there was no way they could talk about it.
- In consequence, the next generations have very little to go on to understand the underlying emotional pain they experience.

One Yugoslav soldier, treated long after the war for a bullet that went right through his chest, told his story when enquired about his inner war wounds: "I went to war with my mates – the worst thing was eating grass – after the war I went to the pub with these same mates for two years to talk it out, so it's over inside me."
This highlights important points.

- The best listeners went through it too, with you
- They are/have become your close friends
- They have the inner experience, so can listen
- It's an exchange
- It takes a lot of time to talk it out
- All likely listeners not involved in the difficult event will find it beyond their ability to listen. It is then a job for experts, but these experts are very few; and we have very few people who know it's a job for experts.

Another aspect of this is that societies go into denial for 50 to 100 years after traumatic events. This is well documented in history books, especially the book *Post-war Europe* cited already.

There was an example in Germany of an old woman being confronted with letters she wrote to the Nazis denouncing her neighbours. What she said on TV when interviewed 50 years after the event was that,

- The letters were in her handwriting
- It was her signature on them
- She didn't write them.

That's denial in a nutshell, beautifully expressed.

Whole nations acted like this, schools acted like this, and history books were written from denial. Often the brutal history was turned into a triumphal conquest. Billions were brainwashed in this way by whitewashing history, omitting key facts, or by gross distortion of facts. It is likely that no one spoke truth. It is likely there is no single truth.
Because of the delay in revealing such events, before people could even become aware of the facts, it was deeply embedded in their family psychology and society's psychology. It was passed down to them/us without anything to make sense of it.

Most importantly, the idea that traumas are psychologically transmitted down through the generations is virtually unknown.

How Pain, Limiting Thoughts and Restrictive Feelings are Inherited

Understanding this process is absolutely core to understanding how to reverse it.

- The first problem is that the people involved in this process – the parents and the children – are deeply buried in pain and suffering already and so cannot operate freely.
- The genetics of the next generation are modified by the previous trauma (see epigenetics discussed earlier).
- Because of the long-running denial stage of 50 to 100 years – people remain ignorant of what is going on inside them.
- Parents also repeat the actions that happened to them as a child when they were growing up.
- In particular, they repeat the actions of incarcerating limiting thoughts and emotional experiences to their child.
- The pain of the adult then becomes the pain of the child as a result.
- Parents do this
  - many times an hour
  - day in and day out for years and for decades
  - with advances and stages as the children grow up
  - mirroring their own experience of upbringing without realising it, and by systematically repeating ineffective actions of parenting, they teach their child to ingrain the parents' limiting thoughts and emotions and how to bury pain.

The most common examples of this are the many ways they:

- Stop children from crying
- Criticise
- Highlight imaginary danger
- Control their children.

By these and other unintended methods, parents who are not making superhuman, effective use of a new-style parenting approach are re-incarcerating their pain into their children by their unconscious actions. It's very hard not to, even when you know you don't want to.

Normal pain recovery

Children get hurt and experience pain of some sort physically and/or emotionally.
It happens all the time and is quite natural.
Normally, infants when they are in physical or emotional pain

- Will cry/weep
- Seek their mother for a cuddle
- Cling
- Get angry and even try to bite or hit
- Want to talk about it as best they can afterwards and if they can
- May conclude with a laugh or giggle and then go back to playing.

In this situation the child can recover fully.

All it requires – but this is in fact a huge requirement – is that the parent ...

- Stays present
- Maintains eye contact in a non-reactive way

- Listens without any interruption for as long as it takes, adding
  - compassion
  - love
  - smiles
  - hugs

... and otherwise doing nothing much else.

But there is an added catch, a very important one that is often missed.

Every little hurt links to emotional or physical limiting thoughts in the family history in both the parent or carer and the child carries these forward from the previous generations of the family.

As a consequence, the child's reactions will be out of proportion to the event and over the top several times over. Almost certainly the parent or carer will feel the exact same pain excessively, too.

So, it is four times as difficult in such situations to manage the natural recovery from simple hurts as above, but not impossible if you possess some simple skills.

The failure to recover

The failure to recover from limiting thoughts and emotions, and the reprogramming of overactive survival instincts comes about by this process.

The parent or other carer will deeply resonate with the pain of the child (because it is their own suppressed pain one generation later) and in consequence will intervene in an inappropriate way.

There is a range of typical inappropriate responses, escalating in severity, that seem common to many parents and carers:

- "There, there, don't cry," is one of the most common inappropriate responses
- "If you don't stop crying I will fuss over you excessively, jiggle you, smack you, hit you, threaten you with hand gestures," etc. is another
- As the child gets older, the threatening responses can be verbal: "If you cry again, I will hit you when we get home."

Obviously, there are a thousand variations on this.

There is another range of inappropriate responses that we can call *distraction*.
A common one is to offer the breast or the bottle or the dummy or something to eat as a distraction from the upset, the crying for example, because it irritates or disturbs the parent because of their resonance with this. This distraction by eating incidentally is a common foundation of eating disorders and cigarette smoking, which is a form of eating disorder.

Another distraction is to

- Switch on the TV
- Plug in a video of Thomas the Tank Engine
- Open up a laptop cartoon
- Suggest a book to read

- Suggest a game to play
- Offer to go outside
- Basically to stop the process of crying or other form of upset.

Distraction is a form of splitting the concentration by seeking freedom through distancing from suffering. This is possibly the primal distress of all human beings.

It puts energy into 'doing' and takes it away from 'being' and creates the primal disturbance of life: split attention, instead of staying present, right in the moment, now.

There is another range of responses that are over-controlling responses, highlighting imaginary dangers. An examples of this is when the child tries to explore and the parent

- Calls him back before he gets very far, as if it is dangerous or
- Shouts at him to come back or
- Grabs him and pulls him back or
- Tells him not to do that or
- Is always instructing him as to what to do and especially what not to do.

This excessive control is likely to stop creativity in its tracks, and if you read about education below, you will see that creativity is thought of as the higher form of intelligence (www.ted.com - Ken Robinson).

The child is also very likely to get the idea of chronic danger at every turn, i.e. to have hyped survival instincts.

This compulsive urge to control children and restrict their activities when there is virtually no danger possible or anywhere in sight is one of the most limiting things parents can do to children. It teaches them that everything they try to do is scary and that they should avoid anything new.

It is a primitive fear pattern handed down without reflective thought compulsively over generations and leads again to the overactive reptilian brain and to the hyperactive child.

There are many other inappropriate responses such as leaving the child alone locked in a room or just ignored until he or she gets over it. Which of course children don't; it just makes their response more intense next time. Or they internalise it into an adaptive and more shut down state.

Here is one example that represents an experience that was regularly expressed in discussions with parents.

A mother smacks her boy for laughing. She is asked why did she smack him? She says because my mother did the same to me. When she is asked why her mother did the same to her she says because her grandmother did the same to her mother.

Put more generally:
When you see a five-year-old girl bossing her three-year-old brother around, you may expect this is learned behaviour. You know this is the way the parent or caretaker is bossing the children in private. And they got this from their mother/father, and so on back to Adam and Eve.

Whatever young children do in a relationship to others is what they learned and are still learning on an hour-to-hour, minute-to-minute basis from their parents and grandparents or at kindergarten or playschool.

The result of controlling our children too carefully is our children becoming like us rather than becoming who they naturally are inside.

If personal pain is left unresolved it will inevitably show up socially or as pathology and typically precipitate personal tragedies like divorce, alcoholism, drug addiction in the child or the parent, criminal violence, domestic violence, smoking and eating disorders, and all forms of chronic disease.

To summarise: Unresolved past experience suppressed by our powerful mind leads to people thinking, for example, that

- They live in a dangerous world, and so they act defensively towards everybody [illegible] within the family (the idea is that everybody is an enemy).
- They are no good and will never succeed (I won't succeed, etc.).
- Their glass is always half empty etc. (I am so poor, nobody loves me, no one appreciates me etc.).

It seems likely that this has directly contributed

- To the breaking up of large extended families
- To people in western society isolating themselves in smaller and smaller private units, as having family is too painful to bear
- To so-called nuclear families and single parent families
- To the idea that current society is turning these old wounds into a new limiting reality.

The over-active survival instincts, limiting thoughts, repressed/overwhelming emotions are dominating society and determining society, as we know it.

There are more consequences to these huge internalised limiting thoughts and emotions.

When a large amount of the population is suffering like this, wars can precipitate, and World War II is an example of this – see the books by Alice Miller (www.alice-miller.com), and of the current wars, the Israeli conflict is a classic example – see *Broken Promises, Broken Dreams* by Alice Rothchild (http://alicerothchild.com), which gives a compassionate/objective Jewish and Israel/Palestinian view of what is happening there.

Recommended reading

Here are some excellent websites and books to help build parenting skills.

- *Making Contact* by Virginia Satir is one of the great classics that has been tested by time - www.avanta.net
  A quote: *I believe the greatest gift I conceive of having from anyone is to be seen by them, heard by them, and to be understood and touched by them. The greatest gift I can give is to see, hear, understand and to touch another person. When this is done contact has been made.*
- *The Continuum Concept* by Jean Liedloff is a must-read for all parents-to-be and deals with the issues of how people come to lose support from the very first day of life. This is one of the great classic books of the 20th century.

- *How Parents Can Counsel Their Children* by Tim Jackins – www.rc.org
  A quote: *If we were to encapsulate what we have learned to do in a sentence or two – it is to explain to people that what they are trying to do all the time, this trying to be listened to, is a very profound process. It will have profound results if it ever gets a chance to operate.*
  What is needed from a listener is a statement like:
  'Yes, I will listen to you and really pay undivided attention to you, for as long as it takes, and I will not repeat what I've heard to anyone'.
  The listener has two tasks:
    - to listen without opening the lips, but keeping eye contact
    - to listen without letting their mind react, or if it does, to rapidly let that thought go.
  No easy task without training!
- *Magical Parent Magical Child* and *From Magical Child to Magical Teen* both by Joseph Clinton Pearce – http://en.wikipedia.org/wiki/Joseph_Chilton_Pearce – is another brilliant resource.
- *Making Sense of Suffering* by J Konrad Stettbecker gives chapter and verse on this subject, which I will attempt to summarise very briefly here.
  The crisis of humankind stems from our incomplete and disrupted consciousness, the unconscious fear that we are deficient, that we are worthless or bad.
  This is the root of all negative compensations and development.
  But as long as parents continue to burden their children and inspire fear in them this sort of fear remains very much alive.
  This produces an overload, which results in distorted attitudes that affect our ability to communicate and act.
  The result is suffering and the impairment of our sense of well-being.
  This book goes in depth into the inner process.

There are many other books:
- *The Drama of the Child* by Alice Miller, www.alice-miller.com. This is a classic and very important book that describes how violent parenting in the 19th century became a forming force for WWI and WWII.
- *The Body Remembers - The Psychophysiology of Trauma and Trauma Treatment* by Babette Rothschild, http://home.webuniverse.net/babette/.
- There are very many other sources of information and whole movements built upon what happens in childhood from parenting. Re-evaluation co-counselling for example - www.rc.org
- *Emotional Healing with Homoeopathy* by Peter Chappell. This book delves into this in some depth.
- *Your Body Speaks Its Mind* by Stanley Kellerman. This early classic is a great way to understand this process - www.amazon.com/Your-Body-Speaks-Its-Mind/dp/0934320012 - 228k
- *Trauma and Recovery* by Judith Herman. This book is a trauma bible of a few generations ago - http://en.wikipedia.org/wiki/Judith_Lewis_Herman http://www.youtube.com/watch?v=USTKmffoQms –

There are many websites full of appropriate information if you search 'parenting skills'.

Toxic Emotions - Experiences of Working with Trauma

Every homeopath is probably aware of the importance of *Staphysagria* after rape. It has become a routine prescription and is highly beneficial. Given that rape has been systematically used in war and is widely a general form of molestation, we can be virtually certain that every woman inherits the experience of rape from the family psychology and that many women have experienced it personally.

Although deeply traumatic at a personal level, the point is that rape is in fact not solely a personal experience. It affects every victim in a roughly similar way. There is a habitual response based on a habitual offence that is rather similar across the planet. By using the same PC RESONANCE for the trauma of rape in different cultures we have tested this idea out and have found reliable results.

The same goes for other traumas, such as those due to catastrophic circumstances, like a sudden accident, a tsunami, an earthquake, genocide and the violence of war, and many such like events. The intensity of the event and the archetypical nature of it overrule the individual aspect.

We respond habitually and this response seems based upon the survival instincts, which we have explained earlier this book, as also in appendix 4.

In homeopathy it seems we have overrated the individuality in such situations and have concentrated too much on that. Looking deeper into the matter there are few fundamental characteristic responses and there is nothing personal about them. We all share habitual responses in times of stress. When we are shouting at the kids, bossing people at work, are subservient to the boss, or the husband or the wife, or being aggressive or argumentative or over-generous or manipulative to our husband, wife or friend; when we are patronizing, or overly kind, or excessively sympathetic, we are acting out of habits, and these are not as personal as we tend to believe they are. Every human being has them to some extent or other; we have our own particular mix, but there is nothing personal about any of it.

The point is that every toxic emotion like guilt, jealousy, rage, envy, hatred, suspicion, secrecy, violent thought, indifference, apathy, making excuses, avoidance, scepticism, dismissal and so on, has nothing personal in it. It is the same for everyone; these are the common habitual responses of the human race based upon the survival instincts. These common responses are like an emotional language. We don't personally own the words we use and neither do we own the emotions we feel.

Many people think that their unique collection of habitual responses is who they are. There are whole systems of therapy based upon this misunderstanding. The reality is that there is no personal part at this level.

Our true nature is to be found in our conscious mind. The true nature of the conscious mind is wisdom and compassion. And the true nature of compassion is that it's the same for everyone.

Homeopaths can then view the habitual responses to trauma as epidemic effects because they are the same for everyone, just as we know about the effects of epidemic diseases, which are essentially the same for everyone because they are caused by a specific germ, virus or bacteria.

Because these traumas have been within the human race for thousands of years and none of them is ever many generations away from an action replay, all of them are present within our psychology as archetypes; trauma miasms. Due to the interaction between for example, a virus and the human race, both change and evolve into something new, but these archetypal processes cover a long time span which may give the false impression that an archetype (miasm) is static.

Homeopaths have always used a limited number of remedies for trauma. Depending on the type of trauma the selection differs. *Arnica* for instance is routinely prescribed in acute physical trauma. So there is actually nothing new in what we present here. We have used single remedies (PC RESONANCES) for numerous epidemic diseases with great success. By testing it in practice we can now state with confidence that a similar approach for trauma is as successful in giving consistent results. We may argue on the theory and the reasoning behind this idea, but seeing large amounts of severely traumatised people releasing the trauma in a matter of days is the reality we have experienced.

The key point here is that treating the effects of survival instincts that have been heightened dramatically in times of unprecedented and severe trauma, works very well – as shown by our results in Rwanda. Perhaps we may need to use this approach in everybody to treat the underlying habitual survival instincts, identified earlier. Most people live with hyperactive survival instincts and the traumas rooted and grown from these survival instincts. Further, we have already discussed how these are inherited and that homeopathic treatment, as it is currently used, often does not get to the core of such issues. In subsequent chapters we will discuss how this could be improved.

We are not stating that, because the experience of trauma is rather universal than individual, there is no place for individualized treatment. Any person with an unresolved history of trauma – which embraces practically everyone – would be best helped by an integrated approach in which there is place for both an individualized prescription and a GENUS TRAUMATICUS prescription. Where to start depends on several factors. A simple rule is to start with what is obvious and visible. The more acute the situation the more likely it is that it is the trauma itself, and not the individual response to it that catches the eye. This is similar to the reflex of giving *Arnica* directly following an injury. The symptoms may later lead to other remedies. If a clear individual picture is visible directly it is obvious to start with that.

Here are some rules of thumb:

- Time clearly influences the ideal approach. The less time that has passed since a trauma the more likely the PC Trauma RESONANCE will be able to cure, and the less chance that an an individual remedy will be needed to complement it.
- Severity of trauma: The more severe the trauma, the more the trauma-specific approach will be the first choice, to be followed by individual treatment.
- Culture: The more individualized a culture, the more important it becomes to prescribe for the individual.
- Circumstances influence strategy. The larger the number of traumatized individuals and the smaller the number of skilled homeopaths, the more a collective approach is the way to start.

Trauma and Mental Health

Treating mental health is fundamentally no different from treating psychological and physical health.

The book *Emotional Healing with Homeopathy* (Peter Chappell), written twenty years ago, gives a fairly complete picture of treatment appropriate to the psychological/mental health field. Admittedly, this doesn't deal with mental health in extremis but it certainly deals with mental health in the early stages of disturbance.

We see mental health issues are really about traumatic emotional disturbances that remain unresolved. Not having managed to process them the person has to adapt to them as in the example of distancing oneself from one's own body while enduring incest, yet being totally freaked out by the reality of it, and its constant repetition. To become split off from your body, schizophrenic, and paranoid, is an intelligent adaptation. True, it handicaps one's functioning in the real world, but it is the best adaptation in such a terrible circumstance. Calling a person a paranoid schizophrenic is solely identifying a person with an adaptation to previous trauma (individual or in the family). The trauma (e.g. incest) needs to be addressed and the victim needs compassionate support, rather than a label and a drug to hide the symptoms whilst clouding the awareness.

Disturbed psychology is the norm

In our assessment everybody alive has a disturbed psychology. It's 'normal' to have this. If the disturbance is strong it can affect weak points in the person's make up, such as a specific organ like the heart or brain or an organ system. One possibility is mental illness. More common by far is physical illness from the same root cause.

To test this idea of disturbed psychology you can carry out this experiment. Think about the people you know who have normal families, really well-functioning normal families where everyone functions well over a long period of time. Then make a list of the families you know and grade them zero to five. Zero equals completely malfunctioning and five equals extremely well-functioning. What do you find?

We have considerable experience from Africa that genocide-like traumas (as just one example) lead directly to high blood pressure, angina, et cetera and that such traumas are also inherited down the generations and result in the full range of illnesses, mental, emotional and physical. See the last case example below for details.

Working in basic village cultures has a lot to recommend it as you can learn how health and disease happen. You see clear processes and effects, unhidden by western over-mentalisation.

It is our conclusion that pretty much everyone in this world is the survivor of genocide, war and other deep traumas (PTSD) one way or another from the last 100 years. If you look at the history of Russia under Stalin, Europe, USA, British Empire, Japan in WWI and WWII, China under Mao, India in partition et cetera you can immediately count half the world's population as having recent war/ genocide/ torture/ rape/ atomic bomb histories that are yet to be resolved. This, in our experience, is one powerful root of disturbed psychology and the reason why it is 'normal' to have a disturbed psychology. In simple terms, the human race as a whole has now a very disturbed psychology. You can read the end results in hospital wards for elderly patients. You can read endless versions of it from the faces of people while walking down any main street.

Symptoms have meaning

As we said before disease is unlived potential.

Further from this it follows that all symptoms are a communication from the semi/un-conscious.

- Chronic diseases are from the collective unconscious (totally unknown)
- Symptoms are from the personal unconscious (completely forgotten)
- Dreams are more related to the subconscious (half forgotten).

Dreams are relatively easy to connect to individual meaning to make good sense of. The meaning can be extracted by a very easy method. But the first point to realize is that only the dreamer knows the meaning of a dream and that you can't work with formulaic dream books. [Here is what you do to understand a dream. On waking you grab your bedside notepad and pen and immediately, even before opening the eyes, scribble down a few key words/ideas of the dream. Then maybe after breakfast or on the train to work you have time to elaborate upon these few points, which act as keys to the dream story. You find, as you write out the dream in full, you extract and realize more meaning and in this process you gain personal insights. If it's really important you might have to repeat it to somebody later, and in the telling of your dream to a silent listener, you understand even more. You don't need outside responses because they are other people's opinions, which are inevitably biased. The only really valuable response is your own insight. This is a powerful form of self-therapy and it's free.]

Symptoms are harder to connect to, yet an intelligent outside observer looking meticulously can often see the stress and the result and make an obvious conclusion. One method is to ask a patient to put the attention while sitting quietly right into the key symptom and see if some sort of understanding comes. You may find some sort of fear comes up in this process or even in the thought of this process. This is the very fear that prevents recovery and is the meaning of the symptom.

Chronic diseases by comparison are difficult to connect personally; they are a deeply hidden message. But since they frequently occur after some traumatic event, after something that was quietly suppressed or something that was overwhelmingly difficult to process, looking back on a timeline to the most obvious events that happened before the disease showed up, is the place to start. Exploring that issue, using the above suggestion for symptoms, may easily reveal the issue. There may be a series of steps like this going back in time to reach the original issue. And an experienced and spiritually aware psychotherapist might be the right person to help with this process, as can the new PC TECHNOLOGY. For the homeopath the response to a PC RESONANCE for a disease can shine light upon the disease-making process or the pathology, so that you see more clearly the future homeopathic steps to take, giving a better chance of a successful outcome. It's like pressing the button on the tape recorder of life. You hear the story that really matters, rather than the intellectually dressed-up theory the patient is keen to tell you.

The expression of anger

The expression of anger, or lack of it, can be a root of mental disturbance. It is repeated experience that, as people get better in health, the process of cure is frequently seen in the more effective expression of anger. The line goes something like this; given there are many options. Anger is not expressed, so they blame others (projection), or if self-esteem is low (very common) they blame themselves for perhaps making a mistake. If this goes deeper, they feel guilty, and if it goes deeper their whole body cringes in guilt, and deeper still they go white or pale and become passive. If it goes deeper then any type of physical or mental pathology can occur now or later. The reverse happens in the process of cure. The patient complains that they are angrier, and when you examine it, it's clearly a step forwards.

A recurring tonsillitis in a young child with a stern father can be easy to understand. The throat is the centre of expression, and expression is suppressed, so the throat becomes toxic and tonsils inflamed. Family therapy is an option that can often resolve illnesses in a member of such a family, allowing the family stress to resolve by providing a safe environment to facilitate examining what has been ignored or blind-sided. These things are often too obvious to miss from the outside, but the family learns to survive as if it is normal, and in many ways the family is a normal one with loving parents and disturbed but functional personalities. The homeopathic way to deal with this, if the constitutional approach to the individual does not work, is to take the case of the family in the way that a family therapist would understand it, and give the remedy to all the family. Another possibility would be to prescribe the PC disease remedy to the patient and to watch closely the dynamic changes within the patient and the family. From that one might understand what is really going on and where the problem actually resides. Remember the adage, every sick child has a sick parent. Many homeopaths learn this the hard way; they have the wrong person in the patient's chair.

Psychiatrists and psychiatric drugs and ECT

We can divide psychiatrists into two categories, with in-betweens. Those that prescribe only drugs for life and do nothing else, (the great majority); and the relatively few whose practice includes kindness, therapy and group work, and who try to understand the patients rather than simply diagnosing and labelling them.

The drugged patient is dulled, confused, shut off, mesmerized by the drugs; seldom gets better, takes drugs for life, exists in a drug-mitigated zombie-land and suffers increasingly from drug side effects. These can be terrible, can shorten life and do not provide a cure.

A typical case of psychiatric abuse is this. A woman weighed 50 kg when she started psychiatric drugs and ten years later in the same mental state or worse, she weighs something like 120 kg of blubber (a known side-effect of the drugs she has been prescribed for ten years) and no cure in sight.

Yet in mental health cases, treatment with drugs and electric shock (Electroconvulsive therapy - ECT) have become the treatment of choice across the world it seems. This is superficial and ignores the cause. The drug aspect is propagated by the pharmaceutical industry (which runs on survival instincts, notably greed). Without offering real cure, drugs often need to be taken for life, a perfect recipe for profit. Social drugs appear to be a cheaper 'solution' to deal with the mentally ill than to offer them individual treatment that may involve internalisation in institutes. This shortsighted vision solves little for the individual and general mental health may even decline. The spin off these profits generate keeps the pharmaceutical system in a totally dominating position, pays for lobbying, funds scientists, and influences at all levels of society.

The evidence in USA is that psychiatrists who base their therapy purely on drugs/ECT earn three times as much as those who base their treatment on psychotherapy and other social interventions. The alternatives to drugs we believe are ultimately cheaper and more effective because cure is a possibility and is often achieved.

So the largely ineffective treatment costs the most and makes huge profits for the drug companies, maximises psychiatrists' income and crucifies the patient into a no-mans-land of drugged semi-oblivion.

Alternatives to psychiatry

Anyone interested in alternatives to psychiatry can read the book *Alternatives Beyond Psychiatry* which is a brilliant book written by 56 authors, equally men and women, active in the field of psychiatric/psychotherapeutic work around Europe and North America. It is cutting edge material (see www.peter-lehmann-publishing.com for full information). It gives access to many resources necessary when treating psychiatric cases. The alternatives suggested are particularly useful during relapsed states, to prevent the patient's recourse to drugs. It includes chapters by psychiatrists, psychologists, social workers, and survivors of psychiatry, legal experts and a full range of opinion in the field alternative to psychiatry.
My overwhelming conclusion (Peter) drawn from this book, and confirming my experience in running an informal supervision clinic based on survivors of psychiatry, is that there is no benefit from treating psychiatric cases with long-term drugs; that there are huge side-effects in doing so and there is no curative effect. But the most important point is that it provides a strong background from the psychiatric point of view and the alternatives that make sense. The basic thesis is that the alternative to psychiatry is to treat a person as a traumatized human being, listen to them and involve the family, friends and social situation with sensitivity, and have an open mind about how to proceed.

I quote from a professor of psychology in the book:

> "Schizophrenia is a human experience with meaning, meaning it is hard to uncover, but it only takes patience, kindness, a tolerance for not understanding, a willingness to understand the human condition at its most painful; a tolerance for desperate defences ... understanding persons with schizophrenia means facing facts about ourselves, about our families, and our society that we do not want to know ... the real tragedy of schizophrenia is not the severity of the symptoms but that we know the psychoanalytic therapies that work and we are not using them." (*Alternatives Beyond Psychiatry* p. 333)

References

- Peter Chappell, *Emotional Healing with Homeopathy*, reprint edition, Homeopathic Educational Services, Berkeley 2003
- Peter Chappell, *The Second Simillimum*, Homeolinks Publishers, Haren Netherlands 2005
- Harry van der Zee, *Miasms in Labour*, Stichting Alonissos, Utrecht Netherlands 2000, reprint Homeolinks Publishers, Haren Netherlands 2009
- Harry van der Zee, *Homeopathy for Birth Trauma*, Homeolinks Publishers, Haren Netherlands 2007
- Peter Stastny / Peter Lehmann (Eds.), *Alternatives Beyond Psychiatry*, Peter Lehman Publishing, Berlin, Germany 2007
- Peter Lehmann (Ed.), *Coming off Psychiatric Drugs: Successful Withdrawal from Neuroleptics, Antidepressants, Lithium, Carbamazepine and Tranquilizers*, Peter Lehman Publishing, Berlin, Germany 2007
- Bruce Lipton, *The Biology of Belief*, Mountain of Love/Elite Books, Santa Rosa CA, 2005
- Christopher Johannes & Harry van der Zee, *Homeopathy and Mental Health Care*, Homeolinks Publishers, Haren Netherlands, 2010

Part IV
Theory of Treating Intoxication

The Toxic Body

Physical toxins undermine health and we live in an increasingly toxic world. The national and international health institutes have failed to prevent our environment from becoming full of potentially disease-inducing toxins.

If you were to try and eat food that is completely free from toxins you would starve. There is now no possibility of eating truly non-toxic food. There is nothing that you can eat that isn't contaminated by some of these toxins. The soil worldwide is contaminated from air pollution. The effects of combinations of these toxins are unknown. We cannot even know what is in the food we eat when we look at it at the supermarket. The supermarkets don't know either and if they did they wouldn't tell us without legislation.

A host of modern ills – like obesity, diabetes, and autism, Attention-Deficit Hyperactivity Disorder – have risen for a generation and have chemical connections. As an example, a recent US study shows that pesticides can influence nerve and brain function, and induce ADHD. Not only do they do that in levels that are above the accepted norm, but also in low levels that were considered innocent by the institutes established to guard our health and that of our children. Chelation studies show that by removing toxins like heavy metals the effects of many chronic diseases can be reduced and reversed.

The alternative health community has demonstrated that autism can be cured in some instances purely by detoxification of chemicals and/or vaccinations.

We can view Autism Spectrum Disorders, affecting increasing percentages of children, as the tip of the iceberg of human toxicity. Within another generation, half the children born could be suffer such disorders. Autistic children also grow up and have children. We can detox them from known toxins by intelligent guesswork, but it has become impossible to know or to measure the full extent of the toxic load. If you go to your doctor, you cannot expect to have a thorough investigation of the level of toxicity in the body. The common toxins in the body will pass unmarked on medical tests.

There are authors writing at the cutting edge of this area of detox, e.g. Tinus Smits – *Autism, Beyond Despair* (http://www.emryss.eu/book_detail.lasso?id=7623&l=eng) and more info can be found at http://www.klinghardt.org/.

The focus in detox is on Autism as it is the clearest and most prescient way the problem may be seen, but detox applies to everybody.

There are published medical research papers on the effectiveness of homeopathic detox. This is an area where homeopathy could really expand its effectiveness.

Another level of toxins is electro-smog, the radiation from mobile phones, Wi-Fi, and laptops, and toxins in vaccinations et cetera. We are all structurally electromagnetic energetic patterns and all forms of radiation do affect us. As may be expected children's brains are much more susceptible to radiation and toxins than adults'. It's easy to show with a magnetic meter you can buy on the internet for less than $100, that the magnetic field of a mobile phone increases 100 to 1000 times when it's in use. The same applies to your wireless mouse, your laptop when it's sitting on your lap, the last place to put it, or your wireless laptop keyboard.

You may be assuming that the manufacturers of laptops, mobiles, and so on are completely aware of the safety limits of electro-magnetic fields. Software industries have overestimated the safe levels and because of commercial interests lobbied to set the safety levels high, just as the chemical giants have overestimated the safe levels of chemicals in the environment and lobbied and controlled the politicians and lawmakers for seven decades. We may expect from the repeated history of toxicity that in 30 years time it will become all too clear, when the damage has been extensive and often irreversible for a generation or two. Ethical medical scientists will then have finally produced the facts that should have been produced before the technology was introduced. In the normal process, as with lead/aluminium and Alzheimer's, or cigarettes and cancer, the manufacturers seek every way possible to continue making a profit until it's an absolute scandal. They lobby governments and lawmakers and continue pursuing profits as long as they can. And they carry out scandalous advertising in other less developed countries to continue their businesses. It's greed, greed and greed all the way to the bank. Why is it that chemical manufacturers are not forced to prove the complete safety for the full life of their products, *before* they enter the marketplace? Why is this not the common rule rather than the reverse, waiting until so many people have died, and then fighting and lobbying to maintain the practice? But that's the state of the world, Mammon to the first and last.

If you want to measure and protect your home, here is where to get the equipment to do so: www.gigahertz-solutions.com. If you want to use a laptop safely, you need to keep a few centimetres away from it, use a plug in mouse and keyboard and sit it on the table. Not so convenient but a lot safer.

Besides avoiding toxins where we can, we need to develop methods of building in permanent resistance to this increasingly toxic world, as well as trying to reduce toxins. The best method we think is to stop being toxic in the mind so that the body has less toxic hot spots to hold toxins in, ensuring we discharge the toxins on a regular basis.

We cannot expect to eliminate over 200 recognised toxins within our bloodstream in a hurry, when the problem has been with us for decades. However, awareness has just reached the tipping point where those in power may do something serious about it. This problem has entered the USA legal agenda as we write. Probably everything we write is an underestimation of the problem, which should be exceedingly well documented by now. They obviously realise it's critical to survival and will suggest laws to force manufacturers to prove chemicals are safe. The world is so completely toxic, that even if production were stopped tomorrow, it would take decades to clean up the mess, assuming it were possible to do so. We can already say the action has come too late. The moves in the USA to strengthen the laws in this area will not prevent the problem escalating in coming years.

The Bhopal disaster – a glaring example

The Bhopal disaster was an industrial catastrophe that occurred at a pesticide plant owned and operated by Union Carbide, a USA business giant, in Bhopal, Madhya Pradesh, India. Around midnight of December 2–3, 1984, the plant released methyl isocyanate gas and other toxins, resulting in the exposure of over 500,000 people. Estimates vary on the death toll. The official immediate death toll was 2,259. Other government agencies estimate 15,000 deaths. Some 25 years after the gas leak, 390 tons of toxic chemicals abandoned at the plant continue to leak and pollute the groundwater in the region and affect thousands of Bhopal residents who depend on it. There are currently civil and criminal cases related to the disaster in the United States District Court, Manhattan and the District Court of Bhopal, India against Union Carbide with an Indian arrest warrant pending against Warren Anderson, CEO of Union Carbide at the time of the disaster. In 2010, 26 years later, the first successful prosecutions occurred but the main players are still free. This shows the cynicism and blatant disregard for human life of a typical mega business.

Vaccination Damage

Vaccination programmes in many countries start on the first day after birth, and have great impact on children's health.

The use of vaccinations has been controversial within homeopathic circles. Several homeopaths have published a wealth of information on possible side-effects including many cases responding to the detoxification of vaccinations. These form an indirect proof of a causal relationship between vaccinations and complaints surfacing after vaccination.

Making up a balance between the advantages and disadvantages of vaccination is no easy task, as both exist and it is not a black-and-white picture. If the balance in a general analysis were to tip to one side this still says nothing about the difficulty of parents' individual decisions whether or not to vaccinate a small child.

The whole debate concerning vaccines is regretfully not an open and honest debate and the forces at work here are not completely clear. Here are some quotes that show the paternalistic and reductionist view of the medical and political powers that either feed conspiracy theories, or worse, cover processes that very seriously threaten world health:

- "Nothing in the world is what it seems. That façade that the media, being part of the ruling powers in the world, present us is based on lies, betrayal and misguidance ... It is known that labs are experimenting with genetic manipulation of micro-organisms in programs for biological warfare. The Spanish flu for instance started at an American army base." [Arend Zeevat, Partij voor Mens en Spirit, Date: 2-7-2009]
- "It is known that in the preparation of vaccines specific components can enter. I'll give you an example: it is known that in living polio vaccine, also in inactivated polio vaccine, two forms of leukaemia and a tumour virus can be present as also the Simian Vacuolating Virus SV40. These Tumour viruses have originally been in the polio vaccines; only later it was discovered that they were in and that they could be

oncogenic – inducing tumours." [Prof. dr. H.H. Cohen, bacteriologist in Johan van Dongen, *Aids de grootste misdaad in de medische geschiedenis* (AIDS the biggest crime in human history)

- "National law and international treaties are insufficient to control the risks of medical research for the development of vaccines due to anarchy of industrial interest groups. Put clearly, profit is more important than wellbeing." [ibid.]
- A polio vaccination program instead of preventing poliomyelitis caused an outbreak of it in Africa. [http://www.nd.nl/artikelen/2007/oktober/05/uitbraak-polio-door-vaccinaties-in-afrika]
- Gardasil that is used to protect young girls from cervical cancer has caused a progressive muscular disorder in several vaccinated girls. [http://www.naturalnews.com/026463_HPV_vaccine_HPV_teenage_girls.html]
- All over the globe governments put their population under pressure to be vaccinated against the Mexican flu, a relatively innocent virus that caused only a few hundreds of deaths where normal winter flu causes thousands every year. Figures were used to manipulate the world population and even the WHO bought the story. [http://tpmcafe.talkingpointsmemo.com/talk/blogs/kstone/2009/06/cdc-was-irresponsible-in-claim.php?ref=reccafe]
- Austrian research journalist Jane Burgermeister investigated the Baxter scandal. Baxer had sent flu vaccines that were contaminated with bird flu virus to sixteen countries. [http://naturalnews.com/z026503_pandemic_swine_flu_bioterrorism.html]
- New Survey In California And Oregon Finds Vaccinated Children Two And A Half Times More Likely To Have Neurological Disorders Like ADHD And Autism: The survey compared vaccinated and unvaccinated children in nine counties in Oregon and California. Among more than 9,000 boys age 4-17, the survey found vaccinated boys were two and a half times (155%) more likely to have neurological disorders compared to their unvaccinated peers. Vaccinated boys were 224% more likely to have Attention Deficit Hyperactivity Disorder (ADHD), and 61% more likely to have autism. For older vaccinated boys in the 11-17 age bracket, the results were even more pronounced. Vaccinated boys were 158% more likely to have a neurological disorder, 317% more likely to have ADHD, and 112% more likely to have autism. ['Medical News Today' August 2007]

A website designed to help people make their own information-based decisions in matters like vaccinations is: www.educateyourself.org

As said before, this may be too grim a picture of reality and for sure there have also been many lives saved through vaccination programmes. A fundamentalist one-sided refusal of them does no justice to that fact or to the reality of their existence. It may be hoped that the vaccination industry will improve their production process as well as develop strategies that follow the natural route for the immune system to respond, e.g. oral vaccines.

There are serious problems concerning vaccination that regular medicine tends to ignore or deny and which deserve the attention of homeopaths, especially as they have the tools to address or prevent them to a considerable extent:

- Consequences for the immune system
- Toxicity

The side-effects that vaccinations can have are either caused by an unbalanced development of the immune system, or by additives present in the vaccines, or a combination of the two.

Vaccination and the immune system

The effects of not having the most common childhood diseases like measles, mumps and chickenpox has consequences as such. If we consider common childhood diseases as positive intelligent forces for strengthening the immune system and for strengthening the individual, by using vaccinations to stop childhood diseases this natural process is disturbed.

The main disadvantage of not having the diseases in childhood is that the immune system in response to the vaccination does not develop as properly as it would in the process of overcoming the disease itself.

In vaccines, a crippled form of the microorganism normally causing the disease is usually forcefully injected into the body. The way it enters the body is different from the normal porte d'entrée of the disease, which forces the immune system to respond in a different way than normal.

In a simple model we can compare it to working out in a gym in an unbalanced way, causing some muscles to be overused and others underdeveloped. Similar to that an athlete, by one-sided exercise, would create a muscular imbalance, vaccinations can disrupt the balance of the immune system.

The fact that often several vaccines are injected at the same time makes it even more difficult for the immune system to create a balanced response. A child would never have the mumps and measles at the same time because the body would not allow it and would instead deal with one after the other, often years apart. Vaccination programmes bypass this safety barrier.

The imbalance of the immune system is further compounded by the excessive use of antibiotics in childhood, which also prevents it developing properly.

The consequence of this is that people develop diseases other than those they would normally, of which allergy is the classic example. Allergies are commonly the result of immature or imbalanced immune development. Besides vaccinations, excessive hygiene is also known to increase the incidence of allergies.

On a deeper level you could say that mankind is playing with nature by using vaccinations programmes as these reduce childhood diseases and epidemic diseases. As a consequence a meaningful relationship is made by many astute physicians to the great rise in chronic diseases. While this is not yet fully proven, we have to consider the possibility that in choosing vaccinations we are risking chronic diseases.

It is therefore necessary to weigh the apparent benefits against the potential disruption of immune development. Authorities offering vaccinations to the people should do so with the greatest care and objectively inform parents and allow them to make their own decision. Although from the viewpoint of maximum effect of vaccination programmes, the present policy of heralding the benefits and denying the side-effects is understandable, it nevertheless is unethical and paternalistic.

It is up to parents to decide which childhood diseases they don't mind their children having, or which they feel are worth having, and which other diseases they definitely do not want to risk, such as polio or tetanus. The main point here is that they themselves need to make an informed decision.

There are several websites and books available that allow parents to inform themselves about the advantages and disadvantages of vaccinations, but not so many of them focus on the most important question, which is the advantages of actually having a simple childhood disease.

Vaccination and toxicity

Vaccinations can have acute but often also long-term and even serious side-effects. Vaccines are often toxic since they can contain heavy metals and other substances that can have serious effects on the health of the child. When injected into the body these toxins can sometimes create severe reactions. This is especially true when vaccinations are used in babies. There is a general consensus amongst doctors who are more aware of the toxic side-effects of vaccinations that it would be better to delay vaccinations until the child has reached at least one, two or even three to five years old.

There are numerous websites documenting the problems of the toxic effects of vaccination/immunisations. We recommend www.tinussmits.com/english by the late Tinus Smits, a Dutch homeopathic doctor who thoroughly studied the subject for many years and developed a system to prevent and treat Post-Vaccination Syndrome.[4] [5] [6] The following quote is from this site:

> 'Post-vaccination syndrome' has for several years now been an increasingly common diagnosis in my daily practice. By degrees I have established an effective method for treating this syndrome. I now consider it a duty to publicize my findings: for doctors, parents and any other persons interested in or concerned with this matter. Conscious of the real significance of this new diagnosis and also of the sensitive nature of the subject, I have compiled this booklet with great care.

Alternatives

Scientists are working on developing vaccines that can enter the body in a more natural way. These are either not available yet or, as in the case of polio, not used in all countries. There are homeopathic alternatives to using vaccinations made with toxic substances and these are given in detail on the site www.homstudy.net by the Australian homeopath Isaac Golden who is the expert on the subject.

---

4 Smits, Tinus, The Post-Vaccination Syndrome - Evaluation of a method and results of a prospective study, Homœopathic links, Vol 14/4, Haren, Netherlands 2001, p214

5 Smits, Tinus & Pernet, Yvonne, The Treatment and Prevention of Post Vaccinal Disease, Homœopathic links, Vol 6/4, Bern, 1994, p34

6 Smits, Tinus, Post-Vaccinal Behavioural Problems - ILL-humour, anxiety, agressiveness, contact disturbances, hysterical behaviour, ADHD, PDD-nos, autism, cured with potentised vaccines, Homœopathic links, Vol 20/2, Stuttgart, 2007

If you Google vaccination/immunisation damage you will get many hits, e.g.

- http://thinktwice.com/
- www.cindeegardner.com/shana.htm
- http://inquirer.gn.apc.org/jabs.html

If you want to read or hear about it, here are a few books and a DVD to consider:

- *Who is Afraid of Tinus Smits* – Documentary on vaccination damage – DVD in Dutch and English.
- *The Vaccine Guide: Risks and Benefits for Children and Adults* by Randall Neustaedter (Author)
- *Vaccines: Are They Really Safe and Effective?* by Neil Z. Miller
- *Vaccinations: Yes or No? – Helping You Decide* by Laura Mary Sussman
- *Vaccination Bible* by Lynne McTaggart
- *How to Raise a Healthy Child* by Robert S. Mendelsohn
- *Handbook of Homoeopathic Alternatives to Immunisation* by Susan Curtis
- *Raising a Vaccine Free Child* by Wendy Lydall
- *Vaccine Free: Homeopathic Alternatives to Vaccination* by Kate Birch
- *Vaccine Damaged Children: Treatment, Prevention, Reasons* by Isaac Golden
- *Vaccination & Homoeoprophylaxis?* A Review of Risks and Alternatives by Isaac Golden
- *Homoeoprophylaxis – A Practical and Philosophical Review* by Isaac Golden

It is incidentally not just childhood vaccinations that can have bad effects; this also applies to adult vaccination of which the flu vaccine is the most widely used. Its efficacy is highly questionable and some studies even show that vaccinated people had more bouts of flu than those that were not. The recent vaccination programme for the Mexican flu is thought to be responsible for a strong increase of narcolepsy in children in Sweden and Finland. In the Netherlands at least one case was reported where the child developed narcolepsy directly following vaccination.

In adult vaccinations it is frequently seen that the onset of a serious chronic disease like Chronic Fatigue Syndrome/ME starts with an influenza vaccination. Also it is widely thought that Gulf War Syndrome was due to the vaccinations given to the soldiers prior to going to the battlefield, as many of the soldiers never actually went into battle but still suffered from Gulf War Syndrome. The fact is that the armies of this world have a habit of filling the soldiers with insufficiently tested vaccines against perceived new threats and might be doing more harm to the soldiers' lifelong health by creating lifelong ill-health, than anything else that happens in the war.

Vaccinations are never a free lunch. They always have consequences. The health industry is driven by profit, regular medicine by the war on microbes. This is a fundamental thing we have to remember, and it's very easy to exploit people's health fears for profit. The interest of the pharmaceutical industry is to get their products to the market rather than to support longitudinal studies as to their long-term side-effects. Organisations which warn against forthcoming flu et cetera are commonly funded by pharmaceutical companies, showing a serious conflict of interest.

PART V

Theory of Treating Chronic Diseases

Genus Epidemicus Applied to Chronic Diseases

Firstly the principles of the Genus epidemicus approach in homeopathy does not only apply to epidemics and trauma but also to chronic diseases, because, as we have discussed before, chronic diseases are really long-running epigenetic (miasmatic) diseases complicated by toxins, both physical and mental, and other factors.

Every chronic disease is in fact a process, often maturing over decades. It is a (slow) moving disease process that has a lot in common with the process millions of other people in the same situation experience. This means that a chronic disease has a collective nature and can be regarded as an archetype. Each chronic disease is one of the paths a human organism can walk.

We think there are several basic processes behind so called chronic diseases.

There are epigenetic (miasmatic) effects compounded by mal-nurturing effects.

We like the adage that all physical pain is repressed emotional pain. Unresolved emotional pain results in tightened places in the body where blood flow and fluid flows are diminished. This results in the accumulation of toxins in hazardous amounts, which can cause pathology.

Disease has a conscious meaning and is a form of communication for the sufferer. The conscious meaning is always rooted in a powerful compassion and a wise intelligence.

The actual pathology has been established by medical science with considerable accuracy and defines the specific nature of the disease. Medical researchers and physicians have invested trillions of man-hours in establishing and diagnosing and proving specific diseases. This is a level of consciousness, which has arisen since the time of Samuel Hahnemann when it simply was not available or known. This and the development of surgical skills is the main contribution of regular medicine.

From the analysis that chronic diseases are slow moving epidemics or miasmatic diseases it is practical to have one remedy for each so called chronic disease that can complement the individualised homeopathic treatment for the patient if that alone is not enough. Some chronic diseases are so much an expression of the collective, the present culture, that a disease specific approach which addresses the collective issues may be more justified and needed than an individual approach. Having said that, ideally each and every patient suffering from a chronic disease receives both, a patient-specific simillimum and a disease specific simillimum. In the chapters on the practical implications of this approach, many cases will show how this approach enriches current homeopathic practice.

The personal patient acceptance of the conscious collective meaning of the disease means that the forming force of the disease as rooted has been removed and that the disease no longer has a basis for existence. The individual simillimum that addresses why, in this particular patient, this disease has surfaced at this point in time addresses the conscious individual meaning of this disease in this person. The two complement each other.

The PC Resonance for a specific disease is then just that – a resonance that will elicit from the disease its raison d'être in terms of meaning to the person. There will be many ways this is expressed, in terms of dreams, relationships et cetera as is well known in homeopathic practice. The key point is that it will bring clarity where there is obscurity.

This approach has to be seen in the context of a complete treatment plan over time.

The PC Resonance is then a conscious resonance aligned to the specific disease. When it amplifies the disease, and resonance is a form of amplification, this sets the stage for the reflected intelligent communication to enter the consciousness of the person and for them to understand the meaning and purpose of the disease.

For some reason homeopaths tend to resist a disease specific approach in principle while their practice very often shows they nevertheless apply it. An example is the use of *Mercurius* as one of the main remedies for treating ulcerative colitis. Here the pathognomic symptoms are used to reach the prescription. In general we can observe that the more severe the pathology, the more homeopaths use remedies that fit the pathology. A good example is the treatment of cancer, where very often several remedies are being used: a remedy fitting the patient, a remedy fitting the specific cancer and/or the tissue involved, and besides that remedies to detox the use of radiation or chemotherapy.

We suggest that cancer treatment shows the truth of what an ideal homeopathic treatment of chronic diseases should look like in general. The resulting picture is then that different methods advocated by different schools of homeopathy together guarantee the best results:

- Individualised prescriptions – classical homeopathy – based on the most highly advanced techniques for finding the individual simillimum
- Disease specific prescriptions – clinical homeopathy – which treat the collective meaning and roots of the disease
- Trauma specific prescriptions – (epigenetic) – including a history of infection, physical/emotional trauma, et cetera – to treat the roots of the disease within the individual
- Detox prescriptions to treat a history of intoxication, vaccination damage et cetera.

Individualised homeopathic treatment completely depends on the skills of the homeopath to find the remedy that mirrors the state of the patient, and besides that relies on the accuracy and development of the Materia Medica. For the other three categories of prescribing this book offers a complete new set of PC Resonances based upon diagnostic criteria.

Part VI

From Theory to Practice

A Summary of the New Theory

We have introduced a number of new concepts and ideas within the theory of homeopathy in the chapters before this one.

We have suggested that Hahnemann's three primary miasms are really three primary forces for good that are motivating humanity in its journey of awakening to its consciousness.

In fact we have shown that everything in the universe is intelligent including diseases. We could say that it is a loving intelligence that is inside every activity, whether we see it or not.

We have called these primary miasms META-MIASMS to distinguish them from disease and call others SPECIFIC MIASMS relating to specific epidemic and chronic disease-like processes, which we have described.

There are many ways of relating these META-MIASMS to other systems that identify three core components. For example we have three core blood groups, three stages of embryonic development, three stages in the birth process (onset, dilatation, expulsion), three stages in pathology (inflammation, proliferation, destruction), three tissue structures (epithelium, endothelium, mesothelium), three core survival instincts (freeze, flight and fight), three doshas in Ayurvedic medicine (vatha, pitta, kapha). There are many more such divisions.

On a more conscious level we would say there are three primary forces in the universal consciousness – power, wisdom and love – and that the META-MIASMS are waking us up to these faculties.

Hahnemann saw the META-MIASMS as the effects of three primary diseases. We are not suggesting this is wrong but that these diseases are specific examples of the consequences of the primary META-MIASMS processes over time. Syphilis for example seems an excellent choice of a disease to represent the fight instinct, and gonorrhoea the flight instinct. But these diseases are not the META-MIASMS, they are just good examples of them. We also suppose that diseases are the logical outcome of millions of years of the intelligent existence of the META-MIASMS. They are the congealed animal and human experience made into form. The diseases are the result of the META-MIASMS, not the cause of them. And we stress again, the META-MIASMS are always intelligent forces and not malevolent forces as the medical profession in its understanding of diseases tends to assume. The very idea of fighting disease is in fact an expression of the hyped fight survival instinct.

We can view the human species as an intelligent process where a new level of awareness is being embedded into a primarily animal form. At one point these two were completely separate. And it is through the multidimensional miasmic (epigenetic) process that this embodying is happening. Consciousness is descending into human form. We are close to achieving it and it can happen at anytime, and it will happen with time.
The point is that these identified Meta-Miasms, have an intelligent role and purpose in the human race, to wake us up to what we really are, a shaped and permanent consciousness that informs a mind-body construct that is temporary.

When it comes to specific miasmic diseases, of which there are hundreds and thousands, each one of these can be routinely treated by a perfect nosode or by one of the resonances made by our new methods. A perfect nosode would in provings and clinically cover the disease totality. Regretfully, most nosodes available are not perfect in that sense. This new technology and the nosode have proven to be both prophylactic/preventative as well as curative. For example herpes, which everyone has heard of, and Ross River Virus, which most people won't have heard of, which is endemic in parts of Australia, can both be effectively treated this way. This is one of the thousands of diseases where the miasmic disease approach is applicable, where the individual approach is usually not.

There has been a lot of confusion in homeopathy in this area. Yet the greatest contribution to human health by homeopathy has been in the area of treating epidemic diseases by using a Genus epidemicus approach. This confusion is shown in the homeopathic literature everywhere, when remedies are suggested for an epidemic disease such as herpes, or malaria, and there is a very long list of such remedies, when theoretically only one is needed which covers the totality of herpes or malaria. Homeopathic literature is full of this misconception. Regretfully, in practice a remedy that covers the disease totality is rarely found, which may partially explain the misconception. PC Technology makes it possible to create disease specific resonances that do cover the totality of signs and symptoms.

The medical profession, with this idea of universal vaccinations, one for each specific epidemic disease and now chronic diseases, does not suffer from this confusion. But it suffers from ignoring or misunderstanding the purposes of miasms and diseases as well as from the way it approaches the problem.

We have shown that the mind-body construct is primarily an inherited phenomenon based upon the epigenetic process, and given flesh and bones by the nurturing we receive as we grow up. The great majority of our nurturing re-forms us in line with the history of our family and our society and in doing so limits us to a specific and limiting form. To come alive to our full potential we have to transform this history to achieve our personal freedom through awareness. That is its purpose. If we don't come alive to our potential, then our energy intelligently stagnates and becomes pathology. So, as we grow older we have a choice of increasingly more painful yet stronger messages if we refuse to heed the original ones.

There are many dimensions to the epigenetic process, which we also call Specific Miasms, which Hahnemann foresaw but was not able to comprehensively explain in his day and age due to the lack of science and the language and the facts of his time.

We suggest that there are many SPECIFIC MIASMS as the scientific research into epigenetics is showing: there are miasms due to diseases, toxins, parasites, trauma in its many forms, fungi and many small forms besides. These all seriously affect our genetic expression from one generation to the next.

From a homeopathic perspective we have drawn lines between individual prescribing and miasmic prescribing theoretically, but in practice there is no such line. If a person presents with a picture of systematic and long lasting Lead or Arsenic poisoning we will prescribe the toxin in potency to great effect because that will be the symptom picture. If the person presents with the picture of homeopathic *Tuberculinum*, we will prescribe *Tuberculinum*. If we look back in history, it is highly probable that in all these cases there is more than one generation involved. It is not so easy then to draw a clean line between such ideas as the individual and the miasmic remedy. This division is possibly a false one.

One thing we think is true is that the more specific the treatment the better. So for example, if we think the person is suffering from heavy metal poisoning, it is better to treat the specific heavy metal if it can be accurately determined rather than prescribing a bottle full of different potentised metals. If the person is suffering from Lyme's disease and perhaps also acquired two other similar diseases from the same tick bite, then it is better to treat all three.

When it comes to chemical toxins in the bloodstream, the average American and probably Western European has several hundred chemical toxins in their bloodstream which should not be there, and eating organic doesn't solve this problem because the soil, water, air et cetera are now polluted. Various sources of fuels that permeate the air on burning can now be found in every soil. We have seriously polluted our planet. This makes it difficult to address. This is an area where homeopathy needs to expand because it has the tools for the job. The difficulty is that you cannot put all the known chemical toxins in potency in one bottle because they cancel each other out. At the same time it is virtually impossible to identify all the toxins in a specific person's bloodstream. Incidentally, a regular sauna would seem like one intelligent approach to this process at the moment since by eating we retox every day, so detox is regularly needed.

Everybody has a history of psychological trauma of various types, given the traumatic history of the human race in the last hundreds of years. We have a post-traumatic human race, whose trauma has also been inflicted upon the planet. For example we can say that almost every woman alive has inherited the trauma of rape. It is often easier to treat the trauma than to identify the individual remedy for a person.

It is probable that those homeopaths that use a few common remedies a great deal, are treating complex patterns of trauma that are common within the human race, and not touching the individual. And this works and shifts consciousness because it addresses serious underlying miasmic processes.

We have suggested that there are in fact three primary survival instincts, freeze, flight and fight based upon the reptilian brain, and two more, food and sex based upon the mammalian brain. These both dominate human behaviour and are largely ignored in homeopathic and other forms of treatment. It may be that over-activation of these causes the primary dysfunctions as well as determining the primary forces for awakening consciousness within the human race. Focusing on these has a lot to commend it. While these forces are theoretically at the primary level of Maslow's hierarchy of needs, they seem to be significantly ignored (See Fig. 3).

We would say that their collective imbalance may be the founding forces leading to the wars of the last century, the banking collapses recently which were based on the food survival instinct, showing up as greed, greed and greed (see the film *The Inside Job* 2011) and other ways in which we are causing great suffering to ourselves and the planet.

In homeopathic prescribing homeopaths tend to work on the consequences of the survival instincts, the total pattern of the person, yet it is very obvious that people who have had long treatments from skilled homeopaths, are usually still dominated by the survival instincts. There is nothing wrong with survival mechanisms, but being dominated by them in situations where they are unnecessary is a problem. So perhaps something is missing in the homeopathic process.

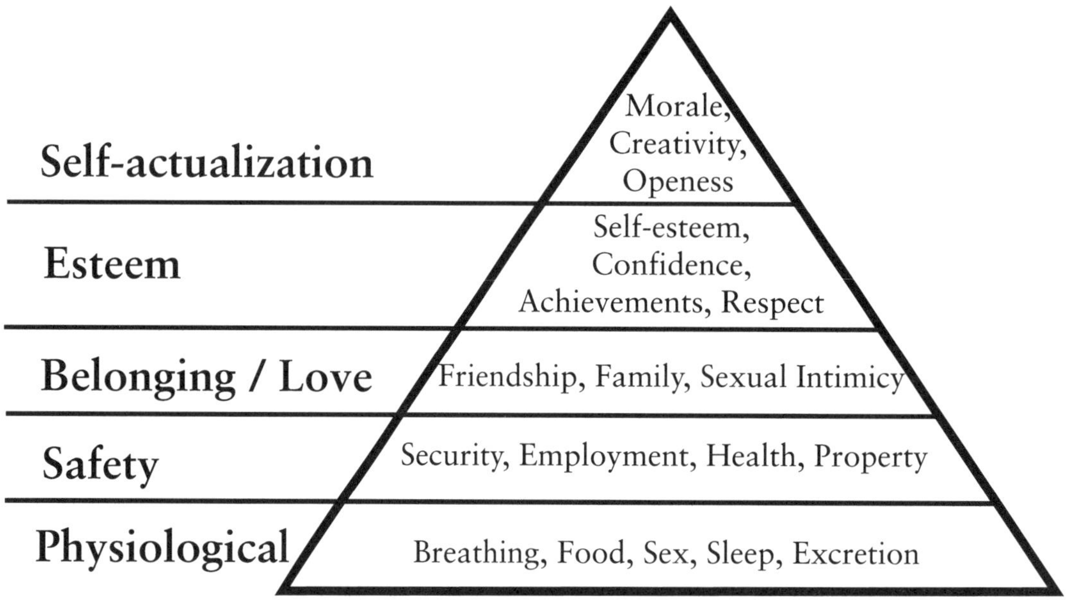

Fig. 3: Maslow's hierarchy of needs

When it comes to Specific Miasms, whatever their roots, we can still see these also as intelligent forces for good seeking to wake us up in specific ways. It is the same with individual prescriptions. The purpose of life seems to become conscious of what we really are, not the mind-body construct that we inhabit temporarily, but the consciousness by which we direct our lives.

We have shown in significant depth that psychological trauma is both very profound and a key root of mental, emotional and physical illness. The same applies to all forms of miasms: spiritual, psychological and physical.

We have developed the hypothesis that diseases are the results of a combination of different types of miasms. They are the combination of miasms derived from epidemic diseases, epidemic toxins and epidemic trauma, combined and aggravated by lifestyle changes towards heavily processed and non-nutritious food and lack of exercise.

We suggest here that these lifestyle changes are possibly the consequences of the suppression of diseases by drugs and vaccinations over generations. When diseases are suppressed, energy drops and the vitality of the human being drops. Consequently when this happens over generations it is reflected in the unhealthy lifestyle.

We suggest that chronic disease remedies, using the disease outcome as a core part of the definition of the remedy, have a part to play in waking people up and reversing specific chronic disease. And when this process is carried on systematically, energy arises and lifestyles change in a more healthy direction and at the same time awareness is enhanced.

Because diseases have been identified since the time of Hahnemann by an amazing effort from the medical profession, we can use this information to prescribe correctly on diseases. By taking the totality of the intelligent purpose of the disease as well as its pathology, which gives it shape, we can make remedies to treat diseases.

In the history of homeopathy we have developed nosodes, remedies made from epidemic disease products exactly for this purpose ~ and sometimes these work. But we have shown, and it is common evidence from the fact that they are not widely used for this purpose, that they are not so successful. We have shown the reason for this is probably partly in the way they are produced. We suggest that the first chronic disease remedy in homeopathy was *Carcinosin*, introduced half a century ago and which no homeopath would like to be without. So, what we are doing is to make these developments systematic and widespread across all types of diseases.

We were very fortunate to be invited to work in Africa in various situations. In Africa you see things much more clearly and dramatically than you find in the West, where the situation is more advanced, more convoluted and more confused. In Africa you see the beginning of the process, that goes on for many generations and in the West you see the result. Africa highlighted dramatically the issues that afflict the human race in a way that was easy to understand. Fortunately we were able to return the benefits of these insights by helping many people recover their health in a safe and effective way.

We will now examine the results of these ideas in practice.

Practical Instructions for Effective Treatment with PC Resonances

This chapter contains the general distillation of our experience with a disease specific approach to trauma, epidemics, intoxication and chronic diseases. In the chapters on several indications for a disease specific approach, whether used primarily or secondarily as a complement, more specific instructions can be found. The disease specific remedies used in the cases that support our theory were PC RESONANCES.

The use of the theory and practice of a disease-oriented approach is not restricted to PC RESONANCES. Any homeopathic remedy or any resonance however prepared can be used within this system as long as it sufficiently covers the totality of the disease it is intended to treat. We are open to the possibility that with a further expansion of the Materia Medica and a deeper and more complete understanding of all the signs and symptoms belonging to individual substances, a disease specific homeopathic remedy can be identified for all possible diseases and states. At this point in time homeopaths have excavated the Materia Medica site for only a small portion of the rich possibilities, bringing into the light far less than 1% of all possible treasures to be found. So, this may prove to be a lengthy process, perhaps hundreds or thousands of years.

Besides the way PC RESONANCES are designed, there are probably many more ways of creating homeopathic like remedies, so the reader is free to use any source of resonances/remedies s/he feels comfortable with and can replace the term PC Resonance with any other simillimum that would cover the disease totality.

This should not be misunderstood as a recommendation to start using all kinds of methods – mechanical, spiritual or otherwise – to create remedies/resonances. The well-being of patients demands health professionals to be professional and not to experiment just for the sake of curiosity. The developments described in this book only came into being because Peter Chappell was confronted with the situation that in 2002 there was no single homeopathic substance known to effectively and consistently treat HIV/AIDS in Africa. It was for the sake of his patients that only then did he seek a way to create a remedy that was not yet in existence.

To be able to cure a patient from a disease a remedy/resonance similar to the disease totality not only needs to include the width and depth of that totality on an informational level but should also have the power to induce healing on a dynamic level. In our experience traditionally made homeopathic remedies and PC RESONANCES meet these qualifications, and only these can we therefore truly recommend.

Ready-to-use PC dropper bottles

For homeopaths and patients living in the West different pharmacies (see end of this book) make ready-to-use PC dropper bottles for patients and these can be mailed directly to a patient on request by a homeopath. This service is easy for the homeopath and the patient and is the best guarantee for a high quality resonance.

How to prepare a PC Resonance for a patient

(These instructions are intended for use in countries and places where high quality service by a homeopathic pharmacy is not available)

PC Resonances are also available as granules. These granules for preparing bottles for patients are provided in tubes. In the final chapters you find information on how to order granules.

If available, prepare the PC Resonance in a dropper bottle, if not, use a sealed bottle of mineral water.

30-50 ml dropper bottles

Put two granules into a clean 30-50 ml dropper bottle. Add to it mineral water or purified water (boiled and cooled down). If properly stored and used this gives at least three months shelf life. If available and no problem for the patient use 80% water and 20% medical alcohol (or 50% water and 50% vodka) to increase shelf life. Leave the bottle standing for a couple of minutes until the granules start to fall apart. Then bang the bottle on a wooden surface or a book five times and that is then prepared for use. Banging the bottle strongly is essential! (Shaking is NOT banging).

250 - 330 - 500 ml mineral water bottles

Use a sealed 250 or 330 to 500 ml plastic or (preferably) glass bottle of still mineral water. Open it and pour out 20% of the content. Put two granules into the bottle. If properly stored and used this gives at least three months shelf life. If available and no problem for the patient add 20% medical alcohol (or pour out 50% and add 50% vodka) to increase shelf life. Leave the bottle standing for a couple of minutes until the granules start to fall apart. Then bang the bottle on a wooden surface or a book five times and that is then prepared for use. Banging the bottle strongly is essential! (Shaking is NOT banging).

Label the bottle with the PC Code (as written on the bottle with granules), add the patient's name and give the patient, preferably in writing, the instructions to use as below (at www.ARHF.nl an instruction card can be downloaded for the use of PC1 for HIV/AIDS). If it's a mineral water bottle first tear off the original label.

How to use a PC Resonance as a patient

For dropper bottles – 555 (5 bangs, 5 drops, 5 seconds)

Before taking a dose bang the bottle on a book or a wooden surface five times to activate and then immediately put five drops into a teaspoon, then into the mouth. Keep into the mouth, under the tongue, for at least five seconds before swallowing. It is recommended to show a patient how to bang the bottle and then ask them to show you how they'll do it so you're sure they've understood and will dynamise the bottle hard enough. (Shaking is NOT banging).

For water bottles – 515 (5 bangs, 1 spoon, 5 seconds)

Before taking a dose bang the bottle on a book or a wooden surface five times to activate and then immediately take one spoonful directly into the mouth. Keep into the mouth, under the tongue, for at least five seconds before swallowing.

In both the above

- The mouth must be relatively clean when taking the Resonance. Do not eat or drink just before or after taking it for fifteen minutes. Also do not brush your teeth or smoke just before or after taking it.

- The water must remain crystal clear. Never contaminate it by putting any liquid back in the bottle. If more than five drops come out just take them all. To overdose is not possible. Never touch the opening of the bottle with the fingers or mouth or by drinking directly from the bottle and always close it properly. If the water is not clear it is contaminated, no longer active, and a fresh bottle must be made.
- Keep the bottle in a cool place out of the extreme heat and direct sunlight.
- If you need to take one dose daily the time of day is not important.

PC Resonances are safe for pregnant women, babies, small children, older people and those using other medication.

Dosage

The dosage of PC Resonances does not essentially differ from how potentised substances are prescribed. For acute conditions regular repetition may be needed as guided by the symptoms (e.g. every 30 minutes in acute flu, acute malaria, acute trauma) with longer intervals as the case improves. In chronic conditions usually once daily five drops as described above is sufficient. In a chronic condition caused by a past event – e.g. post-traumatic stress disorder – repetition is very often only needed for a few days. In case of a relapse after a period of being free from symptoms repetition is indicated until completely well.

With chronic diseases, where well-developed homeopathic skills are needed to successfully and responsibly use PC Resonances, initial aggravations have been reported. Therefore, as with other homeopathic remedies, in cases that are depleted, with low vitality and very limited recuperation ability, it is advisable to start by giving only a few drops of the PC Resonance and then to wait sufficiently long enough to see whether an initial aggravation occurs and if so whether the patients then enters a phase of amelioration. If there is no amelioration after an initial aggravation no more drops can be prescribed and the vitality of the patient will have to be improved through other means than homeopathy first.

Where to start

It may happen that a patient that comes to you suffers from more than one condition at the same time. Often one condition will be most prominent and may push the symptoms of the other(s) to the background. That is the condition to start treating. If it concerns an epidemic or trauma you can start with a disease specific PC Resonance. If the most prominent condition is a chronic constitutional one you start with the indicated simillimum. If that is unclear or not effective you then give a disease specific resonance that can be followed by individual treatment once it has clearly acted, gives no further progress, and has allowed the patient to produce a clear constitutional picture, the sign and symptoms of which were earlier hidden underneath the disease picture.

As long as the response to any remedy that is selected to start with is being observed and analysed carefully there is usually no such thing as a wrong start, as the body will show you whether it agrees with your choice, and if not it will produce signs and symptoms to suggest a better option to you.

It is not advisable to use two PC Resonances simultaneously because it may become difficult for you to properly evaluate the effects. For the same reason we advise not to start with individual treatment together with a disease specific resonance unless the situation the patient is in urges you to do so. We have found no evidence of one approach suppressing or disturbing the other, but rather have seen they complement each other. The time interval in the succession of different remedies/resonances is also dependent on the nature of the condition. The more acute and dynamic the condition the more often one can repeat, change or complement. The same holds true for the more serious a condition is.

A general rule is to start treating the most prominent condition, that which is staring you in the face.

- If a person comes for the treatment of colitis ulcerosa and has to cancel because of the flu, you can start with prescribing for the flu: either a remedy you clearly recognise or routinely the PC Resonance for flu. Later you start treatment for colitis ulcerosa. If you have a very clear picture of say *Mercurius solibulis* as the simillimum you start with that, and complement later with the PC resonance for colitis ulcerosa if no complete cure has been reached. If the simillimum is not easy to detect, as is common in more advanced cases, you start with the indicated PC Resonance. As soon as symptoms start to subside and a constitutional picture clears of say *Arsenicum album*, you can complement the disease specific approach by prescribing *Arsenicum album*.
- If an AIDS-patient has an acute hepatitis you start treating the hepatitis with the PC Resonance for it and let it be followed by PC1 as soon as the hepatitis subsides.

There can be exceptions to this rule though.

- E.g. in a girl who has been raped by an HIV-positive man the symptoms of rape may be very prominent and that of AIDS non-existing. It is too early to do an HIV-test (it takes 2 – 8 weeks before being detectable after infection) but all should be done to prevent a possible infection developing. If available you need to give ARVs and PC1. If no ARVs are available you start PC1 and, on the same day, the PC Resonance for rape trauma to maximally stimulate and restore the immune system. Trauma severely weakens the immune system and since HIV is attacking it, you need to address both immediately (See chapter on AIDS for more detailed recommendations).

A second rule is that if two conditions are connected you give the PC Resonance or appropriate homeopathic remedy for the underlying one unless the subsequent condition is very prominent. Some examples:

- A patient has AIDS and TB, and the TB symptoms are not very prominent. You prescribe PC1 for AIDS, because the immune system is not able to fight TB properly due to AIDS. PC1 is likely to be enough to treat both conditions, and if not it can be followed by the PC Resonance for TB.
- A patient has been raped and is in a clear *Lac caninum* state that dominates her symptom picture. The rape has also resulted in gonorrhoea. You start with *Lac caninum* (complemented with the PC Resonance for the trauma of rape if not sufficiently effective) and follow up with PC Gonorrhoea (also if the gonorrhoea has apparently been treated successfully with antibiotics; its miasmatic effect will still be there).
- A similar patient has strong symptoms of gonorrhoea whereas the symptoms of the rape are less clearly defined. You start with PC Gonorrhoea and let it follow by the PC Resonance for the trauma of rape.

- A young patient is been diagnosed as being autistic. The history makes a causal relationship with vaccination likely. The remedy that seems to fit the case as a simillimum is *Belladonna*. You start to treat the possible cause by prescribing the PC Resonance for vaccination damage (a general resonance for which it is not necessary to know which particular vaccination is the likely candidate), after that has fully shown its action you follow up with Belladonna (or another remedy in case the picture has changed and now clearly points to a better fitting simillimum). If these two remedies do not fully cure the autism the PC Resonance for autistic spectrum disorder can be prescribed.

Another rule is that if a patient suffers from two conditions you start treating the most recent one and then continue with the older one.

- E.g. a 16-year-old patient has been adopted as a baby and still suffers from this; besides that she suffers from recurrent cystitis since she had gonorrhoea one year ago. You start treating the effects of gonorrhoea with the PC Resonance for gonorrhoea and once that has been cured you treat the adoption trauma, either with the PC Resonance for adoption trauma or, provided you are a fully trained homeopath, with a homeopathic remedy in case there is a clear and prominent picture.

In the parts devoted to epidemic diseases, trauma, intoxication and chronic diseases there are chapters that will explain in detail how to use PC Resonances for a variety of indications and we will illustrate this with case examples.

The website www.vitalremedies.com is restricted to homeopaths. Here a complete and regularly updated list of all available PC Resonances can be found. In this book, at the end of the chapters on epidemic diseases, trauma, intoxication and chronic diseases lists of the available remedies for these fields of indication can be found.

Part VII

Practice of Treating Infectious and Epidemic Diseases

The chapters in this section are listed in alphabetical order and can be read selectively or in any sequence preferred. The list of available PC Resonances for infectious and epidemic diseases is much larger. We have restricted ourselves to those indications of which we have direct experience.

Instructions on how to prepare and dose can be found in Part VI: 'Practical Instructions for Effective Treatment with PC Resonances'.

Chapters

- AIDS
- Bilharzia
- Gonorrhoea
- Hepatitis
- Influenza
- Leprosy
- Lyme disease
- Malaria
- Poliomyelitis
- Ringworm
- Scabies
- Streptococcus
- Syphilis
- Toxoplasmosis
- Tuberculosis
- Typhoid

In appendix 5 a list of available PC Resonances for infectious and epidemic diseases can be found. A regularly updated list is available at www.vitalremedies.com.

AIDS

AIDS is a contentious subject. To do justice to our research and answer many critics and important questions around AIDS we investigated the many contentions around AIDS and formed our position. This is found in Appendix 1.

PC1 – A Resonance for HIV/AIDS

In 2001 Peter went to Ethiopia and to determine the Genus epidemicus (totality of the symptoms) of HIV/AIDS in Africa carefully and systematically compiled 70 detailed case studies. From these he deleted those symptoms that were a consequence of the reduced immunity, typically recurring previously acquired infections (typically tuberculosis), and recently acquired infections (typically herpes), and also those symptoms which related to the constitution of the person, as these were seen as the response to the disease, not the disease itself. In simple terms, a *Phosphorus* type person when dying is concerned about the wellbeing of their children, an *Arsenicum* is very anxious about dying, etc and these are just natural responses that would be expected to any threat of imminent death. These are therefore not part of the disease itself.

(For the primary characteristics of AIDS see the discussion in Part II as also *The Second Simillimum* by Peter Chappell)

Peter considered the AIDS nosode (which he noticed caused severe aggravations), constitutional remedies, and tried extensive repertorisation and consideration of existing homeopathic remedies as indicated and consulted many colleagues. He also realised that the common epidemic approach advocated practically by Hahnemann, of a small group of remedies prescribed on the presenting symptoms, was doomed to fail in Africa where skills are in short supply and homeopathic skills virtually non existent, except sparsely in South Africa. He felt that there was no example in homeopathy to date where one remedy treated the totality of any disease in its entirety, even though *China*/quinine for malaria, through which homeopathy was unfolded, was the closest example. He felt that no current known homeopathic approach was in fact likely to be satisfactory.

Peter then took a radical step forward and did something that had not been done before. He decided to create a new technology to design a remedy/resonance. He figured out how to reverse engineer the totality and essence of the symptom picture information and the medical disease description into a remedy for HIV/AIDS he later called PC1. (See Part I on how PC Resonances are made).

Peter's book *The Second Simillimum* gives you the full story of what the building blocks of his consciousness are from which he could create the remedy, and what the first results were with PC1 as well as some other remedies he had created.

The Emoto[1] Laboratory staff in Lichtenstein was reportedly very surprised that a tiny pinhead granule could result in so many well-defined crystal shapes, inferring real and substantial information in the granule. Differences in crystal shapes are also visible between the two different gender formulations of PC1. (See illustrations)

1 www.masaru-emoto.net

Fig. 4: Ice crystal of PC1AF for females

Fig. 5: Ice crystal of PC1AM for males

Since 2002 PC1 has been used in many African countries and India with good results, both as a complement to ARVs or instead of ARVs when these were not available or not yet indicated.

In 2007 the Amma Resonance Healing Foundation (ARHF)[2] was established in the Netherlands. The ARHF focuses on research into the efficacy of PC1 and on making PC1 available

2 www.ARHF.nl

to those that need it. Peter has donated the rights of PC1 and other remedies for the treatment of epidemics and collective trauma to the ARHF. The ARHF is a not-for-profit organization and makes PC1 available at the lowest possible price, which in most situations means for free.

The Advantages of PC1 for HIV/AIDS

- No side effects
- No induction of therapy resistance
- No chemical interference with other medication – but complementary action to drug therapy
- Very cheap production process (1-2 US dollars per patient per month)
- Easy distribution – no cooling or special storage and long keeping qualities
- PC1 in liquid form can be locally produced with low-tech equipment from small stock of granules
- Safe for all ages including babies and pregnant women
- PC1 is a Genus epidemicus remedy, based on the principles of resonance, specifically geared towards AIDS but without the need of lengthy, individualized case-taking, as in individualized homeopathy
- Easy to understand and teach the use (no highly trained staff necessary to monitor proper intake)
- Doesn't contradict local traditions/taboos (one reason why many treatment programmes in developing countries don't work)

Response to PC1

The indicators of a revitalised immune system and the signs of recovery from AIDS using PC1 are:

- Appetite returning to normal; even ravenous appetite
- Regaining of strength
- Ability to walk increased from metres to kilometres
- Increased recovery powers from acute infections
- Gaining weight, getting back to normal weight, is a great sign of improvement (provided there is enough food available)
- Improvement of cough and chest pains
- Reduction of general pains, muscle and joint pains, headaches, usually within weeks
- Feeling well again, hope, happiness, clear minded, sense of increased inner peace/calm and losing those feelings of helplessness, panic, fear of dying and despair. A change in mental health is often the first sign of recovery
- Reduced attacks of malaria
- Elimination of TB

These changes usually happen in days and weeks.

How to Treat HIV/AIDS with PC1

AIDS is one of the most serious diseases in Africa and certainly the one that in this time and age gets most of the attention. Treating AIDS with ARVs (anti-retroviral drugs) is the standard in all African countries, but less than half of those needing it get supplies regularly or at all. The moment it is advised to start with ARVs depends on the state of the immune system, which is measured mainly by the number of white blood cells available to fight HIV and other infections, the so-called CD4 count. A healthy person has a CD4 count of around 1000 units or higher. In an HIV-positive person the CD4 count drops on average by some 50 units per year after an already considerable drop in the acute stage, when after being infected a flu-like state is experienced. After some eleven years the immune system with a CD4 count dropping below 200 units is no longer able to defend the body from infections, and all kinds of viruses and bacteria can freely infect the body. This condition is called AIDS, Acquired Immune Deficiency Syndrome. Treatment with ARVs is started as soon as the CD4 count drops below a certain level, in many countries 200 – 350 units.

PC1 is designed to boost the immune system in HIV-positive patients and can be prescribed in all phases because it is safe and without side-effects.

A different version of PC1 is designed for men and women. The reason for this is that in the totality of the symptoms of HIV/AIDS the socio-economic position and the mental and emotional state of the patient are included, and these differ based on gender. PC1AF is for women, where PC1AM is for men.

For gay people in the West, a very different group context from the general epidemic in Africa, a special PC Resonance has been designed called PC1HW. However it needs to be used as part of a complete programme addressing all the issues addressed previously, and others not discussed as too controversial.

Acute infection

If a patient is possibly very recently infected (unsafe sex, rape, accident with infected needle) this cannot be determined (it takes 2 – 8 weeks before a HIV-test can give a conclusive answer). To be on the safe side precautions need to be taken. The patient should see a doctor immediately to see whether a course of ARVs is indicated for prophylaxis. PC1 should be given also as soon as possible. Since it is possibly an acute state let PC1 be repeated every three hours except during the sleeping period for three days and continue with one dose daily (five drops or one teaspoon) until an HIV-test can be done. If that is positive continue with PC1 once daily.

If there is a flu-like condition possibly due to a recent infection with HIV give PC1 every hour until the symptoms subside. Make the intervals longer gradually until it is given once daily and continue until an HIV-test can be done. If that is positive continue with PC1 once daily.

Pre-AIDS stage

Since PC1 is absolutely safe it can be prescribed also and even preferably in early stages, before AIDS sets in. Although a patient may still have few or no symptoms PC1 can be used to restore the already compromised immune system. It is very important to stress to the patient that PC1 does not cure HIV but only helps boost the immune system to prevent the stage of AIDS from developing. PC1 does not prevent a person from becoming infected nor is it safe to have unprotected sex with an HIV-positive person using PC1. Safe sex is essential in all stages for the patient and their partners. Besides that proper nutrition and a healthy life-style also support the body. In the early stages the CD4 count can be used to see how the state of the patient and the immune system is. Continuous treatment is not necessary in many cases and therapy resistance due to a pause in the treatment cannot develop as with ARVs, so PC1 can be given with intervals depending on the level of CD4 and providing there is safe sex only. It is advised to repeat a CD4 test every three months and to start using a bottle of PC1 again as soon as symptoms arise or the CD4 drops. It is expected that under normal conditions one bottle of PC1, lasting for 2-3 months, every six months should be sufficient.

AIDS

If patients can receive ARVs and their CD4 count indicates they need it they should be advised to take these. ARVs bring the Viral Load (the amount of viruses in the blood) down rapidly, but they do not boost the immune system and due to toxicity even harm the immune system. The immune system when using ARVs only restores slowly. It is therefore advised to complement treatment with ARVs with PC1. PC1 will restore the immune system and due to this other infections will disappear much more rapidly. Besides that, patients suffering from side-effects due to ARVs often see these reduced when also using PC1, because their body is in a better state of health, and is better able to cope with toxins. If despite PC1 a patient still has serious side-effects from ARVs, PC-HAART (PC501a) for the side-effects of ARVs (HAART = Highly Active Anti Retroviral Treatment) can be prescribed alongside ARVs and PC1. It is advised to use PC1 and PC-HAART at different times of the day. If patients improve on ARVs and PC1 they should not stop taking ARVs even if they feel very well, because this can induce therapy resistance, meaning that the patient will no longer respond to the same ARVs in case these would again be needed in the future. Other so-called second line ARVs are much more expensive or less available. Once the CD4 count has been restored to normal it is safe to stop taking PC1 for periods of time. It is advised to take one bottle lasting for two to three months every six months or to start directly if the condition of the patients gets worse or the CD4 count drops. PC1 or ARVs will not make the patient HIV-negative or remove the virus from the body totally. The fact that a patient although well still tests HIV-positive means that the immune system remembers the virus and has learned to live with it. The information of many viruses and bacteria is present in the human body in a similar way, and this as such is not a bad thing but part of human existence.

End stage of AIDS

If started in the very end stage of AIDS ARVs are often not able to save a person's life. The same maybe holds true for PC1 (but see hospice story), but it is believed that combining PC1 with ARVs will at least increase their chance of recovery. It can be observed in these final stages that a patient improves clinically after taking PC1, has a better quality of life, but nevertheless dies.

AIDS and TB

Many AIDS-patients also have TB. ARVs cannot be prescribed together with tuberculostatics (antibiotics for treating TB). The conventional treatment of TB usually takes six months, but even then in many cases TB has not been cured because new forms of TB have come up in recent years that are resistant to conventional treatment. To use PC1 for HIV/AIDS and PC300t for tuberculosis together is no problem. If an AIDS-patient is on tuberculostatics it is advised to start with PC Tuberculosis (PC300t) to assist the tuberculostatics (dosage of PC300t: once daily in the morning – 555 regime; bang the bottle five times – take five drops in case of a dropper bottle or a teaspoon – keep in mouth for at least five seconds). At the same time that PC300t is started PC1 can be taken in the evenings on a daily basis as well. As soon as the symptoms of TB have subsided PC300t can be discontinued. Usually this should be within four to eight weeks. By also giving PC1 while the patient is still on tuberculostatics and PC300t the body can restore the immune system so it can also better fight TB.

AIDS and malaria

If an AIDS-patient has an acute infection of malaria start with PC240m for Malaria. Dosage: start with the five drops or one teaspoon every 30 minutes and make intervals longer as soon as the patient improves. For each dose bang the bottle five times. As soon as the acute attack has been overcome (eight hours to a few days, depending on how far advanced AIDS is) the patient can start on PC1, once daily, the 555-regime.

AIDS and rape

If a person has been raped very recently and was HIV-negative and the status of the rapist was HIV-positive or not known, consult a doctor immediately. The initial main shock to the person is the trauma from rape. Start with PC435p for Rape Trauma, every one hour five drops or one teaspoon. As soon as the shock of rape trauma starts to subside make the intervals longer until once a day, and stop completely if the trauma has been overcome. Tell the patient that if needed she can always start taking it again. After half an hour after starting with PC435p also start with PC1 and repeat every three hours during three days, and from then on daily until the status can be determined. If negative stop, if positive continue as described under pre-AIDS stage. It's important to understand that rape trauma severely impacts the immune system, and makes HIV infection therefore more likely. Treating the trauma of rape is the Number One priority in such situations.

AIDS and orphans

Losing loved ones and the grief that causes is part of the totality of symptoms connected to HIV/AIDS. Especially for little children that have lost both parents this is very traumatic and more than anything else it is love and care that they need. If an AIDS-orphan comes to you this means that at least someone is taking care of it or has adopted it. Within the available PC Resonances you have two options. Children in orphanages or that have been adopted you can prescribe PC309d for Adoption Trauma, one dose daily. The other option is PC343n for Long Lasting Grief, one dose daily. If you have other homeopathic remedies available a single dose of *Ignatia* in any potency you may have can also help.

Other co-infections in an HIV-positive patient, like hepatitis or herpes, can be treated in a similar way as discussed for TB and Malaria. The golden rule is, 'always start with what is staring you into the face', or stated differently, what at that moment is causing most suffering to the patient, whether this is TB or shock from rape trauma or anything else. In general we advise to prioritise trauma over disease.

ARVs and PC1

Some people might wonder why another way to treat AIDS is needed now that antiretroviral drugs are increasingly available in Africa. There are many justifications to continue to engage in such an inquiry as ARVs (Anti-Retro-Viral drugs) have many downsides and limitations. They are:

- ARVs are not available to many of those needing them in Africa
- ARVs can cause serious complications
- ARVs have a limited life, for some people only a year before resistance develops, and the next ARVs are much more expensive, so having a second, even lower cost option seems eminently sensible

- PC1 boosts immunity whereas ARVs kill the virus
- The two together will sometimes be better than either
- PC1 is helpful when ARVs are not found to work well

A positive effect of ARVs on the CD4 count develops only very slowly. Results from the AIDS Therapy Evaluation in the Netherlands (ATHENA) cohort study suggest that restoration of CD4 counts to levels normally seen in uninfected individuals takes a long time and is not feasible within seven years in most patients who initiate treatment with CD4 counts below 350 (Kenyon Farrow - AIDSmeds.com)[3]. Starting all HIV-positive patients in Africa early is practically impossible and would also bring many of the disadvantages of ARVs forward earlier. PC1 or any other effective homeopathic approach is ideal since it can be used in earlier stages at low costs and low risks.

Results with PC1

In the book *The Second Simillimum* already quite a number of reports on the effects of PC1 for HIV/AIDS have been published. We will not repeat these in full here. Here is a summary and some additional reports that show that the nature of the feedback we receive remains the same, namely that patients usually recover rapidly from their AIDS-related symptoms, get their appetite and energy back, and return to a normal life.

Depending on the stage of AIDS the results will be visible within days or weeks. The clinical observation is that people get well from all AIDS-related symptoms including opportunistic infections and can work again, take care of their children, or go back to school soon. They normally feel very well in weeks. Their appetite returns and they gain weight. Their pains disappear and their energy returns.

In Ethiopia Peter Chappell started to collect data of the results with PC1 in 2002. In a group of 95 patients the Karnofsky score – a validated system to measure the general state of health – increased in these patients from 43 out of 100 to 77 (from frequently needing support and being disabled to being able to look after themselves and having moderate symptoms). In eight of these patients he measured CD4 counts after the treatment of three months had stopped. In the first ten weeks after stopping PC1 the CD4 showed a rise of 40% on average in this group, indicating that the immune system was able to further recover on its own. This is very significant since without treatment the CD4 drops 50 counts per year until all kinds of infections have free play inside the body.

If you want to read about a first study of the results by external homeopaths in Malawi 2004 you can read the article 'PC1 – Answer to AIDS in Africa' at www.ARHF.nl. This article describes how 57 patients that had been treated with PC1 for 20 weeks on average were interviewed. They showed significant improvement of all AIDS-related symptoms, including a much lower incidence of Malaria signifying the restoration of the immune system.

3 Wood E, and Montaner JSG. When to initiate HIV antiretroviral therapy: do benefits other than survival deserve greater attention? *J Aquir Immune Defic Syndr* 45 (2):131 - 2, 2007

Gras L, Kesselring AM, Griffin JT, et al. CD4 cell counts of 800 cells/mm3 or greater after 7 years of highly active antiretroviral therapy are feasible in most patients starting with 350 cells/mm3 or greater. *J Aquir Immune Defic Syndr* 45(2):183 -92, 2007

Research in Africa is not easy to organise, so most of the results reported are still anecdotal. Here are some quotes from several doctors in several African countries as well as India:

Malawi 2003

In December a woman is hospitalized weighing 25 kilos and waiting to die. A relative heard about PC1 and brought her a bottle, which she used for three months. She was the only one to leave the ward alive, and ten months later she weighs 52 kilos and has no symptoms. Her husband refused to have only safe sex and to stop seeing other women. She realized that staying with him would bring AIDS back rapidly, so she kicked him out.

Report from Vyara, India

'Within two to three follow-ups almost all the patients got rid of their acute infections, which they used to suffer regularly from. Their strength and mood is also elevated significantly. Many patients had presented with loss of appetite but showed good improvement now; even the significant increase in weight also speaks about the recovery. One more significant thing I had observed. Those patients having less than 200 CD4 count, normally often need medications against common bacteria. We kept them under close observation by calling them every week, but yet they have not suffered from any sort of such illness. This is very marked.'

Report Nigeria

In a small study with ten patients in Nigeria in 2005 CD4 counts could be measured. In only a few weeks time the CD4 raised on average by 25%. A month later the increase had gone up to 43%.

Report Ghana 2007

'A male patient used two ARVs for two years and his CD4 went from 2 to 105, meaning he was still very vulnerable for opportunistic infections. After using PC1 for nine weeks, his CD4 was at 312! Currently we have about 25 people on PC1. After the first month all of them showed marked improvements in weight, some as high as four kg which is unprecedented.'

Report Johannesburg 2007

A man, 35 years old, suffers from symptoms due to AIDS. He is tested HIV+ and his CD4 count is 186 (Ref Ranges 500 - 2010). The CD4% of lymphocytes is 20,60% (data from 16-05-2006). (Normal % of lymphocytes that are CD4 cells is 32 – 68%) After PC1 his symptoms improve quickly. At 10-01-2007 new tests are performed. His CD4 is 773 counts now (415% increase!) and the CD4% of lymphocytes 32,70%. [National Health Laboratory Service - Johannesburg Hospital]

Report Ghana 2007

'I am sure you would like to know about my experience with the remedies. My visit was rather short so I have not been able to experiment with a lot of the remedies but what I saw was quite encouraging. I first made contacts with a local hospital at Nandom where I gathered a team of interested people. I explained the method to them and then we went to visit one AIDS patient at his home. At that moment he was suffering from weakness, perspiration, severe abdominal pain (as if there was some big lump preventing him from sleeping), loss of appetite and diarrhoea. We visited him again on day four; accordingly the abdominal pain had completely disappeared allowing him to sleep now, weakness and perspiration were also better; appetite was still the same; diarrhoea had stopped. It was very uplifting to see this happening and it gave me the confidence also to experiment with the other remedies, especially the one for malaria, which I gave on five occasions. Two of them I was not able to follow up on, the other three went back to farming the next day.'

Report Cambodia 2007 (House of Family - HIV/AIDS Programme for Children)

'17 children received PC1 of which nine girls and eight boys. Thirteen children were already using ARVs. Three girls were not on ARVs. One of them had to start HAART, because of further decrease of CD4. One girl was on second line HAART because of a further decrease of her CD4 count; while using PC1 the CD4 count was increasing more rapidly than before. One girl had doubled her CD4 during the first month of treatment with PC1. All other girls their CD4s kept increasing and clinically also they were very well. One boy was not on ARVs. With initial CD4 below the level we have to start HAART I kept him only on PC1 and after two months his CD4 was far above that critical level so HAART was postponed. One boy suffered from severe thrombocytopenia after HAART was started and there was only slow increase of CD4. After PC1 he doubled his CD4 in two months and recovered from thrombocytopenia as well. There was TB detected in one boy; until then his immune system was not strong enough to start fighting it and TB was not revealed. One boy was always doing poorly, but ever since using PC1 was pretty well. All other boys had increasing CD4s and were very well clinically.' (Henrieta Havrilova, Trnava University and St. Elizabeth university of social sciences and public health in Bratislava).

Seboche Hospital Lesotho (June 2008)

'I have seen a lot of improvement in the patients that are using PC1, although at first it was not all that easy to believe that it works! From the few patients that I do interact with, I haven't got any doubt about it and I do hope that more doctors will actually put more patients on it (Emmanuel Okonga, pharmacist).'

Report from Zambia

'The two members of my family (male and female) have greatly improved. My cousin (female) has improved tremendously and the TB is completely gone. She went to the Doctor and the TB results were negative. She has started work and going about her business normally apart from a bout of malaria which caught her last month but she was able to pull through. The HIV positive colleague I started the PC1 remedy on in September last is still fine and still shows no symptoms at all.'

Report from Rwanda (Mouvement Congolais des Hommes Contre le SIDA)

'In general patients well appreciated the remedy due to its presentation as normal mineral water, easy to keep and easy to use, the figures show also an increasing of CD4 count >10% in average, while the HIV test remain positive.'

Dr. Rainer Schneider, University of Freiburg, analysed the data: 'I performed a non-parametric test since the sample size is small and a number of data are missing. The difference between first and second CD4 test is highly significant (Wilcoxon $Z = -3.23$, $p = .001$) meaning that the number of CD4 increased. The effect as such, however, is rather small ($d = 0.33$).' (Note: 25 patients were included in the study. In eleven of them the first CD4 was taken after the treatment had already started weeks ago. The second CD4 was sometimes taken much later than treatment was stopped and reinfection might have already taken place. The increase of the CD4 measured is most likely lower than if in all cases it

would have been measured exactly at the beginning and the end of the treatment.)
'100% of patients reported an improvement of health status, disappearing of opportunistic infections and weight gain but at the same time the medicine brought hunger while many of them do not have access to enough food.' 'According to the big number of PLWHAs* dying without treatment, PC1 is an alternative for life prolongation especially for those with CD4>200.' (*People Living With HIV Aids)

Report from Bangui, Central African Republic

Schustereder, Schneider & van der Zee

In February 2006 a small team travelled to Bangui to discuss with government officials the possibility of doing a study with PC1 in the AIDS-centre in the capital. The initiative was taken by the minister of health who had spoken to AIDS-patients treated with PC1 by Dr. Klaus Schustereder in Baboua, and had asked to study the remedy as a possible solution for the hundreds of thousands of AIDS-patients in the country that receive no treatment whatsoever due to lack of funds for ARVs. During the visit we treated some patients to give the doctors in the AIDS centre a taste of the results while we were there. The patients were seen back only four days after the treatment was started, and again four weeks later, when Klaus visited Bangui again. Here are in short four cases that mainly show two things: PC1 acts rapidly and if patients recover they get an increased appetite and if needed food should be provided as part of a treatment protocol.

Case of A. 30 years old

Her husband has already died of AIDS. She was tested HIV-positive in 2001. She is on tuberculostatics since seven months since she also has TB. She suffers from pain in the chest, joint pains, weakness, cough and numbness in her right arm.
Follow-up after four days:
The pain in the chest has changed. The joint pains and the weakness are much better. The cough is still the same, the numbness in the right arm better.
Follow-up after four weeks:
She is completely free of symptoms but very hungry because she cannot afford the amount of food her body demands while it is healing.

Case of F. 35 years old

Husband died of AIDS. WHO stage III (> 50% in bed). Pain in the right inguinal region since eight months. Further she has headache, weakness, candida in the mouth which makes eating painful, her joints are painful and she has respiratory complaints.
Follow-up after four days:
The pain in the right inguinal is completely gone. Her headache is 50% better. The other complaints are still the same.
Follow-up after four weeks:
No more symptoms besides hunger.

Case H. 39 years old

Tested HIV-positive in 2004. Extrapulmonary tuberculosis with pain in stomach after eating. Further she has weakness and no appetite. Every day she has chills with sweating at 3-8 PM (pointing to malaria besides AIDS and TB).
Follow-up after four days:
The pain in the stomach, which was there for at least a few months, is gone. Her weakness is much better. Four days ago she was brought by a car because she could not walk the distance, but now she walked the three miles to save money and will walk them back as well. No more chills with sweating at 3 – 8 PM.

Follow-up after four weeks:
Hungry but besides that free of symptoms.

Case C. 40 years old

Tested HIV-positive 1999. Husband died; takes care of nine kids. Back pain. Weakness. Vaginal itch. Palpitations. Cough.
Follow-up after 4 days:
Back pain >, Weakness >, Vaginal itch =, Palpitations =, Cough =.
Follow-up after 4 weeks:
Free from symptoms but hungry. Her sister that received PC1 shortly after she did also symptom free.

Case reported by John Fox, Mzuzu Malawi 2007

"One man came yesterday, nearly at the point of death, on ARVs but unable to take them as he can keep nothing down for more than a few minutes. So he just vomits all his medicines up. It's another reminder of what a huge difference there is in the pain and discomfort threshold between Africans and whites. Here was a guy very, very far down the road to death and he was not feeling sorry for himself or shouting angrily at the gods. Just meekly talking about being 'a bit OK'. I'll let you know if he survives but objectively speaking it would be almost a miracle, just to look at his skeletal form. This chap, Tony, accompanied by his, by the look of it, long-suffering wife, showed me his 'health passport' which detailed staggering amounts of medication he had been prescribed by two different hospitals in this region, one mission and the other government. He also had malaria, for which he had been given quinine tablets. But, as I wrote, he could keep nothing at all down and was near collapse. Just about every ache and pain and debility too, especially badly swollen legs and feet, and tremendous pain when he tried to speak. The health passport also revealed he was a WHO Category 3 patient – pretty hopeless normally. Anyway I ran through my explanation and advice though I was mainly dealing with the missus as poor Tony didn't have the energy to do more than just try to sit upright. I warned them about a possible healing crisis, though from my experience only a minority of PC1 takers report actually going through this. Our normal advice, also written on the instruction sheet we give with the PC1 bottle, is to ride out the storm rather than rush to treat it with heavy drugs. Well! Next day at the same time the unhappy couple rolled up again at the house. This time poor old Tony was so weak he had to be carried out of the minibus by the driver and his wife. The latter was very worried as he had got, if possible, much worse in the preceding 24 hours. Coughing literally all night, and sweating profusely, sore joints and back, severe headache – all the usual malaria symptoms. What to do? It's at times like this that I start to sweat a bit myself, as, given our fairly precarious status here (after six years here we still haven't got an official work permit, just a written acknowledgement that we have applied for one!) and the fact that there is ambivalence and sometimes downright hostility from official health service quarters towards our promotion of homeopathy, it wouldn't actually take all that unlikely a concordance of circumstances to get us turfed out of the country – a reality that doesn't quite cause us sleepless nights but that has kept us from embarking on some of the more outlandish schemes we have thought up to get PC1 more widely known and used.

Follow-up:
And then this morning. I was typing away in the office, doing the staple tasks of sweet-talking some Dutchies in an attempt to loosen their purse-strings in our direction, when Lucy, who helps us in the house, called out "Molendu, molendu!" She was telling me there were visitors on the veranda. I went out to meet whoever was there: Tony and the missus, one Jenny.
I could not believe my eyes and ears. Against all logic, the guy looked and talked like a totally new

man. For one thing he had walked from the minibus unaided, jaunty as you please. All this in a week! Cough almost entirely gone, fever disappeared, vomiting finished and able to eat. Sleeping like a lamb for the first time in months, top half of his body completely normal. Just the swelling in the lower limbs was still causing him a lot of discomfort. What a change, though! We've dispensed PC1 for over three years now, but this revival was certainly the most spectacular I've personally witnessed. Jacqueline has of course seen a lot of this in the centre, me not till now, at least of this magnitude of transformation. I would have guessed that if he were indeed to pull through, he might need at least a few months, not a week, to show clear improvement."

Ghana 2007, doctor reporting via Nico Beentjes in 2007

PCI AF/AM is doing fine. Currently we have about 25 people on the remedies. We haven't been able to get the CD4 count of individuals but we decided to use the weight, reoccurrence of disease and the ability of them to recover from infections as the indicators of improvement and so far after the first month all of them showed marked improvements in weight, some as high as four kg which is unprecedented.

Indian tea taster

An Indian tea taster living in Switzerland most likely got infected with HIV by a dentist in China or India: Ever since 2004 he regularly sends a report on how he is doing including CD4 counts and Viral loads. He showed a marked improvement once the original version of PC1 was replaced with PC1AM, specially designed for males. His CD4 went up from 330 to 550 and his Viral load down from 63,000 to 2,500. Perhaps even more important, on a scale of 0-10 his quality of life went up from four to eight.

Case example Burundi 2009
Harry van der Zee

Seven-year-old Daniela is HIV-positive as are her parents. Since 2006 she has symptoms. She uses bactrim. Her appetite is bad (3), she has an eruption in the mouth, and lacks the energy to play with other children.
Follow-up:
I saw her again two months later. The eruption in the mouth is gone. She is eating normally now, has gained two kilos and plays with other children. She used to be sick all the time, her mother says, but now she is well. Also her sleep has improved.

Case example Congo 2009
Harry van der Zee

Juma is a six-year-old boy. He is an AIDS-orphan and was tested HIV-positive in May 2008 and was immediately put on ARVs. His most recent CD4 count in September was 110 units. His weight is 21 kilos. He suffers from skin eruptions that get infected, and has had malaria or angina many times.
Follow-up after 4 weeks:
Weighing 22 kilos now. The angina, bronchitis and fever are gone and he has no more malaria.
FU after seven weeks:
His CD4 has gone up to 175 units and his Karnofsky score has gone up from 40 to 90.
FU one week later: all the previous symptoms of weakness, lack of appetite, general pains, headache etc. have now all disappeared. He is a normal child now.

Report from Malawi (2012)

Joseph Msumba is AIDS-worker in Malawi and manager of the Amma4Malawi AIDS Project in Chintheche. Joseph has had experience with prescribing PC1 since 2004 and has treated hundreds of cases with success. In 2010 he opened a new clinic in Barwe where he started treating 30 AIDS-patients. In June 2010 the average reversed Karnofsky score of this group was 54,6 for the men (n=15) and 62,6 for the women (n=15). Four months later the same score was 70 resp. 71,4.

In 2011 Joseph writes about B., a 50-year-old man. He was lying on his bed the whole day, because he was completely paralysed from the side-effects of ARVs. First pains, then weakness and ultimately paralysis of the legs is a common side-effect for which we've seen PC1 is very helpful. So in 2010 B. was given his first bottle of PC1. Now in 2011 he is walking around on crutches and has much more energy. His reversed Karnofsky score has gone up from 20 to 60. Now he is only a little tired and has some minor weakness. As the strength in his legs has not completely returned he needs crutches, but besides that he is practically symptom free.

The Chintheche Homeopathy Clinic was opened by Joseph in April 2011. Hundreds of HIV-positive patients have been treated within the first year. The good results have caused the local governmental hospital to refer AIDS-patients to the Chintheche Homeopathy Clinic. They discovered that patients on ARVs had much less side-effects if they were also treated with PC1. Those patients that are not on ARVs yet are also referred as PC1 can be prescribed for them from an early stage on. At the ARHF website a documentary on the clinic can be found. PC Resonances are used in the clinic for infectious and epidemic diseases. For all other conditions regular homeopathic remedies are being used, either or not complemented with a PC Resonance for the indication.

As of 2012 a data-collection project has started. All AIDS-cases will be monitored using a questionnaire that records their subjective symptoms as also objective ones like their weight and CD4-counts.

Also in 2012 a group of 28 people were trained to prescribe for AIDS and Malaria in the villages, so the clinic has now an effective outreach program. From these a group has been selected to receive full education in homeopathy. Homeopaths from Europe and the US visit the clinic on a regular basis to provide training and supervision.

A case example of AIDS
Joseph Msumba, Malawi, 2012

A woman was suffering from malaria frequently and was regularly admitted to hospital. There they advised her to start taking ARVs. But she went to the Homeopathy Clinic instead and received PC1. She was unable to work in the farm, but after PC1 she could work again and the attacks of malaria ceased.

Before starting PC1 in April 2011 she was weighing 40 kg. Now 11 months later she weighs 60 kg and is completely free of symptoms.

Case of a 33-year-old woman with AIDS
Harry van der Zee, Malawi, 2012

Intake 24-02-2012
She is on ARVs since 2008. She has lost 8 kg and is weighing 53 kg now.

"Right now I think I've got malaria and I've got sores all over my body. (She shows dozens of sores on her arms and legs.) My name is Beauty but I'm no longer beautiful. My urine is very hot when I urinate. I've got very little energy. I'm very weak. From where I'm living I walked for almost 2,5 hours to reach here. Because I'm weak I can't walk properly. I stay at home. There is nothing, nothing, nothing ... to eat and to do. I can't live with my own kids because I've got nothing to give them. They live with my brother and my sister in town. My appetite is down because the food I can eat is very bad, so my appetite goes down, down, down. I always have headache, very strong. I cough too much. Sometimes I become dizzy because I have a shortage of blood."

Follow-up after 4 weeks
"I'm doing much, much better these days. All the symptoms have changed now. I'm fit now and a bit strong (laughing). Now I can go to the gardens and work in the gardens. Now I can make cassava pap. I can pound, make the cassava flour and make the pap. Since taking this medicine my headache is a lot better. All my sores are gone. I'm so happy that you good people came here. You help us." "Yes, I feel beautiful again."
On checking her weight it appears she has gained 8 kg.

Case example from Uganda (2011)

J. has been raped, was tested HIV-positive later and started to develop the usual symptoms of AIDS. Ever since the rape she has nightmares and she wakes up in fright at least once a week. Treatment was started with PC435p for rape trauma. This resulted in the nightmares disappearing. She no longer wakes up in fright nor does she fear the night anymore. Before the remedy she was always alert that a rapist might enter the house. Then she starts PC1 and reports feeling well since using it and being completely free of symptoms.

Report by Dr Shangloo from India (2011)

A man is coming to the clinic for several years already and is given the best available treatment. In 2004 he was tested HIV-positive and since 2006 he uses ARVs. Despite the ARVs and other treatment provided he is not doing well. On average he scores four out of five on a Visual Analog Scale for eleven symptoms. He starts using PC1 in November 2010. Within a month the quality of his life already improves a lot and for the same eleven symptoms he now scores an average of three out of five. Another two months later the symptoms have further subsided to an average below two out of five. His wife, who is also HIV-positive, was given PC1 as well and had a similar response.

A given-up case of AIDS
Jules M'Mombwa M'Motoelwa, Burundi

The case concerns a 42-year-old lady, with six children. Her husband died, probably of AIDS. They resorted to traditional medicine for him without success.
Three years later the woman also started to get symptoms. They took her to a room of prayer to get rid of demons that would make her ill. They prayed and prayed, but they could not find a solution. After that she started with modern medicine, consulted a doctor, was tested HIV-positive and put on ARVs. She was hospitalized at the hospital for three months but the ARVs made no change to her condition. She was told her CD4 was already too low, 50. So she was expected to die any day. In the hospital they said: "We have a lot of ill people here. Take your relative, take the pills, go home."
They provided her with a urinary tube and as she was not eating, they also placed a nasal tube to feed her. Then she was told about me and the treatment we have.

I visited her and said to her relatives: "I have something she can take alongside the other medicines." Because swallowing pills was difficult for her she received ARVs in liquid form.

As she also suffered from Tuberculosis we brought her two medicines along, PC1 for AIDS and PC300t for Tuberculosis. Since it was water and she only needed a teaspoon of each remedy it was easy to give it to her. We opened her mouth and then we slipped the remedy in.

After one week she started to move, to turn by herself. From lying so long she had ulcers that we treated with Dettol as other medicines for it were too expensive.
After two weeks I told them: "We will take out the tube", as she had started to open and close her mouth. She didn't talk, only opened and closed her mouth asking for food. So I took out the nasal tube, but I left the urinary tube in place. Now she started to eat a special porridge for AIDS patients. Very nutritious! After one month the lady started to talk! She started to talk! And then, when we helped her, she began to sit up! So we also took out the urinary tube. As soon as we took out the urinary tube, the lady said: "I have to go to the toilet." We transported her to a toilet and she did what she had to do.
And now, after three months treatment, from her waist up, her body has recovered.
Only, because they were inactive for too long she cannot use her lower extremities [this can also be paralysis from ARVS, a known side-effect – the authors].
We could say that she is handicapped for the moment and she goes to physiotherapy. But up until now, the lady moves around through the city with her hand bike.
She has stopped taking ARVs, moves around independently, and as the strength in her legs is coming back, expects to be able to walk again. She is back to work selling things and continues with physiotherapy.

Research into PC1

A research protocol has been designed by the ARHF to scientifically study the efficacy of PC1 for HIV/AIDS.

In 2006 a small pilot study was performed with permission of the prime minister and the minister of health in Bangui, Central African Republic. 27 patients were included in the pilot and similar to the results observed in Malawi in 2004 showed significant improvement on all parameters. Unfortunately the intended measurement of CD4 counts and Viral Loads could not be performed due to problems with the machines at the Institute Pasteur.

Other attempts to perform a study in Africa or India have until this day failed for a variety of reasons, the bottom line of which is a non-cooperative attitude by the very institutions that could provide authorisation or funds.
Doctors and homeopaths interested in performing a study or in testing out PC1 in their clinic are requested to contact the ARHF (www.ARHF.nl – info@ARHF.nl)

Downloads for Data Collection

The aim of the ARHF is to offer treatment to all that can benefit from PC1. To reach that goal doctors and clinics are invited to use the resonance, and if possible also gather data for research purposes, because the more solid proof can be provided concerning the efficacy of

PC1 for HIV/AIDS the closer we will get to having the resonance available on a large scale. It may be clear that to get there a lot of help is needed on many levels. There are a few forms and a manual available that you can download for data collection at www.ARHF.nl:

- PC1 intake form – has the possibility to gather all relevant data at intake
- PC1 follow-up form – has the possibility to gather all relevant data of follow-ups
- PC1 short case management form – intake and follow-ups all on one sheet of paper for easy use
- PC1 instructions for patients
- Amma4Africa Manual (available in English, German, French and Portuguese)

What can Stop Recovery?

Although the overall response to PC1 for HIV/AIDS in Africa is very positive there can be circumstances and reasons why recovery can be problematic.

Factors delaying the recovery are:

- Poverty and all its many complications, lack of education, lack of access to medical support, long distances from clinics, lack of understanding of medicines, intermittent food supplies, specific tribal customs, failure to understand about sexual transmission, prejudices
- Unsafe sex. PC1 does not protect the patient or the partner from (re)-infecting each other
- Other concurrent diseases may reduce or restrict recovery – gonorrhoea, syphilis, hepatitis, chlamydia, parasites, herpes, TB, malaria etc.
- Diet – the better the diet, the quicker the improvement. Virtual starvation or inability to eat can restrict or stop recovery
- Inability to eat due to AIDS symptoms – thrush that invades the mouth and extends down to the stomach and takes away all appetite and makes eating unattractive. The thrush should improve rapidly on PC1, but until it does a fluid diet that is less painful to eat and swallow is recommended
- Degree of sickness – sicker people will obviously take much longer than someone in al most perfect health to improve
- Length of sickness – the longer infected the longer the recovery
- Age – the older in years the longer it can take to achieve an improvement. Children can respond the same day, even after the first dose
- Stress and especially emotional stress and trauma. Homelessness, rejection by family and friends, no income, no support, guilt etc. can all slow down recovery.

What if Recovery is Problematic

Here are some major factors why PC1 might not work or might work only temporarily for a patient:

- Safe Sex Practices: Patients taking PC1 should abstain or follow safe sex practices for their own health and that of their partner
- Concurrent Opportunistic Diseases: In most cases, this will not make a difference. However in certain occasions, if a patient is suffering another serious disease, it may interfere with the action of PC1

- Nutrition: It is still vitally important that a patient has enough to eat, can eat, and eat properly with good enough food
- Regularity & Compliance: PC1 must be taken daily according to the instructions. Banging the bottle before each dose properly is essential. Preventing the bottle from becoming spoiled is also essential
- Care of PC1. It is quite robust but it should be kept clean in a cool, dark place and not be exposed to long sunlight, excessive heat, strong odours or pollution, also away from computers, mobile phones or microwave ovens (especially old, leaky ones).

AIDS – A Love Story

Another appropriate title for this chapter would be: AIDS – The True Story, or AIDS – The Full Story. Yes there is (apparently) this virus, which spreads through intercourse and needles, that multiplies in white blood cells and thus slowly destroys the immune system, and that causes people to ultimately die from emaciation and opportunistic infections. From the point of view that identifies our physical body as our reality this is an impressive story. From this angle the story of AIDS is full of suffering, pain, disease and death, based on which there is only one appropriate response, namely to kill HIV, the monster that causes it. There is though another side to the story of AIDS, one that connects with the reality of the spiritual world. The following case opens up this reality.

I can experience love with anyone

Egmond aan Zee, Netherlands, 2003

At the 2003 ECCH congress Malcolm Smith presented a case which left me (Harry) feeling as if I'd been hit by lightning. As far as I was concerned the rest of the presentations could be cancelled and all available time should be used to discuss the consequences of this impressive case. Let me share this case with you, as it gives essential information as to the roots of HIV/AIDS, and on how in general disease specific resonances can support changes in humanity.

The patient concerned was a gay man that had been treated for his depression for years with all kinds of homeopathic remedies without any success. Since the patient was also HIV-positive the homeopath ultimately prescribed PC1 for him with the idea that if not for the depression he might perhaps at least be able to do something for his AIDS.

Here are some quotes from several interviews before the patient received PC1 to give you an idea about the nature and depth of the depression:

> "I'm like an emotional basket case ... Things are still very gloomy. The fog doesn't seem to be lifting, you know. Clouds. When I get the nerve to get over the daily anxiety to do something, then Bam, it doesn't work. Another signal is telling me you are not worth it; you are not worth doing ... getting anything. You are going down the wrong road again. Every time I'm trying to go to work I end up all depressed. It just doesn't pair up. I don't know how to describe that. Each time it doesn't and I get all depressed it gets worse in a way. I like to think that it is behind me or that I can overcome that.
>
> Everybody should have goals and desires. I have none of that. I'm just trying to deal with this depression. I'd like to set an experiment, a pass or fail, that if this was that if you fail with me I'm gonna be dead. (Meaning he'll end his life – the authors) That is how bad it is with me. I feel sometimes I'm destined to kill myself. I have felt that a long time. People in my family don't know what's going on all the time. If they were called and told it is about me it would be the first thing they would think, that I have killed myself.

Initially you feel nobody is going to touch me again; nobody will want to be intimate with me again. Nobody is ever going to love me. Things that happen can bring me straight down, wham, within seconds or minutes sometimes, and sometimes it is really difficult to get out of that again. It brings all of that back, all that universe against me kind of thing."

Follow-up:
After PC1 the same man explained how PC1 had affected him:

"There was this turning inside of my gut. It wasn't that uncomfortable or anything, but it was more intense and different than I have ever experienced. It was like turmoil in me was being stirred up. Something was happening. It was a little uncomfortable. It wasn't bad or anything. Because it was a change, and a change from where I was had to be good. All those mixed up negative feelings and emotions, and depression and all that stuff was being kicked up in the air and when it was coming down some was still up there because I was in transition, but when it was coming down instead of being mixed up it was coming into place or being sorted or fitting somewhere. I know something good was happening. Thursday I was turning on the music and I was dancing. That is not like me. Tears of joy happening. I was so happy. That it was all going away that was awful. It's like I'd come from hell. I came here from hell today. Literally. Because that is what it has been. And far too long. I'm happy but it doesn't look like it (crying), I know it. I was still alive and stuff but the meters had run out and what was gone has been filled up again. I was always being treated for the depression and now I'm being treated for HIV, and I've never been treated for the HIV and it cures the depression. I've been praying more. I've been meditating. I've been working out every other day. I quit smoking. (Talking about a book) ... Humour and sexuality are at the core of our spirituality, because there are no boundaries. At the core are no boundaries and with humour there are no boundaries. We can make things that are painful real difficult and we can laugh about it. It is the core of our spirituality. Like art, music there is no boundaries in that. It's very spiritual and in nature. I can see that and experience that kind of stuff in a different way. I didn't have that ability really before. It was blocked. The ability I had but it was blocked.

With sexuality same thing. There is no judgment on it I think. I don't feel either. It's not just thinking gay and bi and straight, all that stuff. With sexuality it's a person's freedom. We can do with these things what we want. And that is so like free, liberating, it's amazing.

(Regarding being gay) ... it doesn't make a person burn in hell or anything. I was in hell, so you don't have to die to get there and you do not have to die to go to heaven. That's exactly what that prayer meant. As it is on earth as it is in heaven. It is exactly what that means, literally.

Tuesday everything was going against me, not going my way, and after all the rescheduling it still didn't work, so it all had to be cancelled, but I was okay with it. I was really concerned. It was like ... I opened the door to that depression, and I could see it, and I could have taken one step and been there. That's how close it was. I could see it and I could feel it because it is very familiar still. I could have felt depressed and given up everything very easily. But the thing is that I had needed to know that when those things happen that I don't have to get depressed and go back in that place again.

I was all alone and felt I was really needy again, needing something, and I prayed and I wanted to ... this was wild ... I wanted to know, I wanted help, and I wanted to know that I was going to be okay and that I wasn't going to go back there. And I knew right at the time that I ended the prayer that it had already been answered. And I just said thanks because I didn't go back there. I could see it and feel it and then go.
It had happened in order for me to know. You can't intellectualize it. You must feel it, see it to be able

> to know. That's why it happened. What other people said or did, or didn't say or didn't do determined my self worth and that is so far from reality. But that was how I was then. But I know now there is no way that any one of us – there are so many things I know now – that anything anyone says or does or doesn't say or doesn't do could possibly determine our self worth.
> I couldn't have the self worth because I couldn't connect with the energy. And the love, the spiritual connection that it is, that is where our core energy comes from. And I had no clue. And I thought that certain things that could help me to get out of my depression ...
>
> I was like wanting to be in love with someone that loved me desperately because I felt like that's what I needed maybe to fill that void or recharge that energy or help myself to have some self worth. That was the situation I was in where a person did love me and I didn't believe it. So in other words, I was incapable of experiencing love, whether platonically or whatever, true love, really experiencing and that energy flowing back and forth and now I can so experience it with ... anyone, friends, anyone. It's phenomenal."

The genuine spiritual transformation that this patient was telling about impressed me deeply. This is what I would love all my patients to experience. This is what I'd love to experience myself. The whole idea of not being loveable or able to believe others would love him had completely gone. Instead he was now so full of love that he experienced it with anyone. No boundaries, no restrictions, an unconditional love for everyone.

The implications of this response to PC1 are huge. To me it means that in essence PC1 goes to the core of HIV/AIDS. This of course is an exceptional case where as I understand it the essence of HIV/AIDS happened to be similar to the essence or state of this man. Although PC1 is not a nosode you can compare this to a constitutional *Tuberculinum* patient that has TB and responds very well to *Tuberculinum* for the disease as well as his state. Therefore this patient can teach us about AIDS and about the ability of PC1 to treat AIDS.

The whole story of AIDS is the story of love, or rather the absence of it. The infection with HIV is very often connected to loveless sex or relationships in which respect for the partner is lacking. In the West mainly gay promiscuous men and heroin prostitutes attracted the disease. In Africa it is a heterosexual epidemic based on promiscuity, on women not being able to say no to sex, on a masculine culture of having sex with as many women as possible, on trans-generational sex, on men going to prostitutes because while working in the mines they are far away from their wife and family, on women that due to poverty have to prostitute themselves, on rape being of epidemic proportions in many parts of Africa etc.

The second AIDS-patient I (Harry) met in 1986 was again a gay man. He knew he was HIV-positive, he knew he could infect other men, and still he had anal intercourse with young boys without using condoms. As long as they did not ask him whether he was HIV-positive he would not tell them. To me this indicates a lack of love, care and respect for other people. Don't misunderstand me here. I know lots of gay people that are very loving, caring and respectful, as are many Africans. Many AIDS-patients got infected and infected others being totally unaware of their status or, especially in Africa, lacking any understanding of the disease itself. People that deliberately infect others are probably a minority, but as such in the extreme show what AIDS is actually about. In the Netherlands a few years ago a group of HIV-positive homosexual men were arrested because they deliberately infected other men. In a bar they would drug their victim, have sex with him, and then inject him with their blood. Their absurd reasoning was that this would free the other person, as once infected they no longer needed to protect themselves and could give in to all forms of sex. An extreme example of sex lacking love, care and respect. Now back to the case. That PC1 was reported to work wonders for AIDS-patients in Africa was great, but this case indicated too that it not only treats the symptoms of AIDS but also addresses the very root of it, the reason for its existence. It was this case that motivated me (Harry) to go to Africa and objectify Peter Chappell's results.

A Shamanic Journey to HIV

Later in 2005 we tried to receive insight into the role and purpose of HIV/AIDS via another channel. Eileen Nauman is a Native American shaman and a homeopath. In 2005 she made a shamanic journey for me (Harry) to diagnose a problem I had at that time, and the outcome of her journey both cleared the medical diagnosis as well as the spiritual background of it. She made the journey in Arizona while I was in the Netherlands. The medical diagnosis she made could be confirmed by an MRI and the spiritual background I could confirm from my own experiences. So I had confidence in her abilities to indeed travel to other realms and find meaning. We asked her whether it would also be possible to make a journey to visit a disease entity and learn from it. She replied that she didn't know, because she had never done it before, but that she was willing to try. So she asked her spiritual guides whether she could make a journey to HIV and got permission for it.

A very short summary comes down to the following information on the role of HIV in Africa:

'If men cannot love women, then they will both die. If there is respect between them, they will not. There must be love to create the bond between man and woman. If more men would love the women they take, then I would not affect them.' (For her full report see Part II)

Transformation in Africa

For some taking a shamanic journey to a virus seriously might be a bridge too far, and even the suggestion that an epidemic disease has a role and a purpose and thus an intelligence behind it might be difficult to digest. We're not asking you to believe this nor do you need to. Whether intentional or not, whether part of a bigger plan or not, the AIDS-epidemic has an effect that cannot be denied. In sub-Saharan Africa, where so many millions are infected and AIDS devastates the very fabric of society and family structures, the disease cannot but change the people, their consciousness and their ways.

If you read Stephanie Nolen's *28 stories of AIDS in Africa* or have your own encounters on the continent, the signs of change become clear. AIDS is strongly challenging age old taboos and tribal ways. In the extreme only those will survive that go against some of the dos and don'ts of African culture. Women that do say no to men, that do demand condoms to be used or that demand their husband to be tested and to live monogamously will live. Women that do not dry their vagina with tomato leaves to give more pleasure to men and pain to themselves will have a lower risk of being infected. Men that stay away from prostitutes, that ignore the taboos and get tested for HIV, that respect the women they have a relationship with will live. Little girls that are not being raped because HIV-infected men question the belief that having sex with a virgin cures AIDS will live. There are some courageous men and women that publicly state they have AIDS. The price they pay is often abandonment by the family, ridicule by the tribe, pestering and beatings. Women have been beaten to death by the very men that infected them, because they publicly declared their status and thus brought shame to the family. By going to schools, by speaking to soldiers and minors and by providing care for prostitutes these courageous men and women are role models for a new generation.

Women specially carry the burden of AIDS. They lose their husband and need to take care of the children alone. Women especially are active in all kinds of community initiatives concerning AIDS. The positive side of this is that by doing so they strengthen their self-esteem as well as their capacity to decide for themselves. They develop the ability to think critically about common misconceptions, and the courage to go against priests who forbid prevention. They learn to openly communicate about sexuality which used not to be done. These women establish gender equity; these men discover that masculinity is not related to having many sexual partners.

There is a lot of suffering connected to HIV/AIDS but on the other hand there are also so many beautiful qualities displayed by wonderful people that take their responsibility. There are grandmothers that take care of their grandchildren and have a heart that is big enough to include other orphans from the village as well. Boys and girls take on the responsibility for their younger siblings, see to it that they go to school, get properly dressed and nourished. Africa has many thousands of examples like this. In South Africa many white people have started clinics, hospices and community centres and thus not only help AIDS-patients but also heal the wounds from apartheid. Love and compassion is what motivates them.
In a way homosexual men and African women have a lot in common. Both are being suppressed and are often being treated with disrespect. Both have strong taboos to fight against. Both carry the burden of AIDS, and both can come out with more self-respect and self-love.

Love, respect and care – for other human beings, for the partner, male or female, heterosexual or homosexual – these are we believe the gifts of HIV to mankind. A lesson causing much suffering and learned with pain for sure, but also one that many begin to appreciate. One example of how HIV/AIDS can help an individual to experience a transformation can be found in Gavin Harrison's book *In the Lap of the Buddha.*

Another example is Kevin from Johannesburg. Like Gavin, Kevin is gay and used to have many sexual contacts. It was almost like a sport to have sex with a man he had not had sex with before. A really intimate relationship he did not have. His life of going out, meeting friends, having sex as often as possible completely came to a halt when he got diagnosed with AIDS. He got hospitalised, lost many kilos and was close to death. At that point he realised he could choose to live or to die. Once he made the choice to live he started eating again, got his strength back and healed his relationship with his father. He realised that choosing to live was choosing to love. He found one partner to live with, sold his business and now spends his time on projects concerning AIDS-awareness and education. He has become a completely different person and realises now that the promiscuity of the past had to do with a lack of self-esteem and self-love, that having sex with a person was an ineffective way of trying to find self-worth. Kevin is a living example of the transformation HIV can bring about in people. One day he drove us to Hannah. Hannah is an African mother who besides her own children started to take care of other children that had lost their parents to AIDS. When we met her, Hannah had taken eleven babies and seven older children into her house. The township she used to live in had difficulties with so many children living in a small hut and urged her to either get rid of so many children or to live somewhere else. 21 people in a small house must have been hard for Hannah too. A group of businessmen heard about her and her work of love and bought a house for her in which she now provides love, care and a future for these children. She and Kevin are examples of how AIDS can bring out the best in people – Love. AIDS truly is a love story.

Bilharzia

At http://en.wikipedia.org/wiki/Schistosomiasis we can read the following on Bilharzia:

Schistosomiasis (also known as bilharzia, bilharziosis or snail fever) is a parasitic disease caused by several species of trematodes (platyhelminth infection, or "flukes"), a parasitic worm of the genus *Schistosoma*. Snails serve as the intermediary agent between mammalian hosts. Individuals within developing countries who cannot afford proper sanitation facilities are often exposed to contaminated water containing the infected snails.

Although it has a low mortality rate, schistosomiasis often is a chronic illness that can damage internal organs and, in children, impair growth and cognitive development. The urinary form of schistosomiasis is associated with increased risks for bladder cancer in adults. Schistosomiasis is the second most socioeconomically devastating parasitic disease after malaria.

This disease is most commonly found in Asia, Africa, and South America, especially in areas where the water contains numerous freshwater snails, which may carry the parasite.

The disease affects many people in developing countries, particularly children who may acquire the disease by swimming or playing in infected water. When children come into contact with a contaminated water source, the parasitic larvae easily enter through their skin and further mature within organ tissues. As of 2009, 74 developing countries statistically identified epidemics of Schistosomiasis within their respective populations.

A case of bilharzia

Joseph Msumba, Malawi

In September 2011 a 45-year-old man comes to the clinic with urinary complaints. Before, during and after urination he has pain and the urine is coloured red with blood. He had gone to hospital where they diagnosed bilharzia. Treatment was started but now, at the end of the treatment the complaints are largely unchanged.

He was prescribed PC132d for bilharzia.

One month later there is no more blood in the urine and the pains with urination have improved but not totally yet. Another month later all complaints have gone.

Gonorrhoea

Gonorrhoea is a common sexually transmitted disease (STD) caused by the bacterium Neisseria gonorrhoeae (also called Gonococcus, which is often abbreviated as "GC" by clinicians). In the US, its incidence is second only to Chlamydia among bacterial STDs. In both men and women if gonorrhoea is left untreated, it may spread throughout the body, affecting joints and even heart valves. In his analysis of the sycotic miasm Hahnemann has also described the long-term transgenerational effects that can result from suppressed gonorrhoea. In our understanding Hahnemann's core miasms are to be seen as META-MIASMS, which means that sycosis covers a larger totality than the gonorrhoea miasm, and is even not primarily related to disease and pathology (See Part II), but with a phase in human development. Pathology is then both the result of stunted growth as well as the key to unlock the potential of that phase.

In Europe a homeopath will not often treat a case of gonorrhoea or come across a history of it in a patient. In Africa our experience is that you may see more cases in which gonorrhoea plays a role in a day than in Europe in months or years. This has to do with a mix of circumstances amongst which an enormously high incidence of rape in many areas, promiscuity, unprotected sex, bad hygiene and compromised immunity are some of the main ones.

Because gonorrhoea plays such an important role in Hahnemann's theory of miasms and chronic diseases and because it is so common in Africa where our main focus is, we decided to ask Eileen Nauman to also make a shamanic journey to Neisseria gonorrhoea. A full report of this journey and a discussion of it can be found in Appendix 3. What came forward strongly is that gonorrhoea has to do with honouring yourself as also honouring the choice of any individual to say yes or no to participating in the sexual act. It is connected to loss of respect between genders, with abuse, rape and disempowerment. Its role and purpose would be teaching to approach sex with integrity, honour, respect and a balance between the two consenting parties.

Sycosis in Evolutionary Perspective

As in our analysis Hahnemann's concept of Sycosis is much larger than gonorrhoea and its chronic effects alone, what follows includes the gonorrhoea miasm but is by far not exclusive to it. Malaria for instance (see later) belongs to the end stages of the sycotic process, as does typhoid.

In the birth process, which shows the journey of man on this planet in a nutshell, Sycosis is connected with the irreversible start of the dilatation process and symbolises the descent into the underworld. It is characterised by antagonism between mother and baby, the one being a cause of pain to the other. The previous paradisiacal womb has turned into its opposite. Images of suffering in Hell, entering Hades and confrontation with the Devil belong to this phase. In psychological terms Sycosis is connected with the shadow and the exploration of the unconscious, and with the idea of being a powerless victim. Self-appreciation is the result of this journey into the underworld and many qualities are brought from the darkness into the light – honesty, modesty, endurance, empathy, adaptation, tolerance, friendship and forgiveness are among them. The pathological side is expressed in self-condemnation, feeling bad and evil, and a split between good and bad with the tendency to associate with the latter.

Dissociation is a way of dealing with the suffering. The prisoner is a good symbol of this state and expresses the lack of awareness of a way out. The plant kingdom is connected with Sycosis.

A case of gonorrhoea
Klaus Schustereder, Central African Republic

A 28-year-old woman comes to see me in Baboua. She tells me she has had pain in her abdomen for about ten years. It is especially painful during her menses. I ask her to show me exactly where the pain is. She points to her lower abdomen, both sides where the ovaries are. When I palpate the abdomen, it is very sensitive. She says it is painful. I ask her if her husband had gonorrhoea once. She said yes, that was before they met. Her problems started at the time of the beginning of their relationship.

I give her PC gonorrhoea, five drops a day and ask her to come again in a week.

Follow-up:
A week later she visits me again. She tells me she is so much better. She tells me there is now no pain anymore during sexual intercourse (she did not tell me at the first consultation). Her abdomen is much better. There is still a little pain, but it is not comparable to the pain she still had a week ago. She tells me, every time when she took the remedy, about five minutes later, there was a strong vaginal discharge. She says: "All the dirt came out." I asked her if I could touch her abdomen again, and notice it is clearly less sensitive.

Her husband came also to see me. He suffers from pain in the kidneys. I also gave him PC gonorrhoea. He took about fourteen days till he came back to report to me, that since he took the medicine he had to urinate a lot, but the pain in the kidneys was much less. He furthermore had stronger erections and he can enjoy sex more.

Woman 33 years with pelvic pain and leucorrhoea
Klaus Schustereder, Central African Republic

A 33-year-old woman is in the women's ward. She has pelvic pain and leucorrhoea. I palpate her abdomen and there is a pain on both sides of the ovaries. She tells me she usually has very severe pain during menses. She had already been hospitalised for a week when I first saw her. The nurses had given her two different antibiotics and painkillers. Nevertheless she did not improve. I prescribed PC Gonorrhoea.

Follow-up:
After that I could see her improving day by day. After one week, there was no pain anymore and the leucorrhoea had stopped. She left the hospital happy.

Cases of PC gonorrhoea
Harry van der Zee, Burundi and DCR Congo

During my visits to Bujumbura, Uvira, Kiliba and Bukavu PC gonorrhoea was prescribed to lots of cases of infertility, chronic infections of the lower urinary tract and/or vagina, womb and ovaries.
A fascinating case concerned a woman that was going to be operated on in two weeks. For three months already she was suffering from intense pains in the womb and an echogram she had with her showed cysts in the womb. On inquiring it appeared that two months before all this started she had

an infection, which I assumed, was gonorrhoea. After the first dose of PC gonorrhoea she discharged great lumps of blood that looked like meat. The next day the pains were practically gone and she went back to work. Four days later she was beaming and cancelled the operation. Two months later I saw her again and she was still completely free from symptoms.

For cases of infertility (gonorrhoea cause number one) I have not had enough follow-up to be able to make any judgement about the effectiveness of PC gonorrhoea in those cases. All other cases that I saw for follow-up responded quickly and completely.

An interesting observation was also that people who used to be free from malaria and at some point started to have malaria regularly, often reported that shortly before that they were infected with gonorrhoea. Either the infection itself or its suppression made them more vulnerable to malaria.

A case of gonorrhoea and malaria

Harry van der Zee, Burundi

Christelle is 35-years-old. She has malaria ten times in a year (meaning chronic malaria) and besides that has suffered from vaginitis with itching and discharge for five years. She received PC Malaria (PC240m) and PC180g for gonorrhoea (one in the morning, the other in the evening, to see whether dealing with two diseases simultaneously would work).

Follow-up after five days:
In response to the medication she felt a pain in her right shoulder extending to the head which then went away. The pain she had in the lower abdomen doubled for a short time and then went away together with the discharge. The itching is a lot better since the discharge has stopped.
The headaches and vertigo have improved as well as cramps she used to have all over her body. The pain in her joints is completely gone. Her head is still sensitive to the sun.

Follow-up after four weeks:
All symptoms are gone.
Follow-up after two months:
She is completely fine, also no more malaria.

Conclusion from the above case: using PC Resonances it is possible to successfully treat two conditions simultaneously. Despite that, certainly when you have the opportunity to regularly follow the case, the usual advice is to start with treating the disease that causes most suffering or that started earlier and to start the second remedy as soon as the first condition has been cured. In a case like this it is very likely that PC gonorrhoea alone would have dealt with both diseases as one triggered the other. I have for instance observed this in a case of chronic hepatitis that preceded chronic malaria. Treating the hepatitis was enough to also get rid of malaria. It was the teaching of Hahnemann two centuries ago that two diseases did not coexist in the body, or one was dominant. In our experience many different diseases can be concurrent, although curing one may well cure them all if one compromised the immune system and other diseases came as a consequence of that.

Hepatitis

Hepatitis is an inflammation of the liver. The condition can be self-limiting or can progress to fibrosis and cirrhosis.
Hepatitis may occur with limited or no symptoms, but often leads to jaundice, anorexia and malaise. Hepatitis is acute when it lasts less than six months and chronic when it persists longer. A group of hepatitis viruses (Hep A, B, C) cause most cases of hepatitis worldwide, but it can also be due to toxins, medicines, other infections (bacteria, parasites) and autoimmune diseases.

Acute Hepatitis

Initial features are of nonspecific flu-like symptoms, common to almost all acute viral infections and may include malaise, muscle and joint aches, fever, nausea or vomiting, diarrhoea, and headache. More specific symptoms are: profound loss of appetite, dark urine, colourless stool, jaundice.
Acute viral hepatitis is more likely to be asymptomatic in younger people. Symptomatic individuals may present after convalescent stage of seven to ten days, with the total illness lasting two to six weeks.
A small proportion of people with acute hepatitis progress to acute liver failure (leading to confusion and coma) and produce blood proteins (leading to peripheral oedema and bleeding).

Chronic Hepatitis

Chronic hepatitis often leads to nonspecific symptoms such as malaise, tiredness and weakness, and often leads to no symptoms at all. It is commonly identified on blood tests to evaluate nonspecific symptoms. The occurrence of jaundice indicates advanced liver damage. On physical examination there may be enlargement of the liver.
Extensive damage and scarring of liver (i.e. cirrhosis) leads to weight loss, easy bruising and bleeding tendency, swelling of the legs and accumulation of fluid in the abdominal cavity (ascites). Eventually, cirrhosis may lead to various life-threatening complications.

PC Resonances for Hepatitis

The PC Resonances discussed here are produced for acute and chronic forms of viral hepatitis and have mainly been used in Africa where other forms of treatment are often not available. There are specific PC Resonances for specific forms of viral hepatitis as also a general one as in developing countries facilities to determine which virus is in play are often absent.

A case of chronic hepatitis
Klaus Schustereder, Central African Republic

40-year-old male with chronic hepatitis since his fifteenth year.

Follow-up after PC191i for hepatitis (all types):
After three weeks already his tiredness is better, strength better, sleep improved and he is less slow. His nightmares, which he had because he had been beaten a lot by his father, disappeared with the prescription of an individual simillimum.

A case of acute hepatitis
Klaus Schustereder, Central African Republic

A man 30-years-old and employed in the hospital is diagnosed with acute hepatitis B. He has high fever, icterus, vomiting, pressure in the right hypochondriac region and he can't walk due to weakness.

Follow-up after PC191i 5 drops every hour:
After a few days he is already much better and walking around, where the normal course here is that people either show slow recovery taking months or they die from the hepatitis. In answer to the question whether he felt the remedy had helped him he exclaimed in wonder "are you crazy? "He had seen many cases in hospital and knew how long it took people to recover – if they did.

In Africa and Haiti we've treated several cases of chronic hepatitis. Considering they often had the disease for many years already these patients responded amazingly quickly. Here is an example.

A case of chronic hepatitis
Harry van der Zee, Burundi

Faustin is 33-years-old and has had hepatitis since 2004 (case taken in 2008). He has fever often, can't stand for long due to pain in the liver and also has malaria regularly. His eye sclera are very yellow.

Follow-up eight days after PC191i, 5 drops daily:
What we notice is that his eyes are less yellow. The pain in the liver has gone down from a five to a three/four. He can stand longer and his energy has improved. He continues the drops.
Follow-up two weeks later:
Feels very well. He can work normally again and was able to watch a full soccer game while standing.
After two months:
"The remedy has helped me a lot. As long as I do not overdo it I can walk without a problem and the liver does not become painful. I can stand now for a long time. I feel this is really a good medicine for me."
Three months later:
I receive a report through email saying the hepatitis is no longer bothering him, that his eyes have a normal colour now, and that ever since he started the remedy malaria has not returned, and therefore no follow-up with PC240m for malaria was required.

Herpes

Herpes simplex virus 1 and 2 (HSV-1 and HSV-2) infect humans. Both HSV-1 (which produces cold sores) and HSV-2 (which produces genital herpes) are common and contagious. They can be spread when an infected person is producing and shedding the virus.

Symptoms of herpes simplex virus infection include watery blisters in the skin or mucous membranes of the mouth, lips or genitals. The blisters heal with a scab. After the initial infection, some infected people experience sporadic outbreaks.

Genital herpes is a sexually transmitted disease mostly caused by HSV-2. When it occurs, there are typically one or more blisters on or around the genitals or rectum. The blisters break, leaving tender ulcers (sores) that may take two to four weeks to heal the first time. Typically, another outbreak can appear weeks or months after the first, but it is almost always less severe and shorter than the first. The infection can stay in the body indefinitely, but the number of outbreaks tends to decrease over a period of years.

In the USA about one out of six people between fourteen and 49 years of age have genital HSV-2 infection. Genital HSV-2 infection is more common in women (approximately one out of five women between fourteen and 49 years of age) than in men (about one out of nine men between fourteen and 49 years of age).

PC192j is the PC Resonance developed for both HSV1 and HSV2. As the experience the authors have with herpes is restricted to the use of downloads instead of granules or dilutions we share some cases in Part XII, which discusses sound as carrier of healing resonance.

In that same chapter also a case of chickenpox treated with a download is presented.

Influenza

Influenza, commonly referred to as the flu, is caused by RNA viruses (orthomyxoviridae), and affects birds and mammals. The most common symptoms of the disease are chills, fever, sore throat, muscle pains, severe headache, coughing, weakness and malaise. Influenza is a more severe disease than the common cold and is caused by a different type of virus. Typically, influenza is transmitted through the air by coughs or sneezes, creating aerosols containing the virus. Influenza can also be transmitted by direct contact with bird droppings or nasal secretions, or through contact with contaminated surfaces.
Influenza viruses can be inactivated by sunlight.

Influenza spreads around the world in seasonal epidemics, resulting in the deaths of between 250,000 and 500,000 people every year, up to millions in some pandemic years. So a simple flu takes many lives each year, especially in wintertime. It is nature taking its course and actually a relatively mild way for the old and weak to leave the planet. With homeopathy we can treat flu or prevent it and this is done routinely. If there is anything that should urge decision makers in healthcare to seriously investigate and implement homeopathy it is the results homeopathy has shown in the treatment of epidemics. The stunning results with the 1918-19 avian flu alone should have that impact.

Once every so many decades a dangerous flu pandemic breaks out. Here are some quotes from Maggie Taeger's review of *The Homeopathic Treatment of Influenza: Surviving Influenza Epidemics and Pandemics, Past, Present and Future with Homeopathy* by Sandra Perko:

> "The Spanish Flu pandemic of 1918-19 was estimated to have a global mortality top of 40,000,000. Onset was extremely rapid and death could ensue within 48 hours or less of first symptoms. Conventional doctors were helpless against the disease, and were probably responsible for greatly increasing the death rate through the heavy-handed use of aspirin. Tragically, the young adult population, fourteen to 40 years of age, was the hardest hit and saw the greatest number of fatalities. Homeopathy was the light shining in the darkness. In roughly 50 accounts from homeopaths of the time we hear how they treated patients successfully, mostly with a few well-known remedies (Gelsemium looms largest), and lost astoundingly few patients."

The following quotes on the influenza epidemic of 1918 come from Julian Winston:

> It was called "the Great White Plague." It is hard to imagine the devastation caused by the Flu Epidemic of 1918 - 19. People who lived through it reported that some one who was up and well in the morning could be dead by evening.
> Dr. H. A. Roberts was a physician on a troop ship at the time. Another boat pulled alongside to get any spare coffins – its mortality rate was so high. On his return to port, the commander said to Roberts, "used all your coffins?" To which Roberts, who had been treating his ship with homeopathy, replied, "Yes, and lost not one man!"

The following is an extract from an article entitled "Homeopathy In Influenza - A Chorus Of Fifty In Harmony" by W. A. Dewey, MD that appeared in the Journal of the American Institute of Homeopathy in 1920.

- Dean W. A. Pearson of Philadelphia collected 26,795 cases of influenza treated by homeopathic physicians with a mortality of 1.05%, while the average old school mortality is 30%.

- Thirty physicians in Connecticut responded to my request for data. They reported 6,602 cases with 55 deaths, which is less than 1%. In the transport service I had 81 cases on the way over. All recovered and were landed. Every man received homeopathic treatment. One ship lost 31 on the way. – H. A. Roberts, MD, Derby, Connecticut.
- In a plant of 8,000 workers we had only one death. The patients were not drugged to death. Gelsemium was practically the only remedy used. We used no aspirin and no vaccines. – Frank Wieland, MD, Chicago.
- I did not lose a single case of influenza; my death rate in the pneumonias was 2.1%. The salycilates, including aspirin and quinine, were almost the sole standbys of the old school and it was a common thing to hear them speaking of losing 60% of their pneumonias. – Dudley A. Williams, MD, Providence, Rhode Island.
- Fifteen hundred cases were reported at the Homeopathic Medical Society of the District of Columbia with but fifteen deaths. Recoveries in the National Homeopathic Hospital were 100%. – E. F. Sappington, M. D., Philadelphia.
- I have treated 1,000 cases of influenza. I have the records to show my work. I have no losses. Please give all credit to homeopathy and none to the Scotch-Irish-American! – T. A. McCann, MD, Dayton, Ohio.
- One physician in a Pittsburgh hospital asked a nurse if she knew anything better than what he was doing, because he was losing many cases. "Yes, Doctor, stop aspirin and go down to a homeopathic pharmacy, and get homeopathic remedies." The Doctor replied: "But that is homeopathy." "I know it, but the homeopathic doctors for whom I have nursed have not lost a single case." – W. F. Edmundson, MD, Pittsburgh.
- Three hundred and fifty cases and lost one, a neglected pneumonia that came to me after she had taken one hundred grains of aspirin in twenty-four hours. – Cora Smith King, MD, Washington, DC
- I had a package handed to me containing 1,000 aspirin tablets, which was 994 too many. I think I gave about a half dozen. I could find no place for it. My remedies were few. I almost invariably gave Gelsemium and Bryonia. I hardly ever lost a case if I got there first, unless the patient had been sent to a drug store and bought aspirin, in which event I was likely to have a case of pneumonia on my hands. – J. P. Huff, MD, Olive Branch, Kentucky.

Clearly homeopathy has a lot to offer in flu pandemic and if a serious one breaks out we may better be well prepared. To be prepared knowledge about useful remedies is evidently needed. Maggie Taeger:

> "Perko then gives a 112-page Materia Medica of 68 remedies in which she includes only symptoms relevant to flu ("Influenza Remedy Differential Reference"). This is quite useful since it is hard to get an unencumbered flu picture at a glance from other sources."

Usually a handful of remedies will be sufficient once the Genus epidemicus of the flu pandemic has been established. Even then though homeopathic skills are needed to make the correct choice amongst these. We have to realize that the vast majority of the world population has no skilled homeopath, or even homeopathic remedies in a pharmacy, available.

In 2005 all alarms went off as it was considered highly likely that an avian flu would break out. As it would take months for regular medicine to develop a treatment that would only reach the wealthy part of the global population it was decided to develop a PC Resonance for bird flu. In the worst-case scenario it was clear that a killer pandemic could easily paralyse the whole of society. If the people at the pharmacy would fall ill, or the postman stopped collecting the mail, or the local pharmacy closed shop, no pills or potions would reach those in need of them. At that point Peter decided to create a new way of imprinting homeopathic healing information into sound instead of water or milk sugar granules, so a flu resonance could be downloaded from the internet, a facility that might still be working despite a global panic. (See www.healingdownloads.com where by now also other resonances are available.)

Besides that, to gain insight in the role and purpose of this possible pandemic, Eileen Nauman was asked to make a shamanic journey to the virus.The complete journey can be read in Appendix 3. The main topic that, according to the journey, is connected with avian flu is the way humans damage the planet in general, and pollute the air in particular. The virus becoming virulent to humans would be a consequence of the current ecological situation.

To this day the bird flu pandemic has not yet occurred, and instead the world population and its healthcare institutes overreacted when an epidemic of swine flu broke out and are now dealing with the possible side-effects of mass immunisation. The swine flu pandemic that never happened has clearly awakened the world population to look at vaccination more critically, and not to simply take the words of the specialists that officially have independent positions but usually are advisors of the pharmaceutical industry or dependent on their funding.

About the Conventional Drugs for Flu

Many people think/hope that if a serious flu pandemic breaks out they can rely on vaccinations and drugs like Tamiflu and this may be true for some people but certainly not for everybody for reasons of distribution as well as whether it will be effective or not.
Vaccinations are unlikely to work because the virus mutates fast, faster than the vaccines can be made. Old vaccines just won't work.
While attacking the flu is a bad idea it will still happen. The worst consequences of drugs like Tamiflu is that they encourage the virus to mutate with the possibility of its becoming more deadly. As most governments will want to be seen to do something, this scenario is most likely. The intelligent decision would be to tell people about homeopathic history in pandemics and give them the choice, as also to co-operate with homeopaths in studying homeopathic prophylaxis and cure of influenzas and other epidemics.

PC Resonances for Flu

The following PC Resonances for flu are available and can be used as prophylaxis and curative:

- Influenza – PC200i
- Bird flu – PC202k
- Swine flu – PC579e
- Influenza vaccination toxic effects – PC504d

In the occurrence of a pandemic killer flu downloads for it will be made available for free, so every person world-wide who has access to internet or has a cell phone can receive treatment.

Leprosy

Leprosy is a chronic disease caused by the bacteria Mycobacterium leprae and Mycobacterium lepromatosis. It is primarily a granulomatous disease of the peripheral nerves and mucosa of the upper respiratory tract; skin lesions are the primary external sign. Left untreated, leprosy can be progressive, causing permanent damage to the skin, nerves, limbs and eyes. Contrary to folklore, leprosy does not cause body parts to fall off, although they can become numb or diseased as a result of secondary infections; these occur as a result of the body's defences being compromised by the primary disease. Secondary infections, in turn, can result in tissue loss causing fingers and toes to become shortened and deformed, as cartilage is absorbed into the body. [http://en.wikipedia.org/wiki/Leprosy]

Leprosy case
Peter Chappell, Central African Republic

> A fifty-year old man came to see me with recurring leprosy. He had had it earlier in his life and his nose was a bit eaten away by it. His father had leprosy too. The leprosy on his ear was also in his hair. After one week on PC leprosy it all cleared up. Treatment was stopped. A month later it was still fine and other old symptoms, sores in his nose he already had for a year or so, have also improved.

Lyme Disease (Borreliosis)

Lyme disease is caused by the bacterium Borrelia burgdorferi (B. burgdorferi). Certain ticks carry the bacteria when they bite mice or deer that are infected with Lyme disease. Commonly you get more than one disease from such a tick bite that's infective. Deer ticks can be so small that they are almost impossible to see. Many people with Lyme disease never even saw a tick. Most people who are bitten by a tick do NOT get a disease.

First symptoms resemble the flu and include:

- Chills
- Fever
- Headache
- Lethargy
- Muscle pain
- There may be a 'bulls eye' rash, a flat or slightly raised red spot at the site of the tick bite. Often there is a clear area in the centre. It can be larger than one to three inches wide.

Later stage symptoms of the disease include:

- Body-wide itching
- Joint inflammation
- Stiff neck
- Unusual or strange behaviour
- A physical exam may show heart, joint, or brain problems.

PC232n for Lyme disease

Case of a 53-year-old man with Lyme Disease

Harry van der Zee, Netherlands

Six weeks after his father died he got a rash from a tick bite. Three years ago he also had borreliosis, and he notices that must have been also come six weeks after the death of his sister. He doesn't think it is connected to grief but rather to the fact that in both cases he had to arrange the inheritance. He had to deal with other people's belongings, divide them amongst relatives and keep his share. And although he did nothing wrong and actually what was expected of him, he described the feeling as intruding, as if doing something improper, almost like stealing. As if he was breaking in, going through other's property, taking something that didn't belong to him.

Response to PC 232n for Lyme disease:
A nightly irregularity of his heart which had been present for one year was much better. A pain in his right shoulder which was there for six months already disappeared in a few days, as also a pain at the left lower ribs that used to be there when lying on left side. Another remarkable thing was that close to the nail of his toes of the right foot he had some kind of pimple from which some silicon-like substance would come if he squeezed it empty. It had been there for a year already, and within a few days after starting with PC Lyme disease it completely disappeared. As the rash, which was the reason to seek treatment, was still spreading after one week of treatment he decided to take antibiotics after

all. Considering the response to the remedy the possibility is that all symptoms that had improved so rapidly were related to his earlier borreliosis infection, as arrhythmias and neuralgic pains can belong to the chronic borreliosis picture. The oozing pimple with a substance that looked as if it was the fluid pre-stage of what had to become a nail remains a mystery as there was no description of it found in relation to Lyme.

Follow-up one year later:
He reports that the rash disappeared after the antibiotics but that the other complaints at some point returned. Only the pimple stayed away. So he wonders whether indeed the other complaints were related to the earlier infection with borreliosis and that he should have waited in taking antibiotics.
Prescription: PC232n repeated daily

Follow-up after two weeks:
The arrhythmia has improved and the pain in the shoulder and chest is gone. Interestingly enough after a few days of treatment the pimple at the toe reappeared. He took that as a sign he had taken enough from the remedy and stopped.

In this case the remedy was not given in granules or drops but as download (See Part XII).

The circumstances of both incidences of infection with borreliosis in this case are placed within an interesting context by Eileen Nauman's journey to the parasite (See Appendix 3). Two clear themes come forward that have significance in this case:

> "Lyme Disease is all about strong boundaries, i.e., the boundary of the forest as an example – of stopping people who come to steal/take/disrespect or alter the fabric of the natural environment in some way."

> "This protozoon could be drawn to takers who are selfish and insensitive to anyone but themselves, but also, the other end of this spectrum, people who give away their life blood, their energy, literally and they don't know where to stop, where a healthy boundary exists."

Confronted with these themes the patient of the case above said:

> "When my sister was buried and we walked out of the church I saw a dear friend of mine crying. She told me later she was crying for me. She saw me taking care of everything and everyone and thought 'Who is taking care of you'. To me a strange question as of course I take care of myself, and that realisation shows how correct her observation was. I tend to think of myself as selfish or even insensitive and perhaps I am compensating for that feeling and am therefore seen as being the opposite." He also narrated his sister had actually lived like a parasite. She had heavy pathology, psychologically speaking, and her behaviour was much like that of a parasite. She did not know how to live on her own energy, had no source for that inside herself. So she was taking from others without permission. On the physical level by stealing money, food, things in shops etc. On an emotional level by claiming people and making them her 'friends' whether they liked that or not.

Peter Alex in his book on Lyme disease [*The Homeopathic Treatment of Lyme Disease*, HomeopathyWest Publishing, 2007] proposes *Aurum arsenicosum* as a Genus epidemicus remedy for borreliosis:

- Fear for loneliness (Arsenicum) at an older and mature age (Aurum)
- Wanting to preserve wealth (Western society) (Aurum) and fear of bankruptcy (Arsenicum)

- Make the structure perfect (Aurum) and have perfect control over everything (Arsenicum)
- The end (Arsenicum) of wealth, the king's drama over power (Aurum) has come.

Alex mentions that we are no longer the rulers of the Earth. Borreliosis has a high incidence in industrialised countries, in which the people thought their increasing wealth was secure and now have to experience the opposite. In the light of the shamanic journey above, it is also especially for the consumers in the West that forests in the world are being destroyed, so their houses and furniture can be built and the cattle they consume can be fed.

Much to the benefit of his patients, Peter Alex shows a pragmatic and open attitude as to his prescriptions for Lyme patients. In his book he describes a case of a 70-year-old borreliosis patient where *Nux vomica* as a constitutional remedy had no effect, and *Aurum arsenicosum* as his Genus epidemicus remedy gave 30% improvement. He then gave PC Lyme and saw several complaints get up to 100% better.

Lyme disease case report

Peter Chappell, Czech Republic

> Male, 49 years old.
> He was bitten by a tick in June 2005 in the hollow of his knee, had a large ring around it after that. This was followed by severe weakness, visible trembling and cramping pain in muscles and joints.
> He also had painful skin on his arms, shoulder, neck and chest.
> He felt worn-out, had to do everything in slow-motion and his mind could not cope with the speed of life. He lost confidence in his body because of this.
> His sleep was disturbed; he woke with a start, was restless and left the bed.
> He felt depressed and was not able to work or even drive a car.
>
> I gave him PC232n on 10 September 2005.
>
> *Follow-up:*
> The very first day after the remedy he felt more confident, at ease and wanted to drive the car! Every following day he improved and after three weeks he was 80% better.
> Since then these symptoms never returned. He took the remedy for three weeks every day and after that *Natrum muriaticum* helped him with other complaints.

Lyme Disease Complex

Lyme disease proves even more complicated with associated co-infections urging patients to request testing for three other common tick-borne illnesses.

www.prweb.com/releases/2008/09/prweb1345344.htm:

> The ticks that transmit the bacteria that causes Lyme disease also carry numerous other pathogens that can complicate the treatment and management of the primary infection and lead to a longer-lasting, more devastating illness. The three most common Lyme disease co-infections are: Babesiosis and Erlichiosis (HME or HCE), both parasitic infections, and Bartonellosis, an infection caused by bacteria called Bartonella.
>
> Symptoms and treatment of Lyme co-infections are as complex as Lyme itself, similar to the difficulty with Lyme diagnosis and treatment, as the symptoms of these Lyme co-infections are also non-specific, such as fever, chills, headache and malaise, and the diagnostic procedures often rely on a series of negative tests, since the parasites and bacteria that cause the infections are only detectable in the bloodstream for a short period of time.
>
> *Babesiosis* is an infection caused by a parasite that infects red blood cells. Babesia microti is believed to be the most common piroplasm infecting humans, but scientists have identified over twenty piroplasms carried by ticks. Symptoms of babesiosis are similar to those of Lyme disease but it more often starts with a high fever and chills. As the infection progresses, patients may develop fatigue, headache, drenching sweats, muscle aches, nausea, and vomiting.
>
> *Ehrlichiosis* is common in two forms, both of which are caused by tick-borne parasites called Ehrlichia that infect different kinds of white blood cells. In HME (human monocytic ehrlichiosis), they infect monocytes. In HGE (human granulocytic ehrlichiosis, also called anaplasmosis), they infect granulocytes. Ehrlichiosis and anaplasmosis share the same symptoms: sudden high fever, fatigue, muscle aches and headache. The disease can be mild or life-threatening. Severely ill patients can have low white blood cell count, low platelet count, anaemia, elevated liver enzymes, kidney failure and respiratory insufficiency.
>
> *Bartonellosis* is known to be caused by a bacteria carried by fleas, body lice and ticks. Bartonellosis is often mild but in serious cases it can affect the whole body.
> Early signs are fever, fatigue, headache, poor appetite, and an unusual, streaked rash. Swollen glands are typical, especially around the head, neck and arms. Lymph nodes may be enlarged and the throat can be sore.

A PC Resonance covering borreliosis and all possible co-infections is now available.

Malaria

Although it was AIDS that motivated Peter to go to Africa to see in how much homeopathy could be used to decrease suffering and call this epidemic to a halt, the joint experience of the authors is that even more than AIDS it is malaria that the peoples in Africa and other developing countries struggle with. The consequences and suffering due to AIDS are horrendous and have in some areas wiped out a complete generation. Nevertheless, the consequences of malaria in general go much deeper. Malaria as it were keeps Africa and Africans down as long as the history of mankind goes back, and is deeply connected with the state of the continent and its failure to thrive.
Malaria in humans is caused by one of four protozoon species of the Genus Plasmodium: P. falciparum, P. vivax, P. ovale, or P. malariae. All species are transmitted by the bite of an infected female Anopheles mosquito. Occasionally, transmission occurs by blood transfusion, organ transplantation, needle-sharing, or congenitally from mother to foetus.
Malaria is prevalent in 106 countries and world-wide there are the incredible estimated number of 500 million infections per year, resulting in one million deaths per year. On average 3000 African children die from malaria every day.
Therapy resistance is huge and until recently only one drug was still free from it, artemisinin.

http://news.bbc.co.uk/2/hi/asia-pacific/8073118.stm:

> "International scientists say they have found the first evidence of resistance to the world's most effective drug for treating malaria. They say the trend in western Cambodia has to be urgently contained because full-blown resistance would be a global health catastrophe.
>
> Drugs are taking longer to clear blood of malaria parasites than before. This is an early warning sign of emerging resistance to a disease that kills a million people every year. Until now the most effective drug cleared all malaria parasites from the blood within two or three days but in recent trials this took up to four or five days.
>
> The artemesinin family of drugs is the world's front-line defence against the most prevalent and deadly form of malaria. Two teams of scientists, working on separate clinical trials, have reported seeing the disturbing evidence that the drugs are becoming much less effective."

Professor Nick Day, director of the Mahidol-Oxford Tropical Medicine Research Unit that is carrying out the UK study, said:

> "Twice in the past, South East Asia has made a gift, unwittingly, of drug resistant parasites to the rest of the world, in particular to Africa."
>
> "That's the problem. We've had chloroquine and SP (sulfadoxine pyrimethamine) resistance, both of which have caused major loss of life in Africa," he said in reference to earlier generation anti-malarial drugs.
>
> "If the same thing happens again, the spread of a resistant parasite from Asia to Africa, that will have devastating consequences for malaria control," he said."

From research we know that malaria accompanies humanity from as far as we can look back and it is estimated that in the total history of mankind 50% of all humans that ever lived died from malaria. At present 50% of the world population lives in areas where malaria is endemic.

Considering the magnitude of the impact of malaria it is not only interesting that Hahnemann started the homeopathic adventure with *China*, but possibly also very meaningful. From the figures above we may conclude that the Malaria miasm is probably (one of) the most basic miasm(s) guiding the development of mankind.

The core remedy belonging to the Malaria miasm is *China officinalis*. Typical of the remedy is a combination of a mind full of plans and ideas contrasted by feeling unfortunate:

- Abundant ideas at night
- Reflects upon execution of many plans
- Delusion he is hindered at work
- Delusion he is unfortunate

The fact that the ideas enter the mind at night while during the day he feels hindered at work means that the manifestation of plans does not occur. They remain ideas in the dark that do not see their realization in daylight.

An unfortunate feeling is inherent in the attitude of the victim, a strong sycotic feature, where being full of plans and ideas suggests an active attitude and an expectation of being able to change one's fate. The birth process signifies the individuation process and the psychological and spiritual evolution of mankind as in a nutshell. [van der Zee: *Miasms in Labour* and *Homeopathy for Birth Trauma*] Placed on the grid of the birth process the theme of China suggests a position close to full dilatation. There is a perspective of a way out of one's situation (the opened os uteri) but this is not translated into successful action yet (the expulsion phase has not started). As with Sycosis the situation one lives in can be experienced as a prison, and plans are made to escape from it. Malaria is mainly prevalent in countries with tribal culture. The tribe is typical of a community that on the one hand serves to guarantee support in providing all the primary needs in life (Psora) and on the other hand can become a prison (Sycosis) because it blocks further development and individuation. This suggests that the Malaria miasm might have to do with the process of the individual choosing a path away from the collective, a theme happening in most if not all individual lives (the young adult leaving home), but most relevant in traditional cultures with strong tribal rules and taboos. But one can also think for instance of people raised in an orthodox religious setting that wish to break out because dogma restricts the fulfilment of their needs.

As the history of PC Technology started in Africa with the treatment of AIDS it is obvious that malaria was another disease Peter was confronted with. PC malaria was therefore one of the first other PC Resonances made and experience with it goes back to 2003.

Malaria and Meaning

As in Africa and many other countries its impact is huge (often larger than AIDS) knowing better the intelligence behind the disease would be helpful in dealing with it. So once more we asked Eileen Nauman to make a shamanic journey (See Appendix 3).

The main topic that came forward from this journey was the role malaria plays in the individual's breaking loose from tribal consciousness. In earlier phases of development the collective, the tribe or family, offers safety and support. If rules, customs and taboos are very strong, the safety of the tribe turns into restriction of the individual to follow its own unique path in life.

If one is in a situation that one is not happy with and the awareness and desire for change is there, then making plans is what is needed. During malaria fevers people have a very active mind that is full of plans and ideas or hallucinations, so the role of the disease seems to be connected to leaving what is familiar or pre-ordained behind and designing an individual path. In this light the fact that the remedy *Natrum muriaticum* is considered as one of the main malaria remedies also makes sense. Isn't the first community we need to break loose from the one with our mother? Breaking loose from the mother, family, church or tribe is usually accompanied by mixed feelings. The freedom of breaking loose and the new opportunities are exciting, but there is also a sense of loss and grief. Really losing one's mother, family or even tribe due to disease, war or genocide, something happening a lot in Africa, can also force an individual to create a life without the safety and limitations of them. So the impulse to individualise further comes either from within, if necessary stimulated by malaria, or from external influences.

Breaking loose can require an act of violence or assertion at least, and violence is certainly part of the Malaria miasm. Louis Klein comes to an interesting understanding of violence related to malaria that confirms the above:

> "Many of the personal feelings of hostility, persecution and even homicide, (genocide) ... can be extended to and seen in a larger socio-political way. This is especially true where the individual or group needing help from remedies in this miasm are living in a town, society, or country where they are being taken care of, but not allowed independence. This can be especially seen with refugees, principally those living in a refugee camp. As a result, there is a feeling or sense of being stuck in a cycle of expectation, welfare and constant humiliation. Underlying this forced situation is the injustice but also a belief (parasitic) that they deserve more than they get from those they are dependent on. There can therefore be homicidal rage directed to those they are dependent on." [Klein, 2009]

> "What is distinctive about the Malaria Nosode is that there is an underlying aggressive and revengeful aspect, rather then just a sense of victimization. In the extreme, these individuals will subscribe to violent conspiracy theories as well as a code of violent revenge. In many areas where malaria is endemic, there is much tribal or cultural warfare, torture and genocide." [ibid]

The lack of success in life is projected either on the family or tribe of which the person can become a violent member, or the collective lack of success is projected by one tribe on another with genocide as a result. Plasmodium reproduces best in marshes and swamps where plants decay and rot away. It is as if the situational Materia Medica of malaria is that of a person sinking away in a swamp and that fighting the situation only makes him sink deeper into this desperate state. Especially in the last decades genocide has taken enormous proportions in certain parts of Africa (e.g. Rwanda, DRC Congo, Burundi) and Asia (e.g. Cambodia) and we may wonder whether the suppression of malaria is one of the factors responsible for this outburst.

Considering all acute infections and the vast number of people that are chronically ill it is clear that economically speaking malaria heavily cripples society and prevents it from prospering and flourishing. As discussed above another view is that malaria helps people to move on from a restrictive tribal culture that is preventing individuals to develop and excel. At this moment the balance has not tipped yet and Africa especially suffers in the process.

If we look at the success of the industrialized world and especially Europe where it started, we see that malaria disappeared together with poverty. The people of Europe once left the cradle of mankind (Africa) and moved to Northern regions. A colder climate forced people to create their own circumstances. We suggest malaria is connected to moving from being a victim of circumstances to learning to master them.

We can imagine how Africa would thrive should malaria become history.

Malaria Treatment with PC240m

Report from Malawi 2004

Corrie Hiwat & Harry van der Zee

Due to reduced immunity AIDS-patients tend to have malaria regularly:

> "What was really impressive was the reduced incidence of malaria in patients once they started with PC1 (for HIV/AIDS). Most patients who had regularly suffered from malaria before taking PC1 simply told us that since taking the remedy, no malarial symptoms had occurred. This would indicate an almost immediate and strong improvement in the immune system. The incidence of malaria is season-linked, so we checked the figures at the centre for this. The largest number of patients coming to the centre for the treatment of malaria come in the months April to June, with May as the peak month. Most patients included in our data had started taking PC1 just before or in April. So the sudden reduced incidence of malaria in this group occurred despite the increase of malaria in the area ... [with 57 AIDS-patients the score (0-5 scale) for malaria went from 0.61 to 0.17; an improvement of 72.1% with a significance of 0.004]
>
> ... HIV-negative patients who suffered from malaria were treated with PC-Malaria, a remedy designed in a similar way to PC1, but now for the totality of the malaria epidemic. The results we saw from this remedy were similar to that of PC1. People who suffered from malaria regularly simply stopped having symptoms. In most of these cases we had a follow-up of about six months." [Hiwat & van der Zee, PC1 – Answer to AIDS in Africa, *Homœopathic Links*, Vol 17:4, 2004]

Report from Central African Republic
Klaus Schustereder, 2005

After more than 100 people treated (Nov 2005) with PC Malaria only:

- PC Malaria seems to be highly effective in people who already have a semi-immunity to malaria.
- I treated eight white people and about 92 black people. Most of the 92 black people came with acute malaria, but some of them came with terrible chronic effects caused by malaria.

It was interesting to observe that there seems to be a sequence to how the organism reacts or in other words, how PC Malaria seems to support the organism. First the organism reduces the chills. Usually this happens within 30 to 60 minutes. I recommend staying at the bedside of the patient and to observe the patient. Doing this will teach you a lot and you will get an idea about the tremendous healing force within us, as soon as we start supporting the organism in a way that the organism itself can solve the problem. The second step is a more or less strong perspiration. People usually seem to feel much better when they can perspire. This mostly happens after 30 to 90 minutes.
Headache is a common symptom in malaria and people suffer a lot from it. Unfortunately headache is the last symptom that disappears. This can last up to six to twelve hours. Other symptoms usually associated with malaria, like muscle and joint or back pain are reduced clearly within the first two to three hours. There is another observation which once more underlines the importance of fever. In some patients, not all of them, I guess about 20%, I could observe a rise of the fever up to one degree compared to the fever before PC Malaria. This, according to my observations, seems to happen within one to two hours after starting the treatment. Despite the rise of the fever, patients usually said they felt better.

Conclusions Schustereder:

- Patients say PC240m is superior to everything they had before. (Chinin)
- I sell the remedy for less than one euro (five times cheaper than Chinin treatment)
- PC Malaria has no side effects
- The application is easy (Chinin is often given by infusion)
- In my opinion this is exactly what developing countries need

Case example 1
Klaus Schustereder, Central African Republic

A 27-year-old lady, married, has two children, suffers from a pain in the left ovary. It started with a strange feeling in both legs about three weeks ago. She describes the feeling like a little animal that creeps around in her legs. During the last weeks this feeling ascended from the legs to the lower abdomen. It annoys her day and night. During the night, she says, she cannot sleep.
The physical examination shows a spot in the left lower abdomen, maybe an adnexitis. I ask her, if she suffers a lot from malaria.
She says, she had malaria the last time in 2003 but not the last two years. Before 2003 she had malaria regularly.

I give her PC Malaria, because I read in a book once, people who had malaria suffer from a feeling which is like: a little animal creeping around in the body.

Follow-up:
A week later she came again and tells me, she can sleep now and the strange feeling is almost gone. There is still a pain in the lower abdomen, but she is much better.
Later also the pain in the lower abdomen has gone.

Case example 2
Klaus Schustereder, Central African Republic

Yesterday a man came to see me. Somebody, he says, in the family has got malaria. When I arrive at the house, I see a 35-year-old man lying in front of the house. He has got chills and sweats on the head. He tells me he can hardly move. The back aches and the joints and muscles are painful. The head is painful. He tells me he has already taken Paracetamol and Chinin. Temperature is 38,6. I give him PC Malaria.

Follow-up:
After 1 hour the joint and muscular pain is almost gone. He has a bit of a headache on the occiput but generally feels well. He has no chill. No appetite. No vertigo. After taking the temperature he looks at the thermometer and is surprised to have 39.8. He tells me he does not feel as though he had an almost 40 degree temperature. His skin is hot and he tells me his perspiration disappeared five minutes after taking the remedy the first time. After taking the remedy the second time he feels better than after taking Chinin for two days. He is surprised.

I explain to him that the fever kills the parasites. He understands well and says he will not take paracetamol. Since he lives 100 meters from our house I go there every hour. After three hours he still has 39.8. After four hours still 39.8, but he walks around and feels pretty good. After five hours still the same. After six hours, for the first time his temperature dropped to 38 degrees. He has talked with friends and he asks me if I could tell them more about the medication and how the organism reacts. He seems to be a really clever guy.
When I go there the last time for the day, about eight or nine people are sitting around a fire. My patient is one of them and they talk and wonder. He has been eating meanwhile. It is 9.30 p.m. When I saw him for the first time it was 2 p.m.

Cases like this malaria case from June this year, I saw a lot.

Case of cerebral malaria
Klaus Schustereder, Central African Republic

Eight-year-old boy is in coma for two days; nothing helps to get him out of it. He is given PC Malaria every hour.

Follow-up:
He wakes up the next morning and as a complementary next prescription gets *Hyoscyamus.*

18-month-old boy with malaria
Klaus Schustereder, Central African Republic

One of the nurses comes to me to tell that the father of an eighteen-month-old child does not have enough money for the malaria treatment of his child. I tell them to bring the little one to the children's ward. The lab result confirms malaria as does the clinical observation. There is another child in the children's ward, also with malaria. There is no money for regular medication, so I give the little one PC Malaria. It has a 41-degree fever. I tell the nurse to give the drops once every hour and hope she will do that. Without medication I have seen quite a few children die.

Follow-up:
The next morning I see the boy. The temperature has gone down to 37 degrees; he has a good appetite and sits up in his bed. [The other child with malaria that had been given chinin in allopathic doses still had a fever of 39 degrees and diarrhoea.] I tell the mother to stay another day and in case everything is fine tomorrow, she can go back home. Next day everything is still fine and they go back home. I asked 500 francs for the treatment. If we had treated her child with chinin and paracetamol it would have cost her at least 3000 francs (local currency).

Report by Bruce Frayne (Kenya/South Africa)

If PC1 is the miracle it seems to be from what I have read, then this needs to be become mainstream. As an aside, I took PC1 (in the version that combined remedy for AIDS, TB and malaria) for malaria recently, and within hours I was well again – I still have trouble believing the results , as I have never seen anything quite like it.

I was born in Africa and have been exposed to malaria most of my life, perhaps explaining why the remedy worked despite my being white. Although I have lived in and regularly visit malarial areas, I have never actually had the disease, so contracting it recently was the first. I was not near any medical facility so was sitting it out for a couple of days until I would be back in town, when I remembered that I had PC1 with me (quite by chance). So when I took the PC Resonance as the first option and improved so rapidly, I was both amazed and delighted. Within 24 hours I was pretty close to 100%, and have not had a relapse of any kind.

Report Adjoa Margaret Stack
Ghana September 2007

Dear Peter and Harry,

Sorry for the long delay. But, here's some information on the cases I treated with PC240m this summer.

In total, I treated 196 people at the two clinics I ran this summer. Of those, 57 cases were malaria. Out of the malaria cases, 21 were treated with PC240m. My criteria was; emergency cases and heavily suppressed ones (injections).

Here is a brief outline. They are listed by age/sex [8M= 8years old, male]

Cases with follow-up:

8M: 5 drops every 15 mins. Completely recovered after five doses. Never saw the patient again.

3M: 5 drops every 15 mins. Better after two doses, came back next day, gave two doses again.

8M: 5 drops as needed – sent him home with medicine. He dosed every 30 minutes up until midnight then slept. Needed the remedy for heat at night for three days – after that fully recovered.

4F: treated over four days as needed, patient never fully recovered so I finally worked her case out to the remedy *Nux vomica* and after one dose 200C patient fully recovered.

38F: Best case! Chronic malaria for six months. Patient used PC240m over a period of ten days on and off as needed. She felt fully recovered from the malaria but symptoms of gonorrhoea came up and I treated those with one dose of *Thuja* 30C. After four days all symptoms were gone and she feels better than ever! Like she's 16 yrs old.

8M: five drops every 15 minutes – fully recovered after three doses.

2F: sent patient home with medicine – never heard from them again.

7M: same family as next two patients.

10F: same family – all children returned in two days fully recovered.

8F: sent home with medicine – see above

14F: five drops every fifteen minutes – after four doses patient broke out in sweat and wanted to eat.

40F: five drops every fifteen minutes – after two doses recovered.

2F: five drops every fifteen minutes – after four doses, recovered, no fever, no racing heart.

16M: five drops every fifteen minutes; after five doses – recovered but everything returned after two days very intensely – family took him in for injections – that's what they usually do.

12M: five drops every fifteen minutes – after two doses patient was better; sent home with medicine. Reported took four more doses before recovering.

15M: five drops every 30 minutes – patient fully recovered after two doses.

22M: patient used medicine for one day – no change, malaria got worse. Patient typically gets injections for malaria at least once or twice a year. He didn't respond to homeopathic remedies last year either.

20M: sent patient home with medicine. Reported taking it four times then better.

45F: five drops every 30 minutes – started at six pm and slept by ten pm, woke and took one dose in the morning. Felt fully recovered by twelve noon.

36F: five drops every fifteen minutes – left medicine with patient to use as needed; was recovered after two days.

39M: five drops every 30 minutes – after four doses patient left feeling better.

While in Burundi and East DRC Congo in 2008/2009 I (Harry) mostly treated malaria and PC240m for malaria was almost a sure hit. If a case did not respond I was just amazed, that's how confident I got in its effect. One case did not respond to a daily dose, then took the remedy every hour, and was fine the next day. So I had missed the acuteness of her state and instead had treated her as a chronic case. [ARHF Newsletter November 2008]

The visit to Burundi and Congo in 2009 was a follow-up of the visit of November 2008. The main purpose was to supervise the nurses that have been using the Amma4Africa Kit. Overall their experience is very positive and this made clear that indeed with just a few hours training medically qualified people easily implement the manual and successfully prescribe PC Resonances. The nurses confirmed the good results with HIV/AIDS and malaria witnessed in other African countries and felt very confident in prescribing the PCs for them. 80% of these cases do very well. If the remedies for these indications do not seem to work they look for obstacles to cure and usually find them in terms of wrong diagnosis, patients not taking the remedy properly or as with malaria that there are abdominal symptoms due to another cause (parasites etc.). [ARHF Newsletter February 2009]

Case of acute malaria

Harry van der Zee, Malawi 2012

My assistant in the clinic is starting to fall ill acutely around 10 AM. Within a few minutes she gets a high fever and has to stop working.

"Yesterday I was feeling very tired. This morning I did some duties as a housewife and came here to work. Just 15 minutes ago I'm feeling headache, I'm feeling fever, very much cold. I'm feeling very cold. And I'm feeling pain in the legs. And I'm feeling nausea, like I can vomit. I always have malaria, every two months. And I always take the malaria drug, lariam, and sometimes they can give me quinine."

She has been hospitalised with malaria several times, and had cerebral malaria three times. We prescribed her a mix of *Belladonna* C30 and PC Malaria, to be taken every 30 minutes.

Follow-up
Three hours later I visit her in her house to see how she is doing. She lies in her bed sweating heavily and is hyperventilating, which causes her fingers to get into a cramp.
"Whenever I have malaria my hands get like this. I can't handle anything, I can't get them straight."

I wonder whether a history of regular cerebral malaria causes an anxiety which in turn makes her breath fast. She asks for water with lemon, so I don't change the remedy and advice her to breath more calmly.

The next morning, before going to the clinic, I pay her a visit. To my surprise I find her outside looking completely healthy.
"The night was a little bit fine. All over the night my husband was waking up giving me the remedy,

every 30 minutes. Up till 3 AM when I really fell asleep. So when I wake up in the morning I get out and see my body is so fine. No headache, no fever, completely fine. In the past I would have to go to the hospital, and to be fine they would have to give me a quinine drip. Without that I would not be fine, I would stay with malaria for a week. And I would faint with malaria. I was just surprised that after taking PC Malaria every 30 minutes I'm just fine now. Early in the morning I said, "what's in the house so I can eat something? I want to eat." I'm fine, I'm feeling fine."

A case of splenomegaly
Harry van der Zee, East DRC Congo

N. is 14 years old and small for her age. Due to splenomegaly her abdomen is enormously enlarged and painful. Her spleen must weigh several kilos. She has malaria very often. As splenomegaly is one of the serious complications of malaria she is treated with PC malaria.

Follow-up after two months:
No more malaria. Her abdomen no longer hurts and is a little bit less swollen indicating that the spleen is becoming smaller in size. Although she has no more malaria the swelling of the spleen is reason to let her continue taking PC malaria.

Africa is a wonderful place to learn about the dynamics of diseases, of the forming forces of miasms, about the validity of homeopathic theory and about what does and does not work in practice. The following case is a great teaching.

A case of gonorrhoea and malaria
Harry van der Zee, East DRC Congo

C. is 35 years old and over the last few years has had malaria ten times in a year, with a range of chronic malaria symptoms, and also suffered from vaginitis with itching and discharge for five years (often caused by gonorrhoea).

Prescription: a combination of curiosity and lack of dropper bottles made me combine PC180g for gonorrhoea and PC240m in one bottle.

Follow-up after 5 days:
In response to the medication she felt a pain in her right shoulder extending to her head, which then went away within a day. The pain she had in the lower abdomen doubled in intensity for a short time and then went away together with the discharge. The itching is a lot better since the discharge has stopped. The headaches and vertigo have improved as well as the cramps she used to have all over her body. The pain in her joints is completely gone. Her head is still sensitive to the sun.

After four weeks:
All symptoms of chronic malaria and chronic vaginitis have gone. No malaria as yet.

After ten months:
Feels completely fine. No malaria. No vaginitis.

Comment 1: Despite the combination of remedies she responded according to the laws of healing. She had a short aggravation, and then was relieved of all symptoms and shows increased health with no malaria up to the latest point of follow-up.

Comment 2: In acute malaria PC240m should be given every 30-60 minutes until clear improvement is evident and then the intervals can be increased. Although in an acute attack a patient is supposed to experience relapses of the symptoms every 48-72 hours, once the treatment has started, patients are normally well within twelve hours and stay well. Besides having curative capabilities, the remedy also works prophylactically as once the acute attack is cured the usual short (eight to ten days) or long (two to sixty days) relapses do not occur. We have observed in several cases of chronic malaria that possibly typhoid or parasites is also present. On PC240m the majority of the symptoms disappear but pain in the abdomen may remain, for which complementary treatment is needed. PC302v is an option for that. It is not included in the Amma4Africa Kit and should be ordered separately.

Comment 3: We've observed several cases in which there is a relationship between malaria and gonorrhoea. In areas where malaria is endemic the immune system of healthy people is strong enough to prevent them from getting malaria. Gonorrhoea, and likely also the treatment of it with antibiotics, are possible ways of weakening the immune system, and several cases have been observed where people reported that they never had malaria until a couple of months following gonorrhoea. In those cases it is advisable to start with PC240m (malaria) to be followed by PC180g (gonorrhoea) as soon as the malaria symptoms have gone.

That one infectious disease can reduce immunity against another infectious disease has also been observed in sub-Saharan Africa with malaria and invasive non-typhoid Salmonella (NTS). NTS infection is a common and often fatal complication of Plasmodium falciparum infection. A mechanism in the human body that increases tolerance to malaria impairs resistance to NTS. [Cunnington, Nature Medicine, 18 Dec 2011]

East Africa malaria report
Stuart Deeks, UK

The story as noted down by the patient's mother in England.
F aged 47 consultant. East Africa. (African father, Canadian mother.)

2008: Contracted acute cerebral hepatic malaria. In coma for several days. Hospitalised for ten days. Treated with Artemisia.
2010: Second acute attack, and numerous milder episodes since 2008. The last one was early January 2011, when very busy. These were treated with Artemisia and in some cases antibiotics.
Attacks were preceded by intense work stress, low immunity and flu-like illness. Local conditions offer little or no protection against mosquito bites. Her situation has been described by doctors as potentially life threatening.

Began PC 240m remedy mid January 2011.

Follow-up:
Mid February – has had no further attacks or auras so far, despite heavy workload and tiredness. (Aura – a strange feeling of something coming on.) However no conclusions can be drawn from this till end of rains in September.
She has nine independent malaria strains in her blood at any one time.
She is rushed off her feet, and lacks support generally.
No close family nearby.
End of April 2011 – says that it is the rainy season now, and so far she is feeling fine. She has continued

to take PC 240m daily; it has been ten weeks.
June 2011 she is still malaria free.
Mother gives her insights in respect of the African situation:

Tanzania has long had an independent cultural position and close ties with China, who have encouraged localised use of Artemisia. Malarial support appears better there than in countries that rely on Western knowledge systems. Wherever Western medicine has dominated, malaria treatment and control have been reliant on chemicals. DDT was used to decontaminate swamplands, and quinine-based medicines, to which the mosquitoes have now adapted, to prevent and treat malaria infections.

Child with malaria
Rashid Rissasi W'orgene, Organisation CELA, DRC Congo

My child suffered from malaria and suddenly I said to the nurse not to give her any remedy, because I had with me a very effective remedy that I was going to give to my child and it was PC Malaria. After two days of treatment, the child was healed and up until the present she is not suffering anymore from that disease.

Offering cheap and effective treatment can also create problems like the following story shows. In order not to compromise the involved we've left out their names.

How success can complicate things
A story from DRC Congo

Close to where I take care of the ill people, at a distance of only ten metres, there is the Red Cross hospital.
In September, I received an invitation from the responsible nurse of that hospital. He sent a child to give me a note that read "Mr X, come to see me".
When I arrived, he said: "I have to talk to you. You know, this remedy from that white man of yours, this PC from that white man of yours, it makes that we don't have any ill people anymore."
In this village K. there were many cases of swamp fever, malaria, that made it the hospital's main business.

The Red Cross nurse continued: "we receive 100 to 150 ill people suffering from malaria per month. But this time ... Here is my report of the months of September until November. There is nothing. Here, look in my register!" He opened the register and was leafing through the pages, and we saw that there had been seven people suffering with malaria in the month of October.
He said to me: "Now, how will I pay the nurses? I have no more money."
It was malaria, the patients suffering from malaria that brought a lot of income to the hospital. "But since you have started to give PC, PC, PC, the malaria has finished in the village. What will I do, how can I pay the nurses?"

Offering the Red Cross Hospital free stock of PC240m was the way we decided to deal with this situation and turn it into a win-win situation.

Prophylaxis of Malaria

The PC Resonance for malaria we have tested as prophylaxis. Potentially other PC Resonances for infectious diseases could be tested for prophylactic use as well.

Malaria prophylaxis at a school

Reported by Harry van der Zee, DRC Congo, 2009

In Congo we had the opportunity to treat 600 children (mainly orphans) at a school. We treated for several indications of which the trauma of war and losing parents (from the war or AIDS) was the main one (See Part VIII). In respect to malaria we first gave PC240m to those children that had malaria regularly and after we left the teachers, gave them one dose every week. As a next step we asked the teachers to give all 600 children PC malaria as a prophylaxis – one dose of five drops every month.

Follow-up after 1 year:
The bishop supervising the school wonders whether they should stop the prophylaxis with PC Malaria as "malaria is no longer a problem". As malaria is endemic and all children keep being exposed we suggested to stop now and to continue the monthly doses as soon as there were indications that the incidence of malaria amongst the children was on the rise again.

Malaria prophylaxis at a day care centre

Reported by Harry van der Zee, Malawi, 2012

In Mzuzu the Mbawemi Women's Association provides day care to 305 orphans and children from very poor families. First all orphans were treated for the trauma of losing ones parents. Volunteers have been instructed on how to provide PC Malaria. Each child got one dose for seven days and then once every two weeks. The results were not available yet by the time this book was ready to be printed.

See appendix 5 for different available PC Resonances for treating and preventing malaria.

Poliomyelitis

Poliomyelitis is a viral disease that can affect nerves and can lead to partial or full paralysis caused by infection with the poliovirus. The virus spreads by direct person-to-person contact, by contact with infected mucus or phlegm from the nose or mouth, or by contact with infected faeces.

Risks include:

- Travel to an area that has experienced a polio outbreak
- Changing nappies after vaccination

There have been very few cases of polio in the Western hemisphere since the late 1970s. Occasional outbreaks would typically happen in communities that refuse vaccination. It's still common in parts of Africa.
There are three basic patterns of polio infection: subclinical infections, non-paralytic, and paralytic. Approximately 95% of infections pass quickly and unnoticed.
If the spinal cord and brain are involved disability can be severe.
Post-polio syndrome is a complication that sometimes develops thirty or more years afterwards. Weakness may get worse in muscles that were previously weakened and in other muscles.

Owing to vaccination programmes and improved hygiene Poliomyelitis has become a rare disease in developed countries. The PC Resonance for it was made in Africa to treat a case like the one below. It can be used to treat undesired effects of polio vaccination, acute poliomyelitis or Post Polio Syndrome.

Case of a 15-year-old boy

Klaus Schustereder, Central African Republic

> The boy is severely hindered by contractures due to poliomyelitis he suffered from as a small child. He walks with crutches and has much pain in the joints.
>
> *Follow-up:*
> Following PC Polio ten drops daily he of course remains crippled but the pains have dramatically improved and stayed better for the duration of my two-year-stay in the clinic.

Ringworm

Ringworm is a skin infection caused by a fungus not a worm! Ringworm can affect skin on the scalp, groin area also called jock itch, or feet also called athlete's foot. Often there are several patches of ringworm on the skin at once.

It can be passed from one person to the next by direct skin-to-skin contact or by contact with items such as combs, unwashed clothing, and shower or pool surfaces. One can also catch ringworm from pets that carry the fungus. Cats are common carriers.

The symptoms:

- Itchy, red, raised, scaly patches that may blister and ooze.
- The patches often have sharply-defined edges.
- They are often redder around the outside with normal skin tone in the centre.
- This may create the appearance of a ring.
- The skin may also appear unusually dark or light.
- When the scalp or beard is infected, bald patches appear.
- If nails are infected, they become discoloured, thick, and even crumble.

Ringworm is quite common also in Africa. As anything common depends less on an individual approach, a Genus epidemicus remedy for it can be safely used.

Case of a baby boy of three months old

Peter Chappell, Malawi

> One week after using ten drops of PC Ringworm daily there is clear improvement. When the boy is seen again three weeks later there is no ringworm anymore. Another seven months later he is still okay.

Scabies

Scabies (the seven-year itch) is a contagious skin infection caused by a tiny mite, Sarcoptes scabiei. This parasite burrows under the host's skin, causing intense allergic itching. The word scabies is derived from the Latin word scabere (to scratch). The disease in humans may be transmitted from objects or bedding (like mattresses, etc.), but is most often transmitted by direct skin-to-skin contact, with prolonged contact being more efficient. Initial infections of scabies require four to six weeks to become symptomatic. However, persons having recently been cured of the disease, upon re-infection, may manifest symptoms within as little as 24 hours. Because the symptoms are allergic, their delay in onset is often mirrored by a significant delay in relief after the parasites have been eradicated.

Scabies mites prefer thin hairless skin, and concentrate between fingers, toes, on wrists and in skin folds, avoiding callused areas. Infants may be infected over any part of the body, as may also immuno-suppressed persons.

Crusted scabies, formerly known as 'Norwegian scabies,' is a more severe form of the infection often associated with immuno-suppressed hosts. In crusted scabies, the mites, numbering thousands in such cases, cause scaly rashes and thick crusts of skin.

The characteristic symptoms of a scabies infection include intense itching and rashes. The symptoms are caused by an allergic reaction of the host's body to mite proteins.

The symptoms are usually experienced as being worse at night, and the itch is also made worse by warmth, such as bathing in warm water. In most hosts, the trails of the burrowing mites show as linear or s-shaped tracks in the skin, often accompanied by what appear as rows of small pimple-like mosquito, or insect bites.

The onset of the symptoms typically appear two to six weeks after infestation for individuals never before exposed to scabies. For those having been previously exposed, the symptoms can appear within several days after infestation.

Homeopaths generally connect scabies to Hahnemann's concept of Psora, but several authors have shown its connection to leprosy, and in that sense, although not true in the actual sense, scabies could be seen as a superficial form of leprosy.

Scabies and Psora

As mentioned earlier we feel that Hahnemann's main three miasms – Psora, Sycosis, Syphilis – which we suggest to call META-MIASMS – should not be seen in a narrow sense as representing the long-term effects of these diseases alone. So the Specific Miasm of scabies may belong to the META-MIASM of Psora but Psora includes many more Specific Miasms.

The birth process [van der Zee, 2000, 2007] can be used as a blueprint of human individuation. The onset of labour is connected with the departure from paradise and the onset of separation from the mother. The corresponding miasm is Psora. The prenatal unity is broken and the world of opposites comes into existence. The expulsion from paradise is connected with the myth of the fallen angel and Lucifer. In the individuation process Psora is connected with the development of the persona. Developing self-confidence through gaining the ability to take care of basic needs is a theme in Psora. Qualities developed in this phase are those of curiosity, initiative, expectation and practical knowledge. Shame and insecurity form the shadow side. It is a state of trying and learning through failure and success. The beggar is symbolic of this phase and the kingdom it is chiefly connected with is the mineral kingdom.

Many if not all cultures know the concept of paradise, a situation where man is still living in complete harmony with God and with his surroundings, nature. Everything is God-made and since everything is perfect and man is lacking nothing, there is no need for anything man-made. There are no demands on mankind.

In a healthy pregnancy free from traumatic occurrences the period in the womb resembles paradise. Everything is perfect, and the foetus is free from any desires, since all it could desire is already there even before the idea of 'want' might come up. The temperature and nurturing are constantly just as they should be. The world of opposites, like hot or cold, or overeating and famine, is unknown. There is no developed personality or individual identity, no sense of I and you, internal and external, only a vast ocean of unity. Just as a drop in the ocean doesn't feel separate from the total ocean, the child is completely one with the mother.

Sulphur, Hahnemann's main psoric remedy, signifies Lucifer, the fallen angel that induced in men the curiosity to discover the world of opposites resulting in the expulsion from paradise. The price for this is men's basic delusion, namely that s/he is separated. The onset of labour signifies the onset of separation from the maternal unity, paradise. The chemical changes and muscular contractions change the seemingly eternal paradisiacal state into an increasingly unpleasant one. The circumstances are no longer perfect, thus introducing the concept and experience of 'want', of shortage. Psychologically speaking, the experience of lacking comfort in this phase of birth forces the individual to develop skills in order to provide for himself. This is the very psoric phase of trying, of failure and success, of insecurity and shame at one's inadequacies. It's also a phase of great dependency still. During birth it is still the mother providing all the basic needs, as in the first phase of life, the weeks and months following birth. Life can be considered as the real performance for which birth is the blueprint and final rehearsal.

The role model for a lack of initiative in taking responsibility for one's own life is the beggar, Psora's main character. Even *Sulphur*, with all his abilities and seeming self-confidence, tends to look like a beggar. It is as if he philosophizes about life and how mankind left paradise and how to move on from there but fails to complete a simple practical task like buttoning his shirt properly. *Psorinum* is the homeopathic equivalent of want, with the body lacking heat and food, and with no money in his purse to do something about it.

In terms of relationships the psoric phase is self-centred, for which Eros is a proper term. A partner or sex is something present or lacking, which is essentially a mineral way of keeping the accounts of one's life.

The discomfort of scabies forces one to launder one's clothes, wash the body, make the bed, etc. To improve the quality and ease the discomfort of life one has to exert oneself. In the history of mankind this was especially the case in the colder regions, where most inventions took place and the industrial revolution started. Tropical islands, with shores full of fish and co-

conuts dropping into an outstretched hand, resemble paradise and stimulate the development connected to the psoric miasm much less strongly. To create change under less favourable circumstances men had to develop qualities like curiosity and initiative, to learn a wide variety of skills, and had to gather knowledge about plants, animals and all kinds of materials. All qualities connected to the psoric phase of development and therefore to psoric remedies, just like the pathological side of the coin – of failure, ridicule and shame – are psoric motivators to perform better.

Certainly if it is her first delivery the onset of labour can be connected to psoric uncertainties in the mother. Is she ready for it? Will she be able to deliver? What if she starts screaming? What would people think? She depends a lot on the partner, midwife or mother supporting her.

In Jungian psychology we can connect Psora with the development of the persona. It is the result of a process of adaptation and a compromise between the demands of the individual and those of society. If the latter are strong the individual will hide most of its true nature behind the mask of the persona. The persona has a lot to do with how we come across on many levels, a strong psoric theme and sensitivity.

PC Treatment for Scabies

Like ringworm, scabies is another eruption still quite common in Africa and therefore one of the early PC Resonances made is the one for scabies.

Case of scabies

Klaus Schustereder, Central African Republic

> For four months a boy has itching that keeps him awake all nights. On investigation the diagnosis is scabies.
>
> *Follow-up after PC290s for scabies:*
> The itching is gone already the next day.
> In the following days the eruption also disappears.

Streptococcus

Streptococcus is a genus of spherical Gram-positive bacteria belonging to the lactic acid bacteria group. They grow in chains or pairs, hence the name from Greek (streptos), meaning easily bent or twisted, like a chain (twisted chain). Streptococci are oxidase- and catalase-negative, and many are facultative anaerobes.

In addition to a strep throat, certain Streptococcus species are responsible for many cases of meningitis, pneumonia, endocarditis, erysipelas and necrotizing fasciitis. However, many streptococcal species are non-pathogenic. Indeed, Streptococci are a necessary ingredient in Emmentaler ('Swiss') cheese. Streptococci are also part of the normal commensal microbiome of the mouth, skin, intestine, and upper respiratory tract of humans.

A case of cystitis
Harry van der Zee, Netherlands

A 63-year-old woman is under treatment since 1992. For fourteen years she has responded well to climbing potencies of *Mercurius solubilis* for headaches, back pains, throat infections, abdominal pains and the fears and trauma due to a violent husband she divorced in 1976. With once or twice a year a dose of *Mercurius* she was doing very well, and the indications for treatment were increasingly less severe, indicating cure and not suppression.

January 2007 I see her again. In the past year she has had cystitis a couple of times, went to her family doctor and got antibiotics. Since abdominal pains were recurring, a vaginal smear was done and it appeared she had a chronic streptococcus infection. Since also throat infections were a recurring complaint the conclusion was clear that, despite good results with *Mercurius*, infections were still recurring and a miasmatic approach was indicated to tackle Streptococcus pyogenes.

January 8 2007 she received PC410k for Streptococcus pyogenes, five drops daily.

Follow-up:
After two days her abdomen started to feel distended, accompanied two days later by a drawing sensation in the lower abdomen and burning pain in the vagina. After one week she got cramps in the stomach and the drawing sensation increased, followed by diarrhoea the next day. A day after that her abdomen and throat started to improve, and one day later the pains were much better.

Again two days later she has a strong pain in the middle of the chest extending to the throat followed by chills all over the body. The next day the pains in the vagina and lower abdomen are practically gone and she stops taking PC410k.

Three months later the burning pain and the drawing sensation start again. She starts taking the PC Resonance again and within three to four days the complaints subside where otherwise they used to increase to a much more severe level, which, if she went to the GP, led to a course of antibiotics.

Syphilis

Syphilis is a sexually transmitted disease caused by the spirochetal bacteria Treponema pallidum. The primary route of transmission of syphilis is through sexual contact, however it may also be transmitted from mother to foetus during pregnancy or at birth resulting in congenital syphilis.

The signs and symptoms of syphilis vary, depending on which of the four stages it presents in (primary, secondary, latent, and tertiary). The primary stage typically presents with a single chancre, secondary syphilis with a diffuse rash, latent with little to no symptoms, and tertiary with gummas, neurological, or cardiac symptoms. Diagnosis is usually via blood tests. It can be effectively treated with intramuscular penicillin G.

Syphilis Miasm

Syphilis as a miasm is very interesting to study, as until it was imported from the Americas the disease was not known in Europe. Its influence on Western culture is marked as for instance the syphilitic eruptions in the throat area caused people to wear high collars and may be the original reason for men wearing ties. The horrible smell of the eruptions stimulated the perfume industry and the loss of hair brought wigs in vogue as well as the colouring of eyebrows of prostitutes (which nowadays woman still do), to cover up the loss of hair. It was the megalomania of European kings that caused men like Columbus to sail the oceans with the intention to discover and conquer more land and to bring its gold and other valuables back. So syphilis and imperialism are closely connected. In Europe the syphilis epidemic broke out amongst royalty where infidelity was high and courtesans the norm and then followed the armies and their entourage – the prostitutes – to further spread over Europe.

The whole expression 'survival of the fittest' is syphilitic in nature and has become an unquestioned belief underlying current society.

The destructive aspects of the miasm and its connection to unlimited wealth and power may be easily recognized as being part of the current crises the world is struggling with – bank, economy, environment.
The destructive forces of fanatic religiosity and terrorism are also very syphilitic by nature.

Within the cosmic process of unfolding human potential the META-MIASM Syphilis is connected with the mythological ascent from Hell and the propulsion phase of birth [van der Zee 2000, 2007]. In the birth process the dynamic between mother and child in the syphilitic phase is one of synergism (as opposed to antagonism in the sycotic phase). Both are actively working towards birth. In mythology Syphilis and the journey through the birth canal are expressed as a death-rebirth struggle, the killing of the dragon, ego death and crucifixion. In Jungian psychology the concepts of the anima and animus, the magna mater and the wise old man are connected to the evolutionary force behind Syphilis. It is characterised by self-assertion and expressed in qualities like creativity, courage, altruism, responsibility, service and love. The pathological shadow side of Syphilis is expressed in increasing isolation, egotism and animosity. The king is symbolic of this phase and the animal kingdom mostly identified with it.

In the birth process the propulsion of the baby through the birth canal is a phase in which there is synergy between mother and child, and the mother and those present to assist her. Passivity (dilatation phase – Sycosis) is turned into its opposite - great activity and energetic effort. Once the baby has entered the birth canal a point of no return is reached. This is the most dangerous phase of birth, mainly for the baby, but also for the mother. This is where life and death meet, causing Grof to call this the death-rebirth struggle. The strong emphasis on syphilitic remedies regarding physical fluids and excretions like blood, mucous, urine and faeces, especially related to delusions and abnormal behaviour, strengthens the notion that the Syphilitic miasm fits the end phase of birth where all these excretions are usually encountered by the baby on its way into life.

Mirroring what happens when no synergy is reached during the propulsion phase of birth, a lack of synergy in society causes death and destruction. Syphilitic pathological features like egotism, isolation and animosity have to be overcome to reach altruism, responsibility, service and love.

On an individual level this means taking responsibility for one's own life by creatively using the qualities retrieved from one's shadow in the previous phase. On a society level, syphilitic remedies fit those that take responsibility to lead and serve society. Ultimate isolation and the threat of assassination is their fate if they use their qualities and position solely for their own means and those of their clan. Great respect, admiration and love is their reward if they succeed in rising above their ego and offer their qualities and use their position for the good of all. 'What is best for all is best for the self' is a syphilitic lesson not easily learned.

Where Psora is connected to the expulsion from paradise, the Syphilitic miasm is connected to the expulsion (or perhaps rather, in terms of birth, literally 'narrow escape') from hell, Sycosis. The hopelessness of the sycotic situation, where suffering is never-ending with literally no way out (closed os uteri), is turned into a dangerous endeavour with the hope of success and survival, provided one invests everything in the battle through the birth canal. This translates itself into the body posture of mother and child. While the mother pulls herself together to push the baby out, the baby coming from a bend position to endure the contractions during the dilatation phase straightens its back both physically and psychologically. Where the contractions during dilatation seem never to end, now there is physically an opening out of it, and the awareness that usually within about half an hour the pains will cease, and the reunion of mother and child embracing each other: the happy end.

After the integration of the anima in a man and the animus in a woman the creativity that has now become available needs to be used for a higher purpose than the satisfaction of the ego. This is the syphilitic challenge. In Jungian terminology the acceptance and influx of spiritual inspiration and guidance turns a woman into magna mater, and a man into the wise old man.

If a society is not able to encounter its collective shadow, or to forgive those that have sinned against its rules, and acknowledge its responsibility for the criminal conduct of some of its members, destruction will be its fate. Injustice will prevail, ultimately leading to a rising up of the oppressed. The prisoners will kill their guards, break down the walls, or freedom fighters will attack the establishment. Thus an inability to heal sycotic pathology, either in an individual or a society, tends to lead to syphilitic pathology.

The role of the ruler or king is closely connected to Syphilis. The appreciation of a ruler depends on whether egoistic or altruistic motives determine his reign. Starting with the paradisiacal role of prince (e.g. Gautama) or princess, to beggar, prisoner and revolutionary the status of king or queen is now reached. The heritage is earned by going through the initiation process of individuation, and from having experienced the opposite of power and wealth, a humble attitude of service is the healthy result, and despotic exploitation the pathological one.

With regard to the end of the propulsion phase Stanislav Grof made an interesting observation in many of the cases he gathered of reliving birth. After having given everything to bring birth to a positive end, many experience a short moment where it feels as if everything has failed, and death is imminent. This idea of total existential failure is strong in a syphilitic remedy like *Aurum*. Everything is lost, and total physical and psychological breakdown and destruction is the unavoidable finale. The curtain falls, the lights go out. The End.

Considering the current crises in the world and their syphilitic nature we can predict the logical outcome will be like a death-rebirth experience where it may look like life on this planet comes to an end and only at the last moment the new man will arise from its ashes as a phoenix bird. A mankind that has overcome the delusion of separation that underlies syphilitic behaviour and instead shows the qualities that will emerge as written above.

Treatment of Syphilis

More than 90% of cases occur in the developing world. In diagnosed cases patients need to be advised to follow regular treatment. Because of the miasmatic disturbance and long-term effects homeopathic treatment is advised as well, even if (apparently successful) treatment with antibiotics took place many years ago.

A case of syphilis 1

Klaus Schustereder, Central African Republic

A man came with his wife to see me. They both suffered from sleeplessness, fatigue and very loud bowel movements. They both had Syphilis three years ago. They have these symptoms since their syphilis and never really felt well again. Both were then treated with antibiotics.

I gave them PC293v for syphilis.

Follow-up:
Already on the same night they slept well. There are no bowel sounds anymore and the fatigue disappeared. There is still a pain in the left lower abdomen. Both had exactly the same direction of cure and both still have a pain in the left lower abdomen. Generally they felt much better.

Later all symptoms completely improved.

A case of syphilis 2

Klaus Schustereder, Central African Republic

A 31-year-old man had syphilis ten years ago. Now he has intensive pain in the bladder during urination and burning in the urethra, increased frequency of urination during night. The symptoms are worse when he works in the fields and especially when it is sunny in the afternoon. He usually doesn't sleep because he goes to the toilet very often.

Follow-up:
After the PC Resonance for syphilis – he took the remedy for ten days – no more pain in the bladder, no burning, no increased frequency.

A case of syphilis

Harry van der Zee, Malawi

A 30-years-old man; he works in the maize mill.
"4 years ago they found I had syphilis for which I was given an injection. Now I have an eruption at the penis and pus is coming out. I feel pain on passing urine. I have no sexual power and have not had sex for three weeks now."

Prescription: PC 293v for syphilis, 5 drops daily and advice to send his wife for treatment as well and to use condoms.

Follow-up after 2 weeks
"The discharge of pus has stopped and urination is no longer painful. There is still an itching eruption at the foreskin, but first there were many sores, now only a few.

First I had no desire for sex, but now I have a lot, but I'm still using condoms. First the desire was very little but now I can have sex 2-3 times per day."

Toxoplasmosis

Toxoplasmosis is a parasitic disease caused by the protozoon Toxoplasma gondii. The parasite infects most warm-blooded animals, including humans, but the primary host is the cat family. Animals are infected by eating infected meat, by ingestion of faeces of a cat that has itself recently been infected, or by transmission from mother to foetus. Although cats are often blamed for spreading toxoplasmosis, contact with raw meat is a more significant source of human infections in many countries, and faecal contamination of hands is a greater risk factor.

Up to one third of the world's human population is estimated to carry a Toxoplasma infection. In Western countries seroprevalence among women of childbearing age (15 to 44 years) is around 10%.

During the first few weeks post-exposure, the infection typically causes a mild flu-like illness or no illness. Thereafter, the parasite rarely causes any symptoms in otherwise healthy adults. However, those with a weakened immune system, such as AIDS patients or pregnant women, may become seriously ill, and it can occasionally be fatal. The parasite can cause inflammation of the brain and neurologic diseases, and can affect the heart, liver, inner ears and eyes (chorioretinitis).

A case of chronic headache and toxoplasmosis

Harry van der Zee, Netherlands

April 2003 a 30-year-old mother of three children consults me because she is suffering from headaches. She has red hair and makes a lively and cheerful impression. She has had headaches for as long as she can remember. "It runs in the family", she says. Also she is often tired.
As a young child a brain scan was made to look for a malignancy that might cause the headaches. If she has a headache "everything is pounding and hurting". Behind the eyes she will feel a pressure. During walking she needs to hold her head with her hands. The headache is clearly worse motion. Also stooping makes it worse. She prefers to sit or lie down, but with three young children of whom one is hyperactive and later is diagnosed to have PDD-NOS (most common form of autism), taking the rest she desires is not always possible.
A hot shower helps. The headache decreases "and it brings my mind to rest". A cold east wind can aggravate her headaches.
"If in the morning I have a headache on rising it will stay with me until the evening." The headache can also start later on in the day.
If she doesn't sleep enough she has more headaches, and taking a nap in the afternoon ameliorates a present headache.
During headaches she is irritable.
At puberty she had to study hard to get good marks, so she would be studying until late in the evening. The level was actually too high for her, "but I had started it and wanted to finish it". Besides that she had to travel three to four hours every day, because the type of religious school her parents wanted her to attend was far away from where she lived.
Later, when she trained to become a teacher, she had less headaches. The studies were easier for her, and since the school was near she could go by bike.
In recent years the headache can start in the neck and then extend over the head to the eyes.

"I get stressed easily. I like to do a lot of things, too many, and I'm too stubborn to let go of some of my activities. So I get stressed about how to manage it all, and I have notes hanging everywhere in the house to remind me of the things I need to do. I can't do things half-heartedly, but am rather a perfectionist. I want to do things myself so I know they will be done right, and if they go wrong I can blame myself. If I do something I really go for it.

"I get a headache if I can't oversee everything. I work in a very structured way. If we have guests I make a lot of fuss beforehand. Everything out of the normal rhythm stresses me. I need to plan things."

The vision in her left eye is bad. Every one or two months she gets an inflammation of her retina leaving scar tissue behind. Also the right eye gets infected sometimes but has been less damaged. She sees black spots due to the scars, and can't read the blackboard from a distance. Lines are blurred and not sharp. During her second pregnancy her eyesight deteriorated a lot. A diagnosis of what is going on with her eyes has, as far as she knows, not been made. Later in a letter from the ophthalmologist I read that at that time it was diagnosed as uveïtis posterior of the left eye eci (without a known cause). Later the name choroiditis possibly caused by diffuse retinal pigment epitheliopathy. In another letter toxoplasmosis is mentioned again as a possible cause.

She can fall asleep any time of the day. If she sits on the couch she often falls asleep, and also if travelling by car or train she dozes off easily. "I can't stay awake." If reading a book in the evening she always falls asleep.

When the children were younger she was very sensitive to what other people would think of how she raised them. She would easily feel she wasn't doing things right. Also in discussions she would easily feel that she was not knowledgeable enough about the subject and that others would think her to be stupid.

She resembles her father most. "He is a great person; also very perfectionistic." He is a history teacher and also does all kinds of other activities which he works on until night.

Her mother was always tired, but also always available and busy caring for the children. She is the second of two girls. The eldest sister has quite an explosive character, and she had the role of mediator in the family. Having peace in the house was important. She would respond to her sister calmly. "My mother and sister could say rude things and hurt people without being aware of it. I was easy-going, quiet and shy. My teachers never knew who I was. In a group I will never speak from fear of saying something silly. People didn't hear me or see me.

Her husband is five years older. He is her first love and being rather sloppy, very opposite to her.

She is chilly.
She likes bread, sweets, chocolate, chips.
She dislikes red beets and bell pepper.
Sleeps on her abdomen with her hands under her abdomen.

She dreams about her youngest son dying. "If I dream I startle very much. About things that could have happened in daily life concerning the home or the family. For instance about burglars.

During her menses she used to be very nauseous and have a lot of pain. Because of that she started using contraception at a young age.

Her faith in God is very important to her. "It is a great feeling to know that I am a child of God. Also the church community is important. To enjoy together all the gifts of God, and to be active together for the church."

Analysis:

A repertorisation suggested *Aurum, Silica, Sepia, Natrum muriaticum, Conium, Nux vomica, Calcarea carbonica, Glonoinum, Bryonia, Phosphorus* and *Belladonna*. Combining the commitment to the church community with her headaches *Sanguinaria* also seemed an option. None of these remedies were convincing though. I prescribed *Calcarea phosphorica* 200K for her, since one of her children responded well to it, since *Calcarea carbonica* and *Phosphorus* both came up high and because it fitted her idea that others might think she cannot study well and is stupid. Besides that, on asking whether she liked meat she answered that she especially loved bacon, and she confirmed her fear of thunderstorm.

Follow-up after five weeks:
Following the remedy she had a lot of headaches for a week. Then for three weeks, despite a busy period, no headache at all. Also after the remedy both her eyes got infected. In the mean time the right eye is back to normal.

Plan: wait.

Three months later:
She has had quite a lot of headaches again. Her tiredness is less though. She has stopped participating in the school board because it causes too much stress and therefore headaches. "I like doing it, but it is in my head day and night. I can't go easy with it if others don't do their part properly. I had to decide to stop, because it was just escalating. It is very hard for me to say no."

Plan: *Calcarea phosphorica* 200K

Three months later:
Again she had more headaches initially followed by a few weeks of no headaches at all. Now she has a headache every day but a bit more moderate. But as soon as there is something outside the daily routine, like having someone over for a coffee or going out for an evening, it is worse.

I conclude that the remedy is perhaps close but certainly not close enough. She relapses too quickly and the general improvement in the long run is rather because she skips things from her agenda than that she has internally improved. So I decide to ask her to tell me more about how she experiences the headache.

"It hinders me in my functioning. Because of it I am less happy, less cheerful. It is very frustrating. Consciously I minimise my activities and even then I still have headaches. That is just not nice. I want to be a cheerful mother. The headaches hinder me from enjoying everything."

Analysis:

The frustration due to the feeling of being hindered is a theme of the Rubiaceae. From that plant family *China* comes up strongest in the repertory. The following rubrics support *China* (MacRepertory using Complete 2005):

- Head; PAIN; Motion; agg. (180)
- Head; PAIN; Stooping; agg. (144)
- Head; PAIN; Mental exertion, from; agg. (150)
- Head; PAIN; Heat; amel.; hot; applications (27)
- Head; PAIN; Pressure; amel. (192)
- Vision; COLORS before the eyes; black; spots (102)
- Mind; CONSCIENTIOUS about trifles (100)
- Mind; DELUSIONS, imaginations; Unfortunate, he is (13)
- Mind; DELUSIONS, imaginations; Tormented, he is (5)
- Mind; DELUSIONS, imaginations; Work; hindered at, is (1)
- Mind; DREAMS; Death, of; family, in (23)
- Mind; DREAMS; Misfortune, of (69)
- Mind; DESIRES; Numerous, varies things (24)
- Generalities; FOOD and drinks; Sweets; desires (190)

China is not mentioned under retinitis or under inflammation choroid, but other problems of the retina are mentioned in the Materia Medica: “retinal asthenopia ... black spots before eyes ... anaemic retina”.

Prescription: *China officinalis* 200K (DD Chininum phosphoricum).

After three months:
All in all it is going very well. In three months time she only had a headache twice. This gave her the confidence to resume teaching, which she enjoys a lot. Despite that she has less need to take a nap in the afternoon. She also restarted her work for the school board, and even when she continued work until 12 p.m. this did not result in a headache. Her eyes are still the same, but have at least not deteriorated.
Her sleep is no longer restless and there have been no frightening dreams. She is less chilly, and while it is winter had to start wearing her summer nightgown. Never before was she so comfortably warm in the winter.
She has stopped hanging notes all over the house, and is less stressed if she can’t finish what she is working at.

Plan: wait.

Another month later:
Sleeping worse and also more headaches since a week, without a clear reason.

Plan: *China officinalis* 200K

Four months later:
Again a relapse and *China* 200K is repeated.

Three months later:
Her left eye is getting worse and that also causes headaches.

Plan: *China* 200K

Three months later:
Although she is on *China* for more than a year now the choroiditis continues every one or two months. Since her response to *China* for the rest of her complaints is very good my conclusion is that this choroiditis is beyond the range of what a constitutional remedy can do for her.
The ophthalmologist now confirms the diagnosis: Toxoplasmosis, most likely congenital.

PC toxoplasmosis

At this point there are several options. One is to give the toxoplasmosis nosode, another to, by repertorisation, look for a remedy for choroiditis that could complement *China*. Based on experiences in other cases I felt this case was a perfect example of one where a disease-specific remedy could complement the simillimum. I asked Peter to design a PC Resonance for toxoplasmosis. Soon I received the remedy that is since then available as PC303w.

Prescription: PC303w in liquid; five drops daily after banging the bottle five times.

Follow-up after one month:
The black spots have become smaller. This has never happened before. Until this remedy they would only get bigger each time the infection repeated. In the areas around the black spots she could only see black-and-white. This has changed, and she can see colours again in these areas.

Plan: continue PC303w 5 drops per day until there is no further improvement. Since some of the scars will probably stay and keep influencing her eyesight I didn't expect her eyesight to become completely normal. Because I wasn't sure whether taking the PC Resonance continuously would cause her to become less sensitive to it I choose to let her stop as soon as the symptoms stayed the same for some weeks.

Three months later:
Two months ago she stopped taking the PC Resonance since there was no more change. Since then her eyesight is stable and ever since starting the remedy she has had no attacks any more. Since a few weeks though her headaches have come back.

Plan: *China* 200K.

Four months later:
The headaches vanished soon after *China* and are still gone. A month ago though she had a choroiditis again and restarted taking PC303w.

How to dose the remedy for her was something I still needed to find out, since the experience with these disease-specific remedies was still very limited. The fact that she had no attacks for seven months where she used to have them every one or two months was remarkable, but knowing the scars these inflammations cause can most likely not be completely removed, I would prefer her having no more attacks period.

Plan: continue PC303w until there is no further improvement, and from that point on take the remedy periodically for one month as a prophylaxis followed by two months no remedy.

Two months later:
Headaches back, but no more chorioditis.

Plan: *China* MK

Four months later:
Again some headaches, but absolutely not as bad as it used to be before she started taking *China* more than two years ago. No chorioditis.

Plan: *China* MK

Five months later:
She has had no more inflammation of the eyes for a year now, so using the PC Resonance as an intermittent prophylactic seems to work well.

Plan: PC303w daily for one month every three months. China if indicated. Since the headaches are possibly also associated with the choroiditis due to congenital toxoplasmosis, giving disease-specific remedy prophylactic and the constitutional one as soon as indicated is, in my opinion, the best strategy for this case now.

There has been a *total follow-up of three years* since starting with PC Toxoplasmosis and she has done progressively well.

Tuberculosis

Tuberculosis or TB (short for tubercles bacillus) is found in mummies as old as 6,000 years. It became a major problem in the crowded cities of the early industrial revolution. At that time in Europe tuberculosis was a major cause of death and it was so endemic that practically everyone was infected.

TB is a common and in some cases deadly infectious disease caused by various strains of mycobacteria, usually Mycobacterium tuberculosis in humans. Tuberculosis usually attacks the lungs but can also affect other parts of the body. It is spread through the air when people who have active TB infection cough, sneeze, or spit. Most infections in humans result in an asymptomatic, latent infection, and about one in ten latent infections eventually progresses to active disease, which, if left untreated, kills more than 50% of its victims.

Regular treatment is difficult and requires long courses of multiple antibiotics. Contacts are also screened and treated if necessary. Antibiotic resistance is a growing problem. Prevention relies on screening programmes and vaccination.

One third of the world's population is thought to be infected with M. tuberculosis, and new infections occur at a rate of about one per second.

The distribution of tuberculosis is not uniform across the globe; about 80% of the population in many Asian and African countries test positive in tuberculin tests, while only 5–10% of the US population test positive.

Due to compromised immunity AIDS brought tuberculosis back in developing countries and it has become the main cause of death in African AIDS-patients. The following news item narrates its impact:

> **HIV-TB 'double trouble' warning**
> Story from BBC NEWS: http://news.bbc.co.uk/go/pr/fr/-/2/hi/health/7959399.stm
> Published: 2009/03/24 14:00:25 GMT © BBC MMIX
>
> "One in four TB deaths is HIV-related, twice as many as previously recognised, experts say. Co-infection remains a major challenge and more efforts are needed to spot and treat the two conditions in tandem, says the World Health Organization. HIV and tuberculosis services must be joined up if we are to achieve global disease control, warn disease experts. Despite TB killing more people with HIV than any other disease, in 2008 only 1% of people with HIV had a TB screen.
>
> Problems compounded:
> - HIV disables the immune system, leaving the body vulnerable to opportunistic infections like TB. In Sub-Saharan Africa, HIV has caused TB incidence to triple since the 1990s and in some countries 80% of TB patients are co-infected with HIV.
> - "TB is preventable, treatable and curable yet it kills close to two million people a year" (Archbishop of Canterbury Dr Rowan Williams).
> - In 2007, worldwide there were an estimated 1.37 million new cases of TB among HIV-infected people and 456,000 deaths. The situation is made more urgent by increasing rates of drug-resistant TB in areas with a high prevalence of HIV. Again, in 2007, an estimated 500,000 people had multidrug-resistant TB, but less

than 1% of them were receiving treatments meeting WHO's recommended standards.

- Dr Margaret Chan, Director-General of WHO, said: "These findings point to an urgent need to find, prevent and treat TB in people living with HIV and to test for HIV in all patients with TB. Countries can only do that through stronger collaborative programmes and stronger health systems that address both diseases."
- Another pressure is financing the measures in the current, unstable economic climate. "Now is the time to scale-up financing for effective interventions" (Dr Michel Kazatchkine of The Global Fund to Fight AIDS, TB and Malaria).
- The UK Coalition to Stop TB is urging Gordon Brown and world leaders attending the forthcoming G20 meeting to deliver on their funding pledges to stop TB and to scale up a coordinated and coherent response to TB-HIV.
- It estimates that an investment of US$14 billion would reduce TB deaths in people living with HIV by 80-90%."

The above is a painful example of how mainstream medicine, and its main organ the WHO, find themselves in a Catch 22 situation. Billions are spent on the treatment of diseases like TB with antibiotics, resulting in (often only temporarily) cures but also increasing therapy resistance, making the disease more malicious, the therapy powerless, and causing policy makers to demand more billions to invest in newly developed medicines ... that will only add a new spiral to the same hopeless process. We may only hope that many more people working in healthcare will witness results as reported below and come to realise the potential of homeopathy to truly answer the medical needs of our time.

Being one of the major epidemics on earth we asked Eileen Nauman to also make a shamanic journey to the Tuberculosis bacteria so we may possibly learn more about its dynamics. What came forward as essential to TB is that it is connected to TRUTH. The disease offers the individual the possibility to become still, turn inside, to find their inner suppressed truth, and to speak and live that truth. In Appendix 3 you find the journey and a detailed discussion of it.

In Louis Klein's book 'Nosodes and Miasms' we read:

> "In Chinese medicine, the lungs have to do with soul – the soul lifting energies upward – and this is the deeper meaning of the Tubercular miasm. Patients in this miasm are soulful individuals, swollen with great emotion and mental faculty (figuratively speaking). There is expectancy, a hope of greater connection on a soul level – expectations that, realistically, cannot consistently be satisfied in their lifetime. This intense feeling permeates everything that they do or think ... They will do anything to maintain this passionate connection and reach their soulful ideal – often acting from a compelling feeling that they must abdicate responsibilities even to the point of renouncing anything that might get in the way. They want to break free ... The romantic and passionate idealism can become a torment, experienced as a feeling of easy oppression and of restriction by circumstances which they have to fight to overcome.
> With any slight impingement, the idealistic bubble bursts, and we have the other aspect of the tubercular state – a feeling of being trapped easily. With this feeling, there comes active defiance or contrariness that can lead to active malicious behaviour ...
>
> The presence never seems to live up to the swollen ideal ... This gives the idea of being "burned out as a world traveller," but having a more sophisticated worldview as a result." [Klein, 2009]

Striving and hoping to establish a deeper connection on a soul level (Klein) is another way of saying a person desires to live and speak his inner truth (Nauman), as the one is an unavoidable consequence of the other.

PC Resonance for TB

There is an extensive number of tubercular nosodes and deciding between them demands advanced knowledge and skills. Even then finding the best fitting TB nosode does not automatically result in cure. Considering the results observed in Africa with PC300t for Tuberculosis – one effective remedy for the diagnosis TB – it would be worthwhile to test whether PC Tuberculosis can also replace the multitude of tubercular nosodes as an anti-miasmatic.

Case of a 40-year-old lady with TB

Klaus Schustereder, Central African Republic

She has used tuberculostatics for three months and nevertheless the cough and the pain in the chest remain the same. (Something observed a lot is also that people are better after six months treatment and only a few months later all complaints return.)

Follow-up after PC300t:
After one week there is no significant change yet. After two weeks the cough and pain have much improved.

In my experience with not too advanced cases of TB you can see results with PC Tuberculosis within days. If patients are on tuberculostatics and you add PC Tuberculosis this will speed the healing process.

In a case where a patient had TB and Malaria together I prescribed both PC Tuberculosis and PC Malaria. Already the next day the patient was a lot better.

Case of a 70-year-old lady with tuberculosis

Harry van der Zee, East DRC Congo

M is a 70-year-old woman who has had pulmonary tuberculosis for three years. Initially she was treated with antibiotics for six months and was okay for some time but then the complaints came back. She has a painful cough and coughs up blood every day. Her abdomen has become painful from all the coughing.

Prescription: PC300t (PC Tuberculosis) once daily 5 drops.

Follow-up after 5 days:
On coming home after the first dose she coughed up a lot of blood, much more than normal. That was the last time she coughed up blood. The cough started to become less painful and after the fourth day the cough completely stopped.

After ten weeks:
Still well, with no further cough.

Comment: Despite her age, this woman showed a remarkable cure, starting with an aggravation within hours after the first dose, followed by a very rapid cure. Usually it takes longer for a patient to become well and our advice now is to take the remedy two or three times daily until the symptoms have subsided. Especially in people with AIDS who often also have TB, along with many other infections, the patient may need more time to recover. If in a person with AIDS the symptoms of TB are most prominent, we advise starting with PC300t and to also give PC1 (for AIDS) as soon as the TB symptoms are clearly subsiding. In cases where AIDS-symptoms are most prominent we start with PC1 and I have observed that often the improved immune status is enough for the patient to clear tuberculosis on PC1 alone.

Typhoid

Typhoid fever, also known as typhoid, is a common worldwide illness, transmitted by the ingestion of food or water contaminated with the faeces of an infected person, which contain the bacterium Salmonella enterica enterica (Salmonella typhi). The bacteria then perforate through the intestinal wall and are phagocytosed by macrophages. The organism is a Gram-negative short bacillus that is motile due to its peritrichous flagella. The bacterium grows best at human body temperature.

This fever received various names, such as gastric fever, abdominal typhus, infantile remittent fever, slow fever, nervous fever, pythogenic fever, etc. The name of 'typhoid' was given by Louis in 1829, as a derivative from typhus. [Typhoid fever should not be confused with typhus, as the diseases are unrelated. Typhus is caused by Rickettsia, an obligate parasite that cannot survive for long outside living cells.]
The primary target of the disease is the intestine. It attacks through tissues that are a part of the immune system called Peyer's patches. These tissues on the inner surface of the intestine are normally the first line of defence against food and water-borne infection, but the typhoid bacterium subverts them. It does not have the cell surface features that normally trigger a defensive response but it can fool the cells of the patches to take it in without attacking it. The infected tissue becomes inflamed and the intestine begins to lose function, leading to diarrhoea or constipation. There may be bleeding of the intestine leading to bloody stools. In severe cases, the disease may punch holes in the intestine leading to peritonitis (infection of the abdominal cavity) and death.

The impact of typhoid fever falls sharply with the application of modern sanitation techniques.

With an estimated 16 – 33 million cases of annually resulting in 216,000 deaths in endemic areas, the WHO identifies typhoid as a serious public health problem. Its incidence is highest in children and young adults between five and nineteen years old. An outbreak in the Democratic Republic of Congo in 2004 – 05 recorded more than 42,000 cases and 214 deaths. [Typhoid fever. World Health Organization. Retrieved 2007-08-28.]

The chronic typhoid carrier state can occur following symptomatic or subclinical infections of Salmonella typhi. Chronic carriers of typhoid are, by definition, asymptomatic.

Transmission may occur person-to-person or by ingestion of food or water contaminated by the urine or faeces of acute cases or carriers. Humans are the only known reservoir for S. typhi. Among untreated cases, 10% will shed bacteria for three months after initial onset of symptoms and 2-5% will become chronic carriers. [The most notorious carrier of typhoid fever – but by no means the most destructive – was Mary Mallon, also known as Typhoid Mary. In 1907, she became the first American carrier to be identified and traced. She was a cook in New York. She is closely associated with fifty-three cases and three deaths. Public health authorities told Mary to give up working as a cook or have her gall bladder (where the bacteria houses) removed. Mary quit her job but returned later under a false name. She was detained and quarantined after another typhoid outbreak. She died of pneumonia after 26 years in quarantine.]

The first homeopathic medical school in the United States founded by students of Hahnemann in the late 1800's, gained recognition because of its success in treating typhoid and many other disease epidemics rampant at the time — including scarlet fever, cholera and yellow fever. [www.wholehealthnow.com/homeopathy_info/history.html]

Typhoid Miasm

[From 'Homeopathy and Birth Trauma', van der Zee 2007]
Rajan Sankaran places the Typhoid miasm close to the acute miasm since it is characterized by critical situations. Among the remedies he classifies under the miasm are *Bryonia alba, Nux vomica, Chamomilla, Rhus toxicodendron, Baptisia tinctoria* and *Nux moschata.*

If we look at the birth process being a universal blueprint of any process it is easy to see where the energy of these remedies is mostly expressed. The irritability and sensitivity to pain, touch and disturbance, like in *Bryonia, Nux vomica* and *Chamomilla*, are strongest close to full dilatation, so at the end of the sycotic phase. In this phase there is not only antagonism between mother and child, but the partner, midwife and nurse can also be seen as a cause of suffering, or a subject for projection. Full dilatation is also a critical situation, so in that sense there is still an analogy between the nature of the disease Typhoid and a sudden change, albeit not in connection with the acute miasm as Sankaran suggests (which in my analysis is connected to the actual moment of birth) but with the transition between dilatation and expulsion – full dilatation.

There can be no doubt as to the connection of *Chamomilla* with reaching full dilatation. The repertory and Materia Medica is full of symptoms connected with labour pains. The remedy is typical of anything needing to break through, whether a tooth, an infected ear, or the os uteri. I haven't seen a *Chamomilla* child during whose birth the mother didn't enter a *Chamomilla* state once getting close to full dilatation, including stamping their feet with anger, an aversion to lying down, anger towards everybody around, up to striking the gynaecologist, or cursing people and sending them out of the room.

Rhus toxicodendron fits fixation with a need for and improvement with movement, similar to the improved state of mother and child once full dilatation has been reached and active engagement in the birth process is needed.

One of the responses to strong pains in a situation one cannot change is dissociation, strong features of both *Baptisia* and *Nux moschata.* The idea that one can capture the body but never the mind is also in line with the idea of the prisoner. The body may be confined or even tortured, but the mind is free to roam where it wants to. It is not a real solution but more an escape inward instead of a break through outward.

In DRC Congo I (Harry) have regularly heard reports about typhoid and malaria being together present in one patient. Almost routinely abdominal symptoms, remaining after malaria had been treated successfully with PC240m, were considered as being due to typhoid. As typhoid normally runs a four-week course ending with cure, death or the patient becoming an asymptomatic carrier this diagnosis is most likely incorrect. Just as any form of fever or headache is rapidly called malaria, any form of diarrhoea, at least in East DRC Congo, is rapidly called typhoid.

The typhoid miasm though, follows the malaria miasm very well and the fact that both diseases are mainly seen in the same countries where malaria is endemic is meaningful. With malaria we discussed how people feel frustrated and as if they were imprisoned by tribal rules, taboos and ways. The boiled up frustration is burned up in bouts of malaria that also awaken a vision of an individual path. The typhoid miasm as a next phase signifies a break through and once the individual has been sufficiently able to define its own path and re-establish a new relation with the tribe its role would be considered fulfilled. The vehement energy of typhoid remedies like *Chamomilla* and *Nux vomica* signify the amount of energy needed to bring this transition about.

Like with other infectious/epidemic diseases "in cases who had Typhoid fever in their past, it is so obvious that they never really recovered and they all are still more or less sick. I get such a wonderful idea of miasms here. I think it could not be better." [Schustereder, Central African Republic]
The authors share the experience that in Africa one can observe how miasms leave their marks in patients as in no other place. Not only is it very common to be able to relate a chronic complaint to a history of malaria, typhoid, gonorrhoea, syphilis etcetera, which then, with the Genus epidemicus like PC Resonances, make for easy and reliable anti-miasmatic treatment, but also it can be observed how different infectious diseases can be related in a case history. Gonorrhoea preceding malaria is very common, and (possibly) typhoid complicating or following malaria as well. Their miasms viewed from an evolutionary perspective would also have to be placed in that sequence. The gonorrhoea miasm (the fixed situation that paralyses and frustrates) is followed by the malaria miasm (a vision of a way out of frustration) and as a next step by the typhoid miasm (a break through out of fixation).

Available PC Resonances for Infectious and Epidemic diseases

In the previous chapters we have restricted ourselves to indications on which we have received reliable reports.
For an extensive list of all available PC Resonances for infectious and epidemic diseases, see Appendix 5.

PART VIII

Practice of Treating Trauma

- Terminology
- Experiences in Working with Trauma
- Genus Traumaticus and Instructions
- Amma4Trauma
- Abortion Trauma
- Abuse Trauma
- Adoption trauma
- Birth trauma
- Genocide and War Trauma
- Injuries, burns and accidents
- Nagasaki and Hiroshima Atomic Trauma
- Natural catastrophes
- Sexual abuse and rape
- Shock Trauma
- Torture Trauma
- Unburied Relatives Trauma

Terminology

Trauma is an evolving field. Neurological studies with fMRI are revolutionising our understanding of this area. It used to be called Post Traumatic Stress Disorder but that's very specific, limiting and narrowing. We simply use Trauma, to mean psychological trauma (as well as physical trauma which has psychological components).

Experiences in Working with Trauma

Working in Africa with collective conditions like epidemic diseases and trauma, we have come to understand that in homeopathy we may over-emphasise the individuality of problems a patient presents with. The focus in homeopathic practice is often on finding 'the' simillimum, and despite Hahnemann's directions that without treating the miasms a case may not find real cure, this rarely is systematically practised. Many (if not all) individual problems are expressions of universal themes which can be traced back to the life, family or culture of the individual. We can and need to discover these miasmatic / epigenetic roots. The more time has passed between the epigenetic trauma and the current state, the more individualised the expression of it becomes. The epigenetic root may become overshadowed by the individual unique expression such that homeopaths no longer recognise it or act on it.

Unresolved trauma lies at the root of many chronic conditions. If we look at the language of Vital Sensation (the deepest way in which a patient experiences his state, for instance a sensation of being scattered in pieces – Sankaran[4]) these are expressions of trauma. These are sensations fitting a traumatic experience to a life form. It may therefore be expected that the Vital Sensation method will prove to give longer lasting results – something those experienced in practising it skilfully confirm, as the Simillimum thus found would combine the epigenetic root with the individual response to it.

An Individual Trauma can express itself in an Individual Disease. This is something we know from experience. For instance, an unresolved grief can be expressed in recurrent throat infections, or as a result of sexual abuse a woman can have recurrent bladder infections.

Trauma is hereditary (miasmatic). See also the work of Hellinger (www.hellinger.com). If we go back a few generations, there are lots of traumas that can be at the root of symptoms we come across in our patients. These include wars, periods of starvation, crashing stock markets, stillborn babies, rape, incest, and so on.

A Collective Disease can follow a Collective Trauma. A good example is cholera following the horrors of war. It is interesting to see for instance that *Cuprum* is a remedy fitting both war (the typical *Cuprum* state is that of a soldier) and cholera. Another example is the influenza that we mention elsewhere in 1918 at the end of the First World War. Millions of the most able men died (for no real reason) followed by a massive influenza epidemic requiring *Gelsemium* which cured most cases. And Gelsemium is a great remedy for grief. The flu may well have been an expression of grief. It killed 40 million people, ten times more than the war deaths. It also killed mostly fit and able people primarily, as did the war. The target and the effect similarities are important to see and understand. It is very easy to dismiss this as coincidence rather than cause and effect, and to misunderstand the way life works.

Of course there are also circumstances on the physical level like lack of clean drinking water that contribute to cholera epidemics, but that doesn't mean that trauma at the energetic level is not an essential part of the expression of the disease or susceptibility to it. Again the cause and effect is easy to dismiss if you think materialistically. By looking solely at material manifestations and circumstances, conventional medicine denies the role of energetic disturbances in many conditions. Let's not make that same mistake.

Besides that, we know from research that traumatic events cause malfunctioning of the immune system (Segerstrom and Miller, 2004[5]; Smith and Giannoudis, 1998[6]), so circumstances and susceptibility come together to create disease.

---

4 Sankaran, Rajan [2007] *Sensation Refined.* Mumbai: Homeopathic Medical Publishers

5 Segerstrom, Suzanne Ph.D., and Gregory Miller, Ph.D., How Stress Affects the Immune System, http://mentalhealth.about.com/od/stress/a/stressimmune604.htm

6 Smith, R.M. and Giannoudis, P.V., Trauma and the immune response, http://www.pubmedcentral.nih.gov/articlerender.fgci?artid=1296840

The language of the Vital Sensation (in homeopathy) is the language of Trauma. If we read all the different ways a vital sensation is expressed, this becomes very obvious. Whether it is being pressed together, falling to pieces, torn apart, exploded, scattered, and so forth, these are all very physical expressions of ways in which the integrity of an organism can be threatened. So the sensation of the deepest disturbance in an individual is trauma, and this trauma-based sensation is being expressed in chronic diseases.

There is commonly known homeopathic experience and practice here.

It is common homeopathic practice in physical trauma (which automatically engages our deepest survival instincts; physical trauma by itself is impossible) to start with *Arnica* and then follow up with for instance:

- *Hypericum* for nerve injuries
- *Calendula* in tooth extractions
- *Bellis perennis* in repeated injury of the soft tissue
- *Ruta* for ankle injury
- *Rhus toxicodendron* or *Bryonia* in knee injury
- *Ruta* or *Ledum* in eye injury
- *Hepar sulphuricum* in septic pus filled wound
- *Trillium pendulum* in pelvic complaints
- Surgery where necessary

Notice that none of this is personal and it's assuming that, especially in the acute phase, the human being at a very physical level of localised problems can be treated by Genus epidemicus-like methods (See Part I), the same remedy for everybody in the same situation irrespective of the person. This is what happens in homeopathic practice. For specific kinds of trauma most homeopaths select one remedy from a relatively small group of remedies, and this is not only the case for so termed physical trauma (which at root is always psychological), but also for psychological trauma.

As we have seen in the previous section on epidemic diseases, there is a body of experience that shows that one remedy for one epidemic disease is effective as long it covers the totality of the signs and symptoms of the disease. Selecting one remedy from a small group is rather based on the practical fact that usually not one single remedy covers the disease totality or all of its expressions, so then one that covers it best for a single patient is selected. With PC Technology we have now introduced the possibility to translate the Genus epidemicus of a disease directly into one single remedy.

Genus Traumaticus and Instructions

We want now to introduce a new term and a new concept within the homeopathic mindset. This is Genus Traumaticus which as the name suggests, is the concept of analyzing the symptom totality of a specific traumatic situation. Then to, either select a small group of remedies that covers the Genus Traumaticus, (as the repertory already largely does by grouping remedies for specific indications, e.g. Injury of the spine) or to, as we have done, create one PC Resonance for every specific identified and analysed form of trauma.

For example in cystitis after rape it's common to give one specific homeopathic remedy *Staphysagria* with very good results, and for the trauma of rape in general homeopaths usually tend to have a top three or four that are used in the vast majority of cases. We would argue that these remedies together cover the GENUS TRAUMATICUS for rape and that this idea can be extended to any overwhelming communal trauma, from things like earthquakes and hurricanes, tsunamis, floods and a host of other natural catastrophes. These impinge on the survival instincts in the reptilian brain and the human response varies little if at all in these situations. There is a strong emotional content which has deep roots in the human unconsciousness, going into the survival instincts. These emotional responses are very similar between people, because deep down we are all very similar. The reptilian brain for example evolved over perhaps one billion years, before humans existed so it's likely to be very similar for all of us. On a psychological level these different forms of trauma are archetypal and present in the collective unconscious, i.e. directly below the surface of anyone. Also one usually only has to go back one or two generations to find these traumas present in ancestors, so these could be passed on as traumatic miasms.

In the beginning lines of §70 of the 6th edition of the Organon Hahnemann writes:

> "From what has been stated so far, we cannot fail to recognize that:
> all that the physician can find in diseases, which is really pathological and is to be cured,
>
> - consists only of the patient's state and complaints and the changes of his health perceptible to the senses;
>
> in a word,
>
> - it consists only of the totality of those symptoms by which the disease demands the appropriate medicine for its relief / suited to relieve it. (...)" [exact translation by Monika Grühn]

If we translate the above for an epidemic disease like cholera it reads: Cholera consists solely of the patients' totality of symptoms. By these symptoms, cholera demands the medicine suitable to its aid.

If we include the effects of trauma or intoxication under the term 'diseases'[7], we could say for instance for rape trauma: rape trauma consists solely of the patients' totality of symptoms. By these symptoms, rape trauma demands the medicine suitable to its aid.

By using the plural 'patients' we make the connection to a collective approach for trauma. We could have elaborate discussions on whether or not we can do this and whether or not the *Organon* gives that freedom. The one that heals is right, and we hope to present sufficient case histories in this book that show a GENUS TRAUMATICUS approach is justified by its effects.

We have extended this idea for instance to the traumas of genocide, war, torture, natural catastrophe and more as needed.

7 The following definition of disease allows to include any cause that deranges the life force; Disease: a solely dynamic mistuning of the life force, which is manifested in one's state, in one's condition, and in one's appearance. ... [Wenda Brewster O'Reilly's *Organon*, p 301]

This idea corresponds exactly to the modern research into epigenetics which shows that trauma passes down generations, by modifying the genetics, switching on and off, or tuning up and down, various genetic possibilities from one generation to the next. There is also a field of psychological research, which includes constellation work, which has identified trans-generational trauma which is the same idea as Genus epidemicus on the level of a family constellation. We have also connected this strongly to the survival instincts and we say that GENUS TRAUMATICUS is rooted in the survival instincts.

A first experience with the creation of a GENUS TRAUMATICUS remedy was with War and Genocide Trauma in Rwanda in 2005 (See Part III). Based on the excellent results witnessed in heavily traumatised people we felt confident to extend the concept to other types of trauma, and in the following chapters we will share experiences with those.

For a variety of causes of trauma specific TRAUMA RESONANCES for healing have been designed. These can be used both for healing the actual trauma that happened to a person and inherited traumas.

While it may be that there is one underlying mechanism involved in trauma there are many important aspects that vary according to the type of event, so from a range of resonances it should be possible to pick the one that roughly covers the event or events that happened. There is some overlap between these resonances inevitably. For example shock occurs in war and accidents. It's best to use the simplest resonance that is appropriate.

First Aid - Treating Acute Trauma with PC Resonances

How often a dose of the appropriate PC RESONANCE must be given depends on how acute and how serious the condition is. In acute states like a severe accident or a serious burn the resonance can initially be given every 30 seconds. As soon as the patient starts to respond and his/her condition improves the time between doses can be prolonged. This pattern is similar to that of other homeopathic remedies given in acute diseases.

Treating Post Traumatic Stress Disorder with PC Resonances

In the chronic effects of trauma, like the long term effects of an injury, rape or war, a regular dose – five drops after banging the bottle five times kept in the mouth for at least five seconds – can be given on a daily basis.
The key thing about Post Traumatic Stress Disorder due to psychological trauma is the mental flashbacks, like seeing the goal scored again and again and again, and you can't stop it. The appropriate PC RESONANCE can resolve these flashbacks rapidly. As soon as there is no more improvement the patient can stop taking the PC RESONANCE.

The following article was published in Homœopathic Links, September 2010. As it discusses several trauma resonances we print it here instead of spreading the cases over the appropriate chapters. Caution – it is harrowing reading.

Trial of Peter Chappell's Trauma remedies at the Crossroads Women's Centre Homeopathy Clinic

Report compiled by Jennifer Hautman, United Kingdom

Summary

Report of a trial of Peter Chappell's trauma remedies, including Genocide and War Trauma (PC304x), Rape (PC435p), and Torture (PC311f), at the Crossroads Women's Centre homeopathy clinic, London, during one year (October 2006-2007). Most of the users of the clinic are African women asylum seekers who have fled war and conflict and are fighting for the right to stay here and be reunited with their families. Despite some initial scepticism, we found the PC trauma remedies to be very effective and of great benefit to the women. Out of a total of eighteen cases, four had to be excluded because we were unable to follow up their cases (including one who was deported), or they didn't take the remedies, and three were difficult to assess due to other circumstances. In our view there was significant improvement in almost all the women we were able to follow up (eleven out of fourteen or 79%), and strong improvement in half of them. This is despite potential blocks to treatment such as suppressive allopathic drugs, and extreme anxiety and worry caused by their uncertain immigration status and daily struggle for survival.

Background

Since January 2001, homeopath Jennifer Prescott Dooley, RSHom, has been treating users of the Crossroads Women's Centre (based in Kentish Town, London). In 2006, she was joined by Jennifer Hautman, RSHom (a student during the trial, now a qualified homeopath). The clinic is a free / low cost service that relies on unwaged volunteer work and donations from suppliers and other homeopaths. Most of the patients are women asylum seekers referred by organisations providing frontline services at the Centre such as: the All African Women's Group (AAWG), Black Women's Rape Action Project (BWRAP), Legal Action for Women (LAW), WinVisible (women with visible and invisible disabilities), Wages Due Lesbians and Women Against Rape (WAR).

The Women's Centre has been running for over 30 years, and is a multi-racial, wheelchair-accessible base for grassroots women's self-help services and campaigns, as well as a men's group. Every week, 20-30 women, many with significant health problems, contact the Centre for help with asylum, immigration, benefits, disability discrimination, child contact, housing, sexual and/or racist violence, and to seek justice for themselves and their loved ones. The Women's Centre has been keen to increase grassroots access to homeopathy, especially for women who live in or come from countries of the South. Centre users have also organised a campaign in defence of homeopathy provided free as part of the National Health Service (NHS), particularly to reinstate patient access to the Royal London Homeopathic Hospital (see our Open Letter to Brent Primary Care Trust demanding restoration of its contract with the RLHH, available online).

Users of the clinic

Asylum-seeking women are among the most vulnerable members of any population. Since 2003, 30 to 40 women seeking asylum have been meeting regularly at the Centre as a self-help support group – the All African Women's Group (AAWG). Most are from Burundi, Cameroon, the Democratic Republic of Congo, Eritrea, Ethiopia, Rwanda, Sierra Leone and Uganda. They are struggling to overcome emotional and physical traumas resulting from rape and other torture, witnessing the murder and/or rape and torture of loved ones, and having to leave children and relatives behind. At the same time, they have to deal with the ongoing trauma of an uncertain future. Having arrived in the UK seeking safety, they are often left destitute or at best are surviving on vouchers or £30 a week and in very poor housing. They suffer racism and other discrimination, and are under constant threat of dispersal (being forced to move to another city, away from any support they may have), detention (being locked up in prison-like conditions), and removal to the country they came from (with a renewed risk of torture, including rape, and even death). As is common with survivors of torture and genocide, many feel guilty for having survived while loved ones did not. Many are mothers of babies and small children or are pregnant, some as a result of rape. Some have been on hunger strike while in detention in protest against the conditions there. Some are suicidal and would prefer to die here than be sent back.

According to international agreements, asylum seekers are entitled to healthcare, free at the point of service, but in practice many do not receive this. It is widely recognised that the healthcare needs of asylum seekers are not adequately addressed and that their general level of health deteriorates, often drastically, after entry into Britain. One reason for this is that immigration legislation brought in on 1st April 2004 prohibits people whose claims have been closed from accessing any NHS health care. Many people are thus left untreated regardless of their medical need or disability. Many have no GP, and those who do often receive no proper diagnosis and are simply prescribed anti-depressants, tranquillisers and sleeping pills.

The clinic

The clinic is part of an integrated holistic environment that has the potential to address women's many needs at once. The ethos of the organisations based at the Centre is one of self-help, and therefore of empowerment. Working on a self-help basis is an important part of the healing process, because, as one woman put it:
'When you are tortured, they make you feel that you are helpless to stop them, to help yourself, or to help anyone else. When you come to the Women's Centre, it is the opposite; it is about self-help and collective help. It is not easy but it helps to undo the work of the torture.'

By re-learning through experience that there is always something that can be done, no matter how small, to help themselves and each other, many notice a great improvement in their confidence and wellbeing. As a result, they can become more active protagonists in their own case to demand – and get – respect from lawyers and service providers. Collectively, our experience is that winning justice and protection is crucial to the healing process, and that a lack of justice can be a deep seated maintaining cause of ill health and disease. For this reason campaigning for justice is an important part of self-help.

By supporting women with homeopathy to overcome their traumas and other health issues, the clinic can strengthen their resolve in every other sphere, which can in turn help them to win their cases. As far as we know, this is the only homeopathic clinic in Britain that predominantly treats women seeking asylum.

PC trial October 2006 – October 2009

In 2006, Jennifer Hautman, who has been a volunteer at the Women's Centre since 1995, started sitting in during consultations as a final year homeopathy student, and became a liaison between patients, the homeopath Jennifer Prescott Dooley, and the various organisations referring patients. In the course of her studies, Hautman attended a workshop by a well-known homeopath, Peter Chappell (FSHom), where he presented his work on treating Genocide and War Trauma in Rwanda, using a remedy he developed specifically for the purpose which will be referred to as GWT (available as PC304x). Mindful that his approach may be of benefit to the women in our clinic, Hautman invited him to the Centre to discuss it further, to which he agreed.

Until then, Dooley had mostly only been able to offer acute treatments in the clinic due to time constraints and the number of women needing treatment. While many symptoms improved, she was frustrated with the difficulty of getting lasting benefits while treating the underlying trauma. She found that in some cases, indicated remedies would not hold as expected, usually the patient would relapse each time there was a fresh trauma in their case, as it would cause them to re-live their old traumas. The underlying trauma was a constant block to the case. Remedies such as *Staphysagria, Aconite, Ignatia, Natrum muriaticum,* and *Arsenicum album* were often indicated, but would only palliate the case while the patient continued to be under duress.

Having met with Peter Chappell and discussed the use of his remedies, we decided to try out his PC RESONANCES. He agreed to support a trial and donated all the remedies needed to carry it out.

In October 2006 we began our trial with Dooley as the prescribing homeopath and Hautman taking notes. During the trial, Chappell was contactable for advice about the use of the remedies. Around the halfway point of the trial, in March 2007, we held a weekend Seminar with Chappell on Treating Trauma, Miasms and Diseases, attended by about 40 people, half of whom were practicing homeopaths, and the other half key workers from the Women's Centre, including lay supporters and users of homeopathy. Chappell generously donated the proceeds from this seminar to the clinic.

Method

After initially using MYMOP[8] to record the results of treatment, we found them too time consuming where the patient had difficulties with English. We then agreed with Chappell that we would use an adapted version of his summary sheet for each patient and his scoring system for each key symptom, together with a Karnofsky score[9] that the patients found easier to relate to (examples of this summary sheet and scoring system are available – please contact the author). We asked patients to sign consent forms and made sure they understood the treatment they were receiving, as most were new to homeopathy. We filmed some early cases, in the hope of doing 'before and after' comparisons, but we soon abandoned this as most women preferred anonymity. It was also not practical due to a lack of time and space. Notes of the cases remain confidential and any discussion here must therefore remain anonymous. Our clinic continued every Tuesday as usual. We saw between four and six patients each week. Follow-ups were arranged to be between two and four weeks after initial treatment, or as the women were available.

Demographics

Eighteen women took part in the trial, aged between 19 and 59. They came from Uganda (9), Rwanda (3), Burundi (2), Congo (DRC) (2), Cameroon (1) and Sierra Leone (1). All had been raped and tortured in other ways, both during conflict or while fleeing. Eight had been detained at some time, either in Yarl's Wood Immigration Removal Centre[10] (6), Oakington Immigration Removal Centre[11] (1) or in prison[12] (1). Ten had not been detained. Most (16) of the women had not won their asylum cases when we started

---

8 MYMOP (Measure Your Medical Outcome Profile) a patient generated outcome questionnaire available free online.

9 Performance status to quantify general well-being on a 0-100 scale.

10 Yarl's Wood Immigration Removal Centre, in Bedfordshire, has 405 bedspaces and is the main removal centre for women and families. For more information, please see: "Bleak House" for Our Times: An investigation into Yarl's Wood Removal Centre available from Crossroads Book (www.allwomencount.net/Publications/pamphlets.htm

11 Oakington Immigration Removal Centre, near Cambridge, has a capacity of 408 beds for male detainees. Women (including many rape survivors) are also detained here.

12 One young woman who had escaped her traffickers, was held in an adult prison, despite being under 18, and charged with criminal proceedings because the UK Government Home Office disbelieved her age and identification.

the trial. Of these 16, at least 8 have since won the right to remain in the UK, while 5 are still fighting, including one woman who was deported. One woman returned voluntarily to Uganda. We are no longer in touch with two women.

All but two were mothers of young children, some as a result of rape. For some of them, the children were also a constant reminder of their experiences, and many of them struggled daily with feelings of guilt, and at times anger. Fourteen of the 18 had to leave children behind, which again filled them with guilt and grief, and the daily worry of what might be happening to their children. Four had been diagnosed HIV+. Sixteen were taking allopathic medication, such as anti-depressants, painkillers, and sleeping tablets, as well as anti-psychotics, anti-inflammatories, and so on. The women who were put on anti-psychotic drugs were thought of as suffering from psychosis (with symptoms such as hearing voices), with little understanding of the trauma they had suffered. It is important to note that for these women, many times the voices they were hearing occurred during flashbacks or dreams, and always involved past experiences. This was discovered during the homeopathic case taking process, with many questions exploring their mental state more deeply than their allopathic physician may have been able to. These symptoms cleared after they took the PC Resonances and they were then able to come off the allopathic medication.
Their initial traumas were experienced between two and eight years ago. Trauma symptoms included: suicidal depression, grief, flashbacks, sleeplessness, panic attacks, hallucination, screaming or talking in sleep, hearing voices, palpitations and breathlessness (during panic attacks), uncontrollable crying, depression, lack of appetite, rape trauma syndrome, hopelessness, extreme anxiety, fear of bad news and / or of being detained and deported, fear of death, and anger. Some still had physical scars and wounds from being tortured, including hearing loss, painful broken teeth, bleeding, fibroids, fistulas and other gynaecological problems.

Thirteen were treated with PC GWT (war trauma), including three who also had PC1, a remedy developed to treat HIV in Africa. We tried to space the remedies, PC1 in the morning and GWT before bed. Four were treated with PC Rape (PC435p) together with PC Torture PC311f) – after discussing with Chappell, we used these if the women had been raped and tortured repeatedly over weeks or months rather than in a one off incident (again we tried to space these remedies morning and evening). One was treated with PC1 alone. Almost all (16) of the women were also given other homeopathic remedies at some time. Two had only PC Resonances – one of them was deported
before a follow up could be done, and the other did very well on PC1 and GWT (see summary of Case 2 below). At least 10 had been given homeopathic treatment before joining the study.

Summary of cases
Out of a total of 18 cases, four had to be excluded because we were unable to follow up their cases (including one who was deported), or they didn't take the remedies.

Of the remaining 14, three had no discernible improvement. These were complex cases of older women – one had unstable diabetes and HIV (she was given PC1 and no PC trauma remedies); another was on a long list of blood pressure medications; and the third was sleeping rough at times and on anti-psychotic medication. Due to her circumstances, it was difficult to assess progress and we were uncertain as to whether she took the remedies consistently.

Of the remaining 11 cases, seven showed strong improvement after taking the PC trauma remedies (three of whom were also taking PC1 for HIV/AIDS), and four showed some improvement.

In our view there was significant improvement in almost all of the women we were able to have follow ups with (11 out of 14 or 79%), and strong improvement in half of them. This is despite potential blocks to treatment such as suppressive allopathic drugs and extreme anxiety and worry caused by their uncertain immigration status and daily struggle for survival.

Clearly, our study is of a small group and many of the people taking part were living in difficult situations, but we feel the results we have seen are encouraging and merit attention.

Below are the case summaries of those seven women in whom we could see the most significant improvement. In each case we have included the women's background and immigration status as these factors had a major impact on their wellbeing and ability to deal with health problems.
The symptom scores mentioned in the following cases are graded from 0-5, with 0 being the best it can be, and 5 the worst. Karnofsky scores give an indication of general wellbeing and range from 0-100, with 0 being 'dead' and 100 being completely well.

Case 1

A 36-year-old woman who was imprisoned, raped and tortured in Uganda because of her political activities. Her husband was murdered by government soldiers in front of her and her children. She was taken away to army barracks and raped. She managed to escape and fled Uganda leaving three children behind. She claimed asylum in 2003 but was refused. Her lawyer never appealed the Home Office decision. In 2004 she was arrested and detained – she was over seven months pregnant, was held in a filthy unhygienic cell and denied daily medication. Three doctors signed her 'fit to travel' – to be deported back to Uganda despite high blood pressure and increasingly severe stomach pains. Black Women's Rape Action Project, Women Against Rape and Legal Action for Women succeeded in stopping her deportation at the last minute. She had an appeal hearing in 2006 and won the right to stay and the right to bring her children over from Uganda.

We first saw her in our clinic in October 2006. She had just won her case. She had given birth by Caesarean section a month previously. Despite her victory, she complained of depression and lack of sleep due to flashbacks. We gave her PC GWT and Bellis perennis for the C-section. One month later, she had a flu, which we saw as cleansing, and was given Gelsemium. In March 2007, five months after taking GWT, she said: 'I was depressed, but now I'm going to be fine. I sleep well all night and I feel relaxed.' Her symptom scores went from 4.5 (sleep) and 3.5 (depression) to 0 and 0, and her Karnofsky score from 70 to 100.

Case 2

In April 2007, a 19-year-old woman from Uganda came to see us. She had been raped by soldiers on her way back from school aged 13, and had twins as a result. While in a coma after a Caesarean section birth, her twins were given up for adoption. She woke up to find her twins gone, and to learn that her family had died in the war. In February 2006, she was diagnosed HIV+ and put on ARVs. Following the diagnosis, she tried to kill herself by taking an overdose. She had nightmares, was crying at night, and was self-harming (burning herself). She complained of asthma since she was a child, which had gotten worse since the trauma. She was on anti-depressants and needed immunoglobulin infusions because of her tendency to bruise and bleed. We gave her PC1 and PC GWT.

Two weeks later, she complained of nausea and dizziness from taking the remedy (a symptom mentioned by Case 4 also), but her asthma was improved. One week later again, she felt 'not bad, not as bad as before'. She was not having nightmares and slept 'really well', waking up refreshed, and the flashbacks were not as severe. By June, two months and one week after first treatment, her periods had improved and she was not bruising as easily as before. The medics said she no longer needed immunoglobulin treatment. Laughingly she said, 'I think I'm fine for now, I don't get bruises. I feel good because I don't have to go for injections, I feel relaxed.'

When we first saw her, her viral load count was about 50, and her CD4 count was 98 when diagnosed HIV+. Two months after treatment with PC1 her viral load was less than 40 and her CD4 was 178. In other words, the HIV virus count had reduced and her immune system was much stronger. Her depression and nightmare scores went from 5 and 4 to 1 or 2, and her Karnofsky score went from 10 to 90.

Case 3

A 38-year-old Ugandan woman who fled multiple rape in Uganda and Rwanda, leaving three children behind, one of whom was raped in front of her. She was later diagnosed HIV+. In 2003 her asylum claim was refused. She was detained for three months at the end of 2005, but she couldn't be deported back to Uganda as the Ugandan government refused to accept her. Whilst detained in Yarl's Wood Detention Centre, all medication, including ARVs were stopped. She became very ill, was hospitalized and diagnosed with cryptococcal meningitis.

In July 2006, we gave her PC1. In September she complained of a temperature with inflammation of the brain, which we took to be a return of old symptoms, and treated acutely with *Apis*. The physical symptoms recovered well, but then she became very emotional. In October she was sobbing uncontrollably in the consultation, as she was worried about the children she had left behind. She was depressed, unable to speak for sobbing, holding her head in her hands and rocking back and forth. We gave her PC GWT. Two weeks later, she was crying less, but still complained of lack of motivation. However she seemed to be stronger despite having received news that the Home Office was trying to disperse her to another town.

By the end of November, seven weeks after treatment with the GWT resonance, she reported that her sleep had improved, and that: 'I think about things but I don't cry. I think I've moved from that crying, not that I hold it in, I don't feel it's there.' She felt less weak, and was more philosophical about her situation. By the end of January, three months after taking GWT and seven months after taking PC1, there was a lot of improvement in her crying and depression, although she still complained of headaches, especially when thinking about her children. Given that she had still not won her right to stay and was still separated from her children, she had recovered well from the trauma. When we first met her she couldn't speak for sobbing, but now she had become an accomplished public speaker and a key member of the All African Women's Group. Her crying and depression symptom scores went from 5 to 0 in seven months, and her Karnofsky score from 70 to 90.

Case 4

A 36-year-old woman from the Democratic Republic of Congo, who returned home in 2002 to find her village and house had been burned down by Lendu militia and her two children missing. She was captured and held in a military camp in the forest for three weeks where she was raped, beaten and tortured, including being burnt with cigarettes and beaten so severely on her head that her ears bled and she partially lost her hearing. She was also persecuted for her ethnicity – she is from Eastern Congo, which has born the brunt of the war. She has no idea of what has happened to her children, or if they are still alive.

She arrived in the UK in June 2003. Her asylum claim was refused. A new solicitor was found to reopen her case. She had not had secure housing or support for many years, and was dependent on the goodwill of friends – she was doing housework in exchange for a roof over her head. She was waiting for a decision on a Judicial Review.

In 2004, she started homeopathic treatment for her head injury and a cough from sleeping rough. She did well on *Natrum sulphuricum*. Later she also had *Staphysagria, Rhus toxicodendron, Arnica,* and *Phosphorus*, which were prescribed for various acute symptoms developed while she was homeless. She was also given *Chlamydia* for symptoms of an STD. These remedies helped with the acute and physical trauma symptoms, but they didn't get to the underlying emotional trauma.

In October 2006, she complained of depression and bad dreams. We gave her GWT. Two weeks after taking it she complained of nausea, but she was sleeping well, was less tired and less depressed. In six months she had improved significantly, was less angry, more relaxed, and instead of bad dreams had dreams of hope and was generally much more positive. During the time she was on GWT, her symptom scores went from 4 to 1, and her Karnofsky score remained 80 throughout. In 2009 she won the right to remain in the UK, but we don't know if she knows this as we lost touch with her in January 2008.

Case 5

A 30-year-old woman who fled Uganda in 2000, after she was accused of being a rebel collaborator due to her husband's membership of the Allied Democratic Force. Government soldiers raided her home looking for her husband, and she was violently beaten and suffered multiple rapes. She had a miscarriage as a result and spent about six weeks in hospital. As soon as she was discharged she fled Uganda leaving her five children behind. Her husband was subsequently killed by the Ugandan Peoples Army during a raid on a political meeting.

An initial claim for asylum was refused in 2001 without medical evidence and expert reports having been presented. She complained of poor legal representation – the lawyers lost her files, including her report from the Medical Foundation for the Care of Victims of Torture, and she was not informed of her current legal status for many months. For over three years she had been living with no means of support or lodgings. This put her in an extremely vulnerable position. She was also unable to access medical help for the injuries previously inflicted on her. This everyday struggle compounded her continuing trauma due to the multiple rape and beatings in Uganda, and the loss of her children.

In April 2007, she came to see us complaining of severe tooth pain caused by damage from the beatings, anxiety attacks and flashbacks. Due to all support being removed by the National Asylum Support Service, she was refused any dental treatment. We gave her PC GWT. By mid June, she reported improvement in her tooth pain and said: 'Now when I start to take the medicine [GWT], my anxiety attacks calm down.' Two months after first treatment, she said: 'The tooth pain is still there but it's better. I have no anxiety attacks and no difficulty sleeping.' Her symptom scores for teeth pain, anxiety attacks and flashbacks went from 4 or 5 to 0 or 1 in about six months, and she was able to reduce the amount of painkillers she was taking.

Case 6

A 31-year-old woman from Rwanda, who was repeatedly raped by men she had turned to for help to escape Rwanda. In 2000, she had night sweats and fevers and was given six months of drugs for TB, despite not testing positive for TB. In 2001 she was diagnosed HIV+ and put on ARVs.

We met her in July 2006, and gave her PC1. In September, she complained of bad dreams, anxiety and getting angry with her daughter, but her energy was better. In October, she complained of depression, inability to sleep, lack of appetite, and poor concentration, and we gave her GWT. Three months after taking GWT, and five months after starting PC1, she decided to stop taking ARVs, but did not tell us until January 2007. At this point she had started to get fevers and ulcers, a return of old symptoms from before the ARVs. We treated her acutely (with *Pulsatilla* and other remedies), and since then, to this date, she has been very well, with no relapses. She's only occasionally retaken PC1. Her concentration and sleep improved greatly, and she became more hopeful. In that time her symptom score for depression went from 5 to 2.

Case 7

A 34-year-old woman who came to the UK in 2001 fleeing torture and rape for her political activities, leaving three children behind in Uganda. In 2003, her children were able to join her and also claimed asylum. Her teenage son has mental health problems as a result of his traumas. She then married in the UK, had a child, her husband died, and she later had another child. She and the children were put in detention twice, and faced raids by the Home Office, which further traumatised them all. She was then deported to Uganda with all of her five children (including the two who were born in the UK), and was tortured again. Whilst in Uganda, her teenage daughter was raped. She managed to escape and in 2006 made her way back to the UK, but she had to leave all five children behind.

When we saw her in the clinic in November 2006, her two-year-old son (the eldest of the two born in the UK) was due to be coming back from Uganda the day after. Even so, she was suicidal, couldn't sleep, and was taking anti-depressants. We gave her PC Rape, PC Torture and *Ignatia* 1M to take during the consultation because she broke down and was unable to speak. One week later, she was able to sleep much better. She started taking the PC Resonances the same day her son came back from Uganda. She had 'two nice days' with him, but her son was confused and reminded her of all she'd lost back home, including her four other children. Three months after PC Rape and PC Torture, her youngest son was supposed to join her from Uganda, but this fell through. This disappointment was treated acutely with *Ignatia*. From then on she was treated with other homeopathic remedies (*Sepia*, *Gelsemium*). Despite the multiple problems she was having with her children, we felt there was significant improvement to her sleep and depression from the PC Resonances. Her symptoms scores went from 5 (depression) and 4.5 (sleep) to 1 (both sleep and depression). After a long struggle, in October 2007, she won her case and was eventually reunited with all her children.

Conclusion

General observations in the use of PC Trauma remedies

For the most part, the patients we have seen, especially those who had survived malaria in infancy, were basically strong healthy people, until the trauma happened. Despite the high levels of trauma they have suffered, they responded well to homeopathic treatment. Where patients have been receiving homeopathic treatment for some time, PC Trauma remedies have helped to remove a deeper layer of distress. This may reveal more clearly a constitutional remedy or the return of old suppressed symptoms that are then more responsive to further homeopathic treatment. Once the trauma begins to lift, the women reported that they sleep better and are not so overwhelmed by their emotions; therefore they can express themselves better, which helped us to find the next remedy. We often found that even in the first week after taking a PC Resonance, the response could be dramatic and was then sustained – this included better sleep, anxiety reduced, flashbacks stopped and appetite improved. At least two patients were able to significantly reduce their allopathic medication after treatment with

PC1 and GWT, one stopping ARV's and the other no longer required immunoglobulin treatment. Others were able to stop or reduce their use of anti-depressants, sleeping pills and painkillers after PC Trauma remedies.

Despite Jennifer Dooley's initial scepticism of PC RESONANCES, she is now convinced of their effectiveness. Dooley's experience was that the stress of deep traumas could be a block to conventional homeopathic treatment, and in the previous five years of working at the clinic, that was her greatest frustration. She felt that about a third of the cases just wouldn't budge, but the PC Trauma remedies were able to unlock those cases. Her observation and experience of using them is that they cleared the trauma layer, leaving a clearer picture of the case, so that sometimes, after a PC RESONANCE, just one dose of a constitutional remedy was enough for a woman to be well enough to no longer need treatment. In spite of the different experiences that caused the trauma, the response to those experiences followed the same symptom picture. In Dooley's experience, therefore, (in line with Peter Chappell's *Second Simillimum*[13]), the trauma symptoms can be treated in the same way as an epidemic disease, as all the asylum seeking patients she has treated over the years suffered from the same trauma symptom picture as shown above, and those are the symptoms we were able to clear using the PC Trauma remedies.

The results were extremely convincing, changed both Dooley and Hautman's parameters of what homeopathy is, and now we wouldn't go anywhere without PC RESONANCES in our kit.

Acknowledgements

I wish to thank the women of the All African Women's Group who took part in this trial, all the women at the Crossroads Women's Centre, not least for their commitment to make private space available despite the severe overcrowding, and Jennifer Prescott Dooley RSHom, Lori Nairne RNHom and Nina Lopez for their help in compiling this report.

For more information about the Crossroads Women's Centre Homeopathy Clinic contact: centre@crossroadswomen.net

13 According to Chappell '...you intelligently combine what is common to a lot of cases together to find the totality and essence of the miasm or the disease. In other words there is a Genus Epidemicus an d a GENUS CHRONICUS, both forms of the second simillimum.'

Amma4Trauma

In 2005 Peter had treated war and genocide trauma in Rwanda, and in 2008 and 2009 Harry treated war & genocide trauma as well as rape trauma in Burundi and East DRC Congo (see following chapters). Word about the results must have spread as in 2010 the AMMA RESONANCE HEALING FOUNDATION received an invitation by FEPADE (a women's organization in East DRC Congo) to train a group of professionals connected to several NGOs to become trauma relief workers. The understanding that trauma is widespread and heavily undermines health and the ability to create a happy and fruitful life had already been rooted deeply in our thinking. Based on the invitation we created a training programme for PTSD. A manual was written and a group of PC RESONANCES selected.

Nico Beentjes was asked to give this first training because of his experience in using PC for treating trauma in Haiti and his excellent French. FEPADE announced that 100 trainees would attend. 127 showed up and all completed the training. These trauma relief workers are a wonderful force for positive change and can each treat thousands of people in the months and years to come. Not only will they improve the health and quality of life of many individuals, they will contribute to a transformation of the collective trauma in one of the most traumatized parts of the world.

On the other side of Lake Tanganyika, in Kigoma, another women's organization, WADS (Women Action for Democracy and Solidarity), heard about the experiences of their colleagues in DRC Congo and the ARHF received an invitation to train 100+ trauma relief workers in the Nyarugusu refugees camp near Kigoma.

Trauma Relief Training in Nyarugusu Refugee Camp, Tanzania

Harry van der Zee & Nico Beentjes, November 2011

From Fizi district, East DRC Congo, hundreds of thousands of people fled the country in 1996 and since. They crossed lake Tanganyika on anything that would float to seek refuge at the shores of Tanzania. Several refugee camps were created by UNHCR and the Tanzanian government. Slowly refugees have been repatriated or found asylum in other countries.

Nyarugusu is the last camp providing refuge to 64,000 Congolese (2011). If one listens to the appalling stories of slaughter, torture, humiliation and rape one can understand that even after 15 years the effects are still felt as if it all happened yesterday. Many lost family members, many arrived as orphans with images of their parents being slaughtered, and even inside the camp some were still not sure of their life. Nyarugusu is situated in Kigoma region, the North-West of Tanzania. One of the local NGOs that try to help the refugees is WADS (Women Actions for Development and Solidarity). They invited ARHF to train trauma relief and it was concluded that the ideal place to do this would be inside the camp, so refugees themselves could participate. Through the Ministry of Home Affairs in Dar Es Salaam authorisation was given to provide the training inside the camp. WADS found a partner inside the camp in SOPEFAC (Solidarité Paysanne pour l'Education aux droits des Femmes et des enfants et Anti-Corruption). Antoine Kasongo, whose personal history would make a book by itself, invited members of other NGOs active in the camp and ultimately 122 participants were trained. First they were given basic theory on homeopathy and trauma and then learned how to prepare PC TRAUMA RESONANCES.

After that they took each other's case of war trauma in pairs and treated each other. Soon the first changes of symptoms were reported. Someone who had at least four nightmares per night had his first peaceful sleep in fifteen years. Another reported how she always was harsh with children and to her surprise now observed she treated them with mildness and understanding. Tormenting and repetitive thoughts reduced, fears subsided and faces expressing pain and fear now relaxed and radiated with joy and peace. The group was now clearly motivated to treat their fellow refugees. They formed groups divided over seven zones, and divided each zone into sections. Each group selected a leader. Some members would especially focus on treating orphans with PC Adoption Trauma and some on treating sexual abuse with PC Rape Trauma. Within the remaining two days that we were still in the camp they managed to treat the incredible amount of 5,000 people, and when we left they had enough stock to ultimately be able to treat all inhabitants. After a week Nico returned to take more follow-ups, which indicated that people kept improving and that the number treated kept rising.

What kept the refugees for fifteen long years in the camp was a combination of the ongoing situation in DRC Congo and their deeply rooted fears. If after the upcoming elections it stays calm in DRC Congo UNHCR is planning to repatriate them. When we first met the refugees we met walking stories of a troubled past. We hope that due to the treatment we made available they can return home with joy and hope for the future.

At ARHF.nl a documentary on this project can be seen.

Abortion Trauma

Abortus provocatus is ending a life. We are not suggesting that people should or should not abort, we're just stating the reality, that it is a form of trauma. What an abortion needs, as the trauma is more than just physical, is some kind of closure. Since trauma remains in the body in a timeless way this can be done at any time after the event and even 30 years later. The persons involved can get together and hold a little ceremony like a funeral and bury something symbolic and say prayers and sing songs or whatever would work for them. The main point is to bring about closure.
This remedy is to help bring about closure and the resolution of all the guilt, grief and other associated feelings that can go along with it. PC Abortion Trauma does not apply to miscarriage as that is a natural event and does not carry the same baggage and trauma as deliberately ending the life of a foetus.

Abuse Trauma

PC Abuse Trauma is for where a person has suffered systematic abuse at the hands of another, often a parent, stepparent or relative, especially over a long period. This often creates a deep victim psychology and a repetitive cycle of abuse, including self-abuse, abusive relationships etc. This remedy could be taken daily for one month in conjunction with psychotherapy for example with or without some other form of intelligent monitoring like a homeopath.

Adoption Trauma

Adoption is probably always traumatic as it includes the loss of biological parents, especially the mother, and often also a change of country and culture. The more traumatic the adoption the more it becomes seemingly impossible to meet the love needs of the child. Love is not just accepted by them or is deeply distrusted. An unwanted Chinese girl for example who had been adopted and brought into England by a typical white English couple suffers from a cascade of traumas. They are in effect deeply in trauma.

Besides the adoption itself the process can be traumatic too. For example the original parents are reluctant to let the child go, and there is a period of deep uncertainty. The adopting parents fear to love fully, as their hearts might get broken. Or it can be that the child is abandoned on a doorstep or in a waste bin. It can of course get much worse than this. We have seen on television malnourished, neglected children in Bulgarian orphanages, whose twisted limbs had locked into foetal positions, rocking to and fro, speechless, no light in their eyes. Hopelessly traumatised on all levels. These children's cases are severe and they require the very special needs that few can offer. So multiple traumas can occur in these situations and need systematic unravelling and healing. PC Adoption Trauma will have better results if used in conjunction with individual homeopathic treatment or other holistic treatment.

Case of history of adoption

Ellen van der Voort, Netherlands

A 25-year-old woman was adopted from Sri Lanka as a baby. She is very suicidal and self-mutilates.

Follow-up:
After PC Adoption trauma she completely lost her adoption problem and grew out of it to be a wonderful free women with no suicidal tendencies and no self-mutilation. This change also occurred in a very short time.

Adoption trauma in India

Maggi, Auroville, India (who for a long time was the personal assistant to The Mother, one of the great yet humble self-realised people last century)

It doesn't seem so long ago that I read in "Links" that Peter Chappell claimed not only to have produced a remedy that was showing promising results in curing AIDS in Africa, but that he could produce remedies to combat any disease. Peter, that staunch British disciple of Classical Homeopathy and George Vithoulkas, dealing in specifics! It left a question in my head ... not about the remedies but about Peter. I had followed his great missionary work in the Middle European countries. What now? I didn't give it much thought until I read Harry van der Zee's very moving account of a case, treated by Malcolm Smith, of a severely depressed HIV-positive man, resistant to all remedies but cured in a deep, irrefutable and ideal way with the PC AIDS remedy. An account so impressive that my "what now?" Changed to "what if?"

My correspondence with Harry and Peter fostered a growing interest in their work but I didn't see, or I wasn't sure, how the PC Resonances could be incorporated into a classical approach (they were specifics) though of course nobody doubts the importance and utility of Genus epidemicus remedies. Was it possible that the PC Resonances worked on a similar principle regarding any disease as having a universal common denominator? It was all too mind blowing.

In due course I received a neat little 'Amma4Africa Kit' with a briefing and 18 PC (PC = Peter Chappell) remedies, including remedies for birth trauma, rape trauma, sexual abuse trauma, unburied relatives trauma (evidently a big problem in Africa), AIDS (for men and another for women), three chronics (hypertension, infertility and diabetes) and some other separate PC Resonances for an interesting range of other diseases. Hypertension, diabetes and infertility were listed under 'epidemic remedies'. Well my Oxford dictionary gives me 'widely prevalent' as one of the definitions for 'epidemic' so yes, perhaps it is not so far fetched to think in terms of Genus epidemicus remedies here.

There was also a remedy for adoption trauma: I had a ready candidate for it. I had been living in South India since the late 50's, was responsible for a small home for abandoned Tamil children and had adopted five children myself. They were doing well, but I knew that all adopted children have been traumatized no matter how well adapted they seem. Still it took me some time to open the little blue box and prepare PC309g (adoption trauma), 2 globules in 35 ml of water. None of the below knew that I was giving them something for the trauma of adoption, it was just 'mama dosing them as usual'.

Case 1

My third daughter, a very pretty and intelligent 25-year-old with a Masters in psychology and holding down a responsible job, came home from Bangalore for the 2009 Christmas Holidays. I chose her as the first recipient of the remedy, because she was the most likely to take the drops regularly and correctly. You have to bang the bottle five times and keep five drops under your tongue for five seconds, (once a day) 5-5-5, at least fifteen minutes before or after food or toothpaste.

Being an adoptee in India is particularly traumatic because, though long since outlawed, caste is still an important issue here and an adoptee, no matter how beautiful, talented, intelligent or cultured he/she is, is in a social sense, no better than an outcaste, perhaps especially so here in the South. Three of my children married Westerners, two of them went to live overseas. Many, many times my third daughter has told me what a problem it is for her. For a long time she felt unable to admit being an adopted child even to a boy who was totally in love with her and with whom she was totally in love. When she did, he made it plain that he could never marry her, or even introduce her to his sisters!

Not surprisingly this young woman, whom we will call Usha, suffered from anxiety and insecurity with people and had periods during which she was afraid that something terrible might happen.

She was also suffering from what we called 'jerks' on going to sleep, something that sounded like small convulsions, and which caused her considerable anxiety verging on downright fear. She had reacted minimally to *Lachesis* and *Sepia* and *Natrum muriaticum* (which looked like her constitutional remedy), but the jerks would always return. But it was the sense of insecurity of which she complained, rather than the jerks that had led me to give her the adoption trauma remedy.

Follow-up:

She went back to work in Bangalore on the 26 of December 2009 and on the 2nd January 2010 I received a postcard saying that since she had started the drops there were no more jerks and that she was happy. She was happy! Being a *Natrum muriaticum*, she was not normally given to divulging that sort of information on a postcard. Later when the drops were finished she asked for more and wrote that when she didn't take the drops the jerks started again.

She has been promoted at work and is in charge of training new employees. She is now 80% more confident, the insecurity as well as the jerks are very much reduced: instead of getting the severe jerks several times practically every night, she may get them once in a night perhaps once in ten days and in a very attenuated form.

Case 2

My adopted son of 24 also came home that Christmas. He had a long-standing cough which didn't worry him nearly as much as his beginning vitiligo. But I gave him the PC509g for neither of those problems specifically, but for whatever trauma the separation from his mother and the adoption had caused him and for the social difficulties he had experienced as an adopted child, which were quite similar to those of my daughter.

Follow-up:

Though he is a handsome lad and a football champion who played in the junior national championships, a series of girlfriends broke off the relationship when he found the courage to tell them he was an adoptee. It had been deeply disturbing, but after the drops he shrugs and says he is not going to try and make it work with an Indian girl. He will find a western girl. His vitiligo vanished without his needing the PC vitiligo remedy. After we next saw him after taking the remedy he seemed to be spilling over with an extra energy we had not seen in him before. When talking to us he would get up and literally dance around while talking, hopping from one foot to the other, gesticulating. And I suddenly saw him as a *Phosphorus*. He still had his cough and I checked and found the modalities of the cough fitted *Phosphorus* well. He was cured with *Phosphorous* C200 in just a day where he had it for several years. So dealing with the adoption trauma released his true nature, which helped me to now see his constitutional remedy. He is much more confident now and has had two promotions since early 2010 when he started the drops – a period of nine months.

Case 3

My elder daughter has fewer social problems since she had always mixed with westerners having been adopted at six weeks old. She had a history of several bouts of bronchitis as a very young child and a chronic cough in her thirties, which went away when she took the drops.

I still have to get the drops to my other two children who are overseas.

Case 4

I have kept this till last because of the interesting way in which the adoption trauma remedy worked in this case. The recipient was a 36-year-old woman who had been suffering from chronic diarrhoea for some fifteen years.

Follow-up:
The diarrhoea was soon 85% better, but many fears remained.

Some time after starting the adoption trauma remedy she needed to go to the dentist for an infected wisdom tooth. She had managed to avoid dentists all her life since she was terribly afraid of pain. This time she went, but no sooner had she lain down on the dental couch than she started weeping and trembling and had to be sent home.

What happened?

She had never realized it before but she was afraid of being tied up. If we had been more alert in taking her case we might have seen it before. She had always said, for example, that she didn't want to get married because she didn't want to be "tied down". After taking the drops she was able to go to the dentist and via the experience that followed was able to formulate her fear for the first time. Clearly the trauma drops had worked as a catalysing agent. She also now realized that she didn't like to be held by the forearm. She was afraid of being seized and bound, which is what she feared would happen when she lay down on the dental couch. Her forearm she now admitted would instinctively always jerk away from even the gentlest hold. It was only now she realized this.

What was all this about? How did it originate she asked herself, and so did we. She had never suffered any physical abuse. She came to the conclusion that it belonged either to something that had happened while she was in the womb or in some past life. Well the thing to do was to find a remedy with fear of being bound, fear of being tied. Delusion is bound, or tied, Delirium is bound or tied, Dreams of being bound or tied. None of my repertoires revealed a remedy.

So I asked a colleague who uses a homeopathic software programme (I have a serious physical allergy to electronics). He came back with the information that Rajan Sankaran gives 'binding and unbinding' as the underlying sensation for the *Euphorbia* group and proceeded to read out the remedy names: *Croton tiglion, Mancinella, Cascarilla, Acalypha, Euphorbium, Hura, Stillingia*. I let out a cry, "*Mancinella*"!
It rang a bell. There was something I'd never forgotten entirely though I'd never fully focused upon it. This woman, whom we will call Shanti, had once said, when still a little child, that she liked to sleep with her feet tucked into the blanket, "so that the devil couldn't snatch them." (!!) She should have been given *Mancinella* there and then but there were no concomitants and at the time other remedies seemed more likely. According to Rajan, God bless him, *Mancinella* also doesn't like to be held by the wrist or ankles.

Rx *Mancinella* 1M

Follow-up:
It had a life changing effect: a few days later she reported that she was going to marry her companion of 17 years.
Moreover they had been out walking together when he had suddenly grabbed her forearm to draw her to the side of the road out of the way of an oncoming car and she had not reacted.
Though she had no memory of saying that she liked to keep her feet tucked in out of the way of the devil, what we both remembered was that there had been a nanny we'd had to send away because she threatened the children with stories of 'pei' (devil) when they got out of hand. (Obviously we can never take such remarks too seriously).

I have given this story at some length because I find it amazing that a PC Resonance could work indirectly with such a far reaching effect, acting as a catalyst, as it were, releasing information that had been blocked.

Another aspect of not wanting to be held down was that as an adolescent she had always broken out of school situations. Though a talented dancer and singer with a gift for drawing she had never finished her training or any of her courses. She had gone to an art school overseas and left just as she was really getting started. Later on, she very much regretted not having any degree or diplomas though she was doing something she liked and was good at: arts classes for young children. After the remedy she became much calmer and more contented. She no longer suffers from claustrophobia as she had in the past.
The follow-up since we started with the PC Adoption trauma resonance in this case is now 14 months.

Haiti Dec 17 2010 to Jan 7 2011

Reported by Robert Eklund, MD, Homeopath, USA

Naciketa and I stayed at D's children's home and school. School was not in session but there were seven children that D had accepted because they had no one to care for them. They ranged from two to four years old and most of them were two years old. Within a few days of our arrival she accepted a one-year-old boy who had a reddish tinge to his hair colour – a sign of kwashiorkor, a form of protein malnutrition that is fairly common in very poor countries. An aunt who brought the one-year-old to D explained that the mother would leave him unattended in the streets for long periods of time. The mother was currently in the hospital with cholera. The aunt said she could not raise the baby. He started crying when she left and would not eat – just cry and cry. D said it would take about two weeks for him to adjust.

Amma Resonance Healing Foundation sent us MP3 files by email for many of the remedies since our kits did not arrive before we departed. D was hesitant to let us try our MP3 file for adoption trauma on the baby. We had no idea if it would work so we were not very convincing, but with his continuous crying it didn't take her long to allow us to treat him. He listened to it once and it worked beautifully! He stopped crying except when he wanted to be fed and he regained his appetite. The next one was a two-year-old who began crying when her father left after coming to visit. With one listen to the adoption trauma MP3 file she became her normal, playful, happy self. It normally took her several days to recover. Then D asked us to treat all the children, which we did.

Case of adoption trauma
Reported by Nico Beentjes, Netherlands

An adopted child was taken to see the homeopath under the pretext of doing something about her pimples. A good excuse to lure a 16-year-old teenager into a therapist's practice. Basically, what was wrong was that the child was not very easy to live with – to say the least. PC Adoption trauma was given.

Follow-up:
After two weeks, the mother already reported some change on the telephone. The next visit was set four weeks after the remedy.
During that visit, the mother said she didn't recognize her child anymore – she had totally changed. Whereas before, she never wanted to do household chores, now she was doing dishes voluntarily, without being asked. She would ask her mother: "Mum, shall I make a nice cup of coffee for you?" That was also a first. Now, she would sit on her mother's lap and hug her (at 16!), something she never did before. Love was streaming.

Birth Trauma

Birth trauma can include any number of complex and overlapping traumas for the baby. This is intended for the common possibilities, such as oxygen starvation/suffocation, stuck in the second stage with panic (tunnel phobia), separation from the mother, cutting the cord too soon. If you want to help facilitate a natural birth it's good for the mother to have treatment for her birth trauma as otherwise it is likely to recur when she gives birth herself. Before giving birth, and preferably before getting pregnant, treating any history of trauma, particularly incest or rape trauma, is essential. In mechanical birth injuries use PC Injury; cranial-sacral therapy is brilliant here too.

Caesarean Birth

A normal birth is an initiation into this realm and while often painful, it is necessary and serves a natural purpose. If a person is born by caesarean then it's a potential trauma because a vital life stage has been missed. All sorts of consequences can follow. A lack of gravitas is an obvious possibility, and being ungrounded.

Elective caesareans

A caesarean can either be planned or may become part of the delivery when the situation of mother or child calls for it. An elective caesarean is mainly scheduled when there is a medical reason not to let mother and baby go through the natural birth process.

After a caesarean the mother can have difficulties identifying her newborn as her own. It may take days before this detached feeling leaves her, and it may be clear that this reserved and distant feeling doesn't make for a good start to the relationship between mother and child. Though not unknown, this is observed less after a natural birth, where mother and child have gone through the whole process together, including all the pains and emotions involved. Of course, almost all mothers experience great joy directly after the delivery, no matter how their child was born. In natural birth, under the influence of hormones induced by the pains, this joy can reach an overwhelming state of exaltation. It is thought that the high levels of hormones responsible for this also promote and deepen the bonding between mother and child. Both mother and child also share the experience that if they go for it together they can make it, and for the baby this can be considered as a blueprint for expectations in all other projects it will engage in later in life.

The word 'caesarean' explains a lot of what the implications for the baby in its later life can be. As the word suggests, a Caesar-ean was used to deliver the children of emperors, to avoid the risk of the child's being stillborn. Having an heir to the throne was and still is of the utmost importance to royal families. When a child is born through an elective caesarean it is directly brought from paradise (which a good womb normally is) into this life. From surroundings that always have the right temperature, pleasant subdued light and muffled sounds, and a continuous supply of all nutrients to the baby, it is brought into a room where the supporting walls of the womb are missing, where it is a lot cooler, where the light is brighter and the voices louder and the hands that touch the skin are rough and crude compared to the softness of the wall of the womb. And instead of the floating weightless feeling in the amniotic fluids there is now the force of gravity pulling him down and generating the possibility of falling.

For a baby born after a normal birth the same circumstances exist, but, after having borne hours of uncomfortable and painful contractions followed by a fierce and exhausting battle in the birth canal, these new conditions are a relative improvement, and once the baby is in its mother's arms and sucking her breast the harmonious feelings of paradise return. This child now knows that taking initiative, going for it, not giving up but persevering to the end can result in great satisfaction.

Children born by an elective caesarean can still be very much in touch with the harmonious feelings from paradise, and expect their surroundings still to be able to take care of all their needs. This does not make life easy for the child, since although in the beginning the mother will still do much for it, more and more initiative is needed to gradually take responsibility for its own life. These children can have difficulties in stirring themselves into action in order to achieve what they want. They expect life to provide for them automatically. For the emperor's princes and princesses this was less of a problem. The palace they lived in and the royal household would take care of them just as the womb did, and they were guided step by step through the process leading them to the responsibility of the throne.

In short, what we may expect if more and more children are born by caesarean, is a population that is increasingly dissatisfied and disappointed with what life has to offer them; a population that is not willing or able to endure the pain and hardship that can be part of life, and that does not accept aging and its consequences.

Emergency caesareans

The meaning of an emergency caesarean and its impact on the individual later in life is completely different from that of an elective caesarean. Here birth has been initiated and evolved until at a certain point medical intervention is considered necessary to save the life of mother and/or baby. If the labour pains have not been induced but started naturally, indicating the baby and mother have taken the initiative to end the pregnancy, the typical situation will be that this person each time it later in life enters into a process or starts a project will run into difficulty at some point, similar to the stage in which the birth process was broken off to perform a caesarean. The experience of this difficulty or the situation in which it occurs will often be analogous to how the experience during birth has been.

Genocide and War

This is built from the experiences of Bosnia and Rwanda and other war zones but it applies generally as our experience confirms. In general PTSD/trauma includes flashbacks, this is the key symptom and the other symptoms seem to be consequences of this. There are nightmares of great intensity, there is emotional shutdown and avoidance behaviour and there is hyper arousal. The key thing in genocide is the tormenting memories after a sudden but premeditated, planned, savage, short lasting, attack. Many similar such events occur in war. For the survivors there are flashbacks of exact, extremely scary, horrific moments during war or genocide that were really life threatening, deeply painful, humiliating, remorseful and much more. These flashbacks are occurring daily, even hourly, every minute of every day, and have lasted many years already. Repetitive and vivid flash backs of events that happened.

The consequence of these images, thoughts and responses:

- They cannot get to sleep without tormenting images for a long period into the night.
- They cannot sleep properly at all, only getting light and partial sleep for many years and they are not fully rested or refreshed after sleep.
- They cannot focus on any real daily problem as these get linked immediately to genocidal images, which they normally cannot blank out, and it is in the centre of their mind and any inner thinking goes directly to the 'TV goal' like replays. They cannot make rational decisions because they cannot think, in every thought they go into the genocide images and ruminate and get no further. They stay buried in these overwhelming processes.
- They cannot respond to the needs of others – typically their large family and instead neglect them because they are unable to feel and think.
- They try to avoid anything that will stimulate the flashbacks and hyper arousal and this can lead to extreme behaviour and sometimes they turn to drugs and alcohol or suicide/self harming.
- They feel they could be killed at any moment; any sudden sound frightens them to death day and night. Hyper arousal is the term and it can occur from a child screaming or a loud bang or a stone dropped by a bird hitting the tin roof. There is the immediate expectation of being killed.
- They are very frightened as the killers are still at large, even living next door, even if the killers next door have tried to apologise. They cannot accept or contemplate the apologies.
- They are deeply disturbed by not having been able to bury their relatives. This lack of closure is a very common and serious trauma in its own right.

Also, as a consequence of their internalised fearful and deeply frightened state:

- They fear the neighbours in the community who were the killers and generalise this and don't socialise, don't go to church, don't engage in conversation, never laugh and joke, and instead stay at home, isolated from society. They even become speechless for long periods lasting for years.
- They do not allow themselves to be helped by others.
- They feel it is impossible that anyone could even want to help them.
- They remain dependent victims, having to beg for food, unable to even think of work, of restarting work, instead living in dire poverty, starving (eating a small meal every few days), homeless, rootless yet often having to support large families of orphans.

> Children drop out of school due to the memories and the consequential inability to study. They can become criminals and addicted to drugs and alcohol, not to mention cigarettes.

While this is not the full picture and represents mainly the victim's inner world, it is accurate for the many women and men we interviewed and replicated millions of times across the world in many variations.

Rwanda 2005
Peter Chappell, Czech Republic

(See also Part III)

> 30 survivors of the Rwanda genocide that took place in 1994 who took this PTSD/trauma resonance for the trauma of war and genocide had dramatic improvements:
>
> - The tormenting memories of genocide, which were daily, hourly, even every minute of every day, and had lasted eleven years, virtually disappeared overnight and they had many benefits from this.
> - They could get to sleep without tormenting thoughts.
> - They slept deeply, possibly for the first time in eleven years.
> - They could focus on daily problems without these being linked to genocidal thoughts and could then make rational decisions rather than staying buried in these overwhelming thoughts.
> - They stopped fearing the neighbours in the community who were the killers in the genocide and started again socialising, chatting, going to church, laughing and joking.
> - They stopped feeling they could be killed at any moment, that any sound would frighten them to death day and night.
> - They felt the possibility that they could believe and allow others to help them.
> - They felt able to begin the process of forgiveness and even actively encouraged it with those who killed their relatives.
> - They could respond to the needs of others – typically their large orphan extended family.
> - They decided to stop being dependent and having to beg and to start thinking about a small business and becoming independent.
> - One child that had dropped out of school due to the memories and the consequential inability to study wanted to return.
> - A businessman who took the Trauma Resonance because of high blood pressure and heart palpitations that occurred around the anniversary of the genocide found it resolved his symptoms, which is not surprising. This is just one of what must be millions of people who have a set of symptoms that belong in history, to unresolved trauma and this I suggest is the reason why the medical textbooks are full of comments about most chronic diseases where they say the cause is unknown and there is no known cure. These are the routine before and after comments you find in the bibles of medicine. The amount and intensity of trauma that has been piled up over generations is a most likely cause. Treating these chronic effects of past trauma as miasmatic trauma layers we suggest is the cure.

This Trauma Resonance works for both victims and aggressors, since, in the main, the aggressors are victims to the instigators and their subconscious so it's intended to work for both. Also, for instance the Rwandese rebels that today kill and rape in East DRC Congo were themselves victims of the 1994 genocide. Those people that murder and rape can only do that because of the unresolved trauma inside of themselves. Due to this state, that may be transgenerational as also based on direct experience, they have become unfeeling and able to pass their inside horror on to others. In that sense traumatic events only know victims.

There are wars and conflicts all over the world on a continuous basis adding millions of newly traumatized people. Here is an excerpt showing the consequences of what could be considered to be a more minor conflict.

In Kashmir, Conflict's Psychological Legacy
Mental Health Cases Swell in Two Decades
Muslim protesters shout pro-freedom slogans during a curfew relaxation in Srinagar. Tensions had eased in recent years, but a land-transfer plan stirred anger among Muslims. (By Dar Yasin -- Associated Press)

By Emily Wax

> Washington Post Foreign Service Monday, September 1, 2008; Page A09
> ... Srinagar, a scenic lakeside city nestled in the foothills of the Himalayas, once had among the lowest mental illness rates in the world. But in 1989, leaders of the region's Muslim majority launched an armed separatist movement, one of several said to have been backed by predominantly Muslim, which has fought two wars with Hindu-majority India over Kashmir since India's partition in 1947. Srinagar became a battleground as hundreds of thousands of Indian troops quelled the uprising. The fighting has left a powerful psychological legacy.
>
> The number of patients seeking mental health services surged at the state psychiatric hospital, from 1,700 when the unrest began to more than 100,000 now. Last year, they were treated at the hospital or the recently opened Advanced Institute of Stress and Life Style Problems, where Qadeem works.
>
> "Every home in Kashmir has a heartbreaking history," said Qadeem, who admits she sometimes becomes emotional during sessions. "There is terrible ache when you lose a sibling. Pills can't help. I share that agony of loss with my clients. In Kashmiri society, this pain is everywhere."
>
> India's push to keep Kashmir is taking a toll on Kashmiris as well as Indian soldiers, in ways that are harder to measure than deaths or injuries. Experts say that mental health is an invisible casualty of war and that generations will bear the scars, imperilling Kashmir's prospects for a bright future with or without India.
>
> The patients have insomnia, learning disabilities, anxiety disorders and what Kashmiri therapists call the "midnight-knock syndrome," a fear stemming from the many pre-dawn raids by Indian security forces aimed at rooting out suspected insurgents.
> Mental health groups estimate that 60,000 Kashmiris committed suicide last year, a record number, said Mushtaq Margoob, head of the Government Psychiatric Diseases Hospital in Srinagar.
>
> More than fifteen per cent of Kashmiris are afflicted with post-traumatic stress disorder, according to a recent study by Margoob. Indian troops also are suffering, undertaking long tours without their fam-

ilies in a place where residents are often hostile. In January, the Indian army recruited 400 psychiatrists after more than 100 soldiers, including officers, killed themselves.

Among Kashmiris, the sufferers who reach the hospital are a fraction of those who need help. Remote villages have borne the brunt of the violence, and many who live there do not have the money for the long trip.

"It's really an epidemic in Kashmiri society," said Margoob, who opened Qadeem's hospital to deal with the overflow of cases. "Over decades, Kashmiri society has been stretched beyond its natural capacity to cope. Depression and anxiety can also be passed down from generation to generation."

Part of the problem is that there is little justice, Margoob said, something that in psychological terms would be called "closure." Human rights groups estimate that the conflict has left 77,000 people dead and as many as 10,000 missing. Women whose husbands have gone missing during the conflict are known here as "half-widows."
...

Qadeem said her three-year-old daughter recently asked to pet some puppies she had noticed.

"It hurt. I had to tell her it was a curfew," Qadeem said, as the child screamed in her arms. "Before that, she asked me to take her to the nearby gardens. I also had to tell her no, because there was lots of Indian army there. Suddenly I realized that from childhood, she knows that there is danger. That is Kashmir. That is our reality."

That trauma is being passed on down the generations is something WWII has taught us. As a psychological phenomenon this has become general knowledge. Recent research suggests that trauma even changes the genetic information we pass on to our children. The following case is an example of transgenerational trauma as also of the role a Genus Traumaticus approach can play in individual treatment to complement the simillimum.

Case of a 55-year-old woman with a deep pain
Harry van der Zee, Netherlands

Sarah has troubles with her digestion, but 'that is something I can live with by taking natural medicines to prevent constipation.'

'My mother left the house when I was nine and I was looked after by housekeepers. My father was very ambitious and busy. I also spent months with family attending a different school. There was no basic security. I have felt very lonely. All my sisters were placed at different addresses. I had to adjust to a different family and a different school.'
'My mother was depressed and institutionalised. If I saw her it felt as if I was with a dead person. In my puberty I started to release myself from my mother. I had a sort of allergic feeling to her passivity. To be touched by her was very difficult for me. She lived very much on her own. Only once she died was I able to love her again. Now I feel that I have a more beautiful connection with her.'

'My parents had been hiding during the war and my mother's family was completely extinguished in the concentration camps. That has always been there. It seeped through. I had the feeling I had to take care of my mother. I loved her a lot and missed her enormously. But the relationship with her changed. In her depression she could not be reached. My father remarried with a good woman but it was a very mental family. I felt insecure, not at ease. When I was eighteen I emigrated with my sister to Israel. I have lived there for eighteen years, was married and had children.'

'My marriage was very difficult. Now we have separated the relationship is okay. I missed emotional support. When we were having a fight and I felt no understanding or contact I was sucked into very deep emotions that were beyond my control. Like a very old well of pain. As if I was losing grip. As if I was losing contact with reality. Going to a deep place where this was lying. It is a completely different world, with strong emotions and loneliness. Being cut off. As if everything is useless. As if I can already see the end of things. The grief and pain there are so huge and I don't dare to feel the depth of it. I weep a lot.'

'Already at kindergarten I felt displaced. I didn't belong to the group, had no connection, even though I did have friends. Every morning I feel this heaviness when I need to confront the world again. By using my willpower I have done my work and looked after my children.'

'I have a very intense contact with my little sister and when she started to separate herself from me that was very difficult for me. Each time I have to depart from people I get these feelings. Away from the connection, away from the security.'

'I have tended to overeat and was fourteen kilos overweight. I loved cheese, ice-cream, chocolate and sweet dairy products. Then I would slim down drastically followed again by overeating. This is no longer the case. Now I love salads and raw fish.'

'Ever since I started the relationship with my ex-husband I started having asthma. That has always stayed. Very strong attacks. I get more and more asthmatic until it completely closes off. Very frightening. It is worse from wet weather, in autumn, from cats and dairy products.'

'I don't have nasty dreams, but can wake up in a panic, feeling the contact is gone, I no longer feel the relationship.'

'I'm the eldest of three daughters. Before me my mother had a miscarriage. Three months after I was born she was pregnant again. I have three children. In each pregnancy I would become depressed in the seventh month. The last pregnancy was not planned and I felt my husband was not happy with it. Oh I have been so depressed. I would leave the house in the middle of the night. No support. I felt like wanting to take it away using knitting needles. Because I felt so lonely. I was happy with it first but saw his face change when I told him. My mother was an afterthought. Her mother was very cold and had manic episodes.'

Analysis

What was most striking in the case for me was the pain and grief coming from a well deep inside her that she did not dare to feel, that felt as if it was bigger than her. There are enough reasons in her personal life to have feelings of grief and of being alone, but this feeling of everything being useless and this notion of already seeing the end of things I could not connect with her personal history. I could connect it though to her mother's history and to the collective Jewish trauma of the holocaust.

Prescription: PC War & Genocide Trauma (PC304x), 5 drops daily

Follow-up

Five weeks later:

'I am very much surprised. There is a change I had never expected to be possible. I feel a completely different person. A dramatic change. For a short period I continued crying but since then it has not come back. It is a completely new period. I feel optimism, trust, love for life. It is miraculous. This weeping has travelled with me all of my life. The last couple of years it was constantly there. Before that in episodes.'

'I dream again, quite lucid, remember them better. My sleep is much deeper and I wake up less. On waking up in the morning I am okay. No more panic or fear of being abandoned. I can continue with my life like this. I'm no longer afraid to move on, to be forsaken. A great trust has come. It is okay what happens or is about to happen. There is more peace inside. I can enjoy the simple things in life again. Before this all joy was lacking.'

'Before I started taking this remedy I had the feeling of being wiped out, taking no space. I might just as well not have been there. Now I take a space and that has meaning.'

Prescription: continue with PC304x (trauma of war and genocide) five drops daily.

Two months later:

'A complete layer has been closed off, this layer of collective grief.

The insecurities I have now have to do with every day practicalities. Like building my house. Then I feel a lack of stability and go back to the time our family was broken up. Like a sea without borders. I love the sea because it gives space, quiet and openness.'

'In the morning I have a bit of trouble starting the day, a little sadness. In the evenings I am feeling great. What I didn't tell you before is that I have a strong fear of spiders. In the last couple of months my menses has returned.'

Analysis

She is completely free now from this bottomless impersonal but collective pain and grief, and the complaints she has now she can relate to her own life. So, now it is time to move on to a personal simillimum. Regarding her personal trauma the broken relationship with her mother is essential. She was disconnected from the source of security she was depending on, her mother, causing feelings of forsakenness and insecurity. This definitely happened at the age of nine when her mother could no longer cope, but also before that time her mother was depressed and not the source of warmth and comfort she needed. Later in her life we see a tendency towards bulimia with a desire for sweet dairy products, including ice cream and chocolate.

Prescription: *Lac humanum* MK

Eleven weeks later:

'I'm beautifully out of the dependency in my recent relationship (a friend she got after her divorce). I'm on my own feet now. There have been no dips any more and my base has become firmer. All the symptoms that have improved on the first remedy never returned. Since this last remedy my asthma is a lot better, my stomach problems are gone and I no longer have abdominal pains.'

'I dream about my recent relationship. I dreamt of getting a clear view by literally putting on other glasses to be able to see further away.'

Three months later:
'I'm totally fine and suggest cancelling the appointment. I'll contact you in case anything new comes up.'

Two years later she is still doing well and never needed a repetition of either remedy.

Comment: the fact that she responded so well and needed no repetition of the remedy is remarkable. For a case of such depth that is very uncommon and I expect that if I had started her with *Lac humanum* she would have responded, but less deeply and with recurrent relapses. By realizing the root of her problem was transgenerational trauma and by dealing with that first this provided a deep cure to which *Lac humanum* gave the finishing touch.

All over the world there are cases like the above where a history of war trauma in the family is the forming force of a wide variety of physical and psychological problems. From our experiences in Bosnia and Africa we know this to be the reality and we expect many homeopaths that have worked under similar conditions can confirm this. Individualising all these cases is possible and gives results. The Genus Traumaticus approach we suggest on a theoretical basis and have tested in practice is clearly very effective and in our opinion provides excellent results that are more consistent than with individualising each and every case. As a homeopath you can completely listen and be there for the patient and do not need to watch the homeopathic clockwork inside go over rubrics and remedies, and directly prescribe a remedy you know from experience will work. The main thing you need to be aware of is whether there are other stories besides the war trauma, e.g. was rape involved and are there signs of gonorrhoea or AIDS? Ideally individualised treatment is part of the approach, but with massive trauma or in areas with minimal medical care that can often not be given.

War trauma in Africa
Harry van der Zee, Burundi and DRC Congo (2008-2010)

Congolese adults refer to their trauma as 'hypertension' as the pathology often shows in the heart, with palpitation, hyperventilation and fear of death. Here is a case where PC Resonance and an individually chosen medicine complement each other.

Z. is diagnosed with cardiomyopathy and dilatation of the heart, which started in 1997 in her fourth pregnancy, during the time that the war broke out. One day she woke up and found many dead bodies in the street and saw a dog eating from a dead body. That image has forever stayed with her. 'Maybe,' she says, 'that caused my depression.'

Prescription: *PC304x* (Genocide & War Trauma) once daily five drops.

Follow-up after six days:
After the remedy she first had an aggravation with pain in her chest. That pain is now gone. She is still easily short of breath but the images of the war are gone.

After two months:
When a few days ago the police were searching the house looking for illegal immigrants, the fear came back and she felt as if her heart were breaking in two. The images of the war never came back and she no longer dreams of the war. The heart symptoms are the same.

Prescription: Repeat PC304x daily for one week (for the revived trauma) and then start with *Cactus* 200K one dose per week (for the physical condition).

In these regions trauma can be called endemic or epidemic. Although the individual expression may differ a little from one patient to another, after listening to many of them it is clear to me that they are all speaking about a collective experience.

60% of the 600 children at a primary school in Kiliba (DR Congo) were orphans. Many of them had lost parents in the war. Several had been recruited by rebels against their will (dragged from their parents' huts) to become child soldiers. Trauma is all over their faces, their eyes turned inward or staring into a void. These children were all treated with the PC304x for the trauma of war and genocide.

Follow-up:
When I returned to the school two months later, I interviewed them and they told me how much they had improved. Their tormenting thoughts and dreams had stopped. Their teachers reported the children could concentrate now in class and looked so much brighter.

War trauma in a health professional

Rashid Rissasi W'orgene, Organisation CELA, DRC Congo, 2011

Since I took PC304X for the first time, I find a stability in my heart, because all the time I felt like someone was planning to do me harm. Also I am in balance in my office because the bad ideas I imagined all the time don't come anymore; sometimes I saw that my whole environment is bad. I didn't want to share even my ideas, my breaks with my friends. But thanks to PC War, I find ameliorations that I myself confirm.

Incest Trauma

Sexual abuse by a relative, a person that should belong to the circle of those who can be trusted and relied upon, is a widely spread form of trauma, present in all cultures. It is of archetypal nature and therefore present as part of the human drama in the psychology of everyone. Especially when the abuse has taken place at a very young age, or from a young age onwards, the effects on the psychology of the victim go deep. Typically it is a trauma of transgenerational nature where victims turn into abusers or find relationships in which the abuse continues, with themselves as well as their offspring.
In the case below one of the early PC Trauma Resonances – Long time past trauma – was given. Although it was used with good success we would now advise alongside individualised treatment to prescribe the PC Resonance for incest, possibly followed with PC injury. All types of trauma can at some point be long time past, and prescribing for the type of trauma much more closely covers the psychology and symptom totality of that trauma.

Case of incest trauma

Reported by Myriam Birrer, Switzerland

A German 36-year-old woman is a gardener by profession. She has a hard and complex family history with incest by her father. Her mother completely neglected her. She had an accident involving her head and spinal column resulting in chronic pains and a serious sleeping disorder.
She stays in bed until 11 a.m. and has to lie down during the day regularly because she is weak and exhausted. She wakes up at night regularly and lies in her bed fully awake. She has tried all kinds of therapies and treatments with little avail.
Her financial, social and occupational situation is disorganised and all mixed up. Socially she is going downhill. She is married but totally withdraws from her partner. She has fear of men. She gets to know a doctor the same age as her father and they fall in love. She thinks of him day and night. She visits him at his home and has sex with him. She loves him but at the same time is confused by the situation. The man gets more and more aggressive, and visits her mainly to have sex with her. She wants him close to her and can't let go of him. She feels helpless and dependent like she did as a child. She lies in bed and weeps terribly. She doesn't dare to speak about her situation. Feels ashamed.

Prescription: *PC306a* for Long Time Past Trauma.

[As the history included several types of trauma this more general resonance was selected instead of a more specific one, like for incest trauma.]

Follow-up:
With this remedy her sleeping improves. She wakes up in the morning and gets up spontaneously. She weeps less. She starts calling her friends and tells them what has happened. She takes the remedy for two months, and depending on her needs – once daily or once a week.

After that several doses of *Phosphoricum acidum* C200 further help her.
After four months she takes PC306a again. Then *Psorinum* C200 for the flu. Psorinum also fits because of her pessimism, her being always chilly and her strong appetite.
After six months again she uses PC306a. It takes her 18 months to fully let go of the doctor. Her husband doesn't know anything about the situation, but her relationship with him improves. She communicates more with him, gives him hugs. She recovers more and more and becomes stronger.

PC Incest feedback
Peter Chappell, Czech Republic

This was just one client who had been to five psychologists in a row and had never talked to anyone over a period of eight years. The general pattern was that she never opens up and alternates between depression and self-damage, with several suicidal attempts in her 26 years. She is in psychiatric care now for eight years and sometimes she is institutionalised but mostly she is out in the world. She takes antidepressants and they have no effect at all.

She took the PC Resonance for incest trauma for one month and was followed up for a further five months before this report.

Follow-up:
From the first month she started opening up a tiny bit and then the third month she opened up significantly and finally she sees a future and wants to have children; she has a goal she wants to achieve which is a very positive sign.
For the first time she has explained that she feels guilty and that she was involved not as a victim in the incest which was with her father. She feels better in herself and stopped cutting herself and there has only been one attempt at self-violence which was to use an alkaline substance to burn the skin, which was treated with low potency homeopathic remedies appropriate to the burning pain which helped.
She is now more compassionate than before; before she was as sharp as a razor and lacked compassion. She works as a social carer in a house which is an asylum for women with children in need. Her guilt has reduced a little from ten out of ten self-guilt to now seven or eight out of ten. At previous consultations she would offer two sentences in one hour and now she is opening up a bit more each month and this is a great shift after eight years and five therapists. She is still not capable of expressing negative feelings towards the abuser – her father or to her mother.
The therapist says that she is not the typical incest case. She is the exception and maybe there is something like one wanting a mystical union and that this is the way her father could accept her. She's a bit like a princess and she has a great deal of guilt.
This is still slow progress but it's as if one concrete block has been removed and there are still five to go. Her mind is different and her face has changed even so.
Normally with incest it's difficult to get started but once started the therapy is quite effective in a relatively short period of time. This is not the case with her. In her the guilt is like a steel shield.

The conclusions from this: Here we have a very intractable case of incest, one of the most difficult of all to solve or to help and in a matter of three months the client has opened up the first time in eight years. Obviously a repetition of the incest remedy is indicated and maybe should have been used earlier.

Case woman 49 years old
Harry van der Zee, Netherlands

This woman has been treated with homeopathy since 1991. She has a history of incest by her father, a marriage with a sadist and violence by an alcoholic she lived with later.

When she was seen the first time she suffered from strong fears and nightmares and attacks of violence that were such that she was brought to a mental asylum. In her anger she would be extremely strong and pull a granite windowsill from the wall or lift a washing basin and smash it on the floor.

She was initially treated for a couple of years with *Stramonium* which reduced her fears and violence such that further hospitalisation was not necessary.
Stramonium was followed by *Rhus toxicodendron* for the many symptoms she had due to molestation by her partner. The injuries he had inflicted on her were such that hospitalisation and operations were needed. Nevertheless she still lived with this man.
She had developed psoriasis while her mental state was improving. *Staphysagria* given for a number of years further helped, and in this period she also broke up the relationship with her alcoholic partner.
At some point *Staphysagria* no longer helped her and her case was retaken. This led to the prescription of *Cimicifuga,* another member of the Ranunculaceae, which has been her constitutional remedy for the last three years.

Some symptoms that led to *Cimicifuga* were:

- the general Ranunculaceae theme of being strongly upset about situations
- loquacity
- fear of suffocation
- dreams about forgetting to take her medication
- a delusion of being poisoned
- situations in the past (father, husband, partner) that were depressing and gave her the feeling of being stuck and fixed.

After *Cimicifuga* her respiratory problems and anxiety improve and she feels much better in general. An old symptom of cystitis comes back which she had in her childhood a lot. The cystitis, remains of the sexual abuse in her childhood, responds well to *Cimicifuga*, and after coming back a few times it disappears.
The skin symptoms had improved on *Staphysagria* for some time, but now remained being a serious problem for her. PC Psoriasis was prescribed to complement *Cimicifuga*, after which the psoriasis practically disappears.
She has started therapy to further work with the memories and traumas of the past. As a result dreams and fears come up again and *Cimicifuga* is repeated. Nevertheless the memories of her father and nightmares about the past keep coming back.

At that point PC459p for incest was prescribed to her:
Her fears improved rapidly and strongly after taking five drops daily. She develops problems with eating like she had in her childhood, but this goes away after some weeks. Also she developed auras like she had in the past with half of her vision disappearing, but this did not result in migraines now, and after a few weeks also these disappeared. She has a dream of conducting a funeral ceremony for her father to bury him again.

She has a new relationship with a man that is good to her. Having been able to come to a closure and to bury her past herself, she has followed a training to conduct funeral ceremonies and now leads several funerals a week.

Injuries, Burns and Accidents

PC Injuries is intended for all types of injury and is useful in the first stage of any injury. It includes the shock that goes with injury. So in the case of injuries due to a car accident this is the one to use. It is useful after birth and any injury effect like surgery, followed by a more specific resonance like broken bones or burn. In homeopathic terms it's the equivalent of *Arnica*. It is useful if a past injury shows as a defensive reaction in any new event which in some way mimics the original injury, as the injury memory is held in the tissues locally if it was a local injury as well systemically. This is very useful to use as a routine after any injury as it then allows the normal procedures of recovery to take place and speeds up the healing. The mental picture from injury might be flinching from the flashbacks that occur subconsciously, backing away from perceived threats and taking defensive postures automatically in sleep and in reactions to others.

A case of motor accident

Harry van der Zee, Netherlands

A is a 42-year-old man that had a severe motor accident in 1981, 25 years ago.

'I have psychological complaints. These make my headaches worse. Then I totally block. This all started after the accident.'
The headaches are such that he panics and literally runs against the wall. In panic he can beat his head against the wall or strike his head with his fists. If he panics his eyes are wild and he is very aggressive.
He is still very angry at the doctors as he feels they didn't give him the proper treatment. The fact that they pulled off the bandage without any warning still makes him mad. 'I don't trust doctors anymore. They thought it was better to surprise me, but it's the opposite with me. I can block pain if I have to.'
He was totally confused after the accident and cut his broken leg loose from the construction it was hanging in. He seems to have been talking a lot but can't remember anything about that period. 'I didn't know I was in this world.'

A is very aggressive and can't handle his limitations well. He never was able to go back to study or a job since the accident. 'Without medication it's not safe for me to drive. I tend to beat up everybody getting in my way. The noise your pen makes already makes me mad.'
He gets claustrophobic in churches and likes to leave the toilet door open.
He has a compulsive tendency to buy tools and can't stop talking about something he has seen until he gets it.

Also sexually he wants satisfaction as soon as he feels the desire. He thinks about sex a lot and used to go to prostitutes. When he had his first girlfriend he wanted to have sex with her six or seven times a night.
The same with food. All desires have to be met immediately.
He smokes 30-40 cigarettes a day.

Prescription July 2006: *PC201j* (injury) five drops daily

Follow-up after six weeks:
'If I use it daily I get too irritated, so I take it every other day. I'm getting quieter in my head. My thoughts don't cause me to panic anymore, but a daily dose has the opposite effect. Then I think: where is a knife, cut my throat, the whole world is kicking me.
My dreams are milder and more peaceful.
My feet perspire more offensively.
My headaches are less and I'm less depressed.
During a long visit I didn't panic and didn't have to leave the room.

Prescription: continue PC Injury every second day and *Stramonium* 200K, one dose. (*Hyoscyamus* was not given because jealousy was no item he and his wife explained.)

Six weeks later:
Memories from before the accident start to return. He remembers having been sexually active at a young age. 'I can't look normally at women.' He is less preoccupied with sexual fantasies. He had a dream about his father: 'in a normal way. As if he was still alive. You and your father can call each other easily, a nurse said.' He feels more relaxed and sleeps better.

Prescription: *Stramonium* if indicated, continue PC Injury

Three months later:
Although he responds to *Stramonium* there are fluctuations in his psychological state.

Prescription: *Stramonium* LM3

Two months later:
'I have let go of the accident. It's no longer in my mind. It happened, that's all. And the anger and grief about it are totally gone.'

A common burn in Africa

Rashid Rissasi W'orgene, Organisation CELA, DRC Congo, 2011

A neighbour's child was burned with hot water while his mother was preparing the food in the kitchen. When she told me about it, I immediately treated this child with PC Burns and at present the child is really in good shape and he has even started to play soccer with his friends.

Nagasaki and Hiroshima Atomic Trauma

When people en mass evaporate in a millisecond, an unimaginable trauma happens to the people of that country, and in fact to the whole world. The dying process takes time and it cannot be done in a millisecond. This leaves a lot of souls stranded and a lot of unfinished business for the survivors. We understand that the local homeopaths in Hiroshima find their cases stymied by this trauma. This is no surprise. The recommendation is to prescribe this resonance once daily in cases of first or second generation Atomic Trauma and to complement with individualised prescriptions as indicated by the case.

Natural Catastrophes

This resonance is for the traumatic effects of all natural catastrophes.

Primarily it is for:

- The nightmares and constant replays of the event, the flashbacks.
- For the terrible memories and fears and phobias that started then and continue to this day and prevent sleeping properly and stop effective thinking.

Situations where it will apply:

- In flash floods and tsunamis and seeing the family swept away and drowned, even babies sucked out of the arms of parents, children clinging to trees that get uprooted.
- For the loss of land, crops, home, house, animals that flash floods and volcanoes etc. can cause. The trauma of having even your land swept away so the house cannot be rebuilt. The effects of being terrified and suffocated and nearly drowning. The effects of volcanic eruptions and the river of lava destroying everything, including paper proof of accounts, property, passport, identity etc.
- For the effects of earthquakes that have ruined houses, killed loved ones, paralysed the country.
- For the fear of after shocks and the sensation as if another shock is happening.
- For the inability to sleep properly or deeply after such events for even decades.
- For the inability to think properly, study, learn, function because all thinking leads immediately to thoughts of the terrible event.
- For the inability to accept aid yet living in desperate circumstances.
- For the inability to accept even the slightest affection.
- For the blaming of God or others for what happened.
- For the inability to work, study, run a business, to earn a living since the event.
- For the dependence on begging and aid, where previously productive and hard working.
- For the inability to love one's children or adopted children after such an event, taking it out on the children and all other unloving acts resulting from the trauma events.
- It is also for all those suffering from a family history of such trauma, going back a century or more where family members were sufferers as above, especially if they still recite the stories, and have unexplained fears, phobias, panic attacks, that make sense in the above context as if it had happened to the offspring itself. This of course implicates a large portion of the human race, but then, that IS our history. It is therefore needed in all societies where there are unfinished effects of natural catastrophes. It is for all children in the womb of parents who experienced such trauma during the pregnancy; it's for all children conceived and all subsequent generations conceived and born after such trauma unless it is fully resolved.
- It is especially indicated for all emergency care workers, relief of suffering workers, emergency ward workers/professionals, firemen, ambulance drivers, Red Cross/Red Crescent workers, all people involved in the care of trauma victims. They are naturally attracted to their own inner issues, knowingly or unknowingly.

Report from Sri Lanka
Rita Pasquale, Switzerland

When we went to Sri Lanka in summer 2005 we took some of the PC Trauma Resonances with us and distributed it where we could.

I personally had a very good result on treating myself with the PC Resonance for shock. Some weeks after being back from Sri Lanka, where I saw all the traumatised people after the tsunami, we had a flood in Switzerland as well. Our house and all the area around Lucerne were badly affected; my practice was under water (including a lot of remedies donated for Sri Lanka). The night after our flood, I realised that I was also shocked, it triggered all the shock from my Sri Lankan trip as well. So I took the PC trauma remedy and had a wonderful dream, which restored me immediately and gave me power and belief on my way as a healer for a long time after.

The dream was: I was asleep and a bear came very close to me and was breathing his strength into my ear. I woke up and felt very happy, strong and at the same time relaxed. The time following I had more inspiring meetings with bears in dreams or meditation.

Unfortunately we were in 2005 in Sri Lanka not able to make any registered follow-ups.

The recent tsunami created a big scare in a man. He was given the Natural Catastrophe resonance and he had a profound dream about being in a Roman arena with gladiators. Possibly he was killed there. Or he inherited this ancient ancestral memory, triggered by the tsunami. After the dream he recovered from the effect of the tsunami which had been persistent for one and a half years since the event, preventing sleep and other consequences.

The 2010 Haiti earthquake
Harry van der Zee, Netherlands

Shortly after the event – all Haitians speak of 'January 12', as that is when their internal clock came to a standstill – I realized that homeopathy, in particular a Genus Traumaticus remedy for Natural Catastrophe Trauma (PC305z), would be very valuable in treating trauma in Haiti. But as rescue, first aid operations and supplies clearly had priority in the first weeks I considered it premature to visit Haiti. But when shortly after the earthquake I was invited by Diane Cotman of Volunteers of America to come and work in Haiti and set up a small clinic in the tent city on the Episcopal Church premises of College Ste. Pierre I agreed, as in this setting we would not disturb or use resources of those providing acute relief.

At College Ste. Pierre we treated hundreds of people from the tent city and instructed priests and deacons and several others how to treat the people in the areas they represent. Nico (See next report) followed up on this to realise the goal of treating many thousands more to get their internal clock into motion again, relieve them from the past and bring them back into the here and now.

Similar to treating epidemics in Africa I've used the simplest approach possible so others can easily, safely and effectively disperse the remedy. 555 stands for banging the bottle five times, giving five drops in the mouth that should be kept there for five seconds. As this is not a chronic condition but trauma from an acute event giving one dose is usually enough.

Results

The totality of symptoms related to the earthquake is very diverse, and include: palpitations; fear; the feeling the world is turning, moving or opening up; apathy with just lying or sitting and staring; no appetite or vomiting on trying to eat; restlessness with tendency to move or run; grief over loss; hopelessness; headaches or pain in the heart region or abdomen; pains related to injuries during the event; etcetera.

The usual response to PC305z Diane and I have seen is that in a matter of a day the symptoms clearly improve, and that only those that were severely traumatised either mentally or physically would need an extra dose. Others that we had instructed to go out into tent areas and treat people reported the same.

Case example 1:

M.T. is a 62-year-old woman. Ever since the earthquake she has the feeling the earth is still shaking, so she is on continuous alert. She is depressed and looks miserable. Like many others she lost family members and her house. I see her again two days after one dose of PC305z. She smiles and even looks happy; a totally different woman. When I ask her about the feeling that the earth is shaking she tells me it is completely gone.

Case example 2:

O. is a 23-year-old man. Ever since the earthquake he is afraid, has palpitations, and can't sit still. All of the time he has the feeling he should run. One day later the fear has gone down a lot. He feels much more relaxed. He still doesn't like to be in a building for too long, as aftershocks are still expected; a healthy response I think.

Case example 3:

J. is a 25-year-old man that has the feeling the world is turning. Besides that he wakes up with palpitations and fear at least three times per night. The next morning he tells me he slept all night long without waking up once. At 7 AM he woke up refreshed without any fear, palpitation or turning feeling.

Long-term follow-up:

It may be obvious that even if we have reached several thousands of people to treat their trauma, this is still a fraction of those that could benefit from it. Treating a number as large as possible is not only important to reduce current suffering, but also to bring Haitians back into the driving seat so they can built up a new future for themselves and their country. We were happy to be able to find Nico Beentjes prepared to visit Haiti for a month and follow-up on this [with gratitude for the donations that made it possible].

Treating Post Traumatic Stress Disorder in Haiti

Nico Beentjes, Netherlands

March 2010, the Amma Resonance Healing Foundation approached me, asking if I was interested in treating trauma in Haiti with Peter Chappell's remedy PC305z. Since I had confidence in Peter's remedies, based on my own and first-hand experience in treating AIDS (with PC1) and other conditions in Africa, I said I was. So on June 8th 2010 I landed in Port au Prince to stay there for a month.

The assignment I was given was to administer the remedy to as many people as possible and to observe and record the results. After some initial difficulties, I started treating people in the huge camp on the Champs de Mars, the former park beside the (collapsed) National Palace, right in the centre of the city, with the aid of two translators. Later, our activities spread to two more camps, one in Pétionville, and a camp called Solino. We asked any passers-by about complaints since the earthquake, and these were the complaints they still had:

- Loss of concentration
- Loss of memory
- Un pile de pensées (Creole for: A lot of thoughts)
- Mixed up thoughts
- Stress
- Fear it might happen again
- Loss of sleep
- Nightmares of the event (I checked a group once, asking if they had this. About 50% raised their hand)
- Vertigo, especially when sitting
- Headaches
- Pain in the stomach (the large majority pointed at the sternum, so it was not the stomach)
- Belly pain
- Back pain, high or low. Very often they said "kidney pain"
- Vaginal infection (At first we doubted that this was caused by the quake, but gradually I grew convinced that it just might have been)
- Muscle pains, localized or general

Harry van der Zee, who was in Haiti in February right after the disaster and used the same remedy, confirmed all these symptoms and observed a few more, like apathy and fear to enter a building. I guess these symptoms were the acute response to the quake. I didn't observe them, but maybe I overlooked them. Most people had two to four of the above symptoms. We gave them five drops of PC305z and let them come back next day.

Results:
The result was wonderful. As one of my translators said: "Within 24 hours they all improved, from 60 to 100%". Later we gathered data of a small group (n=42) by following them up during four subsequent days. This gave a more realistic picture. The improvement of symptoms after respectively one, two and three days was 23, 61 and 73%.

If one has ever read the report on the effect of Peter Chappell's war-trauma remedy on victims in Rwanda, one should be prepared for reactions like this, but still, it was unbelievable. It was as if a switch was tripped. Which is of course what happened: An energy-blockage was removed. A lot of people slept well for the first time in five months – the first night after the five drops they got. We made a lot of video recordings of the response, amongst which are two from people who saw their complaints disappear within fifteen minutes – complaints that had existed since the quake. And there was a little bonus: A lady who had no complaints whatsoever from the quake took the remedy anyway and showed a very nice little proving. She had vertigo, palpitations and difficult breathing. It disappeared after two days. We have her statement on video.

If I were to make a rough estimate about the number of people that got the remedy while I was there I'd say about 10,000. And my hope is that at least another 10,000 or more are added after I departed, as a few dedicated Haitians are continuing to distribute and spread the remedy. It has been given now to people in camps in Léogane (the epicentre), Jacmel, Ile de la Gonâve, etc. After the quake a lot of people fled to Cape Haitien. In the meantime someone from our group has also gone there and started treatment. It's like an oil-spill.

The main indication for us of the effect of the treatment given was the faces of those reporting back to us and the relief they experienced. These impressions are hard to turn into figures or graphs but are the most important feedback as they touch the heart and core of what motivated us to be in Haiti after this disaster.

Differential Criteria between War Resonance and Natural Catastrophe Resonance

Some other trauma resonances are close to this one, especially Genocide & War Trauma. The main difference here is that with Genocide & War Trauma Resonance, there is deliberate man-made intent behind it. It's human in origin, which introduces a fundamentally different aspect. There is also PC Shock trauma, which is specifically for the effects of shock and nothing else and will work in this specific area.

If you are using a trauma resonance to heal unknown trauma effects from generations back, you should follow the family store of knowledge or the history of your society to decide which. In Europe genocides/war trauma would seem more common. In the east it would seem that natural catastrophe is more common. One can also imagine both war and natural catastrophe trauma being strongly indicated and we would then suggest first one and then the other in sequence, starting with the more recent unless the older one is clearly on the surface.

Sexual Abuse and Rape

It's fair to say that rape should be assumed to be a traumatic event in all situations unless there is strong evidence to the contrary. The event itself is traumatic and besides that the stigma of rape obviously permeates everyone who has been raped. There are some extreme examples where the woman is gang raped by an invading army of men, deliberately as a form of genocide, becomes pregnant, the race/tribe is polluted and the mother is then stigmatised for life by this. She is disowned by her husband and older children, as is the child, nobody in the community likes her or him, and the whole trauma is taboo and never talked about. The child asks 'Mummy, why doesn't anybody like me? Why can't x play with me?' The typical Bosnian Muslim woman raped due to the Serbian Army situation, or the Rwanda Genocide situation or many other similar events.

Cases of rape
Harry van der Zee, DRC Congo

Four years ago 38-year-old M. was raped by two soldiers and became pregnant. It was an extra-uterine pregnancy and the foetus was aborted. Now during intercourse she has a lot of pain, "as if they are trying to put a tree inside." She has vaginal infection frequently. Every time she has pain she thinks about the rape, and ever since the rape she is fearful on seeing a man. The joy of sex is gone, and instead she is afraid of it because of the pain. During intercourse anger is stimulated.

Prescription: *PC435p* (rape and sexual abuse) once daily five drops.

Comment: I had used this remedy only once in the Netherlands with good results but had no idea whether and how it would work in Congo, where thousands and thousands of women have been raped by rebels or soldiers.

Follow-up after 10 weeks:
"The thoughts about rape have disappeared. I no longer have an aversion to sex but desire it very much now. No more fear; I enjoy it now. When I see men, I'm no longer afraid. No more anger even though having sex is still painful."
Nevertheless, there are still the physical problems of pain with intercourse and vaginal discharge. However, the pain doesn't raise anger anymore and doesn't prevent her from enjoying intercourse. Most likely the pain is caused by gonorrhoea due to the rape.

Prescription: *PC180g* (gonorrhoea) after which also the physical symptoms disappear.

The collective case of rape in Bukavu
Harry van der Zee, DRC Congo

Witnessing PC1 giving life back to severely ill AIDS-patients is a dramatic experience. Even more impressive to me was meeting the traumatised women of Bukavu. I dropped silent at hearing stories of so much suffering and was filled with deep respect for their strength. To then see how much their suffering was relieved by Peter's trauma resonances left me with deep gratitude. I love sharing this with you.
During my first trip to DR Congo in 2008, entering from Burundi into Kivu province, the above case was one of several people who had been raped whom I treated, and all responded well. We were ad-

vised not go deeper into Congo then, but on my second trip in 2009 it seemed to be more quiet and we went to Bukavu, a city that saw the number of inhabitants double due to streams of refugees. There I treated more women and with the help of a Congolese bishop we were able to set up a small clinic there. The women who shared their experiences with me made me aware of how the act of rape is only part, sometimes even a smaller part, of their trauma. Let me present a composite story:

Rebels enter the house and demand that a woman should undress. She refuses, after which they torture her in brutal and humiliating ways with guns, knives and sticks. Many women still carry scars from the severe wounds inflicted. Then several of the rebels rape her in front of her children, or the children have escaped the house and try to hide in the woods. They may take the older children with them and kill them later or use them for their purposes as child soldiers or prostitutes. If the husband is there, they kill him before or after abusing his wife. One way is to lock him in the hut and to set fire to it and then rape his wife. If the husband was not there and finds out about the situation, he usually chases his wife and the (remaining) children away. They walk to the city where she tries to earn some money by carrying heavy loads. She earns just enough to buy some food for herself and the children, but as she cannot pay school fees, her children are expelled from school, and have, as the women express it, no future. So many of these women experience trauma piled on trauma and end up doing the heaviest work for the lowest fee while their children roam the streets.

After I had taken their cases and started their treatment they were followed up by two nurses who had been trained in using PC Resonances properly. This is a summary of what they reported a couple of months later:

"All the rape cases are doing very well and are much brighter than before. The only problem is that they have little prospects and are still facing a hard life, which can bring more trauma to them. Here are some quotes by them:

- I have improved and live free of the past now. I have no more dreams and fear. The scars have disappeared but when I was not taking the medicine they came back. I continued with medication and today I am okay.
- I can sleep well now. I was thinking a lot about my past and my hard life, but now I am okay. I am confident that my thoughts about the past will disappear because this medication has helped me a lot.
- I am happier than before. I am much better. I am no more lost in my dreams and hatred towards men. The past cannot disappear completely at once but it is much better now and I thank God.
- I am more positive. I focus now more on my life and family than on my past.
- I am much better and can work well now. I have no more fear and no feeling of being a victim any more.
- I accept the past now. I am no longer the slave of my past. My thoughts are more orientated on my future than the past.
- I can still think about what happened but I don't cry anymore."

No longer being a slave of the past is the essence of a happy life for all of us. We all struggle to get or stay in the here and now, and it is amazing that women that have been so deeply traumatised have the capacity to respond to the treatment so well and in such a short span of time. As I said, this left me with great gratitude!

Haiti Dec 17 2010 to Jan 7 2011
Robert Eklund, USA

A 17-year-old woman was brought by her mother. Her mother had left her alone in a church for a couple of hours and the minister raped her. That was two months prior to her visit to D's. She was still having flashbacks, frequent crying, poor sleep, poor appetite, and aversion to men. [Amma Resonance Healing Foundation sent us MP3 files by email for many of the remedies since our Amma4Africa Kits did not arrive before we departed.]

Follow-up:
After one listen to the MP3 for abuse trauma she stopped crying and having flashbacks. The improvement was dramatic. After a couple of days the complaints reappeared and she needed a second treatment but they left before we could communicate with them again.

Case of sexual abuse
Reported by Maggi, Auroville, India

I had emailed the PC Resonances listed in the little Amma4Africa Kit to some homeopaths and other friends with the asterisk besides the remedies actually included in my kit.

Case 1
I soon received a call from a friend who said she had a candidate for the sexual abuse trauma. This woman of about sixty-five bore the imprint (what else to call it?) of sexual abuse received between the age of six and twelve at the hands of a "friend of the family".

Follow-up:
After taking the drops of PC435p for sexual abuse for four or five days, she reported that a chronic sense of anguish experienced at the level of the solar plexus had disappeared. That was a year ago: it has never returned. The recurrent nightmares in which this man used to knock at the door and come for her stopped entirely. What a grace!

Case 2
A friend who had been raped and in whom there was a deep-seated sense of indignation and shame, something so ever-present that (being a writer) she finally tried to exorcise it by writing a novel in which she recounted the event. It hadn't worked, but after taking the drops she felt she was finally released: a weight had dropped from her. There was a feeling of closure.

A case of medical 'rape'
Ellen van der Voort, Netherlands

There was a boy with kidney problems in the past with a nephrectomy in the end, with very traumatic experiences in hospital such as cystoscopies without anaesthesia, so that his whole genital area has become a sort of "forbidden" place for him.
He was diagnosed as an autistic child, but in my opinion he was just traumatised by his experiences in the past. After PC Long Time Past Trauma (PC306a), he came out of his shell, and is now better treatable for his other complaints.

Shock

This is for any shock which is overwhelming. It's also for the shock of something terrible that happens to somebody else. For example the shock of a parent or child being killed, where the shock is sudden, overwhelming and does not resolve. In shock causing trauma there will be flashbacks which recur and which cannot be erased from memory and recur easily. It's also for the history of the shock in the family and this might be a mining accident, a car accident, or similar event in the family history. For injuries due to a car accident use the injury resonance. In homeopathic terms PC11c (PC Shock) is the equivalent of *Aconitum, Opium, Stramonium* and other shock remedies.

Peter Chappell: I have treated shock trauma extensively, from birth trauma to the siege and torment of Sarajevo, with great success using homeopathic remedies like *Stramonium, Aconitum, Opium, Camphora* etc, each selected with care and precision. But it again gradually dawned on me that this is a total phenomenon that is basically similar for everyone. There is an initial impact and this reaches deep into the human economy, at a speed that defeats logic and reasoning and detachment, and resonates within everyone similarly, like a burn or bruise, and then moves into one or another state, being stunned or in panic, according to the inner nature. It occurred to me that like burns there is no totality remedy for shock, so I made one. It also occurred to me that the reason people cannot focus on the every present wonderment of NOW, this sacred place where God resides, is because they are often in shock and reacting as if every contact with reality is shocking. So treating shock is important for almost everyone. PC Shock strengthens resistance to acute infection as well as improves concentration.

I suspect that those people with photographic memories have deeper present moment concentration and therefore PC Shock should help that unfold, as well as help process all those long lasting shocks and terrible catastrophes people go through. Experience to date looks very promising.

Cases of shock

Peter Chappell, Czech Republic

Case 1

A 35-year-old woman took the shock resonance and the first reaction she had was that she started seeing images of her grandfather. She then asked her family about her grandfather and found out that he had been trapped in a mine disaster as a young man.

Follow-up:

The next thing that happened was that her back started being very painful. This was a replay of her back being injured in the birthing process. The story is that the obstetrician pushed very hard on her mother's abdomen to force her out of the womb. And in consequence she was injured and in the first months of her life her parents had to hold her in a spine stretching position to relieve the pain of the injury to the spine. As an adult she has had 'hundreds' of people trying to relieve the pain in her sacral region to no effect throughout her life. After the PC Shock and her back pain coming back she lay in bed for a day curled up like a baby in the womb. After that the back pain completely disappeared for the first time as an adult. That is quite amazing.

Sometime after this her inner situation became very clear, her right to exist, and an individual homeopathic prescription was used to address this situation, *Hydrogenium*. This well illustrates the use of trauma resonances as complementary to individual homeopathic remedies.

Case 2

Another young woman took PC Shock for exam nerves and reported a remarkable increase in vitality and concentration, and even more after she stopped taking it! In my understanding when you are in shock you find it hard to concentrate.

Case 3

I gave it to a man in a crisis dating from the time in the womb when his mother was threatening to miscarry for the third time in succession. The unconscious fear from this had dominated his whole life of 45 years to the point of being serious emotionally handicapped and he calmed down enormously in all ways possible. (I considered *Stramonium, Aconitum, Gelsemium, Opium* etc. but none fitted so I successfully used PC Shock).

Case of speechless
Klaus Schustereder, Central African Republic

A lady in the Tamale clinic has received PC Shock. She didn't talk for years; it started after she gave birth to a child. I couldn't figure this lady out at that time, but I gave her PC Shock on the assumption that since there were no physical reasons why she shouldn't talk, it was emotional.

Follow-up:
The latest news is that she started to talk again, and my contact writes that her husband is very glad. Only afterwards, I realized that this was probably a case of rape or incest. Since our immune system wants us to survive, and since talking at the time might have been perceived as life-threatening. Who knows? But what is also nice, is that it was the doctor (the one least open to homeopathy) that got me to see her and asked me if I could do something for her.

"I'm suffering from chronic shock"
Case report by Myriam Birrer, Switzerland

This is a complicated case of a 34-year-old woman with a very difficult history. She often can't or is unwilling to speak. She comes from a problematic family and was often completely neglected. She was living on the street. For some time she was in the drugs scene and prostituted herself. She was badly treated by several men and was suffering from disappointed love. She was moving from one place to the other continuously, and in a short period had countless different jobs. Never enough money to support her, always deceived or exploited. She had several accidents (malleolus, left ankle, brain concussion); she has pain continuously. She was a victim of a flood and had pneumonia twice. She has a fever regularly and suffers from colds. She has had bad experiences with doctors. She wants to be alone, can only be with people for a short time because she doesn't like talking. She is afraid of medical treatment and of doctors because she fears things will only get worse. She says: "I'm severely shocked; I'm suffering from chronic shock."

Prescription: *PC11c* for Shock

Follow-up:
She takes it in the evening. The next morning she walks into the street weeping and wants to see peo-

ple. She meets a woman that knows her a little. She spontaneously takes this woman's hand and talks to her for a long time. (Luckily the woman responds with understanding and calm.) Never has she wept and talked like this. Later she tells me: "I have re-established contact with people."
She keeps taking the remedy for a couple of months and experiences relief of all her symptoms. I had lost track of her, but 1.5 years later I hear how much this remedy has helped her.

Case of crying all night

Reported by Rita Pasquale, Switzerland

I am back from the rainforest in Ecuador, enriched with deep impressions of the wisdom of the people Shuar and the richness of nature there.

I could give PC11 to Jomaira, the eleventh and last child of our Shuar-host family. Jomaira was breast fed until recently. She is already two and was crying in the night because she wanted mother's breast ... When I saw the face of the child I had the impression that she is under shock, missing what she had during her first two years. There might have been more shocks in her young life, because already last year, I noticed something like that in her expression.

The parents allowed me to give her PC11, which had the immediate effect of a good and undisturbed sleep during the following nights, a relief for everybody.

Torture Trauma

For where someone has been systematically tortured by others, especially over a long period and systematically, using methods that are cruel, violent, brutal and extremely painful. It is suitable for the torturers too and the supervisors; all those involved as victims or persecutors, and in recovery programmes. It is for the effects on all levels, emotional, spiritual, physical, and ancestral. Amnesty says that most countries do not abide by torture treaties. Just a few years ago the USA in collusion with EU states, flew people to countries to torture them for years under the G.W. Bush administration. Torture was widespread in British Colonial rule and with Chairman Mao it was endemic in China. Torture was widely used by the church in the Inquisition. Everyone alive must have ancestral memories of it.

Case of torture
Klaus Schustereder, Central African Republic

> A captain of a riverboat is tortured by the police for two or three days. Austrian guests on the boat give him PC Shock. After a few days he is over it, whereas in the past (it was, unfortunately for him, routine for the police to harass boat captains like this) this would have taken months. (PC torture would have been more appropriate but was not in their possession.)

Unburied Loved Ones Trauma

When a presumed dead relative is not buried it affects the whole family structure and psychology. It is the worst kind of unfinished business. Obviously this is much worse if for example a young girl disappears never to be found. It leaves an open wound that will pass on for generations if not healed. This remedy is for this purpose, whatever the reason the person is not buried. It is for closure in the most difficult circumstances. This subject is well documented in books by Bert Hellinger. You find this situation after wars – the man went to fight and never returned. The wife waits, even after everyone else has returned, in denial, and still hoping that one day he will walk back into his family. Or be reported dead. But it never happens. In Argentina tens of thousands disappeared with the generals in power, dumped out to sea from airplanes etc. Likewise under Stalin and Hitler. Chairman Mao was the worst by far according to recent documented evidence, terrorising a whole country as well as killing millions etc. Wars, and criminal rulers still do that to people. It's the 'disappeared without a trace' trauma.

Available PC Resonances for Injuries & Trauma

In Appendix 5 all available PC Resonances for injuries and trauma are listed.

Part IX
The Practice of Treating Intoxication

- Intoxication
- Vaccination, Vaccination damage and Homeoprophylaxis
- PC Vaccination Damage

Intoxication

In a world in which new organic and inorganic substances are being invented and introduced on a daily basis toxins have become a great problem. We are long past a relatively safe environment in which poisonous bites and berries can mean an acute but detectable threat, and have entered a world in which poisons of all sorts enter our bodies through the food chain, the air we inhale or directly via the skin. We usually can't see, smell or taste them and it is almost impossible to determine their effect on our constitution. In case of a clear history or suspicion that a particular substance may have caused a diseased state the logical thing to do is to have a potency produced from that very substance as (a complement to) the simillimum.

If intoxication is for some reason suspected to play an essential role but the precise toxin stays unclear the general PC Resonance for intoxication can be used. In acute cases the remedy can be repeated as often as needed until improvement sets in and the time between doses can be prolonged. In cases with a history of intoxication a daily dose of five to ten drops will be sufficient. In case of a strong response (a good sign) it is advised to wait with the subsequent dose until the initial aggravation is over.

A worldwide overused form of intoxication and suppression is antibiotics. To treat and antidote the long-term effects of antibiotics PC Penicillin was made. It is named after the first antibiotic that came into regular use but is designed to cover the unwanted effects of all.

The PC Penicillin case below is remarkable, where potentised Penicillin did not cure, the PC Resonance did.

Case of a 17-year-old girl with vaginitis since antibiotics

Ries IJsseldijk, Netherlands

Intake September 2004

She has a vaginal infection for one year now.
It is burning, itching, and the labia are swollen and raw. The leucorrhoea is with little clots, and sometimes the vagina is very dry.
It all started after she had received penicillin for an otitis media.
Two months ago she again had an ear infection with pus coming out.
Four years ago she had herpes zoster on the shoulder.

Mind: Two years ago she got overworked due to too much study combined with a job on Saturdays and Sundays. There were dollar signs in her eyes.
She is very enthusiastic, she loves company, is very sympathetic, soft and hard. She shows her emotions. She weeps if seeing a film or hearing special music.
She has a fear of mice and thunderstorm and is afraid on the street if it is dark.
Also she suffers from anticipation. She wants to be the best.
Her grandmother died seven years ago, which is still difficult for her.
She had a very close relationship with her grandfather, whom she saw every day and whom she told all her intimate stories.
Now her grandfather has a new friend and she hardly sees him anymore. She is very angry with him.
She hates injustice. She tells her grandfather right to his face that she does not like it that he makes no contact. She is very disappointed, and says she hates him.

Her hobbies are kickboxing and handball.
Sleep: okay, perspiration during sleep (3).
Menses: profuse, painful back and abdomen.

Treatment:
Nitricum acidum MK without result.
Then *Natrum muriaticum* MK also without result.
After *Causticum* MK there was little amelioration.

I waited and repeated the same potency when there was a relapse, after which there was again a slight improvement. When after another relapse *Causticum* XMK was given there was no response.

After *Penicillin* 200K no reaction.

PC Penicillin:
Then I decided to try Peter Chappell's remedy for the after effects of penicillin, PC261q, five drops per day after banging the bottle five times. She started taking the remedy in June 2005.

Follow-up:
She responded with a dramatic amelioration! No leucorrhoea anymore. Besides that she responded with a slight pain in her ear, which disappeared after a few days. Since then even her menses are okay, with only a little headache before. No problems anymore till now! The duration of the follow-up is more than one year.

Penicillin detox

Peter Chappell, Czech Republic

An athletic, healthy adult used PC Penicillin to detox from the repeated use of penicillin he was given as a young child for throat infections. After the detox, which laid him low for a while, he found a new level of self-expression in speech. This is interesting as apparently penicillin for throat infections was actually suppressing his expression and even after many years this blockage was still there.

Detox for Anti Retroviral Therapy

Joseph Msumba, Malawi

Report on PC501a for the side effects of ARVs (HAART = Highly Active Anti Retroviral Therapy)

Most of the AIDS-patients in this area are on ARVS with lots of side-effects: e.g. numbness of feet/hands, eye problems, nausea and vomiting, abnormal swelling of some body part etc. They get better after taking PC HAART for two to three weeks.
Chinteche Government Hospital has included our Amma4Malawi AIDS Project on their partnership list and is referring patients to our clinic. This because of PC HAART. Patients on ARVs have testified themselves how PC HAART has helped them after long years of suffering and this motivated the hospital to refer its patients to our clinic.

A case of ARVs detox

Harry van der Zee, Malawi

A 3 weeks old baby is brought to us who has a terrible rash all over the body. 4 days after delivery the rash broke out especially under the diaper but also under the armpits, on the back, the extremities etc. Parts of skin are hanging loose as if large blisters have come off. The mother is HIV+ and at the end of the pregnancy used ARVs to prevent mother-child transmission. Also, the mother has a history of gonorrhoea.

Analysis: especially the area under the diaper resembled strongly the rash we know can be treated with *Medorrhinum*, and based on gonorrhoea in the history this was one option. As the rash also covered other parts of the body another option was that it was a response to the ARVs the mother (and the baby) had received at the end of pregnancy. On top of that we had to consider the possibility that the child was infected with HIV, something that can only be tested with some confidence at 6 months old. I therefore decided to make a mix of three PC Resonances to cover all possible causes.

Prescription: PC gonorrhoea + PC1 + PC HAART; twice daily 5 drops
(HAART = Highly Active Anti Retroviral Treatment)

Follow-up:
After 8 days all wounds have healed. The mother is advised to continue giving PC1 to herself and to give it out of precaution to the baby until it can be tested at 6 months old.

Vaccination, Vaccination Damage & Homeoprophylaxis

In *The History of Homeprophylaxis and Review of the Evidence to Support its Efficacy* Janette Mackay (United Kingdom) writes:

> "There is growing concern regarding side effects that occur following vaccination which include convulsions, neurological complications, arthritis, temporary coma, asthma and auto immune diseases.[14] Lankinen et al.[15] highlight an urgent need to improve vaccine safety systems, as only six people are employed in this field to monitor seventeen countries. The lack of structure for reporting side effects following vaccination may mean that the adverse symptoms logged are only the tip of the iceberg."

The general public is made to believe that vaccination is highly effective which is often not the case. Mackay:

> "The Medical Research Council shows conventional vaccination is effective in 61%-89% of cases."[16] With the yearly flu vaccination it is even worse as not only is the vaccine not consistently effective and only prepared for one of the many viruses active each winter, it also causes instead of prevents problems in many people.

Homeopathy can be used in four ways with regard to vaccinations. We claim no expertise on vaccinations but will summarise here some recommendations from other homeopaths and add our own:
Where a child has complaints due to vaccinations the homeopath can help by administering the vaccine in a homeopathic dose as a kind of antidote, or use PC Vaccination Damage or find the homeopathic simillimum for the complaints. Ideally the vaccination damage is treated through detox and followed by constitutional treatment.

Secondly, in cases where the child has not been vaccinated yet, a homeopath can help to guide the parents on the strategy they wish to follow, and give the child remedies to minimise the possible side-effects of vaccines they do decide to give. These remedies can include the appropriate vaccination nosodes or the general PC RESONANCE for vaccination damage.

Thirdly, there are protocols for homeoprophylaxis in which homeopathic remedies are used to build up immunity instead of injected vaccines. The work of Isaac Golden[17][18][19] and Gus-

14 Brody, M. and Sorley, R. (1947) Neurological Complications Following the Administration of Pertussis Vaccine. New York State Journal of Medicine. 47: p.1016. Klugman, K. (2003) Vaccine Trialist Group. New England Journal of Medicine. 349:13: p.1341-8, Schwarz, G., Lanzer, G. and List, W. (1988) Acute Mid Brain Syndrome as an Adverse Reaction to Tetanus Immunisation. Intensive Care Medicine. 15: p.53-54, Scheibner, V. (2000) Behavioural Problems in Childhood, The Link to Vaccination. Australia: Blackheath.

15 Lankinen, K.; Pastila, S.; Kilpi, T.; Nohynek, H.; Makela, P. and Olin, P. (2004) Vaccinovigilance in Europe – Need for Timeliness, Standardisation and Resources. Bull. World Health Organisation. Nov: 82 (11): p.828-835.

16 Medical Research Council. (1951) The Prevention of Whooping Cough by Vaccination. British Medical Journal. 1: p.1463-1471.

17 Golden, Isaac, The Safety of Long-term Homeoprophylaxis - Research findings, *Homœopathic Links* Vol 17/4, Haren, Netherlands 2004, p261

18 Golden, Isaac. *Homeoprophylaxis - A Fifteen year Clinical Study: A Statistical Review of the Efficacy and Safety of Long-Term Homeoprophylaxis*, Isaac Golden Publications, Gisborne (Australia) 2004.

19 *Golden, Isaac.* Vaccination and Homeoprophylaxis? A Review of Risks and Alternatives, 6th edition, Isaac Golden Publications, Gisborne (Australia) 2005 (revised 2007).

tavo Bracho[20] deserves to be mentioned here. There have been extensive studies of homeopathic prophylaxis and this is a very controversial subject. Golden showed that prophylaxis using homeopathic remedies prevents infectious diseases and chronic diseases that would result from vaccination for them, while Bracho showed for two subsequent years that using homeoprophylaxis for leptospirosis with millions of people gave a significant lowered incidence during the rainy season.
There was another study in Brazil involving 65,000 plus children who were homeopathically protected against meningitis with a control group of 25,000 children. The protection by the homeopathic method was shown to be 90% effective over a one-year period (Mattos et al)[21]. Homeopaths have routinely used nosodes to protect people from epidemic disease for two centuries and in every time period it's been used it has been effective. However there are some diseases where homeopathic protection is not so easy or effective, for example in malaria in white people who have never been exposed to it before. The immune system seems to need a long time to become effective in dealing with malaria and it only remains on a higher level of alertness in countries where malaria is a chronic condition i.e. it is happening all the time as in Africa. If Africans leave Africa for a few years, they lose their residual immunity to malaria.

From experience we know that for malaria the PC Resonance for it (PC240m) can be used as prophylaxis in Africans (See chapter on malaria). Logically it may be expected that other PC Resonances for other infectious diseases could also be effectively used as prophylaxis, but here the authors lack proof and can only recommend to use it in low risk situations.

And fourthly, in case your child gets the mumps, whooping cough, measles or any of the other children's diseases, the homeopath can usually treat these very successfully.

The experience of homeopaths in dealing with vaccinations differs from one country to another. One of the countries that have developed an advanced system is Israel. There the director of the Israeli School of Homeopathy, Dr. Chaim Rosenthal, has instituted alternative clinics that monitor and vaccinate infants (*Homœopathic Links* Issue 4/2001). These clinics carry the name 'A drop of nature' in contrast to the conservative clinics in Israel, which are known as 'A drop of milk'.

Drop of Nature

The purposes of 'A Drop of Nature' are:

- Guidance and explanation concerning vaccination.
- Guidance and explanation of how to raise children in a homeopathic and natural way.
- Treatment of vaccine damage.
- General homeopathic treatment when necessary.

The team in each clinic consists of a paediatrician (who has also been trained as a homeopath) and a homeopathic practitioner. The paediatrician gives instructions and guidance. Homeopathic treatment, if necessary, is given by the homeopath.

---

20 Isaac Golden, Australia & Gustavo Bracho, Cuba. The Adaptability of Homeoprophylaxis in Endemic, Epidemic and Stable Background Conditions. *Homœopathic Links* 2009; Vol 22/4 pp 211-213

21 Mattos et al. Meningococcinum; Its protective effect against meningococcal disease, *Homœopathic Links* issue Vol 14/4, Haren (Netherlands) 2001, p230

Infants are invited for monitoring seven times during the first year of life (which is similar to the conservative clinic). The general recommendation is not to vaccinate during the first year of life at least. If the parents insist on specific vaccines being given, they give them to the child only under certain conditions. For this they have formulated the following general principles and recommendations.

- The child should not be vaccinated indiscriminately.
- For most children they recommend avoiding vaccination during the first year of life. They see the child again at the age of one year and then decide whether to give it any of the vaccines or not. It depends on the general health of the child, its hereditary state, environmental conditions etc.
- They consider the possible harm that may be caused by a vaccine against its benefit.
- Every case is considered individually.
- If the parents express extreme anxiety regarding meningitis caused by Hemophilus Influenza B, they are willing to administer the vaccine during the first year of life.
- Vaccines that should be delayed until an older age (five to six years old), and may even not be necessary (every case individually) are: hepatitis-B, hepatitis-A, tetanus, pertussis, measles, mumps, rubella (M.M.R.), and chickenpox.
- Vaccination should only be carried out when the child is in perfect health. The child should be healthy for at least three months prior to any vaccination. Vaccination in the summer months (May to September) is preferred.
- Vaccination should not be carried out close to childhood milestones such as weaning, or learning to walk or leaving the home for the first time (nursery or kindergarten), dentition etc.
- The child should not receive several vaccines at a time (they should be staggered).
- If there is a reason to suspect that the child suffered from vaccine damage in the past, or reacted strongly to a vaccine, the next vaccine scheduled should be postponed to an older age. Many cases of vaccine damage could have been prevented if the vaccine had been avoided after a bad reaction to the previous one. In many severe cases of vaccine damage a bad reaction to the previous vaccine can be detected.
- In children with any suspected neurological damage (hypotonia, slow development, difficult delivery etc.), postponing vaccination is important. The possibility of forgoing them completely should also be considered.
- When one child in the family has suffered some vaccine damage, greater care must be taken with the other children. The 'Drop of Nature' homeopaths try to postpone vaccinating them for as long as possible.
- If the child seems to be suffering from vaccine damage, homeopathic help should be sought immediately.
- In any case of disease developing during the first year of life, especially if the child is still nursing, the possibility of vaccine damage should be checked carefully.
- The new vaccines like Hepatitis-A and Varicella are not recommended.
- If there is an outbreak of a local epidemic, and the child has not been vaccinated, the child should be taken to the attending homeopath and given a homeopathic vaccine.

PC Vaccination Damage

The advantage of this remedy is that it is not necessary to use different potencies of all different vaccines used or to establish which specific one caused the problems as it is designed to cover the negative consequences of all types of vaccinations. If the exact vaccine that causes problems in a patient is clearly known, it is advised to use the homeopathic potency of that. In other cases PC Vaccination Damage can be used.

A nine-year-old boy with ADHD and PDD-nos

Harry van der Zee, Netherlands

Dale is restless, moves about, touches everything and keeps asking me questions, while avoiding looking me in the eye.

After each vaccination he had high fever. Once he even got convulsions while shrieking, according to his parents either from pain or fear. He turned into himself more and more and developed strong preoccupations. He would for instance drag his clothes out of the wardrobe and stare at the patterns on a sweater or the sole of a shoe. At 2.5 years old the doctors estimated his IQ to be 50 and told the parents he would never learn to speak. Luckily Dale proved them wrong and did start speaking, be it that the l and r are not pronounced well, and from talking to him it is clear his IQ is closer to 100 than to 50. He has had several fears, especially for the dark, ghosts and Dracula. He dislikes silence and makes sure there is always a radio or TV on.

After other children had teased him he started to become violent for a period. He told his parents that there were eight voices in him, three sweet ones and five bad ones dictating him to strike and attack his parents. Besides these episodes he is always good-humoured, outgoing and talks to everyone.

His parents were not successful in conceiving a child and ultimately a pregnancy was reached using IVF. Pregnancy and birth all went prosperously. The moment that Dale was born though was exceptional. His mother was taking a shower to help deal with the labour pains. Suddenly she said to her husband, he is coming now!!! Standing under the shower she delivered the little boy and both totally wet she slowly walked towards her bed, where she herself cut the umbilical cord. Because he was all wet and not covered and dried soon enough, Dale got under-temperature. His sugar levels were low and it took six days before he was able to balance his sugar levels and temperature properly.

Treatment

Both IVF and vaccination have been mentioned to increase the incidence of autism.

I decided to start the treatment with a remedy for the vaccination damage, to then prescribe orthomolecular treatment to further improve his ADHD and autistic symptoms and individual treatment as soon as I could be sure of the remedy. Dale started with PC32ov remedy for vaccination damage to treat the effects of the vaccination programme. Dale got five drops of *PC32ov* per day.

Follow-up five weeks later:
Dale was already coughing for months, and this cough was quickly gone. The voices he had have disappeared. Four days after the remedy he starts to read subtitles while watching TV and also suddenly he has learned to read the time from a clock. In a matter of weeks he has learned to write and now uses hotmail.

His parents are amazed about the very fast progress he's making in his development. He perspires strongly at night, which he also had when he started taking Risperdal, and is becoming more thirsty.

He started looking his parents in the eyes since the third day of taking the remedy. When watching TV he always had to look away regularly to digest all the impressions, but now he doesn't do that anymore. In the first days he still regularly made remarks like 'I'm going to kill you', but showed no real aggression. Right now he is better able to control his anger. Also new is that he is now able to wait for something, whereas before everything had to be done immediately. He has no more epistaxis, a symptom the parents didn't narrate in the first interview. Before bleeding he would always be very restless and afterwards he would calm down.

An amazing improvement in a very short time, and I haven't even started prescribing a simillimum for him, but only gave a specific remedy for the supposed vaccination damage, a diagnosis confirmed by this fast improvement.

The simillimum:
Father says he had lots of nosebleeds as a child with pressure above the nose. A constitutional sign that might be helpful to find a simillimum. Expecting a constitutional match between Dale and his father I ask him whether there is more in Dale that he recognizes. Based on that interview a clear picture of *Belladonna* arises for the father.

Regarding Dale the parents narrate one other symptom, and that is that he grinds his teeth during sleep.

Repertorising the symptoms of Dale and his father 'as if one person' three remedies come up very strong: *Stramonium, Hyoscyamus* and *Belladonna.*

For *Stramonium* the usual nightmares are missing and also although his birth was different from usual, it was not experienced as traumatic by the mother nor had there been clear distress in Dale.

For *Hyoscyamus* jealousy or sex related symptoms are missing.

For *Belladonna,* besides the many rubrics that cover his behaviour there are some other symptoms that confirm the prescription:

- Nose, Epistaxis in children: Bell. (3)
- Generalities, Vaccination, after: Bell. (3)
- Generalities, Convulsions, Heat, during: Bell. (3)

Regarding his birth, it is fascinating to see that of all the hundreds of birth histories I have heard, this is the only one with problems after birth because of cooling down from being wet, a keynote for *Belladonna.*

- Chills, Wet, after getting: Bell. (1)
- Generalities, Wet, getting agg.: Bell. (3)

I prescribe *Belladonna* 200K for the father and tell the parents that if he responds favourably to it I will also give it to Dale as a next step in his treatment. For now he should continue taking PC320v and to that I add orthomolecular treatment as advised by Tinus Smits.[22] [23] [24]

---

22 www.tinussmits.nl

23 See also Post-Vaccinal Behavioural Problems - Ill-humour, anxiety, aggressiveness, contact disturbances, hysterical behaviour, ADHD, PDD-nos, ADD, autism, cured with potentised vaccines by Tinus Smits in *Homeopathic Links* issue 2/2007.

24 Tinus Smits, *Autism – Beyond Despair,* Emryss Publishers, Haarlem 2010.

Follow-up on Belladonna:
One week later father calls to say that he has improved very much after the remedy. He feels a lot calmer. He has never felt so relaxed in his life.

Now I feel confident to prescribe *Belladonna* 200K for Dale as well. After it he has no immediate strong response but similar to his father becomes more calm and keeps improving on all levels. One month later he gets a high fever with all the symptoms typical for *Belladonna* which indicated a repetition of *Belladonna* 200K. Three months later he has an acute again and responds to *Belladonna* 200K with rapid and good results. He is now on Belladonna Q3 daily and is doing extremely well at school and at home ... without Risperdal which he stopped taking after he started improving on PC Vaccination Damage remedy.

PC Resonances for Intoxication

A list of available PC Resonances concerning intoxication and vaccination is presented in Appendix 5.

PART X

Practice of Treating Chronic Diseases

- Controversial ideas
- Aggravations
- Failures and obstacles to cure
- Alcoholism
- Alzheimer
- Asthma
- Autism
- Bulimia
- Cancer
- Chronic Fatigue Syndrome
- Complex Regional Pain Syndrome
- Crohn's Disease
- Diabetes
- Eczema
- Epilepsy
- Fibromyalgia
- Gilles de la Tourette
- Hypertension
- Multiple Sclerosis
- Myasthenia Gravis
- Obsessive Compulsive Disorder
- Old Age
- Parkinson's disease
- Scleroderma
- Ulcer

Controversial Ideas

This book contains several controversial concepts, some of which may be difficult for homeopaths to accept but where in our opinion the results invite serious consideration of them.

One inconvenient concept for many homeopaths is that of a disease specific resonance for a chronic disease. A remedy for a disease in the case of epidemics is in line with Hahnemann's concept of Genus epidemicus, and to stretch the idea to also include collective trauma for which we have introduced the term GENUS TRAUMATICUS is not such a difficult one to make. But a resonance for a chronic disease (GENUS CHRONICUS) for many homeopaths is like cursing in church.

There is clear logic behind this concept though, one that bridges the gap between classical and clinical homeopathy. There are several prominent homeopaths practising today who, on a very practical level, realised they also have to prescribe for the condition, and this is mainly seen in the treatment of severe pathology, like cancer. If, as part of a treatment plan, prescribing for the disease is successful and acceptable in cancer cases, this approach should be effective in other types of pathology, where the simillimum alone does not fully cure / cover the case, as well.

Although for many homeopaths there is a strong division between classical homeopathy and clinical homeopathy, Hahnemann's legacy gives a very clear way of how both approaches can and should be integrated. This is an area of significant misunderstanding and prejudice.

According to classical homeopathic methodology a homeopath should prescribe a simillimum based on the totality of the symptoms and ignore in the analysis disease specific symptoms. This remedy should then be applied until it no longer gives any improvement. If that means that the patient is totally cured the treatment ends. If the patient is not totally cured the homeopath should continue treatment by selecting a remedy based on the remaining symptoms. If indeed the simillimum is similar enough to balance all constitutional signs and symptoms, the patient would be left with the symptoms of the disease that has not been totally cured. Repertorising these symptoms would lead to a remedy similar to the disease.

The conclusion is that in cases where the simillimum is not enough to cure a patient a second disease specific simillimum is needed to complement the action of the first. Clinical homeopathy is thus not in discord with classical homeopathy but the perfect complement and vice versa.

It follows from this that it is part of a complete homeopathic treatment programme to focus upon treating chronic diseases directly. Opposite to what many regard, this is not a new departure in homeopathic philosophy, principles and practice!

We got to this point because it's a logical outcome of treating epidemic diseases directly. The realization came to us that chronic diseases are in fact slow-moving epidemic diseases which move and adapt through the generations by the epigenetic process.

This realization made us understand that every chronic disease is a freestanding entity that can be treated by the same principles that Hahnemann outlined over 200 years ago.

An important additional point has to be made here. Although conventional medicine is fundamentally based upon physical realities that can be measured, the main origin of all chronic diseases is psychological. This is the dominant factor beyond all others. And as we discussed in the first part of this book, the psychological origins of chronic diseases are our survival instincts. These are the same for all of us, evolved as they were, before the human race started. They live in our reptilian brain and influence us, in terms of obvious fears, phobias and pathologies, but we can't influence them as the pathways connecting the reptilian brain to our mammalian and thinking brains mostly flow in one direction only. The consequence of all this is the understanding that chronic diseases are the same in essence for all of us, and can be treated as if they are epidemic diseases, which means one remedy per disease which is the same conclusion as conventional medicine. The key difference is however critical. We see chronic disease as an intelligent communication between our unconscious and conscious selves, which is to be facilitated to bring about a resolution of the disease. Conventional medicine sees chronic disease as of physical origin to be eliminated by any means possible, and not at all as intelligent.

In our opinion – confirmed by our experience – the ideal way of treating a chronic disease is by combining a patient specific approach (first simillimum) with a disease specific approach (second simillimum).

Aggravations

Where in the treatment of epidemic disease no aggravations of any importance have been observed, in chronic diseases they have. It is needless to let a patient suffer more than necessary, so in the treatment of chronic diseases it is advised to start with one dose and then wait for a few days to ascertain the response. In a minority of cases the patient will respond with an aggravation without being able to overcome it. These are the same patients that similarly respond to a well-chosen individual simillimum, and the response indicates that these patients are regretfully beyond homeopathic treatment, or another approach is needed, such as detoxification first. So, in very depleted or progressive cases with a particularly low vitality and few individual symptoms, one should give one or two drops and then wait for at least a week.

In general an aggravation is a good sign, also for PC Resonances. Wait until the aggravation is over and give another dose. There may again be an aggravation but now shorter and less severe. Wait again. Continue with this process until the resonance can be given on a daily basis (once daily 555) or any other dosage that fits the patient best.

In the following chapters cases will be shared that underline the validity of complementing individual treatment with a disease specific approach. Our contemporary equivalent to Hahnemann's 'mach's nach' is to 'give it a try'. Patients usually don't have any strong convictions as to how a remedy is selected for them; they are open to anything that is safe, has no side-effects and is effective.

Every homeopath knows the experience that 'nothing works'. At times in a situation like that a disease-specific resonance can help. The following quote by Dr L. Raghavan from India gives some examples:

Dr L. Raghavan, India, August 2008

> "I would like to state a couple of cases in which PC Resonances did wonders.
>
> The case of a 56-year-old female suffering from chronic leg ulcer treated unsuccessfully using homeopathic remedies. Her condition improved with PC330u and the ulcer dramatically almost vanished within a week.
>
> We have used PC254s to successfully treat a patient suffering from OCD (obsessive compulsive disorder) recently. After taking the PC Resonance, the condition improved by 90% within a week. The OCD disappeared completely without taking any further remedies. This case is unique because we had only PC254s for the treatment.
> Based on our clinical observations and experiences with PC Resonances, we would like to share a couple of pointers:
>
> - The time taken to treat a chronic case has reduced significantly after using PC Resonances in conjunction with homeopathic remedies selected using the classical method. We were able to achieve palliative care of our patients remarkably using PC Resonances.
> - We have not seen any aggravation till now though we had a mild aggravation in one case that subsided on the very same day.
> - Usually it would suffice to repeat the PC Resonances for three days continuously in most of the cases. In some cases, we use it for seven days and in some for more than a month."

Failures and Obstacles to Cure

The success rate of the use of PC Resonances for chronic diseases varies from one patient to the other, and from one homeopath to the other. Why this is so remains an open question to us as for one thing we can't investigate all practices, case-taking and case-management skills. There are clearly chronic conditions that show more success (e.g. CFS) and others that show less results (e.g. tinnitus). We have received reports varying from 80% effect in 28 cases of various diagnoses to 0% results in eleven cases.
There are many complicating issues here:

- Some so-called chronic diseases are very ill defined and have no measurements to determine them. In consequence diagnostics is a bit like guesswork.
- Sometimes there is a lot of toxicity affecting the person and this is the dominant influence. For example lead, aluminium and mercury poisoning lead to dementia and many other neurological problems and these have to be the key way of treatment. Homeopathy has a very successful track record in this.
- Some homeopaths have a very strong therapeutic bias in their practices which are more like therapeutic practices. The client or patient gets support from the relationship

which is more important than resolving their diseases. In such cases the practitioner-patient dynamic will negate the effects of any remedy trying to treat the disease.
- Homeopaths using classical homeopathy in the western world who restrict themselves primarily to maybe 20 remedies in 80% of the cases may not be prescribing very deeply. While this is common practice judging from pharmacy sales, it means that the disturbing causes of the diseases have not been addressed. Therefore the PC Resonance may not be able to act because the cause is still operating.
- Also among subscribers who use the vital sensation approach, there are still very many inaccurate prescriptions. This is because vital sensation prescribing requires a very high level of skill.

PC Resonances work better when the Simillimum has worked well according to case management rules but fails to (fully) affect the pathology.

Often PC Resonances for chronic diseases are used in cases where individualised homeopathy and other approaches have failed. These are the difficult cases every homeopath wrestles with from time to time. Even if the simillimum seems very clear there are cases that simply fail to respond to it in any potency selected. Similarly a case of a chronic disease can fail to respond to the correct PC Resonance and this should not be a surprise. In prescribing for the disease the same obstacles to cure can be present as when prescribing for the patient. Individualized prescriptions complemented with disease specific prescriptions will raise the percentage of success, but still cases will fail to respond.

Within the tools provided with PC Resonances some of the obstacles to cure can be managed if through proper case taking these have been identified: e.g. vaccination, past (transgenerational) trauma, intoxication, past (transgenerational) infections etcetera. Other obstacles to cure may have to do with age, genetics, life circumstances, life style, habits etcetera, and these are clearly often beyond the reach of the homeopath to change through the use of remedies.

Being used to consistent results with conditions like AIDS, malaria and various forms of trauma we were initially disheartened to find that in chronic diseases this was not the case; we would have loved to see reliable and consistent results here as well. Someone with inside knowledge in the pharmaceutical industry in finding new medicines told us that if PC Resonances for chronic diseases would solve 10% of otherwise incurable cases that would indeed be remarkable by itself. Our experience is that the success rate is higher than that, and much higher in cases where individualized prescribing gives improvement but no full cure. So we ask the reader to realise that PC Resonances for chronic diseases are an option to improve results and not a 100% panacea in all cases.

Alcoholism

A case of alcoholism

Reported by Maggi, Auroville, India

A friend has a 25-year-old Tamil watchman who had drunk himself into a stupor every night for the past five years. Within two days of taking the *PC120a* drops for alcoholism he became absolutely abstemious and a most useful and friendly assistant in the guesthouse that she runs, somebody with initiative and humour, newborn as it were. In seven months he had two relapses of one day each. But he has become more conscious of his problem and has even joined an A.A. circle. He continues to take the drops daily. It is almost a year since he started the drops and besides the two exceptions mentioned he hasn't touched alcohol.

Alzheimer

Alzheimer's disease is the most common form of dementia. This degenerative disease is most often diagnosed in people over 65 years of age, although the less-prevalent early-onset Alzheimer's can occur much earlier.

Although the course of Alzheimer's disease is unique for every individual, there are many common symptoms. The earliest observable symptoms are often mistakenly thought to be 'age-related' concerns, or manifestations of stress. In the early stages, the most common symptom is inability to acquire new memories, observed as difficulty in recalling recently observed events. When Alzheimer's is suspected, the diagnosis is usually confirmed with behavioural assessments and cognitive tests, often followed by a brain scan if available.

As the disease advances, symptoms include confusion, irritability and aggression, mood swings, language breakdown, long-term memory loss, and the general withdrawal of the sufferer as their senses decline. Gradually, bodily functions are lost, ultimately leading to death.

The cause and progression of Alzheimer's disease are not well understood. Research indicates that the disease is associated with plaques and tangles in the brain. Currently used treatments offer a small symptomatic benefit; no treatments to delay or halt the progression of the disease are, as of yet, available.

Alzheimer's disease is known for placing a great burden on care-givers; the pressures can be wide-ranging, involving social, psychological, physical, and economic elements of the caregiver's life.

The following case illustrates how individual and disease prescribing together can help a patient.

Case of an 84-year-old man

Ellen van der Voort, Netherlands

> My father is 84 years old and now stays in a home for people with dementia.
> He never has been violent in his life, a very calm man, a hard worker.
> About 30 years ago he started to have high blood pressure and took drugs every day, as homeopathy could not help.
>
> The whole story started about 16 years ago. Then my father had a strange accident with the car. He drove across a street where many cars came towards him. I think he lost consciousness (not enough oxygen?). Nobody knows how it happened. He never did a thing like this before. After that accident he also had a strange fall with his bicycle once or twice a year, even when he walked normally. So this is for me a confirmation of blackouts. The same thing happened in later years when he got out of bed in the morning. He fell on the floor trembling.
>
> He took PC Alzheimer's every day.

Follow-up:
After four days he became more attentive and he knew better what was happening. I saw his mind was clearing up and he was calmer. Then I also gave *Stramonium* for three days.

To the amazement of the nurses the violence disappeared totally. My father slept well every night (before he never slept well and was always restless).
In the morning he helped the nurses and he could put on his clothes by himself (before the nurses had to dress him).
He could also shave himself (before the nurses had shaved him). And last but not least, the nurses told me he had a very clear mind.

Asthma

Asthma is the common chronic inflammatory disease of the airways characterized by variable and recurring symptoms, reversible airflow obstruction, and bronchospasm. Symptoms include wheezing, coughing, chest tightness, and shortness of breath. Asthma may be classified as atopic (extrinsic) or non-atopic (intrinsic).

It is thought to be caused by a combination of genetic and environmental factors, and can be triggered for instance by allergens and irritants.

The prevalence of asthma has increased significantly since the 1970s.

Case of an 8-year-old boy with asthma
Reported by Harry van der Zee, Burundi

The father of the boy is a priest that helped to translate for many patients suffering from AIDS and the trauma of war and genocide. He asked whether I could give him something for his asthmatic son. I wasn't able to properly take the case and told him that diseases like asthma deserve to be treated individually and that the disease specific treatment I could offer him would most likely not be effective if the individual remedy wasn't given either. He pressed me to nevertheless give it to him, and as I felt there wasn't much to lose I prepared a bottle of PC asthma for him, five drops daily.

Follow-up:
Two months later he reports his son is symptom free and a few months later he informs me that is still the case. I ask about the influence of the season or other beneficial circumstances, but he states that before his son would have symptoms almost daily the year through.

Clearly not the recommended way to treat asthma but I didn't want to withhold the reader the results the remedy nevertheless had.

Autism

Autism is characterized by impaired social interaction and communication, and by restricted and repetitive behaviour. These signs all begin before a child is three years old. Autism affects information processing in the brain by altering how nerve cells and their synapses connect and organize; how this occurs is not well understood. It is one of three recognized disorders in the autism spectrum (ASDs), the other two being Asperger syndrome, which lacks delays in cognitive development and language, and Pervasive Developmental Disorder-Not Otherwise Specified (commonly abbreviated as PDD-NOS), which is diagnosed when the full set of criteria for autism or Asperger syndrome are not met.

Autism has a strong genetic basis, but can also be associated with agents that cause birth defects and environmental causes, such as heavy metals, pesticides or childhood vaccines. The number of people diagnosed with autism has increased dramatically since the 1980s, partly due to changes in diagnostic practice; the question of whether actual prevalence has increased is unresolved.

Parents usually notice signs in the first two years of their child's life. The signs usually develop gradually, but some autistic children first develop more normally and then regress. An autistic culture has developed, with some individuals seeking a cure and others believing autism should be accepted as a difference and not treated as a disorder.

Homeopathy can help autistic children very well (See *Homœopathic Links* issues 1-3/2011). Besides individualized treatment there is the possibility to also address the condition itself directly.

Case of a four year old girl with autism

Ambika Wauters, USA

> Harry, oh me oh my! I just had the most severely autistic kid here who I've worked with in many homeopathic ways for over a year ... miasmatic, constitutional, Tinus Smits' vaccination detox remedies ... and this kid has been on PC autism for one full month and is doing GREAT!
>
> She is talking, asking practical questions, making eye contact, no temper tantrums, pooping regularly. Happy and content and learning in school. I am tickled beyond belief and had to tell you the good news. The mom is thrilled, the family is happy, the child is a real delight and she was a total monster one year ago. I had to rent space to see them because she was so destructive.
> Today she sat on my lap playing and was affectionate, gentle and looking me eye to eye. I am so thrilled I just had to write.
>
> Thanks, Harry. Give Peter Chappell big blessings and gratitude from me. Thank you for your encouragement. Spread the word about this. I'll do some case write-ups for an article any time you like.
>
> I will be singing your praises so if your ears burn its just me!
> Love, Ambika

Case in detail

B came to me through Head Start, a pre-school programme run by the government for children of poverty level families in March 2009. Her parents were in their early 30's, immigrants from Mexico; the father works sporadically at farm labour and green house construction. Both parents had been immunized to meet US immigration standards and the father had a history of cannabis and cocaine use in his youth. B was the second of two girls. E, age 6, her older sister, was very quiet, shy and sweet. B was wild, savage, very loud and destructive. Anything in her wake was pulled, yanked, tortured and abused. I met with her in special offices used for seeing difficult children. The room had a sofa, a large open space for running about and some games the children could play with.

In the initial interview B was loud, raucous, and always moving. She would bang into things and people, acting unaware of her environment. She could not concentrate on any activity. She could not sit still or be quiet. Her mother said she was constipated, not moving her bowels for days at a time. She described temper tantrums that lasted for an hour with B screaming loudly. These recurred five to seven times a day and were very destructive.

The parents were uneducated Mexican peasants who had a very deep love for their children and would do anything to help. They had, at that point, tried everything for their daughter that they knew. Her family doctor diagnosed autism in February 2007. She was put on AzEIP (Arizona Early Intervention Programme) for one year, at which point her medical services were stopped.

The family applied to the Department of Developmental Delay, a state facility that offered services from many other therapists. She attended a special needs school for two hours a day. Her teacher saw no improvement in B and mentions this in her last IEP. She also attends the local Head Start class for one day a week. Her parents began to search out alternative treatments for autism on the web. They managed to locate information regarding gluten/casein free diet, chelation, vitamins and mineral supplements, cranial sacral therapy and several other 'autism' treatments that they used over a two-year period.

B's medical history includes full immunization, with recurring otitis media after vaccination that was so severe drains were placed in her ears. She would often slam her hands over her ears and shout when we first met her.
She had a tympanic belly that was full, bloated and ached often. She disliked touch, being talked to and was often seen 'flapping' her hands in the air, typical of many children with autistic tendencies.

Homeopathic treatment

Because B was so constipated and angry she was given *Nux vomica* 6C, three times daily in water, and *Gaertner* 30C, a single dose. *Gaertner* is for constipated children and Nux vomica for chronic constipation with angry and destructive behaviour. This began a gentle detoxification and stimulated her bowels to move. We ordered *Carcinocinum* LM1 and while it was en route from England her case worker called and said she was 'back'. B began to speak a few words at that time. Mother reported her bowels became more regular and she has less tantrums. She didn't think the treatment was working and had to be reminded in a gentle way these were big shifts for her child.

Three weeks after the *Nux vomica* 6C we put her onto *Carcinosinum* LM1 for two months. She began talking, calming down, responding to instructions and went from savage to a reasonably quiet but disoriented kid who was beginning to wake up to her world. She entered nursery school at this time with two aids. The father, by the way, took *Coca* 200C for his previous addiction and substance abuse of Cocaine. He reported feeling much better after the remedy.

Two months after the *Carcinosinum* LM1 B started to walk on her toes, and complaining of pain in her ears. Her constipation returned and her sleep patterns were again disruptive. In her development she was talking more and understanding more, and she was engaging with other children at school but had great difficulty concentrating on any one task or experience. Mother wanted something to help the child sleep.

I suggested castor oil liver packs to soothe her nervous system and mother said it worked well for her. At this point we stopped the *Carcinosinum* LM1 and began the Tinus Smits vaccination detox process (see his book on *CEASE therapy* for autism). The first vaccine detox was *DPT* in sequential doses beginning with a 30C twice weekly and moving weekly from 200C, 1M, to 10M). She experienced a major response to this with a high fever and earaches. She complained her bottom itched and she developed white spots on her dark, café au lait skin.

At this point she was able to be in nursery without the assistance of aids. She was talking spontaneously but was still very hyperactive. In August she entered our Heart of Peace programme on a full scholarship from a donor and had extensive neurological reflex integration work which included the Masgutova method from Russia, Rhythmic Movement Training from Sweden, Cranial Sacral therapy and movement therapy with Bal-vis-x and wobble board word. These are therapies used in developmental delay and autism. They help integrate the primitive reflexes (Masgutova method and Rhythmic Movement Training specialize in this) and they bring visual and proprioceptive acuity to the developing brain. Cranial Sacral therapy helps stabilize the cranial pulse and release lesions on the spine and in the dural tubes around the brain. It is effective in soothing and calming children with ASD and DD. She ate a sugar free, dairy free, grain free diet and her mother learned how to apply Rhythmic Movement Training exercises for her on a daily basis. She did very well in the programme.

The next remedy was prescribed in September 2009, six months after the initial treatment. It was *Opium* 200C, a single dose. She had begun crying with fear and was constipated again after the programme. Opium worked very well for her and her mother reported she was entering Kindergarten without an aid and began learning at a very accelerated pace after the remedy.

When I saw her at that time she was still doing some echolalia. Her favourite words were "tikatikatika" and we dubbed her Princess Tikatika. She had become a favourite amongst the staff and everyone adored her. She did not let anyone near to her and you could not hold her or engage her for too long. Her mother received state aid and they brought in an ABA teacher who helped improve her vocabulary and cognition skills. It is a rote way of learning but, in truth, she needed to catch up with her age group and it helped her a lot. She was still robotic in her movements and hyperactive at times but a much more responsive person all together.

In November she was given a single dose of *Tuberculinum aviare* 200C. TB is rife in Mexico and they say all immigrants carry it with them when they flee Mexico and legally or illegally enter the States. Her mother is very tubercular and this seemed to be the next good remedy for B. We did not see dramatic changes with this remedy but she continued to strive to learn. She did grow physically with the remedy and started to lose her baby face. Her clothes were appearing too small for her and it was evident she was starting to shoot up. I have often observed that *Tuberculinium* helps children grow.

PC Autism

In December I met Harry van der Zee. He told me about the PC Resonances and I felt it was a good time to introduce them to B.

Follow-up:
I saw her in January after she had been on Peter Chappell's remedy for Autism (PC124e) for four weeks. Her mother reported that she was talking a lot, and emphasized "A LOT". She was asking questions, asking for help, responding to conversation, engaging with people in a natural and authentic way. She was affectionate and, for the first time in one year, came and sat on my lap, played with me, looked at me directly, asked me questions in English and in Spanish, gave me a hug and kiss and was quiet, receptive and very tender. Her mother and I both filled up with emotion when we saw this. Her mother reported her constipation had really cleared on this remedy. She could not say thanks enough times. We still have two more months to go on the remedy. I can't wait to see what develops. This is a truly transformed, loving and graceful little girl who has her life in front of her. The PC Resonances just capped off treatment in a wonderful and wholesome way. Thank you PC.

Bulimia

Bulimia nervosa is an eating disorder characterized by restraining of food intake for a period of time followed by an over intake or binging period that results in feelings of guilt and low self-esteem. The median age of onset is eighteen. Sufferers attempt to overcome these feelings in a number of ways. The most common form is defensive vomiting, sometimes called purging; fasting, the use of laxatives, enemas, diuretics, and over exercising are also common. Bulimia nervosa is nine times more likely to occur in women than men.

Ten cases of bulimia

Reported through Peter Chappell, Czech Republic

An experienced psychotherapist with a big reliable practice over many years tried PC bulimia resonance with ten clients. Each one took it in drops form for one month and then they were followed up for six months in total, so one month taking the resonance and five more months of monitoring. The age range of these clients was between 20 to 40 years and the average age about 25 years and they were all long-term bulimic cases.

Follow-up:
The person who had been in therapy the shortest time noticed no change and nor did the therapist. The other nine all opened up and started talking about topics which they had not talked about before, for example the tendency to be perfect, to want to be perfect, and the tendency to start perceiving their bodies.

The frequency of bingeing reduced very significantly and 50% of them said that they stopped vomiting altogether.

There were several themes that came to the surface:

- the relationship with the parents
- the feeling of not being accepted
- of not being accepted by important male figures such as the men in the family: brothers, uncles, fathers
- two women opened up on religious topics which had never been mentioned before
- three clients admitted to the theme of suppressed aggression
- three clients opened up on sexual topics which had never been mentioned before
- the dominant theme for all of them was not being accepted
- two clients admitted to having an alcoholic problem, that they were depressed and they drank and neither of them then continued with the drinking

Some of them started dealing with this problem of not being accepted and others just realised this is a problem they need to deal with.
All of them, including the one who said nothing changed at all, said they felt better psychologically.
One client had bad psoriasis for almost a year prior to treatment and within a month it had virtually disappeared and did not return.

One client had a repetitive cystitis and there was a very significant improvement.

One client had an aggravation of an allergic bronchitis which took her back to the time when the bulimia first started, the classic return of old symptoms.

Conclusion
This remedy helps speed up the therapy of almost all these clients suffering from bulimia and probably will reduce the time they need to be in therapy.
Bulimic cases are not so fast to resolve but the fact that they started opening up is quite a significant change from the normal pattern of bulimic clients in therapy.

Cancer

In terms of miasms and human development cancer is connected to the transition from the passive role of the victim (Sycosis) to the active role of a person taking responsibility and asserting himself (Syphilis). The disease cancer itself has also both sycotic and syphilitic features, growth and destruction respectively.
The cancer pathology lies in the fact that the individual lacks a balance between the responsibility felt and taken for him/herself and that taken for others. *Carcinosinum*, the best known and most widely used cancer nosode (and the first chronic diseases remedy), tends to neglect his own needs or allows suppression of them by others, but is very aware of the needs of others and feels responsible for their fulfilment.

Cancer stands for the ideal member of a family, tribe or society. These people avoid being sent to the real prisons of life by leading a perfect life in terms of what is expected of them. A different prison is the price paid, for now the individual is held prisoner by his inner drive to consent, please and comply. This at the cost of his own desires and needs, and the lack of space given to himself translates into a physical process that is invading space, by destroying functional well individualized cells and replacing them with clones of dysfunctional cells.
Studying the role and purpose of several cancer-related infectious diseases and finding proper treatment for the underlying patterns that, in a manner of speaking, invite these infective agents in and don't prevent them from entering the body should result in the prevention of cancer. An absence of proper psychological borders translates itself into partners invading borders, an inability of the immune system to defend the integrity of the body, resulting in infectious diseases and ultimately cancer.

The absence of childhood diseases in many *Carcinosinum* cases is meaningful in this respect as well. These childhood diseases can be seen as training the physical and psychological immune system, and without this proper training the individual lacks resistance to defend itself properly later in life. This also places big question marks with regard to vaccination programmes for childhood diseases. Is there a relation between the increased incidence of cancer in our society and the suppression of childhood diseases?

The Cancer miasm has a lot to do with the dynamics between male and female. In Jungian terms creativity is based on the cooperation of male and female energy, similar to the conception of new life being the result of a male spermatozoa meeting a female ovum. The investigation of the shadow and bringing to awareness of its contents are needed before a man can discover and productively use his female side, the anima, and a women her male side, the animus.

PC Resonances for Cancer

Initially one general cancer resonance was prepared. A proving of that remedy was conducted by Dr. Chetna Shukla and is presented in this book in the section on provings (Part XI). In the following case of breast cancer also this general cancer remedy was used. Later several specific cancer resonances were prepared.
Cancer treatment is a good example of homeopathic treatment in which several remedies in different sequences are used together. This can be from the viewpoint of layers in a case or

based on the idea to prescribe for different totalities. Besides the individual simillimum homeopaths can use remedies specific for the tissue involved, the type of cancer, to detox for regular treatment etcetera.

A case of breast cancer

Harry van der Zee, Netherlands

A woman with an advanced breast cancer was treated with surgery, radiation and chemotherapy. The prognosis was actually considered to be hopeless.
"Then they don't know me yet!" is how the patient responded.
She now suffers from treatment complications: infection, oedema and pain.
"I feel burnt inside and outside".

She suffers from a severe depression and feels she has come to an end. "My battery is empty."
She narrates a history with a lot of misery and indignation about how she was treated. She suffers from chronic sinusitis and feels the joints of ankles and knees have been "eaten up".
Further she has strabismus.
"I'm a Don Quixote type, trying to get bananas straight."

Prescription: *Causticum* 200K

Follow-up:
The fire inside is less. "I'm less angry and more sad." The joints are much better and the depression has cleared up so much that she stopped the antidepressants she was using.
Also the sinuses are better so she could stop using steroids for them.
"I worked out stuff with my mother in a dream."

Conclusion: as she responds very well on many levels I conclude that also the breast cancer most likely has a good prognosis.

Prescription: *PC140c* for Cancer ten drops daily, started seven months after Causticum.

Follow-up:
Aggravation with floating sensation and upset stomach lasting for many weeks, but shorter after each dose.
"Then all of a sudden I was fine." "Now my energy is back."
Now she is even feeling better than after *Causticum*, and has become active again:
"I'm of value again; who had ever dared to dream that?"

Report radiologist: doing well beyond all expectations.

Case Management
Next remedy: *Radium bromatum* for after effects of radiation.
Causticum to be repeated in case of a general relapse. *PC Cancer* used as intercurrent and prophylactic.
Six years later the patient is still doing well.

A case of prostate cancer in Tanzania

Nina Lopez, UK

Communication about this case is per email and the excerpt below is from that.

"It started with the prostate and is now in his bones and lungs. He is in great pain and one of his legs is very swollen. They are saying they cannot deal with the cancer but want to operate (we don't know what yet) or give him regular injections to deal with the pain and swelling. We'll know more tomorrow hopefully.
We would like to consult with you regarding PC Resonances or any other homeopathic approach which may help."
"M. is 69 years old. The cancer is very advanced (what they would call stage four) – has spread from prostate to liver and spine. Scrotum is tremendously swollen, testicles are like grapefruit, and his left leg very swollen, like elephantiasis with the skin about to burst in places. M. is in constant pain, with waves of excruciating pain, which takes all his energy. He can sit for a short while about five minutes but then it gets so uncomfortable he has to stand up leaning forward against the bunk bed, then that gets uncomfortable and he sits down again. He has a lot of anxiety. But physically he is still a strong muscular man and he may have the energy and strength to go on for some months."
"E. prescribed first *Conium* C200 with plussing – take a teaspoon every fifteen minutes for two and half hours every morning for a week, followed by *Carcinosinum* C200 for a week ... (and later) *Apis* C200 ... to help with the swelling and oedema."

Prescription: *PC2149h* for prostate cancer.

Follow-up:
"... PC prostate cancer got a remarkable improvement; then there was a sudden crisis and no one on the spot to deal with it homeopathically so the doctors want to operate again, which the family and M. himself seem to have consented to. But we don't know the date of the operation yet and we hope to get improvement homeopathically again and so prevent the op."
"I've caught up with A. [friend of M., taking the PC Resonance to him a couple of weeks ago] after her return from Tanzania. She said the homeopathic remedies had been really helping and healed the sores on his legs. Then after taking the PC Resonance the improvement was remarkable. He managed the journey from Dar to Ruvuma OK, the swelling in his leg was going down and his urination was normalising, the pain was less, he was sleeping for much longer periods – three hours at a time, having managed only minutes before and there were no signs of the mental confusion which was there before. He was much brighter. They felt it was a miracle and M. was saying, "God wants me to carry on doing my work." [He became Christian last year.]

M. died in peace surrounded by his loved ones.

Available PC Resonances for Cancer

A list of available PC Resonances for cancer can be found in Appendix 5.

Chronic Fatigue Syndrome

The first to report on the PC Resonance for Chronic Fatigue Syndrome was Anne Vervarcke from Leuven, Belgium. Together with some colleagues she organized a trial and followed up the patients for several years. The initial results were published in *The Second Simillimum* (Chappell, 2005) and will not be repeated here. A short summary is given below.

The main conclusion was that every patient responded to the remedy, and that the results were beyond what they knew could be achieved with individualised homeopathy. Based on their experience they warned for initial aggravations, as some patients were not able to transform these into a healing response. The advice with CFS in severe cases is therefore to first try to improve general health through non-homeopathic measures, and then to be very careful and start treatment with only one drop and then wait for several weeks.

CFS project Leuven, Belgium

Anne Vervarcke (Published in Homœopathic Links CFS Trial in Leuven with PC-CFS - Conclusions after one year; HL Vol 18 4/05 pp 207-208.)

The purpose of the project was to discover how to treat Chronic Fatigue Syndrome (ME) with a single homeopathic remedy - PC CFS/ME - Chronic Fatigue Syndrome.

Currently, homeopathy aimed at individuals, is unsuccessful in most cases once Chronic Fatigue Syndrome has become well established, after a year or so generally, and other systems of unorthodox treatment are likewise unsuccessful or offer little but welcome improvements. Conventional treatment is likewise unsuccessful. Long courses of antibiotics offer little. Long courses of fairly intensive therapy offer some help in some cases. Partial improvements are mild, common and most welcome.

There were dramatic first day responses, going back to the very day Chronic Fatigue Syndrome started. In retrospect these could have been managed better if for a week or month before starting the remedy the person was instructed to live well within their energy limits, something that allows some energy for recovery. The results for five of the seven patients over a one year period were excellent and far better than any other treatment they had received over a period of up to 20 years. The results of the other two cases could have been equally dramatic except for over-cautious prescribing restrictions (not repeating the remedy enough).

Case of PC CFS

Reported by a homeopathic doctor who treated herself

She has CFS since multiple abdominal operations and also has fibromyalgia.
Besides that she has neurovascular compression syndrome N VIII with vertigo.

Follow-up after PC CFS:
Nauseous, vertigo and sick within one hour.
Never had such a strong response to any other homeopathic remedy.
The next week I was a lot better: less vertigo, less headache, more energy.
I can use the remedy daily and keep improving slowly.
I stop if there is a relapse.
I'm not completely well yet but this is already quite a difference.

Case of 26-year-old woman with CFS

Ries IJsseldijk, Netherlands

Her main complaint is ME for which she even has to use a wheelchair. She had mononucleosis in 2000 and was sick for a whole year. In that time she had a stressful job and a very domineering boss. She is fond of animals.
In 2005 she got very tired, nauseous and her liver was enlarged. Now (2006) she has a constant cold and feels like she has the flu. Her legs got weak like jelly and heavy and she can't use them anymore. She loves animals more than humans and feels like an outcast. She used to be very shy and other people's opinion about her was very important. She tends to sacrifice herself for others. She doesn't easily trust people and feels hurt easily. She is a perfectionist and perseveres. She puts high demands on herself and has low self-esteem.

She has vertigo regularly and the feeling as if she has cotton in her head. Her head is never clear and the vertigo is better by closing her eyes.
Menses: very painful, labour like and cramping pains that extend to her knees. Menses is copious the first day. Before she has back pains, is very tired, irritable and emotional.
She is very chilly lately and sweats at night.
Skin: café au lait spot.

Prescription: *PC CFS* 5 drops daily.

Follow-up after 4 weeks:
The lower limbs have improved a lot. Her right arm is very painful. She is still tired but her concentration has improved.
Emotionally she is more in balance. The vertigo is gone and there is no more nausea. Her eating habits have become more healthy and less focused on sweets.

One month later:
Return of symptoms from several years ago. She is emotional and weeps a lot.

Six weeks later:
She is calm and feels better. Feels more satisfied and less stressed.
She needs to plan her day but her energy is good until 4 p.m. She no longer uses her wheelchair and feels 70% better.
She is less emotional and doesn't get angry so easily anymore. Only when tired in the evening she is still easily irritated.
Menses: less pain.
She was obese and is now losing weight.
Skin: mild psoriasis on her scalp.

Prescription: continue PC CFS plus *Carcinosinum* MK 1 diluted dose.

Six weeks later:
Menses directly after the remedy with less pain and normal bleeding.
Her energy is stable, six out of ten, and sometimes even eight or nine.
Walking is going very well; she can think clearly and can study again.

Six weeks later:
A lot of energy, especially in the morning. She does her housekeeping except for heavy chores and works ten hours per week. She recuperates much more quickly from exertion and if she passes the line she uses PC CFS immediately and feels an improvement usually within an hour.

A case of Chronic Fatigue Syndrome

Veronika Netušilová, Czech Republic

Patient: woman 41 years old

Family: married; she has a very nice relationship full of love; no children.
She was raised by her grandparents since the age of two, since her mother left her.
She works as Operation Director (logistics).

Medical history: CFS medically confirmed since 2002, mononucleosis 1991, salmonella 1997, Lyme disease (borreliosis) 1998. Back injury 1999.
Surgeries: 3x lower abdomen + 2x unsuccessful insemination + appendectomy.
Vaccination – she claims strong reactions resulting in negative impact on her health/feeling in general: tetanus ± 1997, influenza ± 1998.

Current physical problems:
Food allergy since 2001, repeating Candida infections, during last six moths neuralgic pains of head (she reports not having these kind of problems in past), but "nothing can be found" so "she cannot be ill".

Symptoms of CFS – fatigue as the illness:

- Subfebrile fever
- Ague, shake, fever
- Uncomfortable feelings in throat, enlarged lymphomas
- Weakness and pain in muscles, joints and head
- Impoverishment with sensitivity on sound, touch and light
- Chilliness
- Collapse due to fatigue (+ vertigo)
- Lot of different allergic reactions
- Fatigue without relevant stress, long-lasting
- Depression, irritation, poor concentration
- Sleep disturbances
- Mental fatigue – memory troubles, delayed reactions...

Current mental problems:

- Constantly increasing discomfort – feeling tired, poor concentration and aggravation by talking, sleepy, palpitations without clear reason
- No capacity for sport (in past lot of activities) – but she "cannot move", as her brain is "switching off" the control of body locomotion
- Morning – problems getting up and getting started or to communicate
- Evening – progressive worsening of concentration; she hears, but does not understand what people say, she is not able to read – no understanding of text
- Problems in her work as her position requires a lot of her attention, dealing with

people and a lot of responsibility. She likes her work but she is too tired to do it or stop it.

Other symptoms:
Constantly chilly, hot bath ameliorates, sensitive to noise and food (vomiting).

Why she came:
Fed up with her mental disability, last drop was when she felt down in work "because I was only able to order one of my legs", sometimes falls asleep in work.

Main Points:
- Fear for future, fear of poverty, but mainly fear to be dependent on anybody
- Problem with borders (overworking) – not able to say "enough"
- Problems with memory, concentration
- Burn-out
- Tiredness
- People do not believe she is ill

Previous homeopathic treatment:
Lac caninum
Carcinosinum cum Cuprum LM II

This gave temporary improvement and helped understanding the meaning of personal borders (but still poor in setting up borders).
Staphysagria LM VI – reaction on physical body (Candida), for short period (ca 1 month) appeared a new ability to say "NO".

All remedies showed short-term improvement ("did something and that was great") but no stable or significant progress.

Key Words: Control, independence, responsibility

Prescription: *PC 142e* for CFS

Follow-up one week later:
She calls "I am feeling so much better". But she is also very afraid of new short-term improvement.
She is able to communicate in the evening at home.
She starts to care about how she looks.
She is more „alive" now.
Subfebriles fade away (her long-lasting problem was evening 38+C)
BUT: Constantly has the phobia of being dependent.

Three weeks later:
"As you have promised: the aggravation is here!"

Physically:
- First symptom: backache – she cannot move
- Rheumatic pains in joints
- Nausea and vertigo appeared

- Continuous diarrhoea and vomiting (four days)
- Headache – neuralgic + trigeminal pains
- Cannot get off to sleep properly (forgotten symptom)

Mentally:

- Concentration is at a good level
- Communicative and positive
- She is nervous – afraid not to finish work in time (she has started two new projects as she feels better.)

Remedy stopped for eight days.

Eight weeks later:
Different woman.
Lively, like after a sip of Aqua Viva.
Independent, proud on herself, her achievements, her life.
She is able to talk about her childhood!
She is active again (dancing).
She went to kennels and she has a new four year old dog and she decides to change her work ... "for something less stressful and more meaningful."

Note: She is no longer repeatedly saying "I must earn money to be independent" but instead "I feel independent now".

Complex Regional Pain Syndrome

Complex regional pain syndrome (CRPS) is a chronic progressive disease characterized by severe pain, swelling and changes in the skin. In regular medicine there is no cure. The International Association for the Study of Pain has divided CRPS into two types based on the presence of nerve lesion following the injury.

- Type I, formerly known as reflex sympathetic dystrophy (RSD), Sudeck's atrophy, reflex neurovascular dystrophy (RND) or algoneurodystrophy, does not have demonstrable nerve lesions.
- Type II, formerly known as causalgia, has evidence of obvious nerve damage.

The cause of this syndrome is currently unknown. Precipitating factors include injury and surgery, although there are documented cases that have no demonstrable injury to the original site.

The abnormal physiological response to trauma of an extremity can cause:

- Inflammatory symptoms: pain, heat, colour, oedema
- Neurological symptoms: paralysis, tremor, cramp, hypersensitivity, numbness, pain
- Sympathetic symptoms: perspiration, abnormal growth of hair or nails
- Atrophy / dystrophy: skin, nails, muscles, bones

PC143f has been designed to treat CRPS.

Caught in limitless pain
Lyanne Verheij-de Schrijver, Netherlands

Lyanne wrote a thesis for the Homeopathic School in Amersfoort on Complex Regional Pain Syndrome. For this project she treated several cases and also used PC143f in the management of these cases. Her experience proved to be very instructive.

Case 1
After each dose of *PC143f* the patient experienced an aggravation: "as if my body weeps."
She showed improvement of CRPS after eleven days. Interestingly enough she didn't only respond on the level of CRPS but also showed a general response with amelioration of headaches, migraines and the return of her menses.

Comment: When disease-specific symptoms reduce it is generally seen that constitutional symptoms come forward more clearly, making it possible to find a better fitting constitutional remedy to complement the disease specific resonance.
In this case the following constitutional symptoms appeared: acne, feelings of disgust with menses, falling of hair, palpitations.

Constitutional treatment was now clearly indicated but the patient was about to marry and decided for tetracycline instead so her skin would look better on her wedding day.

Case 2

After taking the remedy the patient experienced a "bubbling sensation" in the muscles. Improvement started in the second week and with ups and downs she gradually got better. Also in this case, following the improvement constitutional symptoms came up. She developed a cold, got herpes and experienced emotional aggravation during menses.

Constitutional treatment was actually indicated but within the context of the thesis Lyanne decided to continue with *Plumbum phosphoricum* 200K, as this remedy is suggested for nerve injury by Jan Scholten.

Comment: The above cases show a clear pattern that is illustrative for how disease specific remedies can act. After an initial aggravation the patients show slow improvement and increased constitutional symptoms, for which a constitutional remedy is then indicated to complement the case. Also interesting is the observation that the response to the disease specific remedy is not necessarily restricted to the disease alone. Following the improvement of the disease specific symptoms the general condition is also improving, with reduced symptoms outside of the strict diagnosis as a result.

PC Resonances and constitutional remedies can clearly complement each other and PC Resonances can be used to open up a case, as the following case illustrates.

Case of CRPS

Harry van der Zee, Netherlands

A man had been suffering from Complex Regional Pain Syndrome for many years. He was not open to individual treatment, but when his wife told him it would be possible to take a disease specific remedy for his complaints he agreed to that.

Follow-up:

After starting with *PC143f* he showed improvement of his pain. Following that he started to suffer from anxieties, the very ones that had always kept him from individual treatment, as he feared to face them. Now, being confronted with the anxieties, he decided to follow individual treatment after all and an underlying story of life long trauma came forward.

Three cases of CRPS

Reported by Myriam Birrer, Switzerland

Case 1

43-year-old woman with four children. Ever since the first delivery she has pains in the symphysis pubis and the sacro-iliac joint. The pains improved with homeopathy and osteopathy, but always kept coming back. She is a fearful woman with regular headaches. After some time the pains would also involve the knees, the shoulders and the complete spinal column. Several remedies and therapies (TCM, spiritual healing, massage etc.) give relief, but no lasting improvement. She has had panic attacks for many years and is powerless against them. The panic went away after one dose *Medorrhinum* C200, but the pains remained the same. They got so bad that she had to lie in bed for days. From three different doctors she received three different diagnoses.

Prescription: *PC143f* (Complex Regional Pain Syndrome)

Follow-up:
For a few days and nights she has terrible pain. She was unable to sleep, but nevertheless felt a lot better and had much more energy. Then the pains started to subside. For a period of two months she takes the remedy daily with great improvement. She then goes for acupuncture which now helps much more than before. Somehow the PC RESONANCE has helped to reach a deeper layer. She keeps using the remedy every now and then. She is better than she has been in fifteen years. She trusts that soon she'll be completely free from pain.

Case 2
A 49-year-old woman has backaches for twenty years, a burning pain in the spinal column. For fifteen years she has a burning pain in the left arm due to a chronic nerve inflammation. She has burning headaches and can't stand the heat. At night she has pain in the legs, which keeps her awake. She weeps a lot and has inner restlessness.

She suffers from a fall on her spine and her head, and from grief.
She has a bad history with her family, and was often badly beaten by her father.
For years she suffers from colds, sneezing and coughing.
In the past her menses were very painful. She has pain in the abdomen in the morning. She suffers from the consequences of a wrong homeopathic treatment – incorrect remedy in too high potency. TCM was tried to no avail and only gave aggravations. Osteopathy was used to deal with aggravations. She has pain in the neck, ears and pain in the extremities. She is oversensitive to touch.

Treatment October 2010: *PC143f* (Complex Regional Pain Syndrome)

Follow-up:
Already the next day she has more energy even though she could not sleep. After a week she has slept deeply for several hours and she had two nice dreams. Suddenly she could sleep in the afternoon for an hour and then during the night for five hours without interruption. She feels happy. The improvement lasts for three weeks during which the pains subside.
Then she enters into a crisis. All the stories, happenings and memories come up. She weeps for several days.

Prescription: two doses of *PC306a* (long time past grief)

Psychologically she improves and again she feels this energy after the remedy. She likes to undertake things, goes to a party and seeks contact with other people.

Prescription: PC143f 1-2 x per week one dose.

She takes the remedy for five months and slowly improves. In the winter she gets the flu and since March visits a Tibetan doctor for remedies and acupuncture. Where in the past these only gave aggravations, now these help her to further improve. The pains have subsided to the extent that she can now be touched and she takes massage. She has a lot more energy and sleeps six to seven hours per night.

Case 3
A 56-year-old woman is teacher of gymnastics and dance. She has pain in the pelvic region and the lower back for some 25 years. She has a slight scoliosis. After a car accident eleven years ago she broke her skull and left lower leg. She has burning pains in the back and burning pains in the lungs during

cough. She is oversensitive to strong sensory impressions. Her energy is low and she desires to withdraw. She sleeps badly and has often pain in her thigh.
Her marriage is difficult. They have one child.
She is better from motion, which is followed by weakness. She has to lie down regularly. She is timid and doesn't dare to speak in a group.

Prescription November 2010: *PC143f* (Complex Regional Pain Syndrome) 1 dose

Follow-up:
As a reaction she has horrible pain for some days, a return of old symptoms and old pains. Mentally though she feels very alert and she feels a boost of energy. She waits for a few days and then the pains subside while the energy remains better.
After a week she takes three more doses and has a similar response. Ten days later she takes another dose again followed by an aggravation. Then the pains start to improve for two weeks. When she then repeats the remedy there is no aggravation, only further improvement She has a lot of energy now. She gave a speech to her fellow teachers, and approached her boss to discuss problems at work.
After five months she decides to take a break and stops the remedy. She starts massage and osteopathy. In October 2011 the pains return, especially at night. As there is now a picture of *Sulphur* this is prescribed with rapid results. The pains subside and she is again able to sleep.

Crohn's Disease

Crohn's disease, also known as regional enteritis, is an inflammatory disease of the intestines that may affect any part of the gastrointestinal tract, causing a wide variety of symptoms. It primarily causes abdominal pain, (bloody) diarrhoea, vomiting or weight loss, but may also cause complications outside the gastrointestinal tract such as skin rashes, arthritis, inflammation of the eyes, tiredness, and lack of concentration.

Crohn's disease is thought to be an autoimmune disease, in which the body's immune system attacks the gastrointestinal tract. There is evidence of a genetic link to Crohn's disease, putting individuals with siblings afflicted with the disease at higher risk. It is thought to have a large environmental component as evidenced by a higher incidence in western industrialized nations compared to other parts of the world. Males and females are equally affected. Smokers are twice as likely to develop Crohn's disease as non-smokers.

24 year old man with Crohn's Disease

Edson Sampauo, Brazil

March 3, 2001 – was the first time I saw him: a young man, thin, 24 years old, a public employee in a village, single. He seems to me a little bit shy; he waited for questions and answered in a slow and precise way.

Past history: In 1989 a rectal fistula appeared which was submitted to surgery. Some months after: inflammation in perineum and more fistulae purging (pus); by anus also.
In 1993 strong diarrhoea accompanied by vomiting. He lost 20 kilos. From the fistula runs pus, catarrh and blood with bad odour, like a foot smell — we call 'chulé'. He took some calming pills without relief. He was sent to our state capital (Curitiba) where they diagnosed Crohn's disease along with episodes of urine infections. Now and then scrotal swelling, right testicle pain and new local fistula. Begin steroids and azatioprine until 1999 when he discontinued the drugs and took homeopathic medicines *Pulsatilla* and *Nux vomica*. In 2001 he came to me because his homeopath died.

Main complaint: Some days he felt like a ring constricting the anus. He feels the anus is obstructed. Stools formed and escape through the fistulae. Occasionally he loses stool involuntarily. Episodes with bile vomits; better after vomiting. He got nauseous during meals. When the anus is obstructed the faeces are thin. < morning and > afternoon; but in evening isn't feeling so good and the vision is blurred.
He said the fistulae are worse in winter (our place gets cold in winter, often 0°c) and he prefers warm weather. He got fever and night sweating. He is anxious and afraid the treatment isn't successful.

School: good student, never repeated, good opinion of his teachers. Not prone to cry, even as a child. He had an amorous disappointment in adolescence which he thinks wasn't an issue: a girl he liked moved to another place. In speaking he's precise, chooses the words. "I'm determined. What I take on I'll end. Regarding relationships it's not the same." He is intelligent, proper and cautious and keeps some distance from me (suspicious).

Endoscopy: (after removing a little towel he uses as protection under the shorts) 'multiple inflamed fistulae peri-anal including the scrotum base; pus discharging'.

Direct examination of anus: I only could put the tip of the 5th finger. He felt strong pain.

From the start of the treatment until now I accompanied this young man in a roller-coaster treatment, as frightened as him, only more confident after the PC RESONANCE. (In fact I could never find his simillimum). I was reading Scholten and Sankaran. Observing, he seemed to me a mineral remedy.

I began with *Silica* CM, 1 dose, according to Scholten the 'fistulae remedy'.

30 days after: He said the fistulae closed and came back slowly after fifteen days. He had an episode: he woke after midnight with fever, bleeding a lot, bile vomiting and trembling, burning in fistulae, purging abundantly. Burning in fistulae when urinating.
Endoscopy: fistulae with better aspect and stool coming out.

60 days after placebo: Purging a lot; night sweating on thorax, no smell nor bad feeling. Faecal incontinence (if doesn't attend to urge) and pus (he noted it has no colour) through fistulae. Everything > during stool. Persisted anus obstruction sensation. He said he's less anxious. After one month he gained weight – one kg.

After that the symptoms come and go: blood (clotted and fluid), faeces and pus alternating through fistulae, eventually fever crises and I gave him *Phosphorus, Phosphoricum acidum, Carcinosinum* and other remedies according to the symptoms, but I was half-lost.

One year after the situation not much difference: fistulae goes and opens again; dark and painful urine; no more fever nor nausea and vomiting; just one fistula bled; he gained seven kg; rectal touch the same.

Looking for the right remedy I find in Vithoulkas' *Materia Medica Viva* the *Calcarea silicata* case. June 2002 I begin with C30.

I forgot to say he always came with his mother. She said almost nothing, always seated quietly by his side. He doesn't go after relationships (25 years old) because of his illness. Declares no intention to date or marry and no sexual contact. Masturbation occasionally.

August 2002: Better appearance, his hair loss >. Inflammation without colour running from fistulae. Some of them are closed. Yet with hypothermia and weakness, followed by low fever, but it isn't like before. Urine OK. Anus canal 'sometimes large sometimes small' (sic).

30 days later recurrence: Closing anus, stool running through fistulae.

March 2003 (two years after) – After *Calcarea silicata* I went to *Natrum silicata* because the mother always accompanied him. Long talks with the patient; he is eager to collaborate but I couldn't prescribe with confidence. In October 2002 just two fistulae remain in perineum. The *Calcarea silicata* was increased to M and, with each dose,
aggravation with faeces exploding by fistulae. His weight 75.5 kg (a little bit obese).

Patient impression: "I'm getting better but I want to heal. I'm depressed because I can't manage with the opposite sex. I lack courage". It's not like that in his job where he's OK.
He went on diet and his weight went to 71 kg.

Always looking for the remedy, in June, 2004 I gave him *Ferrum oxidatum* after a long mineral study: ("I must hold on to be cured" – he holds his faeces, he holds on to me). *Ferrum oxidatum* provoked a strong aggravation with fever and diarrhoea; poor sphincter control stools coming through fistulae, but with rare and small bleeding. His impression: "This was the only remedy closer to a healing".

Examination: Just one fistula remains (at 1 o'clock), and for the first time he takes off the little towel without stool, just moisture.

September 2004 – change of job: Now he's a schoolteacher having difficulty maintaining discipline in classroom. This is upsetting to him: "My tendency is to be hard line". He teaches geography. He alternates between euphoria and mild depression, apparently without reason.
Now he's dating a girl. Many changes in his life!

March, 2006: five years after beginning treatment: He got married. He doesn't come with his mother. Now he always comes together with his wife. Holding hands! "My state depends on my evacuation" – "When I had diarrhoea my concern was to retain; now it's to lose." "Despair to cure." "Blocked inside, a torture, no way to get out of this situation."

I got lost in the case, despite the improvement in many ways. Still uses his towel but it doesn't stain anymore. I changed the remedy many times, gave *Cactus* in March, 2006. (His sensation was growing up and shrinking.)

In Nov 2006 I wrote: two fistulae remain, aqueous secretion, not stool. No inflammation.

January 1, 2008 (almost seven years of treatment): Fistula peri-anal still active. He's concerned because his wife doesn't get pregnant. They want a child and he wants a solution! For the first time he came without the little flowered towel. His perineum is dry but the fistula is there, the surrounding is sensitive to touch but without secretion.

PC Crohn

Voilà! Now I have *PC Crohn*. Thanks to God! He took it for three months according to PC instructions. Since then there was just one day he did not feel good. The anus spasm came only in the morning.

June, 2008 – "I have no difficulty evacuating but another fistula reopened (one or two in low part) but it disappeared again." "I still have the feeling that the anus is shut but I can pass stool without difficulty." "My throat was inflamed, I had a high fever. This occurred once before a long time ago." He's more worried because his wife doesn't get pregnant. Ask new spermogram. The first one was 0 active spermatozoid. PC Crohn continued.

Nov, 2008 – His wife had three embryos implanted but it didn't 'hold'. Next attempt in January. He got fatter. I recommend diet and exercises. Prescription: *Carcinosinum* M + PC Crohn.

Jan, 2009 – He is married and lives with his parents, joint-family. This kind of thing doesn't function with us: his wife and his mother quarrelled and he exploded. He was rude, threw things away. This was a surprise to me because he's gentle. His father never appeared in any conversation. He says everything is OK now, no hard feelings. They moved to their own house. Difficult stools. The anus is the size of the fifth finger, but sometimes it's like a thumb. He goes to the bathroom many times, unsatisfactory. The fistulae bulges and sometimes it expels faeces.

Relates his problems as a teacher and says "we are managing". He was reprimanded because he took a pupil by arm and threw him out of the classroom. He admits he was rude. "I am calm but I'm explosive". He has many gasses but it doesn't go out by fistulae.

Medications: *Staphysagria* C200 and PC Crohn.

Last visit (march, 2009): It opened one fistula more but the intestine is working better. New insemination and his wife is pregnant – this time the spermatozoids were taken directly from testicle (biopsy) and not frozen. Faeces are not thick but are sufficient.

He declares: "The last one (PC) was the better remedy you gave me". On a scale of one to ten, he gives himself an eight now.

Endoscopy: Fistulae in 16 and 23 hour around anus, small, with puncture form, no inflammatory signs. Continue with PC Crohn.

January 2010: I'm happy to say all the fistulae closed completely. A little son has been born; we say a 'polaquinho' (little polish). Everybody is happy.

Diabetes

Diabetes deserves some extra thought as it is an increasing disease worldwide. Even WHO speaks about diabetes and associated obesity in terms of an epidemic. For a homeopathic approach this means that although preferable, an individualized approach may be less needed or not enough as we are dealing with a collective phenomenon based on today's culture. If obesity even reaches percentages like 75% (Urban Samoa) and the prevalence of Type 2 diabetes in elderly goes up to 70% (Libya) it may be clear that an as-if-one-person approach (GENUS CHRONICUS is the term we propose) is very likely to be fruitful as a complement to individualized treatment or even as primary form of homeopathic treatment.

Let's start with giving some figures on the consumption of sugars today.

"At the beginning of the last century [19th] world sugar production amounted to no more than 11 million tons raw value ... and by the end of the century it was around 129 million tons ... Sugar consumption in North and Central America is close to 38 kg per head. South America has a per capita consumption of 46.5/kg which is increasing at an annual compound rate of more than two per cent." [Trends in global sugar consumption by Javed Kayani - www.dawn.com/2005/10/31/ebr13]

"Around 1600 a UK person would use around 2.5 teaspoons of sugar per day. His offspring in the US would use 56 teaspoons per day in 2003. Between 1958 and 1994 the prevalence of Diabetes mellitus in the US has increased by 500%." [The Sugar Consumption to Diabetes Connection - www.neprimer.com/ePress]

"In the last 20 years, we have increased sugar consumption in the U.S. from 26 pounds to 135 lbs. of sugar per person per year! Prior to the turn of this century (1887-1890), the average consumption was only 5 lbs. per person per year!" [www.healingdaily.com/detoxification-diet/sugar]

Diabetes and Obesity

That hugely increased sugar consumption causes a problem to the human organism should be no surprise, especially if that increase coincides with enormously decreased motility. One result is increased obesity:

"Currently, more than 64% of US adults are either overweight or obese, according to results from the 1999-2000 National Health and Nutrition Examination Survey (NHANES)." [www.obesity.org/statistics/obesity_trends]

The WHO writes: "Obesity has reached epidemic proportions globally, with more than one billion adults overweight." [www.who.int/dietphysicalactivity/publications/facts/obesity/en/]

"The number of cases of diabetes worldwide in 2000 among adults 20 years of age is estimated to be 171 million. Even if the prevalence of obesity remains stable until 2030, which seems unlikely, it is anticipated that the number of people with diabetes will more than double as a consequence of population aging and urbanization. ...

In summary, these data provide an updated quantification of the growing public health burden of diabetes across the world. The human and economic costs of this epidemic are enormous. Mortality from communicable diseases and infant and maternal mortality in less-developed countries are declining. In association with increasing diabetes prevalence, this will inevitably result in increasing proportions of deaths from cardiovascular disease in these countries, as well as increased prevalence and associated consequences of other complications of diabetes. A concerted, global initiative is required to address the diabetes epidemic." [www.who.int/diabetes/facts/en/diabcare0504]

Diabetes in Africa

The experience of the authors with PC Resonances for diabetes is mainly restricted to Africa. In most African countries diabetes, if diagnosed, is often not or only partially treated. Depending on the availability of health facilities and the financial situation of a patient treatment is given. In practice this often means that a diabetic patient only uses oral medication or insulin injections if there is money. Every now and then they buy some tablets or injections and for many days and weeks they go on untreated. A homeopathic remedy specific and effective for diabetes would be ideal for them as the costs are just a fraction of regular treatment.

Also in Africa diabetes is on the rise:

"Diabetes is an increasing problem in sub-Saharan Africa. Type 2 diabetes, the most common form, is becoming more prevalent owing to rising rates of obesity, physical inactivity and urbanisation." [Diabetes in Africa: epidemiology, management and healthcare challenges; N.S. Levitt, Groote Schuur Hospital, Cape Town, Published Online First: 2 June 2008. doi:10.1136/hrt.2008.147306. Heart 2008;94:1376-1382]

"Diabetes is an important cause of morbidity and mortality in Africa ... Mortality associated with diabetes is unacceptably high and is disproportionately due to preventable acute metabolic and infective causes ... Efforts to prevent this disease and its complications in Africa are impeded by inadequate health care infrastructure, inadequate supply of medications, absence of educational programmes, and lack of available health care facilities and providers." [Diabetes trends in Africa, Ayesha A. Motala, Diabetes Unit Department of Medicine, Nelson R. Mandela School of Medicine, University of Natal, Durban, South Africa.]

In Africa famine is in the subconscious of every individual as a lack of food in shorter or longer periods has been part of the collective experience for ages. This, together with other motivations like trauma and stress, drives people to eat excessively. Added to that in Africa is the deep-seated appreciation of obesity as a sign of wealth.

"We have gone from under-nutrition to over-nutrition without ever having passed healthy nutrition." [Krisela Stayn, a retired professor with the SA Medical Research Council.]

"Worldwide, analysts say, an estimated one billion people are overweight while 800 million are undernourished. Health experts say the poor are the most vulnerable ...
Health experts warn that the high cost of medicines means that the majority of the poor often goes untreated or has no regular treatment ..."

"This epidemic is responsible for so much suffering and loss of life, yet so little is being done to tackle it," says an official of the Diabetics Federation. "Doing nothing in the face of the epidemic will place significant stress on the economic development of many countries and jeopardise the Millennium Development Goals." ...
"With more diabetic deaths, Africans will realise the wisdom of their ancestors."
[Diabetes in Africa; Sifelani Tsiko, Harare, Zimbabwe (Dec 14 2006);
http://www3.interscience.wiley.com/journal/98518095/abstract?CRETRY=1&SRETRY=0]

Treating Diabetes with PC

For the treatment of diabetes and obesity the following PC Resonances are available. A combined resonance for types 1&2 was added for developing countries where proper diagnosis is often not possible and a good case history may be lacking.

- Diabetes Type 1 -- PC157m
- Diabetes Type 2 -- PC158n
- Diabetes Types 1&2 -- PC150d
- Obesity due to famine reflex -- PC170f

Treating diabetes in Congo and Burundi

Harry van der Zee, Netherlands

In november 2008 I treated at least twelve cases of diabetes in Burundi and East DRC Congo. At least twelve, because at some point due to the large amount of patients I stopped filling in two forms, one for the clinic and one for myself. Those that I could follow up responded well, and from the pastors I heard that they received a lot of positive feedback from diabetes patients. Often people are officially on medication, but depending on the money available they only sometimes take some tablets or sporadically inject insulin. So to have a very cheap remedy available now is wonderful for them. One lady who had a blood sugar of 19 was drinking five litres of water every evening, was sweating profusely and all the teeth in her mouth were loose. After the remedy the sweating and the exessive thirst totally disappeared and the blood sugar went down to 16 in a couple of days.

Follow-up two months later:
The nurses that I have instructed on how to use PC Resonances are very positive about PC158n for diabetes. 90% of their cases show remarkable improvement and I have been able to follow-up several of them myself. Blood sugar levels return to normal in a matter of weeks and diabetes related symptoms improve rapidly. Although the nurses did not recommend this, some patients even stopped their regular medication, including a patient that was injecting insulin, without any of them relapsing. Instead their sugar levels remained normal and their symptoms did not return. Remarkable results as in my twenty years of experience in the Netherlands diabetes was not one of the easy indications to treat with homeopathy.

Case example

55 year old P. has diabetes and weighs 80 kilos. Glycaemia 289 mg/dl (N 55-115) or 16.53 Mmol/l.

Follow-up after two months:
"I used to doze all the time but no more. I have lost weight because I'm much more active. Before I felt hungry all the time but now it's finished. I can walk now without getting tired." The last blood sugar level measured on December 12 was normal: 4.8 Mmol/l.

Case of a diabetes patient and his walking stick

Harry van der Zee, Malawi

AL is a 74-year-old male who was diagnosed with diabetes in 1994

Intake 07-03-2012

"I've been sick for 18 years, since 1994 up to now. Sometimes my body breaks everywhere. Penis, anus, muscles. And I have rheumatism – all fingers and all toes.

I can just feel when I've too much sugar in my body. Then I use glibenclamide (2 x 10 mg). When I feel right then I might say I am free (meaning he doesn't take it). But in most cases sugar comes in, very frequently.

The body becomes heavy. Passing urine several times, every 30 minutes I go. Passing urine frequently ... ten times sometimes. Up to now I don't sleep.

I feel like I'm stepping on some stuff when I walk barefooted. And the legs become heavy.

And my eyes, I'm losing eyesight now. I see foggy."

At the end of the consultation I had made A. a compliment about his beautiful walking stick. "I have another one", he said, "which I give to you". "An old man needs a stick", he added.

Being considered an old man dented my ego, but more than that I felt grateful for the gift.

Prescription: PC158n for diabetes, 5 drops daily

Follow-up

A week later, I decided to pay A. a visit to collect my walking stick. I find him sitting in front of his house, from where he has a wonderful view on Lake Malawi. Above his house weaverbirds feed their young. I share my groundnuts with his grandchildren, and receive some oranges in return. A. sends his eldest son out to bring me a coke.

Of course I'm curious as to how A. is responding to the medicine.

"I feel alright, a bit becoming alright. No foggy eyesight now. I see clearly and I see very far. Rheumatism has gone on my fingers and toes, and I'm standing up from my chair now without having to support myself."

He shows me how he stands up quickly without any help, and I remember with how much difficulty he stood up after the consultation, only one week ago.

"I'm feeling I'll be alright. I had a lot of feelings under my soles but it seems it is vanishing. There is a big change. I've got strength. There is a change in passing urine. I used to go 10 times per night, but now I'm going 3 times. I'm sleeping now."

Before I leave he shows me around on his plot of land. I observe that he does not use his walking stick. When I mention that to him he replies, "I no longer need it". I leave with gratitude for his improvement ... and with a beautiful walking stick. And the coke? It never arrived.

Another two weeks later I meet A. again in front of his house. All improvements have stayed but as the hospital is lacking materials they couldn't test his blood sugar level. He didn't use any oral medication for two weeks as he didn't need it, but when he had no more tea sweetener and started using sugar instead he started feeling some pain with urination, so he took glibenclamide again until he would have a new supply of sweetex. That he still had to urinate a few times per night he felt disappointing and I explained that at his age he probably had some prostate problems alongside the diabetes. He would come to the clinic soon for a new bottle of PC Diabetes and to see what could be done for his prostate. This was going to be followed up after I left Malawi.

A case of diabetes
Harry van der Zee, Malawi

60-year-old woman.

"My blood sugar is always high and I'm most of the time weak." She is keeping a diet and takes oral medication (glibenclamide) but can't get the blood sugar level below 100 mg/dl.

Prescription: PC 158n, 5 drops daily

Follow-up after 5 weeks
"The blood sugar is now always normal. It used to be 10 and above, but now it remains in between 6 and 7 (60-70 mg/dl). I used glibenclamide but since I'm using your medicine I've never used it again."

As she is overweight and besides the diabetes has pains in the knees, I advice her to lose weight. As I meet her in a lodge on my way to the airport I refer her to the clinic in Chintheche for further treatment. *Calcarea carbonica* might well be a good next choice for her.

Based on the above (and we have seen dozens of cases like that) we hope homeopaths and other practitioners all over the world will try out the abovementioned PC Resonances for diabetes in their clinics and send their reports back to us. This is clearly one of the areas where homeopathy can show to be a reliable, effective and cost-efficient alternative to current treatment. As stated before, this disease specific approach is ideally complemented with an individualised approach alongside guidelines on a healthy lifestyle.

Eczema

Eczema is one of the often-mentioned indications for homeopathy. This doesn't mean that treating it with homeopathy is always that simple. Having an eczema specific resonance to complement the simillimum or to buy time until it is found may be a great relief to the patient, parents as well as the homeopath.

37 year old man with eczema

Harry van der Zee, Netherlands

This man had eczema all of his life. It was situated around the eyes, between his fingers and on his scrotum. He was also asthmatic from cats. After taking a full case I had no idea what to prescribe him. So I decided to start the case with a disease specific remedy.

He started taking a daily dose of the PC Resonance for asthma & eczema. First he responded with an aggravation and then amelioration set in. After six months of treatment his complaints had improved by 60%. I retook the case, but again a constitutional remedy could not be determined, so he continued with *PC160e*.

He was actually so happy with the results that he didn't feel a need to continue searching for a constitutional remedy, and for years he would only call every now and then for a new bottle of the PC Resonance if the symptoms started to come back.

Epilepsy

Case of a two year old boy with epilepsy

Ries IJsseldijk, Netherlands

F. is born on March 21 2003 as his parents' first child. He was born in Europe and later moved with his parents to Israel. He received a vaccination programme including HIB, Hepatitis B, DTWP, BMR and Meningitis C.
He responded with side affects to the last vaccination (meningitis C) by being very angry.

Epilepsy

Report from an Israeli child neurologist: His mother was treated during pregnancy with Progesteron and Aspirine, but there were no complications. F. was born at 38 weeks and had a normal perinatal period and a normal development.
At nineteen months old he started having seizures. The seizures appeared with an aura of fear and were followed by freezing, occasionally accompanied by automatic behaviour that looked like a kind of laughter.
In the beginning the seizures were very short, ten to twenty seconds, and he had one or two per day. The seizures appeared only during waking time. Treatment started with Tegretol, and the result was that he was free from seizures for two months. At present the seizures occur five to nine times per day, some of them nocturnal. Sometimes they occur in clusters and have tonic components, with bilateral arm extension and cyanosis lasting ten to forty seconds, and with the eyes turned to the left side. Despite elevation of the medication, the seizures kept on evolving. He received Valproic, but nevertheless had aggravation of the seizures. Then Ospolote was added, without benefit and with side effects. Now he is on Topiramate, in escalating dosage.

EEG: relatively normal background with epileptiform abnormality on the left side of his brain.

It is possible for F. to fight a seizure. He feels it when it comes, and knows when it stops.

Further history

Mother was pregnant three times before she got pregnant with F. Her first pregnancy ended after two months in an abortion. During the second pregnancy the foetus had no heartbeat, and in the third pregnancy the same happened. In her fourth pregnancy the mother was prescribed progesterone and aspirin, had some bleeding, but ultimately F. was born.
The mother had insufficient contractions to deliver the baby. There was meconium in the fluids when F. was born. The Agpar score though was good, nine/ten.
F. was breastfed till eleven months old.

Mind: He makes jokes, loves friends, and is a sweet and social child.
He needs his mother, but there is no panic when she is not there.
He has no fears.

Sleep: his sleep is restless; he is crawling through his bed. He sleeps in genupectoral position.
Food: desires meat (3).

Family history: some allergies, asthma.

Prescription: I decided to give him the PC RESONANCE designed for epilepsy: *PC162g*
5 drops each day after banging the bottle five times.

Follow-up:
In response to the remedy he had an aggravation that lasted three days, with five seizures during the day and seven during the night. The following list shows how he improved after that:

Table of seizures

	day	night
8th	5	0
9th	6	1
10th	7	0
11th	6	0
12th	6	0
13th	1	2
14th	5	11

This nightly increase showed different, less heavy seizures; one though lasted for one hour and Valium was given.

15th	10	0
16th	5	0
17th	2	1
18th	4	2
19th	1	2
20th	2	0
21th	0	0

One year later he has not had any seizures anymore, and he takes the PC162g every day. When he stops taking it the seizures come back. He has no further medication.

How to proceed from here is the question. Maybe something with PC vaccination is needed as well? Or his homeopathic constitutional remedy together with PC162g, or separated?

Comment by the authors: The way to further treat this case could include both options. If a constitutional remedy is clearly visible starting with that would be the first option. If after that seizures keep coming back when PC epilepsy is stopped, starting with *PC vaccination* to detox for possible vaccination damage would be indicated in combination with *PC epilepsy*. The constitutional remedy needs to be repeated if there are constitutional symptoms coming up besides the seizures. Any change in constitutional symptoms after starting a PC RESONANCE indicates a next constitutional remedy should be selected.

Case of epilepsy

Corrie Hiwat and Harry van der Zee, Malawi

A 20-year-old male has epilepsy ± 1 x per week since he was six months old. After each attack it takes him a day to recover.
He was seen early 2004 by Peter Chappell, who at the time could not establish a simillimum and instead gave him PC epilepsy, five drops daily.

Follow-up:
We saw him six months later. He reported that although he still had epileptic attacks these have reduced considerably. Where before it would take him a full day to recover, now he would be back to normal in only five to ten minutes.
On retaking the case there was now a clear picture for a constitutional remedy, and treatment was continued with a single dose of *Cuprum* 200C.

Case of epilepsy

Klaus Schustereder, Central African Republic

This concerns a man with epilepsy at full moon. He is prescribed PC162g, once daily five drops.

Following the remedy he has no attacks for three months. After stopping the remedy the attacks come back so he continues.

Comment by the authors: The conclusion is that now ideally individual treatment would be called for, but in the circumstances that could regretfully not be provided.
The authors have seen several more cases of epilepsy in Africa. PC162g is in our experience very reliable and can be prescribed with confidence.

Fibromyalgia

Fibromyalgia is characterized by chronic widespread pain and a heightened and painful response to pressure. Fibromyalgia symptoms are not restricted to pain, leading to the use of the alternative term fibromyalgia syndrome for the condition. Other symptoms amongst others include debilitating fatigue, sleep disturbance, joint stiffness. Fibromyalgia is frequently comorbid with psychiatric conditions such as depression and anxiety and stress-related disorders such as post-traumatic stress disorder. Not all people with fibromyalgia experience all associated symptoms.

Fibromyalgia is considered a controversial diagnosis, due to lacking scientific consensus as to its cause. Not all members of the medical community consider fibromyalgia a disease because of a lack of abnormalities on physical examination and the absence of objective diagnostic tests. Although a lot has improved in recent years, for many patients this meant that their complaints were not taken seriously. The increasing recognition of the condition and progress made in its research has not led to consistently effective treatment.

Homeopaths have treated fibromyalgia patients with often limited success as finding the simillimum is often not easy in these cases. A disease specific approach can complement a simillimum if it has been found, or can help to get the picture clear once the symptoms start to subside and constitutional signs and symptoms come more clearly to the for.

Report by G.T.

So far I have done well with PC Resonances and have a lot of proof that only these remedies actually have been helping me so far. A lot of symptoms have improved since I started taking PC Resonances for Fibromyalgia ten months ago, particularly disturbed sleep.

Initially I was not quite sure if PC172h was helping me even though I was taking it religiously from May onwards, I think. But before that, as have many ME/ Fibromyalgia sufferers, I tried everything under the sun in the hope of easing the suffering and pain.

Then recently I had a computer test done by "Oberon", the bio-resonance computer system developed in Russia. To my surprise it was found that I actually started to have a small healing progress, which started from the time I started taking PC172h. The young doctor said that he had never had such a result with a chronic condition.

My best regards and wishes.
G.T.

Case of fibromyalgia

Reported by Ellen van der Voort, Netherlands

My patient is now two months on PC Fibromyalgia.
When she started she was limping and could only climb stairs sideways, crab-like. It hurt to reach out or up with the arms. The muscles are very tense all over for years; and she has much pain and stiffness.

The joints are OK; she can move; and an orthopaedic check for soundness of nerves showed that is OK.
No rheumatoid arthritis factor, either.

After starting PC Fibromyalgia once a day, she felt better, less grinding pain.
After a few weeks the limp had disappeared.
She was tiring less.
A week ago she went up a flight of stairs the normal way.
She sleeps at night without pain waking her up.
Things are slowly improving.
And she had a bad cold and a fever along the way; the skin has rashes everywhere. It is very exciting.

Gilles de la Tourette

7 year old boy with Gilles de la Tourette

Reported by Beverly Welbourne, USA

Spontaneous jerky movements are mostly in his right arm, face, and neck. I can see it clearly in the initial interview. He also is having trouble in school, as he frequently yells loudly at other students.

Prescription: *PC525b*

Follow-up:
We start with one half-teaspoon dose of the solution, after which he gets worse for two weeks – the movements get larger, and occur more frequently. He also seems irritable as reported by his mother, and tries to hit his older brother on three occasions. He has done this before but not three times in two weeks.

Then he gets calmer, and the movements become less frequent. The improvement seems to stall about a month after the initial dose, so we give it again. Again, he is worse, but only for a few days. The remedy is repeated a total of five times in a five month period, after which he does not appear to have any abnormal neurological nor social condition. The outbursts at school have decreased substantially, as reported by his primary teacher.

Treatment is discontinued, no relapse after nine months.

It has been a year now, and he is still doing well.

Hypertension

Similar to obesity and diabetes the prevalence of hypertension is increasing based on cultural changes – urbanization, low motility, changing food habits etcetera. This means that hypertension in a patient can be approached from an individual point of view (E.g. the *Nux vomica* or *Aurum* type) as well as from a collective point of view (overweight urban person with lack of exercise and bad eating habits leading a stressful life). Ideally a patient with hypertension receives individualized homeopathic treatment, if needed complemented with hypertension specific approach. For developing countries with often only low skill homeopathy available or no homeopathy at all, hypertension is one of the indications we felt it would be worthwhile to see whether a disease specific approach alone would be of help. Supported by positive results in Africa PC423z for hypertension was therefore added to the AMMA4AFRICA KIT.

Here is some information on hypertension in Africa:

"Last month, the diagnosis and treatment of hypertension in African countries received special attention, highlighted in a special section devoted to "heart disease in Africa" in the American Heart Association's journal Circulation and on the occasion of the First Pan-African meeting on Hypertension, which took place December 2-5, 2005 in Yaoundé, Cameroon.

Africa is in "epidemiological transition," due to a move by many people from a rural to an urban lifestyle, bringing with it "advances of civilization" such as an increased cardiovascular disease burden, several authors noted. Hypertension in Africa is a widespread problem of immense economic importance because of its high prevalence in urban areas, it's frequent underdiagnosis, and the severity of its complications. For example, the INTERHEART Africa study has shown that hypertension is the strongest risk factor for myocardial infarction (MI) in black Africans, with an odds ratio of 6.99 compared with 2.3-3.9 in other ethnic groups. The latest estimate of the World Health Organization (WHO) is that more than 30 million people in Africa have hypertension. WHO predicts that if nothing is done about it, by 2020 three quarters of all deaths in Africa will be attributable to hypertension. The African Union has called hypertension "one of the continent's greatest health challenges after AIDS."

In Circulation, two South African researchers, Lionel H. Opie, MD, DPhil (University of Cape Town) and Yackoob K. Seedat, MD, PhD (University of KwaZulu Natal, Durban), focused on hypertension in Sub-Saharan Africa ... They have reservations about applying proposals about hypertension in black Americans to Africans living in Africa, and even about applying proposals for one African group to another elsewhere in Africa. They believe that environmental rather than genetic factors may account for observed differences in hypertension between black and white hypertensives.

The First Pan-African Congress on Hypertension was set up by the International Forum for Hypertension control and prevention in Africa (IFHA), which also published the first guidelines for the management of hypertension and cardiovascular risk in Sub-Saharan Africa in 2003. The theme of the congress was "averting a hypertension pandemic in Africa."

The difficulty of paying for antihypertensive drugs was addressed by Marc Twagirumukiza, MD (University Hospital, Butare, Rwanda). "In most Sub-Saharan African Countries, medi-

cines are paid out of pocket by individual patients, rather than being subsidized through social insurance. The price of drugs is therefore a major obstacle to adherence to long-term treatment with agents such as antihypertensives, but too little is known about the prices paid for medicines in low income countries," Prof. Twagirumukiza said.
[http://www.medscape.com/viewarticle/521325_3 Local Experts Focus on Problems of Detecting and Treating Hypertension in Africa]

Report from the Chintheche Homeopathy Clinic
Joseph Msumba, Malawi

> The PC RESONANCE for hypertension is working great. I have fourteen patients on it for two months now and none reported with high blood pressure since.

A case of hypertension
Harry van der Zee, Malawi

> A 75-year-old man is running two motels and together with his wife two private schools. His problem is hypertension. Despite a hospital prescription of Maxide (Triamterene and hydrochlorothiazide) the systolic pressure is regularly way over 200 and the diastolic pressure 110-120.
>
> Prescription: PC Hypertension, once daily 5 drops
>
> After 5 weeks the blood pressure, regularly measured by his doctor, is between 140/90 and 130/80. "When the blood pressure was still high I was feeling weak and I couldn't move properly." He was still taking Maxide in the same dosage as before.

From Kenya, where the resonance for hypertension has been used since 2007, we have received similar feedback (verbal information from Mary Kemunto).

Multiple Sclerosis

Here's what the conventional medicine says about the treatment of MS:

"Several therapies for multiple sclerosis (MS) exist, although there is no known cure. Multiple sclerosis is a chronic inflammatory demyelinating disease that affects the central nervous system (CNS).
The primary aims of therapy are returning function after an attack, preventing new attacks, and preventing disability. As with any medical treatment, medications used in the management of MS may have several adverse effects, ... At the same time different alternative treatments are pursued by many patients, despite the paucity of supporting, comparable, replicated scientific study.
During symptomatic attacks, patients may be hospitalized. As of 2007, administration of high doses of intravenous corticosteroids, such as methylprednisolone, is the routine therapy for acute relapses. Although generally effective in the short term for relieving symptoms, corticosteroid treatments do not appear to have a significant impact on long-term recovery. Mitoxantrone, also used in cancer chemotherapy, is probably the most effective in the short term, however its use is limited by severe toxic effects on the heart."
[en.wikipedia.org/wike/multiple_slerosis]

Case of a 52-year-old woman with MS
Ries IJsseldijk, Netherlands

Consultation: June 2005

A brain scan shows white spots in the brain. Lesions in the spinal marrow are not clearly visible.
She is very tired, and every day feels numbness on her head, mainly the occiput.
Also she feels a trembling inside and there is numbness of the fingers.
In the morning she wakes up with weakness of the lower limbs.
The MS started in 2002. Before it she was never ill, and she hates it that she is ill now.

Two years ago the friend of her son died of cancer, but she can talk about that in a normal way. Also a few years ago her son was drinking too much alcohol, and got into contact with the police. It was an awful period. She worries about everything and she takes too much care of her children.

She has been using birth control pills for twenty years and she has no menses since then. She takes the pill for three weeks and then stops one week, but there is no bleeding in that week.
Before the stop week she gets migraines, pain in the abdomen and mammae.
She has vertigo a few times a week.

Prescription: I gave her the PC Resonance for MS, *PC243p*, five drops in the morning after banging the bottle five times.

Follow-up seven weeks later:
No weakness anymore. The numbness is much less, occurs only once a day and even disappeared for days sometimes. Before she felt it every hour of the day.
The trembling inside has disappeared and she no longer has tired lower limbs.

Also mentally she feels no stress anymore. Before even shopping was stressful.
No more vertigo.

One month later:
The last days she is tired again and on the head some numbness has reappeared. There is no numbness in her fingers anymore.
The trembling inside is still gone. The lower limbs feel tired again though.
Last week she did sports again for the first time in years.
No more vertigo.

I decide to continue with PC243p and to give her besides that *Cocculus* MK in a dilution once daily.

Four weeks later:
No weakness anymore.
Everything is okay.

Three months later:
She has not taken any remedies for five weeks now.
There is a new source of stress though. Her husband is due to have heart surgery.
Her lower limbs are tired again.
The vertigo is still okay, as well as the numbness of the fingers.
The numbness in her head starts again.
Her energy level is relatively good.

I decided to start again with the PC243p and *Cocculus* MK.

Five months later:
After a week everything was okay again. She continued taking both remedies for one more week and then stopped taking them. She has stayed well the past five months.

55 year old woman with MS
Peter Chappell, Czech Republic

"Dear Peter,

Thank you so much for doing the work you do! I am so happy to go on the homeopathic medicine PC243p for my MS. There has been tremendous change in my health condition. I have been bicycling for the first time in over twenty years since I was diagnosed. And I have had my first separate art performance with my paintings and drawings.

In 1989 at the age of 35 I was diagnosed with Multiple Sclerosis. This was a time when I was finishing my second education as a music-therapist. I remember how exhausted I was from the illness and from the way I lived my life.
At that time I never allowed myself to sit down and was always occupied with something, always in a hurry, and my whole body was so tense and tired of the situation that it finally collapsed. My feet were almost paralysed and for months I was linked to my bed. Instinctively and due to my education I knew I had to work with my inner life. At this point I understood how important it was to take responsibility and work with my inner state of mind and give myself positive feed-back and the rest I needed.
I used classical music together with self-hypnosis and visualization. This combination was unique as it worked for me and my body, and gave me back my inner strength.

For years I went on with my life the best I could, always looking for natural treatments which could help me with the different symptoms going on in my body. I tried Homeopathic medicine, Tibetan acupuncture, Feldenkreiss, Anthroposophic medicine, and many other sorts of treatments which helped me in dealing with all the different symptoms of this illness.

In 1999 after my children became grown ups and left home, I moved up to a beautiful little place in the mountains of Norway. I needed to live in a quiet place and in Nature.

For years I did quite well, but these last years from 2002 until 2005, my body suddenly again became weaker. I was living with a man that had an alcoholic problem, and I had forgotten to take enough care of myself.

There were difficulties with my sleep, and I could not relax. My body and muscles were again very tense and I had much pain. At that time I saw a neurologist in Germany who said cortisone was the only treatment for my MS which is the secondary progressive type. I went onto Prednisolon for a year or so, having the treatment with infusion of Prednisolon every third month. This was not good at all as my body would not accept this medicine. Again I had to find another way to handle my situation and find a natural treatment which my body would accept and handle.

I met with a very intelligent homeopath who ordered the PC243p.

Follow-up:
After just some months I felt positive changes coming and I became both mentally and physically stronger. I also went onto other homeopathic medicines such as *Causticum, Aurum* and others.

PC243p works for me. That's for sure! Of course I have my symptoms with bad days, but now I can cope with them also using other therapies such as EFT (Emotional Freedom Technique), art and music-therapies. Just as important as all these therapies is my diet. No sugar, no milk, little meat and no wheat flour. I live a peaceful and good life in spite of my Multiple Sclerosis, and have much hope for my body in the future. PC243p is my "security medicine" which I am convinced has turned the MS diagnosis into a new and positive direction. I feel more secure and have developed strategies to handle my MS.

So thank you Peter, and if you can use my story just go ahead. All the best to you and your work!

Thank you so much again Peter. Sincerely,

M. in Norway"

Case of a 38 year old woman with MS
Harry van der Zee, Netherlands

The first symptoms of MS were probably in 1984 when she had a visual disturbance. The diagnosis was made in 1992 shortly after she had come to my practice. She had been to two other homeopaths before in the period 1987-1989 and had received *Belladonna, China* and *Ferrum*.

So when she comes to me in 1991 the diagnosis of MS has not been made yet. She starts telling how many cares she has had regarding her children and their illnesses. Especially her daughter has been in and out the hospital with severe asthma. She complains of nausea after dinner and tells she is very sensitive to noise, which irritates her. She has pressing frontal headaches that are worse from noise.

She is very tired, which is aggravated by loss of sleep, and she likes to be alone. She is full of emotions due to all the cares but not able to release them. She is the kind of person that takes care of others and forgets to take care of herself.

She is chilly, has a desire for cheese, and dislikes eggs and ice cream. Since she had gallbladder problems after her second delivery she has an aversion for fat.

Rubrics:

- Mind; CARES, worries; Agg. (52)
- Mind; CARES, worries; Full of; others, about (14)
- Generalities; SLEEP; Loss of, from (53)
- Stomach; NAUSEA; Eating; after (188)
- Mind; SENSITIVE, oversensitive; General; noise, to (271)
- Head; PAIN; Noise, from (138)
- Mind; IRRITABILITY; Noise, from (55)

Prescription: *Cocculus indica* MK

Follow-up after two weeks:
First she was even more tired but then this improved. Also she started to feel calmer. Then after her son's sinuses had to be rinsed she felt worse again. The nausea though is a lot better and her appetite has improved. An eruption has started in the neck. From the time she was a baby until she was 25 years old she had suffered from eczema.

Prescription: wait

One month later:
She has no more nausea or headache. Also she feels less tired and her sensitivity to noise is less. She feels irritable though, which as I understand it might be a sign she still needs to be left alone to restore.

One year later:
Again she is very tired. New is that she complains of ascending numbness in left arm and left leg. There is also numbness of the tongue and vertigo. She experiences a loss of strength and her left hand is awkward.

Prescription: *Cocculus* MK

In the meantime a neurologist confirms the diagnosis Multiple Sclerosis.

From 1992 to 2004:
Every now and then she receives *Cocculus* since 1992 and for many years she responds 'well' to this remedy. Nevertheless she has off and on acute flare-ups of the MS and her condition slowly deteriorates. Pulling the brakes is all the remedy can offer her. She gets more and more restricted in her activities, can only walk short distances and needs a wheelchair if she goes out.

In these years I gather more symptoms, dig deeper in the past, retake the case and try several other remedies, all, except if indicated for an acute, to no avail: *Natrum muriaticum, Colchicum, Natrum carbonicum, Pulsatilla, Gelsemium, Silica, Cistus canadensis, Sepia, Asterias rubens, Ptelea, Sarsaparilla.*

In 2004 she is mentally and physically in a really bad state. There are several problems concerning her children and her husband is chronically depressed and seems to be suffering from dementia.
She has a strong twitch-like cramping of the eyes, is very depressed and fears the future now that her husband, on whom she is depending due to the MS, is in such a bad state.
This time the response to *Cocculus* is less than usual. Considering her bad circumstances I prescribe *Cocculus* LM3 daily. There is some effect, but not enough.
She takes *Conium maculatum* 200K and later MK with little result.

Her husband remains a big problem for her and added to that her son enters a very difficult puberty, her daughter discovers she is lesbian and her mother-in-law is found in her house on the ground disoriented and with a broken leg.
The circumstances are so unfavourable for her that I wonder whether at this point there is much I can do for her.
Around that time I had read interesting reports about a remedy designed by Peter Chappell for AIDS. While discussing the results in Africa and planning a visit to Malawi to monitor his work he informed me that he had also designed some remedies for chronic diseases that could complement the simillimum if needed. I offered to try some of these out in my practice in cases where I ran out of options and the patient would give consent. Among the remedies I received was a remedy designed for MS.

Prescription: *PC243p* five drops daily after banging the bottle five times

One month later:
Despite the fact that there are no changes in the circumstances there is quick improvement of her symptoms. Even her mood is much better and she feels fitter. The numbness under her feet goes away shortly after each dose.

After six months:
She is firmer on her feet than in years. She can even wear slippers again, where for the past ten years she could only walk on high solid shoes. She can take longer walks now, can stand and work in the kitchen longer, and makes less use of her wheelchair. The twitching of the eyes is still there but a lot less than before.

After ten months:
She has warts all over, and there are more and more. She can't remember she had warts before. They are big cauliflower dry warts especially on the right hand.
If she stops taking PC the tingling gets worse again. She has decided to take the remedy every three days. Her lower limbs are very good, much stronger. Mentally she feels 100% okay again. The twitching of the eyes is a lot better.

Conclusion: due to the PC Resonance the MS symptoms subside and new constitutional symptoms come up.

Prescription: wait

Two months later:
She is still very satisfied regarding her MS. 'I can do 50% more than a year ago', she says.
The warts though are getting bigger and bigger.

I decide to follow her body in the symptoms it produces and prescribe *Thuja occidentalis* 200K.

One month later:
The warts were getting smaller quickly and seem to dry out.
Since by taking PC MS every three days the tingling under her feet comes back each time I suggest that she continue PC243p on a daily basis.

Three months later:
The warts are totally gone. Her eczema, which had come back after the very first dose of *Cocculus*, is now moving downwards. Also she reports the return of an allergy she had many years ago, as well as a knee pain of many years ago.

I ask her whether *Thuja* has brought about other changes: "I feel more at peace with the fact that I can do less than before the MS ... I have noticed that I can be very useful for elderly people ... I can put my husband's problems aside more easily ... I just go my own way ... I'm more happy with myself. Earlier I used to feel useless, that I meant nothing."

Since taking PC MS daily the tingling no longer tends to return but is for 95% gone.
This summer she has taken a walk on her bare feet on the beach, something which was impossible for more than ten years. Walking and standing remain better without relapses.

Prescription: stop PC

Ten weeks later:
The tingling comes back as well as the twitching.

Prescription: PC MS daily until stable

Two and a half years after starting with PC:
MS is stable. Taking three drops of PC MS daily works best for her, and once the improvement is stable she can stop taking it for weeks to months.

Myasthenia Gravis

80 year old woman with myastenia gravis

Harry van der Zee, Netherlands

Her eyelids hang down and on chewing her food she gets cramps. On speaking she can lose her voice. She can't keep her head straight for a long time. She has heaviness of the legs, and weakness of her hands.
She is a nervous type that panics easily. Bad news can paralyse her. The main problem in her life is her relationship. She craves love and attention, but her husband is a very distant and cold man that avoids physical contact.

Prescription: *Gelsemium* 200K

Follow-up:
After Gelsemium she has no more drooping eyelids. Also the other symptoms improve but keep relapsing as soon as there is a circumstance that provokes them.

Ignatia is tried instead but gives no response. Also *Curare* is given without any result. Her specialist describes her Mestinon which she discontinues as it causes diarrhoea.

She then improves on a combination of Buscopan and *Gelsemium* in LM potency but keeps having regular relapses and shows no further improvement.

Then I have *PC245r* for Myasthenia gravis prepared for her, which she takes daily,
five drops.

Follow-up:
She responds with rapid further improvement of speech, eating and swallowing.
She can do more, feels more fit, but more importantly shows no more relapses from emotional conversations with her husband or others, whereas on Gelsemium these kept occurring.

The follow-up on PC245r is ten months.

Obsessive Compulsive Disorder

Report from India
Dr Lakhsmanan Raghavan

We have used PC254s to successfully treat a patient suffering from OCD (obsessive compulsive disorder) recently. After taking the PC RESONANCE, the condition improved by 90% within a week. The OCD disappeared completely without taking any further remedies. This case is unique because we had only PC254s for the treatment.

Old Age

Death is the certain outcome of a human life and time has therefore been called a fatal disease we all suffer from. With ageing we develop more complaints and if there is no other clear diagnosis or remedy, giving a PC RESONANCE for ageing is an option that can prove to be helpful.

Case of an 88 year old man
Ellen van der Voort, Netherlands

To my old father who nearly died some months ago due to old age, diabetes Type 2 and heart failure, I prescribed the corresponding medicines (PC RESONANCES for ageing, diabetes, heart failure) with very good results. He improved remarkably, and got much better than he had been in the previous year.

Parkinson's Disease

This patient was the first patient I (Harry) prescribed a PC Resonance for. Once I had decided to study Peter Chappell's results with HIV/AIDS in Africa Peter had given me a few PC Resonances he had prepared for chronic diseases, with the invitation to try them out. This Parkinson's patient happened to be the first patient I asked whether he was interested in trying out something completely new. I gave him the instructions on how to use it and planned a follow-up three months later. The day after the follow-up happened to be the day I would go to Malawi to monitor the effects of PC1 for AIDS. Shortly before leaving I was a bit anxious to what I would encounter in Africa. Would PC1 indeed show the effects reported, or would we have to conclude that after initial good responses patients were still dying of AIDS? Had Peter Chappell indeed created a big step forward in homeopathy or would it all be a hoax? With all these questions in my mind I did my last consultations before flying off to Johannesburg and then on to Lilongwe. Here is a summarized history of the case.

Case of a 63 year old man with Parkinson

Harry van der Zee, Netherlands

He stands up from his chair in the waiting room slowly and his arms hardly move while walking into the office. The diagnosis is obvious, Parkinson's. His speech tends to be a bit stammering.

In the last few years his handwriting has become smaller and smaller. Sometimes it looks more like drawing a line. This is worse if he feels stressed, especially if he has to do more things at the same time. He used to take notes during meetings of the church board, but had to give that up. Reading has become difficult because he loses track. Also conversations are hard to follow, so he tends to withdraw if in company.
His right arm is often trembling, especially if he brings something to his mouth.
He tends to mumble if tired.
He is very slow.
At times he has to urinate very frequently, up to four to six times per hour. The urologist couldn't find a cause and suggested it might be due to nervousness.

During cycling he sometimes gets a pain in the chest. The cardiologist couldn't find a cardiac cause for it.
He has a tired feeling in his head bordering on dizziness.
His hands and feet are cold.
He has aphthae regularly.
He has tartar due to profuse salivation.
Ejaculation used to come very quickly.

Aversion to sour and herring. Desire for sweets and fat.

In his sleep he tends to shout "go away", "get out of here". He is always threatened in his dreams.
He dreams of burglars standing in his bedroom.
He also dreams of being at his work and in his dreams he wonders "what am I doing here, I have retired".

Since he was very young he has suffered from headaches, which were worse lying, and better standing and walking. They start from the neck. He either wakes up with it, or it starts around noon.

He is a very meticulous person and is afraid of making mistakes. He used to do the administration for a printing firm and checked all his calculations a few times. When computers entered his life, not being able to check by hand whether the calculations were correct gave him a lot of stress. He doesn't like to take risks.
Religion is the most important thing in his life, and the Sunday sermons are a preview of heavenly joy.

He tends to get diarrhoea from anticipation.
He has a strong fear of water.

Some ten years ago he was been treated with *Argentum nitricum* with some success. On *Arsenicum album* he then did not respond.

Analysis

A repertorisation (MacRepertory – expert analysis) suggests *Plumbum metallicum* as the first remedy. Some of the rubrics confirming the remedy are:

- Clinical; PARKINSON, morbus (74)
- Extremities; TREMBLING; General; upper limbs; hands (218)
- Extremities; TREMBLING; General; upper limbs; hands; writing; while (46)
- Extremities; TREMBLING; General; upper limbs; hands; mouth, carrying something to, when (5)
- Mind; CONSCIENTIOUS about trifles (100)
- Mind; FASTIDIOUS (75)
- Mind; FEAR; Failure, of (53)
- Mind; HYDROPHOBIA (70)
- Mind; DREAMS; Robbers (76)
- Speech & Voice; SPEECH; Stammering (104)
- Head; PAIN; Standing; amel. (14)
- Head; PAIN; Walk, walking; amel. (113)
- Mouth; APHTHAE (209)
- Mouth; SALIVATION; General (405)
- Male; EJACULATION of semen; Premature, too quick (49)
- Generalities; FOOD and drinks; Sweets; desires (190)
- Bladder; URINATION; Frequent (356)
- Teeth; TARTAR (17)

Prescription: *Plumbum metallicum* 200K once a month

Follow-up after five weeks:
He is less tired in his head and more relaxed. Urination is less frequent. His wife noticed that since the remedy he is livelier, and makes jokes again as he used to in the past. "We had almost forgotten that he used to be like that", she says.

Two months later:
His dreams are less restless. The PSA has decreased from 8.6 to 4.9, and he has less frequent urging for urination. He used to be cold in the evenings, but this has changed completely. He has more strength in his hands. His handwriting was normal again for one day, but after that stayed the same. He mumbles and stumbles less.

Three months later:
No more aphthae; no more restless dreams. The other improvements have stayed. In general the Parkinson's has improved a little and then stabilised. He feels no response to Plumbum 200K anymore, and the tired feeling in his head is still there.

Prescription: *Plumbum* MK in a dilution, five drops daily.

Three months later:
Parkinson still a little better than it was nine months ago and stays that way.

Introducing PC

This is what I believed were the limits of homeopathy with Parkinson's – some improvement and then preventing rapid deterioration. I asked the patient whether he would be willing to try out a new remedy. I told him I knew nothing about it, not how it was made, not whether it had ever worked. All I knew was that its maker had reported amazing results with another remedy he had prepared for AIDS. The patient agreed to take it and I explained to him that he could use it daily.

Prescription: *PC260p* in dilution; five drops daily after banging bottle five times.

Three months later:
When Mr. R. enters my office I can't believe my eyes. He walks normally and I see no trace of Parkinson's.
"My writing has improved so much that I can write again like I did in the old days" he says enthusiastically. "The neurologist even told me he had never witnessed an improvement like this." "Also, I can now bring a spoon to my mouth without the least trembling." His wife adds, "I have never seen him so relaxed".

He also reports that his backaches, which he didn't mention before, have improved a lot.

Based on how Peter instructed AIDS-patients to use PC1 I had told Mr. R. to use PC Parkinson on a daily basis. Aggravations had never been reported with PC1. After starting with the remedy though he had a strong reaction, so he decided to stop taking it until the aggravation was over. After the next doses he had shorter and shorter aggravations until he could take the remedy daily and only kept improving.
I was totally impressed by the quick and impressive improvement and left for Malawi in the best of spirits.

Four months later:
The Parkinson's symptoms are still a lot better, but he feels he no longer responds to the remedy. The PSA has increased to 11. In his head he feels very tired.

Prescription: stop PC and take *Plumbum* XMK.

Four months later:
The tired feeling in his head remains, and is what mainly bothers him. He feels like sleeping a lot, but that doesn't help at all.
Some time ago he started taking the PC RESONANCE again, after which he improved. By the time he started to relapse he stopped taking it, after which he started to improve again.

Prescription: *Plumbum* LM2 and restart PC if the Parkinson's symptoms get worse.

Five months later:
Had a reasonably well period and when indicated took the PC RESONANCE for a month. The tired feeling in his head remains and responds to no remedy.

Prescription: *Germanium* 200K

Three weeks later:
No response.

Prescription: *Mercurius* 200K

Two weeks later:
Was very well for two weeks and now starts to relapse.

Prescription: *Mercurius* MK

Three weeks later:
Again felt very well, than after a week started to relapse, but now improves again gradually.

Prescription: wait; PM *Mercurius* LM3 if needed; PC260p if indicated and stop when no more improvement.

Three years after starting PC Parkinson:
His symptoms are still clearly better than before, but nevertheless he slowly but surely has grown worse after an initial impressive improvement after PC Parkinson and a stable phase sustained by using PC Parkinson and constitutional remedies when indicated. My impression is that I still have not prescribed the right simillimum for him. He no longer responds to *Mercurius* or *Plumbum* both given in K potencies as well as LM potencies. Each time he starts taking PC260p again he responds to it and improves until there is no more improvement and then he stops taking it for several months.

Six months later:
He has a flu, something he has had off and on in the past. It starts with diarrhoea, and then he got very cold and his vocal cords started to trouble him. He is hoarse and his throat is sore. His wife says that he made a humming sound all night as if his throat was narrow.

Prescription: *Influenzinum* 200K. My motivation is that a long history of influenza might be connected to the onset of Parkinson, and possibly this is the nosode that can break open the case again.

Two months later:
He responded to *Influenzinum* very well and got over the flu rapidly but no real further changes after that. The Parkinson is stable and he has found out that seven drops once a week works best for him. Since I have been prescribing metals mostly, his wife asks whether the fact that he has been using a shampoo based on zinc for more than 30 years is significant. As he wasn't sure about that, he has already stopped using it for a month, without the dandruff returning. I remember he used to dream of parting from his job and when I ask him about those dreams he says that he still very regularly has those dreams, although he stopped working years ago. In the Iron series *Zincum, Arsenicum, Selenium* and *Bromium* are connected with the end of work (Scholten). *Arsenicum* is connected to the loss of work, *Selenium* with indifference to work and *Bromium* to work coming to an end. *Zincum* is repeating

routines and would fit before the actual leave of work, but what is typical in his dreams is that he tells the colleagues to keep doing everything the way he had done it. He is not so much concerned with the loss of work or income (*Arsenicum*), and he is far from indifferent to it (*Selenium*). So letting go of control regarding his work (Bromium) or concerns regarding the maintaining of the routines (*Zincum*) are the main options to consider. Following the simple directions that life tends to offer us, his wife's remark about *Zincum* is significant. Besides that, guilt (*Bromium*) is not a real issue for him.

Prescription: *Zincum* 200K

Six weeks later:
He initially reacted by becoming more tired but after that his weakness started to improve slowly, and he has had much less need to urinate frequently. He got some eczema on his forehead, which disappeared again. The dandruff returned, but without doing anything about it, also disappeared. His sleep is less restless and he does not wake up his wife any more by shouting in his sleep. The dreams about his work have stopped. He had one dream, but it was not about parting from the job, now he was only making coffee at the office.

Prescription: *Zincum* 200K, one dose once a month and PC260p once a week seven drops.

Three months later:
The improvements that started after the first dose of *Zincum* hold so we decide to continue with *Zincum* 200K one dose per month. He notices now that once a week seven drops of PC Parkinson is not enough to keep his energy level and the Parkinson symptoms stable, so we decide to go back to once a day five drops.
It seems like *Zincum* does not help to further improve the Parkinson symptoms. That taking PC Parkinson once a week is no longer sufficient is an observation made in more cases. After reaching a stable plateau by giving it daily at some point the drops can be stopped, or as he decided to do, taken less. For some months the plateau will hold and then as soon as symptoms start to increase again five drops daily are indicated again.

Scleroderma

49 year old woman scleroderma

Harry van der Zee, Netherlands

According to the specialist the diagnosis is CREST Syndrome, an auto-immune disease also called Limited Systemic Sclerosis, resulting in excessive deposits of collagen. The symptoms of the syndrome consist of:

- Calcinosis cutis (mainly fingers)
- Raynaud phenomenon
- Oesophageal dysmotility (with difficult swallowing)
- Sclerodactyly (deformity fingers)
- Teleangiectasia (red spots on fingers, face and in the mouth)

During the first consultation it is not the symptoms of the disease but rather the news of the diagnosis that bothers her.

"My psychological condition is the main thing now. Since I heard the diagnosis I come to nothing. Nothing can be done about this disease. It's the uncertainty – what will my future look like? What can I do? How does it look like from the inside? It is as if I've fallen still. I just sit or sleep and weep a lot."

She doesn't have all the symptoms of the syndrome. The CREST related symptoms that she has are:

- Episodes of extreme pains in kidney regions (not typical for CREST?!)
- Lack of energy
- Hot and tingling hands
- Pain behind sternum at night
- Dryness of throat extending to chest
- Very thirsty at night
- Dryness of eyes (Secondary Sjøgren)
- Little red spots all over
- Drawing skin in the face

August 2006 she receives *Phosphoricum acidum* 200K.

Two weeks later she calls to tell me that after the remedy she wept a lot and after that started feeling much better emotionally.
"I recognise myself as I was long ago. I ask things instead of always doing it myself, and I can express myself about things that bother me without being angry. I'm much less angry. Things upset me less, like I used to be until some years ago. My sleep has improved, and I'm less hot and perspire less."

She responded to the remedy with frequent stools, like after food poisoning twelve years ago; a diarrhoea that lasted for five years.
The symptoms of the CREST syndrome did not respond to the remedy. Dryness of eyes and throat keeps getting worse.

She had a dream: "I closed myself in while making a wooden shed. Help. I can't get out. I closed myself in by something stupid. A claustrophobic sensation."

She likes to be on her own: "I don't want people to come close, but I'm very fond of animals; always brought sick birds home; had lots of cats before getting married." She has horses now and used to work in an animal shelter, followed trainings for dealing with animals and used to breed dogs. She also has always been afraid she was not good enough.

I wonder whether *Aethusa* might be a deeper remedy for her that would also influence the CREST symptoms, but she has no response whatsoever.

In the mean time a PC Resonance for scleroderma and CREST syndrome was prepared, and she starts taking it daily November 2006.

Follow-up:
The response to PC Scleroderma shows a dramatic a rapid improvement.

She started taking the PC Resonance during an attack of pain in her kidneys. The attack was shorter and the pains were less severe than usual. The dryness of the eyes is much better. She doesn't wake up anymore with difficulty opening or closing her eyes, and she can wear lenses again the whole day.
One hour after the first dose she has extremely cold hands and a cold right foot with tingling, which lasted for two hours.
The pain in her right foot is then soon gone, the numbness much better and the pain in the right shoulder better.
The dryness in the mouth is better. There is no more dryness of the throat; no thirst at night; no pain in the oesophagus. Also the drawing sensation in her face is almost gone.
The feeling that the muscles in her neck are like cables is gone.
The number of stains in her face nevertheless still increase and the nose still feels dry and painful.

Two months later the physical symptoms are so much better that the specialist starts doubting the diagnosis. As she feels depressed again *Phosphoricum acidum* 200K is repeated. Again three months later *Phosphoricum acidum* MK.

Ulcer

A case of leg ulcer

Dr Lakhsmanan Raghavan, India

A case of 56-year-old female suffering from chronic leg ulcer was treated unsuccessfully using homeopathic remedies. Her condition improved with *PC330u* and the ulcer dramatically almost vanished within a week.

Based on our clinical observations and experiences with PC Resonances, we would like to share a couple of pointers.

The time taken to treat a chronic case has reduced significantly after using PC Resonances in conjunction with homeopathic remedies selected using the classical method.

We were able to achieve palliative care of our patients remarkably using PC Resonances.

We have not seen any aggravation till now though we had a mild aggravation in one case, which got subsided on the very same day.

Usually it would suffice to repeat the PC Resonances for three days continuously in most of the cases. In some cases, we use for seven days and in some more than a month.

Available PC Resonances for Chronic Diseases and Behavioural Disorders

A complete list of all available PC Resonances for chronic diseases and behavioural disorders can be found in Appendix 5.

PART XI

Provings of PC Resonances

- Proving of PC1 for HIV/AIDS
- Proving of PC140c Cancer, general disposition
- Proving of PC240m Malaria

Strictly speaking, doing a proving of a PC RESONANCE is not needed as the remedy has been designed for a symptom totality that is already known.
There are two main reasons why nevertheless several provings have been performed:
1 – to establish besides clinical experience through a proving that the PC RESONANCE indeed can be used for the disease totality for which it is designed.
2 – to make it possible to include PC RESONANCES into pharmacopeiae so their production and distribution can take place within the rules and regulations laid down for homeopathic remedies.
Anybody interested in performing an open or blind proving of any of the PC RESONANCES can contact info@ARHF.nl.

Proving of PC1 for HIV/AIDS

A blind proving of the general resonance for AIDS was conducted by Dr. Chetna Shukla in Mumbai. The following is her report.

The Qualitative Synthesis of PC1 Proving

The following groupings of symptoms have come forward.

Love, Sex

I feel the need for an intimate friend. All my friends are married! I also feel I should get married (bashful)(P5).
Marriage has become a question. I miss my old days with him. I was happy with him. Sex is the last thing on my mind. Can say... it is not on my mind at all. I don't even share the bed with him. There is no physical contact at all. I don't want it (P4).
I had a dream that I am getting married. I can't remember the details but my pink lips were prominent in the dream (P6).

Attractiveness

I feel no need for sexual attraction. I need to wax but I don't do it (P4).
Now I am conscious of my physical appearance. I comb my hair very often; I wash my face three or four times a day (P5).
Desire to be naked (P6) I feel very conscious of how I look. I saw myself in the mirror more than four or five times (P6)

Unnatural Sex

Big brother/Big Boss shows ... It is kind of voyeuristic. It is a weird kind of pleasure that one gets after watching such shows (P1).
In Russia there was Ivan the Terrible, the king (3). It is believed he suffered from Syphilis and took mercury for its treatment (P1)/ Count Dracula (P1)
The indulging in different kinds of sex play that is not natural ... (Spoke with disgust)! I can't speak further ... but this is very much on my mind. What have you given? (P4)
There is too much sex on my mind. The vaginal discharge could be impurity. But sex is not bad, but too much sex is bad. It can lead to rape and crime (P6).

Love, Cruelty

In Russia there was Ivan the Terrible, the king (3). It is believed he suffered from Syphilis and took mercury for its treatment (P1).
Count Dracula (P1)
I feel my love betrayed. I want to kill him by strangulating him (smiling) and leave his dead body somewhere in his house (P6).

Food

Desire coffee, brewing coffee, cappuccino (P1)
Aversion tea, Tea does not relieve (P2)
Desire sev puri, milk chocolates (P3)
Desire pav vada, salt, lemonade (Indian burger) (P4)

Desire onions, tea buttermilk (P5)
Desire for spicy (P6), juices, chocolates, coffee (P6)

Urticaria

I had urticaria only on the hands (P1)
I had severe urticaria on the trunk and the forehands. There were severe blotches. I was shocked! I felt as if some insect bit me (P5)
I had an urticarial rash over chin near the corner of the mouth (P6)

Terminal stages/Incurable

Dream: I see my mother very withered and weak, with swollen eyes and in a terrible condition. She looked like an old lady about to die. She was as if in her end stage of life suffering from a disease that is not curable. We are waiting for her to die (P1)
Dream: He tells me that his son has a cancer of the white cells. He gives me the name of a type of cancer of a certain type of white cells called ... what I don't remember at all now! I tried so much to remember but I cannot remember. In the dream I feel what has this little child done to suffer so much? Such an innocent boy, come into existence some while ago and he already has an incurable disease (P2)
She had to nurse her and care for her in the hospital. She was suffering from age related problems and it was as if she would die any moment (P3)

Pelvic affinity

The whole day I had dragging pain in the hypogastria as if menses would appear more in the evening (P2)
I had developed a furuncle on the leg, in this proving I got it in my genital area. It is just one on the pubic region (P3)
... it is the uterus, the pelvis is sore (P4)
I also have a foul smelling vaginal discharge for the first time in life (P4)
I got severe pain in the testes going upwards along the spermatic cord (P5)
I dream that I had an orange coloured mucus discharge from my vagina (P6)

Mood Depressed/ Cheerful

I feel melancholic (P1)
It alternated between talking less and talkativeness, cheerful with young people and gloom and less talkative with elderly people (P3)
I actually have a feeling of 'I don't care', 'I am in my own world'. There is no brooding anymore (P4)
But overall the mood was cheerful. I was contented (P5)
Cheerful mood the whole day (P6)

Abdomen

I had pain in the stomach region as if I had peptic ulcer (P1)
While I tried to have an extra morsel I had a very bad cramp in the abdomen. It was as if my intestines were being twisted like we wring clothes (P2)
I felt as if a load or a stone, as if overloaded and felt much uneasiness in the stomach (P5)

Legs / Calf muscles

I had a cramp in the right calf muscle (P3)
Cramps in the left calf muscles (P2)

I have severe leg cramps. My legs weigh so hard. I want him to press them point-by-point over the calf to release the hardness (P4)

Small / Miniscule / Worthless

There are so many good doctors in homoeopathy and I am a 'miniscule' particle (P1)
I felt we were treated like garbage. We have no worth (P6)

The Synthesis...

Jung (I follow Jung's technique) has laid emphasis on the universal character of collective conscious.

> "... it has contents that are more or less the same everywhere and in all individuals. It is in other words identical in all men and thus constitutes a common psyche substrate of a supra-personal nature that is present in every one of us."

This is true in health!
This is true in disease/s too!
... Because disease is but an altered state of health.

If there is a collective unconscious in health, than there is a collective unconscious in disease too. Therefore diseases although being individual to an individual have a collective unconscious such that it has symptoms (contents) that are more or less the same everywhere and in all individuals. Each disease has a common psyche substrate of a supra personal nature that is lived by every one of us who suffer from that particular disease!
This happens in/is termed epidemic disease.

In §100 (6th edition), regarding the investigation of epidemic diseases Hahnemann says:

> "In investigating the totality of the symptoms of epidemic or sporadic diseases it is quite immaterial whether or not something similar has appeared in the world before under the same or any other name. The novelty or peculiarity of a disease of that kind makes no difference either in the mode of examining or treating it, as the physician must any way regard the pure picture of ever prevailing disease as if it were something new and unknown, and investigate it thoroughly for itself, if he desire ... with the exception of those epidemics resulting from a contagious principle that always remains the same, such as small pox, measles, etc.

In §101 he continues:

> "It may happen that in the first case of an epidemic disease that presents itself to the physician's notice he does not at once obtain a knowledge of its complete picture, as it is only by a close observation of several cases of every such collective disease that he can become conversant with the totality of its signs and symptoms. The carefully observing physician can, however from the first and second patients, often arrive so nearly at a knowledge of the true state as to have in his mind a characteristic portrait of it, and even to succeed in finding a suitable, homeopathically adapted remedy for it."

... Approximating to a homeopathic specific.

Epidemic according to dictionary 'is a disease prevalent among a people or community (common character) at a special time, and produced by some special causes not generally present in the affected locality'. Many epidemic diseases from Hahnemann's/former times have (believed by the medical community at large) apparently been eradicated! But in actuality the same disease now displays itself, to the champions of practitioners of medicine, as another morbid form and is now called as a new disease altogether. But they remain epidemic still.

One amongst these so called new diseases next to cancer is AIDS. From what has come up in the proving of PC1 it is proof enough for me that this medicine is a homeopathic specific for HIV/AIDS.

Proving of PC140c Cancer, general disposition

A blind proving of the general PC RESONANCE for Cancer was conducted by Dr. Chetna Shukla in Mumbai. The following is her report.

The Qualitative Synthesis of PC Cancer Proving

The following groupings of symptoms have come forward.

Extreme behaviour / Lack of Control

(P1) I had impulse to bang my head. I hit so hard that I have an injury mark. If you can harm yourself, it proves to what extent you are serious.
(P2) My feeling was I want to get them punished. One is behind bars and the others fled.
(P2) I was very tensed I literally shouted and screamed at them, calling them names standing outside the house (I have never done this before) openly as like a rebel. I wanted to take immediate revenge.
(P3) Dream ... While I was urinating there just to show that she loves me (or to attract me) she started to urinate in the passage in the standing position behind me. There were some other boys in the toilet too.
(P5) I also fought in the class that I have never done till this 4th year. I am the C.R. (Class Representative) ... Now I feel that they are 'taking me for granted'
(P6) I usually get angry very fast but now I feel I can control myself.
(P6) I always tend to think of incurable disease. If there is headache then I have brain tumour! I will die of cancer! If I have hoarseness then I think of throat cancer, cancer of larynx! If I tremor I think of hyperthyroidism. I have this great fear of disease – incurable and I will die.
(P7) Yesterday there was a bomb scare at Dadar station. But I was not so bothered.
(P4) In anger I wanted to strike them. I wanted to become violent. I wanted to destroy something. I felt angry with her and in anger I broke a pencil.
(P5) At this I felt like committing suicide. I wanted to die by cutting my wrists.

Danger

(P3) Dream: danger from water.
(P3) Dream: But the feeling I had was this man is so furious that he might start to get 'physical' with me (start beating me up!).
(P3) There were two dogs and they started barking at me. I got slightly frightened.
(P3) Sea energy has tremendous power to cause Tsunami's that cause destruction.
(P3) It was stormy weather. The houses were of wood (as in the U.S). The people around were not Indians. We were searching for a safe place.
(P3) Dream: Thunderstorm with earthquake.
(P3) I had a fear of communal riots.

Exhaustion

(P1) I get easily exhausted. By 10-10.30 at night I am tired.
(P4) No weakness, that I usually have, after tea.
(P5) Exhaustion after stools.

Sweets/Sugar

(P1) There was a strong craving for sweets – kheer (sweetened milk with rice, spices and dry fruits), jaggery, apart from chocolates. I felt unsatisfied after eating. I wanted more and more of it.
(P2) I got the desire to eat something sweet throughout the day. In the evening I ate two handfuls of homeopathic pills.
(P6) Normally also I crave for sweets but the other day I ate, I ate and I ate them but I could not feel satisfied after eating them. I just did not feel the satiation after eating sweets.

Dictating

(P1) It is like … like rules, that you have to follow … follow this and follow that!
(P1) They feel I am dominating.
(P2) Dream: I am searching for place and there is an empty chair besides me, I see prover 1, I call for him and ask him to sit here in a very authoritative tone.
(P4) I feel she is bossing.
(P5) But I feel they do not include me in decision-making and just inform me and I have to follow! They only order me, don't consider me and I don't like it now.

Sensitive

(P1) Offended easily.
(P4) I feel hurt when she shouts.
(P5) We had clinics and my teacher asked me if I had done my homework. I had not done and she fired me. After that I lost my confidence.

Cancer

(P1) It is an inner 'self' conflict! Between two extreme thoughts: Freedom to decide and imposition!
(P3) Dream: I was in our college. Somebody has arranged a discussion on "how to build a union" and "how to find out loopholes (ambiguity) in the union".
(P3) Dream: The trustee of the hospital (who in real life is very stern, dominating, perfectionist, faultfinding, fastidious, clean, faultless, and rigid) is sitting there on a bench and smiling. His demeanour is very mild and friendly. He is sitting there with a huge sub-mandibular swelling waiting for his turn for a sonographic investigation. In the dream I feel this swelling is cancer.
(P4,5) It is like in cancer – one/few cells misbehave and all the cells suffer the brunt of chemotherapy! Other cells are not guilty but they have to suffer despite not having done any wrong, having not misbehaved! (Both provers 4 and 6 reaffirmed the same and spoke this simultaneously!)
(P6) I always tend to think of incurable disease. If there is headache then I have brain tumour! I will die of cancer! If I have hoarseness then I think of throat cancer, cancer of larynx!
Family history of cancer: P2 (aunt: breast cancer), P3 (mother: ovarian cancer), P6 (aunt: breast cancer) P7 (mother: ovarian cancer) and the conductor (aunt and mother: both had breast cancer).
Personal history: P3, P4, P6 talked of cancer while describing the disposition of the proving substance.

Physical Symptoms / Sphere of action

Index finger PIP joint (P1-Rt, P3-Lt)
Elbow (P1-Rt, P7 Lt)
Eyes (P2, P4 Lt, P7 Lt, P6 Lt)

Head Temples (P3, P2, P4)
Stomach (P1, P4, P5, P6)
Urinary (P7, P4)
Teeth molars (P6, P2)
Neck (P3, P4)
There are no qualifying physical symptoms except heaviness in head pain, pain in general, bloating in the stomach or abdomen, itching in the skin and dull pain in the abdomen, umbilicus or hypochondria.

The Synthesis...

From what has come up in the proving of PC Cancer it is proof enough for me that this medicine is a homeopathic specific for a most prevalent global epidemic called Cancer.
Why do I call it a homeopathic specific for Cancer?

What is Cancer according to pathology?

Cancer is a class of diseases or disorders characterized by uncontrolled division of cells and the ability of these cells to invade other tissues, either by direct growth into adjacent tissue through invasion or by implantation into distant sites by metastasis.

Cancer is, ultimately, a disease of genes. In order for cells to start dividing uncontrollably, genes that regulate cell growth must be damaged. Proto-oncogenes are genes that promote cell growth and mitosis, a process of cell division, and tumour suppressor genes discourage cell growth, or temporarily halt cell division in order to carry out DNA repair. Typically, a series of several mutations to these genes is required before a normal cell transforms into a cancer cell. It is only when enough proto-oncogenes have mutated into oncogenes, and enough tumour suppressor genes are deactivated or damaged, that the signals for cell growth overwhelm the signals to regulate it, that cell growth quickly spirals out of control.

Cancer is about lack of control
Cancer is about lack of regulation.

The disposition of PC Cancer...

The same is seen in the proving in the state of (altered) disposition of the mind as in extreme behaviour/lack of control. The other theme is regulation itself (laws/dictating/order). The other facets are danger and craving of 'sugar' on which the cancer cells thrive. And the USP (Unique Symptom for Portrait) is Cancer itself. The provers that unconsciously got drawn to this proving have a family history of Cancer and the ones that did not have but still were a part of this experience connected their altered state to the Cancer disposition itself (which is as (P1))...

"An inner conflict between two extreme thoughts: Freedom to decide and imposition!"

And therefore I say that PC Cancer is a homeopathic specific for Cancer.

Proving of PC240m Malaria

A blind proving of *PC240m* for malaria was conducted by Dr. Chetna Shukla in Mumbai, India in 2010. Dose taken: 27th August 2010

PROVER 1 (Male)

First meeting: 03 September 2010

Should be target oriented, be systematic in the work, whatever I am doing.
Sunday I had twitching, involuntary jerky movements in the right hypothenar prominence. (Hypothenar muscles – a group of three in the palm of the hand that control the motion of the little finger.) Right-sided chest pain like angina, right hypochondrium till chest up. Discontented with my efforts. Whatever I am putting in I am not getting desired results. So I feel frustrated and dejected. Heaviness in the head. Desire to change and overcome negative things in me. Find things that are lacking and do the necessary. We had training and there are four levels of working:

- Unconscious incompetence
- Conscious incompetence
- Conscious competence
- Unconscious competence

I know where I may be lacking. I am in the 2nd level.

Ego issues going on. Having conflict with the partner. There is no matching or adjustments with the person. I did not like what he did, not in agreement with what he did. Now it is too much to take. There should be a balance within the religion and the work you are doing. There should be independence, not dependent on anybody. I should not need any help from anyone. That starts with understanding all the negative things in me and I have to correct these.
The negative things:

- Lack of knowledge
- Lack of consistency
- Lack of commitment
- Prioritizing
- Organizing things

A lot is going on in my head. I should be able to decide what I want to do. A prior commitment that was given to me so I could not go for a business meeting as it was decided at the last moment. I said no.
I feel very depressed during the week. Feel I am not committing, not finishing targets and not getting results. I had to stay awake last night and pray and then wake up and do things as I have committed. I felt I was pushing myself … I needed to sleep. I feel frustrated. Maybe I was not pushing enough. If I push enough than I will get the desired results. I cannot give commitment to someone after 6 ‘o clock as it is Ramadan. I cannot do things. I feel dejected.

C: Where is the conflict?
Head!

C: What is the conflict?
Deciding what you want. Give 100% for business or spiritual. What to give priority ... material existence or spirituality? An inner conflict ... you cannot lose one thing for the other. What do I want? I have to balance; if I put all my efforts on one side the other side will be affected.

C: What does this conflict make you feel?
Irritated, frustrated, dejected, confused, feeling like giving up but ... I cannot give up also. Discontent. I need to do those five things. Lower my ego. Decide on one thing. If I don't the balance will be affected ... if one thing is affected then the other thing will also get affected.

C: Imagine, if this goes on what will happen to you?
Losing out on something. Everything will be affected because of one part. Timing of everything is important. Now also I have to go by 5.30 and it got late ... It will lead to a destructive thing ... affect me ... affect my life ... living ... existence. My whole body is affected right now; I cannot say what is happening. Feeling restless. I am destructive against my own existence. It is finished. I will blow up. I feel very impatient and restless ... These negative things in me are my weakness. These five points I need to work at.

I wake up at five a.m. but if I sleep at two or three a.m. than I cannot wake up that early. I had to go today at nine thirty; everything gets out of balance.

PROVER 2 (Female)

First meeting: 03 September 2010

2nd day: Fever blister, used to come earlier but after taking constitutional medicine, it had stopped; fever blister, herpes simplex, on middle part of upper lip.
Disappointed to have only few symptoms.
Lot of itching and dryness.
This week, I was quite organized , which otherwise I am not.
I was not angry even once, which is very rare.
I laughed a lot, especially today. It was raining a lot and then too I had craving for ice-cream.
Fasting.
No other change.

C: Mood, dreams.
Fluctuating mood. Overall it was good since I was not angry.

I cried yesterday since I was watching a TV series and those ladies were crying. The girl was crying since she didn't have a mother. She realized about mother's love.

C: What was the emotion?
I thought mother is so precious in our life. Something that we should really treasure which we don't. Especially I don't.
People who don't have a mother, they actually know the value of one.
Yesterday mother was complaining of epigastric discomfort. She was on an antibiotic. Since she is diabetic she had gone to the ophthalmologist because of pain and redness of her eyes, so I was feeling "what if it is angina and I missed the diagnosis?" I had wild thoughts in the night and when I woke up in the morning, I thought she should be alright.

When I saw her moving in the morning, I felt okay, fine.
No other change, it was routine.

C: Dreams?
Had many but couldn't remember.
Was happy that I didn't get any single scolding from work place.
Felt as if doctor had taken proving dose, and changed.

C: What do you feel like doing?
I will take for seven more days.

PROVER 3 (Male)

First meeting: 03 September 2010

1st day no symptoms.
2nd day: Heaviness of eyes. I feel sleepy. In the night a lot of gas in stomach, itching in the eyes. I feel constipated.
6th day: Dream of my mother She is suffering from rheumatoid arthritis. I dreamt mother is well and running.
Dream of friends who are dead. A friend is roaming with me in school.
Dream of mountain that is surrounded by sea. It was in Tibet. In sometime the mountain was scattered.
7th day: I felt pain in left shoulder. It aches when I raise my arm, then it feels like pain. I feel some tendon is twisted.

C: Moods?
I am feeling depressed. My mother is suffering, she is crying. Today I am going to the village. I will come back after five days.

C: What is this depressed feeling?
She is alone with my father. She says nobody is there. I cannot tolerate her suffering. She has rheumatism since fifteen years. I feel she will succumb to the disease. She says she has fainting, dizziness and she has boils in the breast; that recurs. I feel she will die, during the day I feel she will die (looking blank into space).

C: Still describe this feeling?
What will people say; her son is a doctor and he could not treat his mother. On the 'phone she tells she is fine but I feel she will die. She is suffering. I feel that I could not do anything for her. Last October she was fine. I asked her to come to Mumbai, but she said "No". So I brought my wife here. I feel why did I get my wife here, she should have stayed to care for my mother. I feel grief that I made a mistake by bringing her here. Grief that I left my mother alone … this thought continuously is there.
I feel shivering under this fan. I don't want the fan.
I feel angry with myself and guilty also (weeping). I am leaving tonight. I feel I left my mother alone. She suffered a lot. She cannot raise her hand.

Plan: Stop medicine. To be taken for seven days after returning from the village.

C: What is more the grief, the anger or the guilt?
I feel anger at myself.

C: What is this anger at self?
That I left my mother! This is the first time I left my mother alone. My father is there, he said go take your wife, I will cook and take care of her. So for the first time I left her alone. There was bitterness between me and my mother. She was angry with the decision that I took my wife last year, last October. Since then she does not talk to me properly. She answered only in 'yes' or 'no'. She did not talk to me on 'phone. From this week I feel as if I did some wrong.

PROVER 4 (Male)

First meeting: 03 September 2010

1st day: no symptoms
2nd day: no symptoms
3rd and 4th day: Heaviness of eyes; can't keep eyes open. Sleeping even in train.
Even after arriving heaviness of eyes; went to sleep.
Once I slept, I slept like a log.
First two days slept heavily. Itching in lower margin of eyelid.
Since last two days headaches.
This morning got up at five a.m, getting headache, pain behind eyes, temples.
The whole week I didn't take lunch. Didn't feel like eating since there was no hunger.
Time management was a big issue for me.
But I felt I'm wasting my time and not getting time for anything.

C: Where?
I don't know, but time is just going away.
I had two holidays this week of rakshabandhan (celebrates brotherhood and love) and janmasthami (marks the birth of Krishna). I did plan many things but I just played with the baby.

C: What do you want to do?
Arrange papers, arranging shelf, but did nothing.

C: Mood?
Only I felt I am wasting time, time is just flying away, wasting time, going with friends, whiling away time.
Postponing things, why to sit at computer for half an hour, I will plan for two to three hours but I don't get such hours.

C: Dreams?
No.

C: Appetite, craving, aversions?
Craving for potatoes, okra.

Heaviness of eyes gone – today.

C: He called me one evening requesting me to help him with the pain in the chest. He sounded breathless over the phone and said he felt as if he would die as he could not breathe and could not walk. It was acute and unbearable. He could not sleep nor lie down nor move. (He was asked to wait and bear it and if it did not subside to take *Bryonia* 10M one dose.) He did not take anything to interfere with the remedy action. When he met me after three days I asked him questions to activate his imagination.

C: Close your eyes and imagine what disease picture it presented to you?
Acute breathlessness … no not exactly it was like Angina pain as if arising from the heart. It could also be acute acidity?

The Synthesis ...
(Written by the authors)

There are several symptoms in this proving that point to the malaria miasm:
- Target oriented.
- Discontented ... not getting desired results.
- I feel frustrated.
- Competence.
- Disappointed. Depressed.
- Wild thoughts in the night ... Awake last night.
- Time wasted, going away.
- Mother / disease / death / alone

Part XII
Sound as Carrier

Some years ago when a bird flu pandemic was expected, the question arose as to how to get a Genus epidemicus remedy to all those needing it as prevention or cure? Clearly in a worst case scenario, with millions of people getting infected in a short amount of time with high rates of casualties, sending granules to pharmacies and homeopaths might be very difficult and slow. If an epidemic, as the world experienced with the Spanish flu, were to happen today the world as we know it might stop functioning. Absenteeism through sickness and the fear of infection could paralyze economics. Pharmacies might not receive stock or be forced to close; distribution might not function etcetera. With this worst case scenario in mind Peter experimented with imprinting a healing resonance in music instead of water.

A rather revolutionary idea but in the theory of quantum mechanics it is a feasible idea, to attach healing information, resonance, to any kind of substratum – besides water, sound would be one possibility. As sound can be added to emails as attachment, downloaded from a website, forwarded by cell phones, played on cell phones, computers, iPads, iPods etcetera this was thought to be the best option for rapid world-wide availability of a healing resonance should the need arise. Although luckily a massive need for it has not been necessary so far, the technique was tested out on several conditions and has proven to be effective, as the examples below will show.

Making healing resonances available through the internet or by email is not only a potentially effective tool in the case of pandemics. Also in cases where a patient cannot easily see a homeopath or rapidly needs to receive a remedy it would be a great advantage if a resonance can be made available directly through a phone-call.

After the first experiences showed that sound could indeed be used to carry healing information a system was developed to adjust a healing download to the personal circumstances of the person intending to use it. This in no way replaces individualized homeopathic treatment but it does make a disease specific download more tailor-made for the individual.

Downloads Technology

The preparation of Healing Downloads, similar to that of PC Resonances as pills or dilutions, is a new technology that can't be described in old concepts as these do no justice to the advance. For example we don't use frequencies in the normal way these are understood (e.g. as seen by oscilloscope, made by any machine, heard from a voice or musical instrument, which are physical, material resonances).

We understand that the basic conclusion of quantum mechanical experiments over the last century is that the basic (non) material reality of the universe is consciousness (mystics and physicists agree on this). Material reality is then a specialised field effect of applied consciousness. Put simply, our brain makes up reality as we know it (in time/space and 3D working very fast so we don't see it happening).

For example, if a group of psychologists hold a positive case conference around one client, frequently the client's situation improves. This is a targeted consciousness field effect, and a well-known phenomenon, but outside the material paradigm. Similar field effects are evident in all group work, Oponopono (traditional healing method of Hawaï) and Constellation Workshops (Bert Hellinger).

We use a specialised consciousness intelligent field effect resonances

- for a specific purpose
- to create an intended effect in a person.

With downloads we embed the specialised consciousness field resonance into sound instead of liquids (from which pills can be prepared).

Listening Instructions

You can put the Healing Download available at www.healingdownloads.com on a mobile 'phone or on an MP3/4 player, a CD or on a desktop, play it on the HIFI, or on all of these. This acts both as a preventative strategy and as a treatment.

Depending on the indication one should listen once a day or more or less frequently similar to the way a remedy would be dosed if it were in drops or granules.

Downloads

There are several downloads available. Here are some of the still limited experiences we have with them. These are not case studies with depth to them, just unsolicited feedback.

AIDS

> An AIDS Healing Download was listened to three times a day by a 36-year-old woman and full recovery of her symptoms was clear seventeen days later. She was better in all ways, could walk long distances (for example five km instead of 100 metres), could work, could eat well, and all the symptoms had disappeared.

Athlete's foot

"Trivial yes but over the course of a week it became painful, soggy, crusty and burning despite topical citricidal, tea tree, aloe vera, hypercal and internal homeopathic remedies as well. By the time I started using the tailor-made download, it was too painful to walk on. First day I listened hourly then four times daily. A minor miracle. Within four hours the pain had stopped and within 36 hours the skin is almost completely healed. Thank you so much."

RS, UK

Chickenpox

"My ten-month-old son Samuel got Chickenpox while we were visiting family in Europe so I purchased the healing downloads for Chickenpox and played it to him every night while he slept for about fifteen minutes. After only one time new spots stopped appearing and the current ones have reduced by at least 30%. He had no fever, spots did not itch at all and the whole illness thanks to the download was very mild and lasted a very short time. Thank you!"

PO, USA

Common cold

"I listened to the common cold download and felt a shift almost immediately, with my symptoms resolving entirely in fifteen minutes. I kept the music playing, and in twenty minutes all symptoms returned full force! I stopped the sound and by another fifteen minutes my symptoms were about 75% gone."

KH, USA

Cystitis

"I had haemorrhagic cystitis. One hour after listening three times to the download I stopped urinating bloody urine. I developed a low grade fever, after eight hours this disappeared, and I had no more problems of dysuria."

HW, Belgium

Detox Penicillin

"For several years I was trying, in many different ways, to get rid of small inflammatory problems of tonsils and skin. *Hepar sulphuricum* or *Silica* had only short-lived effect, about three weeks. During the cleansing process (using Detox Penicillin) of the physical body I was more impulsive, or assertive, in solving my business issues in a way that I would not have done before – and thus cleansing effectively some of my personal issues in business contacts. Today, about a month after the detox, there is no tonsil inflammation or abscesses and the state of my skin is about 95% improved. Since PC Penicillin Detox I haven't used any other homeopathic remedy."

What actually happened:
"After two days of listening (several times a day, altogether it would come to one hour of listening time) the following started to happen:

Third day: sore throat as in laryngitis, without redness in the throat, without coated tongue, almost lost voice
Fourth day: pains and aches in joints all over the body, lymphatic glands swelling in the throat, thick yellow phlegm, pains under the left shoulder blade.
Fifth day: the joint pain better by 90%, a bad cold began with yellow green phlegm like a glue, and the abscesses on the tonsils. A strong headache.
Seventh day: a pressure in the sinuses under the left eye, sharp poking under the left shoulder blade, breathing difficult, a pressure on the sternum.
Tenth day: all problems are disappearing. For the whole time I did not have a temperature, I did not sweat, and did not feel the need to lie in bed."

JC, Czech Republic

Fear and food Issues

"I found out about this system from my homeopath. I found several downloads that I felt would be good to test, that actually all fit together for me. So I decided to add them in groups, and listened to them the first week three times a day and then after that once a day. I did this for two months, then I listen when I get the feeling. I feel that there are great changes happening. I had severe fear issues and food issues. I can now eat a meal in six minutes instead of four large bites in less than 30 seconds. I actually chew my food, and am starting to enjoy it. The fear issue is not as severe, the people around me have noticed the change; I can do things calmly (for me), that I would not have done before at all. I do recommend this system as it is the least stressful and most effective method I have tried to relax. Thanks."

DT, Canada

Herpes

"I listened to the herpes download four times a year ago when I had an outbreak of cold sores. I haven't experienced an outbreak since then, which I would have expected by now. Also one of my clients hasn't experienced an outbreak of genital herpes in over a year, after listening to the herpes download."

MS, USA

"After having had mouth herpes as long as I can remember, and having worse and worse outbreaks this winter, I had had enough and started searching for a cure. I found HealingDownloads.com and downloaded both the herpes 1+2 and influenza mp3 files, that both were free at that time. I tried them both several times a day and, lo and behold, they worked! It's now over three months ago, and I haven't had ANY SIGN of herpes around my mouth, and no sign of cold or flu. Looks like the virus is gone, or at least gone for a long sleep. Thank you!! I will try something for my stiff back and joints next ... :)"

HS, Norway

Comment: A number of people with herpes, including experienced holistic practitioners of various disciplines, have listened to the herpes download at the start of an attack and it stopped immediately. There were no side effects, nor were powerful drugs needed. There is nothing personal about herpes. All alternative and holistic therapies will boost immunity generally, but herpes will often continue, usually less often. Here we are boosting the immune defences holistically and specifically for herpes, so it's much more effective.

Malaria

An African patient that volunteered to test a Healing Download for malaria was better from malaria symptoms, after listening non-stop for twenty minutes in an hour, with no other treatment. Normal treatment takes three to four days, often only half works and has complications/weakness that remains for a week. In this case, the morning after the night of malaria the man is standing at his kiln of 4000 bricks he is firing for building his house; this was such a rapid recovery that it is almost unheard of.

Phobia – snakes

"My boyfriend had a terrible phobia of snakes. Since I have one at home, he would constantly go to check if the snake indeed hadn't escaped or slithered under the door. When he went to check it took barely a minute – he said he could not stay and look at the animal, that it gave him the creeps and I could see the fear in his eyes. After two days of listening to the download, something apparently clicked in his head (he compared it to some sort of click of the joint), and then he dreamt about a snake and in the dream he felt clearly in danger (from the snake). It has now been three weeks and he can actually touch the snake now, and he doesn't mind looking at it either, at our live snake or some snakes on TV. I consider this a major shift and improvement as his fear of snakes was really profound."

IH, Czech Republic

Poverty consciousness

"I used a personalized healing download for poverty consciousness because I have never been able to 'have' things of my own. I never felt that I really deserved it. After using the download daily for a couple of weeks, things in my mind and in my life started rapidly changing. I began to see that I am worth it and I no longer just settle for the crumbs that come my way!"

LDN, United Arab Emirates

Prostate

"My husband listened to the enlarged prostate download and went in one night from getting up every two hours to urinate during the night to getting up one time in the night to urinate. That has continued. It improved him in other ways as well."

SS, Michigan USA

Shock and trauma

"I downloaded the shock and trauma mp3 to complement the final stage of treatment my homeopath/radionics practitioner was giving me for psychic shock. The main reason I decided to try it was because I felt the format and usage would work in harmony with my current healing protocol versus interfering. Plus, I love music!

I listened to the music two or three times per day and at first I found the music agitated me and seemed to aggravate my symptoms during listening. I found after three days that only certain sections of the music would agitate me and others now provided me a sense of relief.

After a week and a half, the music no longer bothered me and soon afterwards the psychic shock was released. I truly feel that the shock and trauma healing download helped me to get to that point of release."

TH, Canada

Teething

"My son Gabriel, 1.5 years old is diabetic and he has been treated only with homeopathic remedies. Because I didn't want to influence his treatment using any other kind of remedy, the only thing I used to do when he was screaming and irritable in the night because of his teeth, was to play the teething mp3 (Teething Healing Download) between seven and ten times and it was the only thing that would put him back to sleep.

Thank you for your help. It is amazing!"

VCB, Spain

Thrombophilia

"I experienced a very odd health situation: a middle finger on the right hand became numb, red, swollen, painful. Since I did not hurt it I had a big dilemma. *Arnica* helped but not completely. Since I have thrombophilia I played your resonance for phlebitis for a couple of minutes. Instantly the pain diminished and the second day everything disappeared. It was astonishing. Thank you."

IB, Croatia

Tooth ache, tooth abscess

"I had problems with my tooth which was filled temporarily (the dentist was working on the root filling). Soon after I returned home it already felt uncomfortable, but it usually does anyway, and I did not pay much attention. Next day though, the pain did not go away, as expected, but grew stronger and more intense. I felt throbbing in my tooth and gum and so it was difficult to concentrate on any activity without being aware of the pain.

The dentist was away and weekend coming and the pain was still growing ... I did something I don't do, I bought myself painkillers. After hours of pain this worked for about an hour or so and the pain disappeared totally, but soon after it came back again and I was back to my painkillers checking the instructions about how often I am allowed to pop a pill. By the next day I worked slowly through the box of Ibuprofen and started feeling its negative effects, I guess I am sensitive, I do not take painkillers at all really – my skin was hot and itchy and made me feel very unpleasant especially in my facial area, I was tired and restless. Dilemma at hand, how to handle the pain till Monday morning and not stuff myself with chemicals?

I remembered what I knew about Peter Chappell's Healing Downloads and so I decided to give it a try. I downloaded the personalised Toothache and Tooth Abscess downloads. Initially I sat down and listened about five to ten times and then just walked about with my MP3 and listened often.

Soon I realised that though still aware of my toothache, I was not disturbed by it at all. The pulsing diminished and the pain, though still there, was somewhat veiled over, soothed and not intense any longer. The result was exactly what I wanted, to soothe the pain so I can concentrate on my weekend activities without burdening my body with chemicals. "

HR, Czech Republic

Tinnitus

"I have suffered with constant Tinnitus for around seven years. Two days after listening to the tailor-made Tinnitus HEALING DOWNLOAD, my tinnitus completely disappeared! This had never happened before. However, after a wonderfully quiet 48hrs, it returned. After a week of listening daily, the sound changed to a higher pitch. Again, this has never happened before.

Following the advice of my homeopath, I am now listening to the tailor-made Injury HEALING DOWNLOAD as the root cause of my tinnitus may possibly be due to a former head injury I suffered as a child and the way it was explained was that it's better to treat the root cause rather than just the resulting symptom. This makes sense to me! It is early days yet but since listening, the usual sound I hear 'za-aaaaaaaaaaaa' has changed to shorter bursts of 'zaa zaa zaa' and the pitch has returned to the original level. It is quite obvious to me that these downloads are having some kind of effect. Hopefully, I will see more improvement soon. I will keep you updated."

YD, Japan

Weight loss

"This morning I realized that after listening to the weight loss download I felt like my clothes were looser. I figured it was just my imagination because I just got the download one week ago and I have not had any chance to 'diet'. So I concluded it was O.K. to feel better even if it was just in my mind. Then I put on an old jacket I could not close before and the seams with the buttons overlapped. Thanks. "

DW, USA

Part XIII

Creating Collective Coherence

We humans are intelligent consciousness manifesting through a mind-body. This mind-body is in fact a complete recapitulation and encapsulation of the history of the human race, and responds according to history to what is happening.

Our consciousness has the qualities of absolute intelligence in the biggest sense of the word, which encapsulates love, joy, compassion, creativity etcetera.

Our consciousness flows through us all the time but is corrupted by our mind-body responses. There is intelligent purpose to this in that our corrupted responses create various degrees of suffering to wake us up essentially to the fact that we are conscious beings and not just our mind-bodies.

The suffering that is induced can take the form of simple suffering, all forms of dysfunction and diseases – including epidemic and chronic diseases.

There is a growing body of evidence that individual human consciousness is connected to collective human consciousness and that the two do not only influence each other but effect life on this planet in many other ways. There is a global project that investigates this phenomenon.

> The Global Consciousness Project (GCP) is an international effort involving researchers from several institutions and countries, designed to explore whether the construct of interconnected consciousness can be scientifically validated through objective measurement. The project builds on excellent experiments conducted over the past 35 years at a number of laboratories, demonstrating that human consciousness interacts with random event generators (REGs), apparently "causing" them to produce non-random patterns ... The experimental results clearly show that a broader examination of this phenomenon is warranted. In recent work, prior to the Global Consciousness Project, an array of REG devices in Europe and the US showed non-random activity during widely shared experiences of deeply engaging events. For example, the funeral ceremonies for Princess Diana, and the international Winter Olympics in Nagano, Japan, created shared emotions and a coherence of consciousness that appeared to be correlated with structure in the otherwise random data. In the fully developed project, a

world-spanning array of labile REG detectors is connected to computers running software to collect data and send it to a central server via the Internet. This network is designed to document and display any subtle, but direct effects of our collective consciousness reacting to global events. The research hypothesis predicts the appearance of coherence and structure in the globally distributed data collected during major events that engage the world population.

The effect of interconnected consciousness as discussed above highlights situations where humans share a similar experience. In the above examples this involves interconnectedness through the media. There are different ways in which large numbers of people share a similar experience in which the media may not be involved, but the same phenomenon may nevertheless occur.

As we have discussed in this book we have found that many diseases and conditions may be expressed in an individual but are actually manifestations of a collective derangement of the state of health.

In homeopathy we are used to treat with an individualized approach one person at the time. With epidemics and collective trauma we have shown that a collective approach, with one remedy for all suffering from the same condition, is effective. Ideally everyone suffering from the condition would receive that treatment. Although at an individual level that may be desirable or even needed, the question is, whether for the fulfillment of the role and purpose of the collective condition treating all parts that make up the sum is required, or whether the interconnectedness of human consciousness would cause the collective derangement to change much earlier.

Our hypothesis is that when we cure (and not suppress or contain) a disease like malaria, the purpose of the disease, which is to wake the human race up to some aspect of its own consciousness, is fulfilled. We postulate that to do this only relatively few effective cures are required. Once a limited number of people have experienced the conscious shift that results from curing malaria, it is available to the whole of humanity, because consciousness is universal and available instantly to everybody. The effect just has to pass the point of critical mass where the critical mass of the new consciousness has gained enough momentum to replace the old unconsciousness. The numbers required for this collective shift to occur may be lower than we would expect, because once a few people have responded to the new treatment, the transformation they experience enters the collective consciousness and will seep through to everyone. This is similar to what is known as the 'hundredth monkey effect'[25]. Disease is chaos and health is harmony. In many fields of science it has been shown that a chaotic system can be brought to harmony as soon as only a small part of it becomes coherent. Once that critical mass has been reached the whole system transforms rapidly.

Tipping points, at which complex systems can shift abruptly from one state to another, are notoriously difficult to predict[26]. In studies to the effect of group meditation on society we find possible support for our hypothesis and possible indicators as to the numbers needed to reach a tipping point.

[25] The story of the hundredth monkey effect was published in the foreword to Lawrence Blair's *Rhythms of Vision* in 1975.[2] The claim spread with the appearance of *Lifetide*, a 1979 book by Lyall Watson. Rupert Sheldrake has cited that a phenomenon like the hundredth monkey effect would be an evidence of Morphic fields bringing about non-local effects in consciousness and learning.

[26] Veraert et al, Nature 25 December 2011, www.nature.com/nature/journal/vaop/ncurrent/full/nature10723.html

By tapping into pure consciousness — the Unified Field in the language of modern physics — it has been demonstrated that meditation of a group of people can reduce societal stress and tensions, causing associated reductions in crime and social violence, and an upsurge of peace and positivity throughout the population.[27] "This phenomenon of increased coherence and peace throughout society was first reported in research published in 1976, which found that when 1% of a community practiced the Transcendental Meditation programme, the crime rate dropped by an average of 16%. This phenomenon was named the "Maharishi Effect" in honour of Maharishi, who first predicted it in 1960." [www.tm.org/benefits-society-and-peace]

Using advanced meditation programmes (TM-Sidhi programme) showed that even the square root of 1% of a community would be sufficient to create measurable changes in social trends. This phenomenon has been repeatedly proven in several studies. It is fascinating and opens huge possibilities, also for homeopathy.

In homeopathic provings it has regularly been reported that people not participating in the proving nevertheless showed proving symptoms. This suggests that the effect of a homeopathic substance taken by a group has effects beyond the members of the group. There is no research that shows how far those effects reach. Does it involve just a few others and is it almost to be neglected, or would it come near the effects of meditation? Would this explain the synchronicities observed in the world during several provings? If the effect would come anywhere near the percentages that came up in the TM-studies the implications can be huge. A proving conducted with ten participants could then influence 100 (1%) to 10,000 people (square root of 1%). Based on this possible scenario a first global proving was organized in 2005 [Shukla & van der Zee, The Global Proving of Himalayan Crystal Salt, *Homœopathic Links* 2010, issue 2 pp 85-90].

The implications for the treatment of collective conditions are even more important. Let us look at a few examples:

- For instance, if there is a collective form of trauma involving one million people, it might be enough to treat 10,000 (1%) or 100 (square root of 1%) to bring about change in the collective. As with meditation we may assume that it would be necessary that these 100-10,000 people receive their treatment simultaneously. But this is just an assumption, that may not be true, and cumulative results may also occur when people are treated over time.
- If there is a pandemic of for instance bird flu, giving the Genus epidemicus remedy – either curatively or as prophylaxis – to a part of the infected or endangered population

---

[27] Alleviating political violence through reducing collective tension: Impact assessment analyses of the Lebanon war. Journal of Social Behavior and Personality 17(1): 285–338 (2005).
The Transcendental Meditation and TM-Sidhi programme and decreased urban crime. Journal of Mind and Behavior, 9(4), 457–486 (1988).
Consciousness as a field: The Transcendental Meditation and TM-Sidhi programme and changes in social indicators. Journal of Mind and Behavior, 8(1), 67–104 (1987).
The Maharishi Effect: A model for social improvement. Time series analysis of a phase transition to reduced crime in Merseyside metropolitan area. Psychology, Crime & Law, 2(3), 165–174 1996).
Preventing terrorism and international conflict: Effects of large assemblies of participants in the Transcendental Meditation and TM-Sidhi programmes. Journal of Offender Rehabilitation, 36 (1-4), 283–302 (2003).

> might be enough to let infection and casualty rates decline. This may, simply, be the effective answer to all potentially devastating epidemics. Even a small group, not infected, taking the Genus epidemicus could then help terminate the epidemic.

A prerequisite would be that the treatment used is able to bring about changes in consciousness similar to deep meditation. In homeopathic terms this means that the similarity of the remedy must be close to perfect. It may be expected that the higher the similarity of the remedy is to the state of the collective condition treated, the more profound its effect will be qualitatively and quantitatively.

This concept of creating coherence completely supports all the work we've done in identifying the intelligence behind diseases and the idea that to overcome a disease you have to replace it with a more intelligent process. You can't do this by suppressing its symptoms and fighting it, you have to reveal its intelligent purpose and achieve it and then it's over.

The whole is greater than the sum of its parts. Besides with acute conditions, like collective trauma and epidemics, it is very likely that this also holds true for chronic diseases:

- For instance, the number of diabetes patients benefiting from homeopathic treatment, may be much larger than the number of diabetes patients treated with homeopathy. Essential for this to be true would be that the homeopathic treatment really touches the core of the problem, not only at an individual level, but also at a collective level – the archetype diabetes. We think PC Resonances may prove to be very useful to help diabetes to fulfill its role and purpose. Diabetes and many other conditions are based on cultural trends and a collective approach is then fully justified.

In 2009 we gave malaria prophylaxis with PC240m to 600 children at a school for the duration of a whole year. By the end of the year the teachers suggested to stop, as there had been no malaria at the school for many months. The prophylaxis was intended for the children only and a collective effect was at the time not considered. But when we hear that the number of cases of malaria dropped dramatically in the whole region we need to consider this possibility. Actually malaria has dramatically dropped not only in that part of DRC Congo, but also in many neighboring countries. Scientists have no clear explanation for the sudden decrease. Even though the decrease at the school started immediately once all kids received PC240m, it may be much more likely that the drop of malaria we observed in the school was part of a general trend, which incidentally took place in synchronicity with our prophylaxis project. We're open to that possibility. Also, if PC240m was fully responsible for the disappearance of malaria at the school, it seems unlikely that it would influence the malaria statistics anywhere beyond the borders of the village. And, we're open to the possibility that treating 600 children simultaneously during a year could change the incidence of malaria in a much larger population – perhaps even 60,000 (1% of which would be 600) or 36 million (of which the square root of 1% would be 600).

If using PC Resonances would address the epidemic at a deeper collective level it may then be expected that all other activities undertaken to control malaria (mosquito nets, spraying etcetera) would suddenly become a lot more effective too. In individual cases we've observed that suppression of a disease can be very effective provided it's real cause has been taken care of, and we see no reasons why that wouldn't apply to a collective disease. Suppression then can be a quick way of getting a result that would come naturally anyway.

Clearly, what we suggest here is still highly speculative and none of it can be taken as a fact. We do feel though that the possible implications make this a field where studies would be justified. Studies that could answer questions similar to the following ones:

- We know that the 1918 influenza epidemic was treated by homeopaths using *Gelsemium* primarily. During this epidemic 20-40 million people died. We know that some tens of thousands of people were treated with homeopathy during that influenza outbreak with extremely good results. Would it be possible that treatment of the disease with homeopathy helped to bring the epidemic disease outbreak of influenza to an end because the conscious purpose was achieved using *Gelsemium*? (*Gelsemium* also treats grief, and millions of young men died in World War I, which ended as the flu outbreak began; not perhaps a coincidence as previously assumed. Did the resolution of the grief allow a new human-wide collective insight into the futility of the war?) The numbers add up here. Based on the square root of 1% rule about 13,000 people needed to be treated to affect the whole world population at that time.
- Did treating more than 10,000 people after the Haiti 2010 earthquake (which ARHF carried out) reduce trauma in the collective?
- Did treating 5,000 refugees in a refugee camp help to reduce the level of trauma in the whole camp of 64,000 refugees, or the whole of The Congo? Would it have helped to maintain peace following the elections? (ARHF November 2011)

Clearly this is an area where we have many more questions than answers. At this point of time we can only guess, but we assume all this is possible, and we suggest that if homeopathy be used for collective conditions (trauma, epidemics, diseases), an effect on the collective may be produced if as many people as possible are treated within a short period.

Impossible? 'Impossible' is a word that has been used a lot in the history of mankind, and as history shows, the impossible has often turned into its opposite – possible, reality.

We like to invite others to think and act with us. Please contact Amma Resonance Healing Foundation at info@arhf.nl if PC Resonances are needed for a study along these lines, or if you would like to join our team.

Part XIV

Advances in PC Technology

There are more possible applications of super intelligent resonance beyond treating diseases. Resonance can be used to invoke a specific quality as much as to treat a disease, and actually there is no difference, as one follows the other anyway. Peter is already working on it for raising human potential. It can in principle be used by anybody within his or her specialized field. There are potential applications for creating new energy sources, new music beyond anything ever heard yet, and basically anything is possible.

Having established the way of connecting into this new technology, which was a whole lifetime type process in itself, Peter is interested in training people to use this new technology in their own specialized fields of human endeavour. What personal attributes are needed for this is not clear, but it might include these: A clear in-depth specialisation; An openness and commitment to go beyond the materialistic science world view into the world of consciousness; An integrity and driving force beyond materialistic concerns; An inventive, original streak. Too much identification with the intellect is probably not helpful, whereas being well-grounded is probably essential.

Also here we like to invite others to think and act with us. Please contact Peter at peterchappell@gmail.com.

Part XV

Conclusion

In the above chapters we have shared the preliminary results with PC Resonances for a wide variety of conditions and diseases, as also the first feedback on the use of Healing Downloads.

Our conclusion is that all symptoms and diseases are really a manifestation of our unconscious that communicates with us in a way we often don't recognise or do not pay attention to. And if we do, we may not know what to do with the information.

We see a chronic disease as the end result of a series of limiting habits, suppressed diseases and repressed emotions and unfinished business handed down from previous generations, along with toxic effects transmitted to us from our genetics and the environment, which is possibly more toxic now than ever before.

The process culminating in disease starts out as a gift, the grain of sand intended to create the pearl of wisdom in us. Because we tend to follow old habitual responses we miss the message so it becomes disease.

The PC Resonance simply highlights the intelligence underlying a disease and brings it to our subconscious or even conscious attention. As it were it finds the pearl for us. If we then manage to relate to that, connect the dots, we wake up sufficiently to mitigate or cure the disease. As the disease has brought about its intended change it can leave us. It's that simple. Its purpose has been achieved. All diseases are simply ways of waking us up from our old, habitual, mostly animal behaviour to help us become conscious humans.

We recognise that while our results are largely anecdotal and many more cases and research are needed to further build a case for the efficacy of a disease specific approach. Nevertheless, the sheer number of reports and the diversity of sources show that this may be a very important step forward for homeopathy and medicine in general.

We have tried to perform research on PC1 for HIV/AIDS. We have designed study protocols, looked for partners and sponsors in several countries, have been very close to starting a study several times, and for a variety of reasons this has not happened until today.

And HIV/AIDS would only be one of the conditions for which research would be indicated, as this book shows that a disease specific approach using PC Resonances can be effective for many more indications.

This book is a travel diary of our ongoing journey. We hope it will be helpful to you on your journey and to that of humanity as a whole.

Other Sources on PC Resonances

The following writings can be ordered at www.homeolinks.nl

- Peter Chappell, The Second Simillimum, Homeolinks Publishers, Haren (NL) 2005
- Harry van der Zee, Amma4Africa Manual, Homeolinks Publishers, Haren (NL) 2008

At www.arhf.nl the following texts can be downloaded for free:

- PC1 instructions in English, French, German, Portuguese, Swahili, Timbuka
- Amma4Africa manual in English, French, German and Portuguese
- Amma4Trauma manual in English and French

By contacting info@arhf.nl the following DVD can be ordered:

- Amma4Africa DVD with documentaries on AIDS, malaria, the trauma of war and rape and natural catastrophe trauma

At www.arhf.nl short video's can be watched on several topics and conditions.

Pharmacies

Pharmacies supplying PC Resonances:

Helios Homeopathic Pharmacy (English)
97 Camden Road
Tunbridge Wells, Kent
TN1 2QR
United Kingdom

Tel: +44 1892 536393 (24hr)
Tel: +44 1892 537254 (9:45 am-5:30 pm)
Fax +44 1892 546850

www.helios.co.uk (enter the Helios shop and click on 'Peter Chappell')

Hahnemann Apotheek (Dutch)
Postbus 69
1850AB Heiloo
Netherlands

Tel: +31 72-53 25 373
Fax. +31 72-53 25 375

recept@hahnemann.nl
www.hahnemann.nl

Apotheke zum hl. Florian (German)
Wiedner Hauptstrase 60
1040 Wien
Austria

Tel: +43 1 587 93 01
Fax: +43 1 586 72 44

pcremedies-hl.florian@utanet.at

A list of available PC Resonances can be found in Appendix 5.
An up-to-date list of all available PC Resonances is available at www.vitalremedies.com

Homeopaths and other health professionals active in developing countries, and their organisations, can also approach Amma Resonance Healing Foundation to obtain PC Resonances.

Healing downloads can be found at www.healingdownloads.com

Appendix 1: AIDS

Introduction

The knowledge of Acquired Immune Deficiency Syndrome, generally known as AIDS, was first begun in 1981, the first case being diagnosed in the United States. I (Harry) remember that during my internship somewhere around 1984 the first case was hospitalized in Groningen, Netherlands. Since little was known yet about contagion the patient, typically a homosexual man, was put in quarantine and doctors and medical students took blood samples with the greatest care. Since that time over 67 million people have been diagnosed with HIV and over 25 million have died. This eclipses the Black Death plague in the Middle Ages and therefore AIDS is one the most lethal pandemics in human history.

Practical matters about AIDS and HIV from Our Experience

There has been much conflicting information about HIV and AIDS over the last years, some of which we seek to clarify here, especially since there is a big difference between AIDS in Africa and in the West.

The confusion between Africa and the West in AIDS and HIV

We want to make a very clear distinction between AIDS in Africa and its spread amongst the heterosexual population, and AIDS in the West primarily amongst drug addicts and gay drug users. AIDS in gay men occurred in a group who were often very heavily using amyl nitrate and other drugs and still do. These so-called poppers are still openly on sale in gay bars, for instance in 2010 at the time of the big AIDS conference in Vienna. There are other street and medically prescribed drugs too that cause damage to the immune system. These drugs can be lethal to the immune system in sufficient doses and could easily be described as a main cause of the gay AIDS problem. It's a similar situation but worse among drug addicts.

The situation in Africa is completely different. AIDS there is a disease of sexually active heterosexual people.

When people try to transfer the medical understanding of AIDS in the West to AIDS in Africa it simply doesn't compute. The clinical situation is completely different.

Treating AIDS in the West

The intelligent holistic treatment of the gay and drug addict community with AIDS relates to eliminating the toxic effects of drugs which suppress immunity and which seems a prime causative factor with any infective agent like HIV as a secondary consequence, which once established, also needs treatment, whereas in Africa it's clear to us that AIDS has an infective origin and that is the main problem. So from a holistic clinical treatment point of view, and from the understanding of the problem and its solution, the approach is significantly different.

Denial amongst the gay community

We understand that there has been a huge denial amongst the gay community and possibly the scientific/medical community that the lifestyle of drugs has contributed to AIDS amongst their community. And this problem has still not been fully addressed and is as yet suppressed in the gay press. At the time of writing http://www.youtube.com/watch?v=1vxf7be0XWY gives a clear illustration of this problem from medical Nobel Prize winners and many others.

While gay men are very experienced with the effects of denial in the form of homophobia etc, this does not make them an open-minded community, and in fact, like any community, they tend to believe in their own zeitgeist, which includes vehement opposition to anything which would make their version of AIDS their responsibility.

This is no different from the human race in general which prefers to acknowledge the concept of disease, rather than disease as an actual expression of their own personal unexpressed pain, or even the purpose of the pain, which is to wake us up to our true nature. From this point of view denial of reality is a common feature of everyone within the human race and both gay and heterosexual people are in the same boat.

Our experience with AIDS in Africa

We want to state our personal experience with AIDS in Africa, having had very little previous experience of AIDS at all in the West. It was from a practical point of view and experience that we learned to regard AIDS in Africa as completely different to AIDS in the West in the gay and drug addict populations.

Peter went to Africa, in the nadir of the AIDS crisis, and worked in a clinic in Addis Ababa, Ethiopia and took just AIDS cases. He wrote about this in depth in his book *The Second Simillimum* so we will only mention the barest details here. In the beginning he investigated 70 cases in as much depth as he could. His experience was repeated in many other countries in Africa by himself, by Harry since 2004 and by others. There were no AIDS drugs in use at that time in Ethiopia except maybe amongst a tiny rich elite Peter didn't know about.

Our point is that our position is based on our experience, with a relatively open mind and based on what we found in reality.

AIDS and sexual transmission

AIDS was related to sexual activity and commonly one partner died and the other one started to get sick in exactly the same way as the previous one had. They realized they had the same disease. With clear exceptions – children and other non-sexually active people – no one else in the family got it, which seems to eliminate any other route of infection. Commonly these AIDS infected people were in their thirties, having already produced a family of typically seven to eight children, and their first concern was often the care of the children if they too died.

It was clear that a few of the children were infected, maybe one in ten, and often, if they had been infected, they had already died. These children, typically the last ones born, were sick from birth and were presumably infected through the birthing process and interchange of fluids or through breast-feeding. Surviving children were healthy and well.

There were other people in the same families sharing the same dwellings, food, water and local environment who did not get sick and the prime difference, as we stress again, was that they were not sexually active. This eliminates lots of other possibilities of explaining AIDS other than some infective agent.

AIDS is a new disease

This disease did not seem to link into any disease we've previously heard about, knew about or was evidenced. Not that we were experts on this subject but it was easy to consult with others who were, if needed. It was not primarily tuberculosis, or syphilis or gonorrhoea or malaria. These have definite symptom profiles, timelines etc.

It was not a common epidemic either because of the very slow way it developed. It was neither highly infectious nor did it proceed rapidly (and as we later realized, it was race selective). We can see now from the worldwide experience that it does not spread rapidly through the world population as had been predicted. Like the false flu pandemics, the estimates are proved to be gross overestimates, even in Africa and especially outside of Africa. There are racial/epigenetic issues that have not been realized until now. These we will discuss later.

Immune system collapse

It was clear that the immune system collapsed systematically and this allowed any previous infections, such as herpes or tuberculosis and numerous others that they already acquired and treated and put to bed so to speak, to break out again and/or come to the surface in a much more violent way. For example, normally herpes is contained to an occasional outbreak by the immune system as in the West, and tuberculosis is contained by the tubercles which seal it up and keep it semi-permanently contained. When the immune system collapses they come into play again and much more dramatically. For example herpes develops all over the mouth and tongue and extends across the face etc. Likewise people develop TB but with other separate diseases at the same time so we know the tuberculosis is not the prime cause or event. This is a common feature of the disease, many common diseases all happening to the same person at the same time.

With a collapsed immune system people could contract some relatively trivial problem but it would become something much stronger. For example, a headache would become permanent and never go away. Whatever was previously common but trivial became permanent and intense. That was another key feature of AIDS.

The complete hallmark of AIDS is the collapse of the immune system. It allows a range of common problems, a series of common diseases to all happen at once which in itself is uncommon.

Slim's disease

One common feature that stands out in the early stages of AIDS is the systematic loss of weight while eating normally over a long period of time and it was originally called Slim's disease for this reason. In many parts of Africa this century it was easy to spot a potential AIDS person simply because their clothes no longer fitted them (they were too poor to buy new ones). With this loss of weight and the energy loss, shown in their walking by the lack of vigour, such people were easy to identify. They became shadows of their former selves. You could mistake this for poverty but this was not the key reason in our experience as we've stated elsewhere.

A small percentage doesn't get infected

There was occasionally a husband or wife who did not get infected when their partner was infected, and this was also seen in some places amongst a small percentage of prostitutes who did not get infected. There is a genetic explanation for this which we understood later.

AIDS and poverty

This disease did not seem to relate to poverty directly. When people had no more food to eat than a cup of tea and a bread roll a day, we found that they did not recover from AIDS under our treatment. But when we fed them for two weeks, after failing to recover before, they then recovered as normal. This was Peter's first experience with people living with starvation and it was easy to see that one could jump to, what seems to me a false conclusion, that AIDS is solely a disease of poverty.

This poverty idea does not fit in at all with the situation of the Afro-Americans who are suffering from AIDS in a similar way to the Africans. No one is saying that in the United States they are suffering from a disease caused by poverty.

The reality was that in Africa when people were strong enough to work they could earn the money to feed themselves. But as soon as they lost the ability to work due to AIDS, and if they had no other support, which was fairly common, then they would start to starve to death.

In an AIDS hospice where the people were dying in the final stages of AIDS, the treatment Peter devised stopped the whole hospice from dying and for the first time people started going home, having recovered. The problem with this was that the AIDS hospice didn't have a budget for food so the patients didn't eat. As soon as they started recovering, they had ravenous appetites which couldn't be satisfied.

So the idea that AIDS was due to poverty only did not fully tie in with our experience, anywhere in Africa or from the United States Afro-American experience.

It's not due to more sexual partners

And it's not because they have more sexual partners than white people. Africans may even have less sexual partners on average than white people.

From our observation we didn't observe any obvious differences between Western and African heterosexual practices and think it is easy to have unexamined racial prejudices here.

Africans are much more susceptible to AIDS than white people

Although it was mainly the white gay community where AIDS manifested itself first, African-Americans in the USA are much more likely to be infected with HIV than white Americans in the USA. Race and income has a significant influence on susceptability to HIV-infection; Afro-Americans are 1.33 times more likely to be infected than whites.

Injections and vaccinations

We did not see any obvious connection between injections or vaccinations and AIDS in Africa. It seemed to us that everyone received the same sorts of vaccinations and injections yet it was only the sexually active who got AIDS.

Antibiotics, intoxication, overmedication

The use of pesticides, insecticides and medicines like antibiotics in Africa has often been badly controlled, and substances that were long forbidden in other countries were and still are used in Africa. Of several toxins a causal relationship to acquired immune deficiency exists, but to our knowledge it has never been proven that the current AIDS-epidemic in Africa is connected to this.

AIDS is only mildly infective

It seems that AIDS is not so easily transmitted, it is not highly infectious; one might say it is mildly infectious. For example the research shows that hospital people who are potentially infected accidentally by needles, needle stick injuries, in practice are much less than 1% likely to become infected in reality. This suggests at least that other factors play a role besides HIV. There is also the claim that none of 10,000+ AIDS researchers have contracted the virus from the lab samples. And of course there is the other fact that the epidemic that was predicted has not taken off outside of African-Americans and Africans.

AIDS Delay

There is a long period between the time of infection and the time that AIDS appears, and the official figures of about eleven years ties in with our experience. Commonly people started having sex from sixteen years onwards. Young people are not so likely to get infected as their first partners may be virgins like themselves and not infected, but as people reach their late teens and early 20's and have by then had a few more sexual partners the likelihood of infection is increased. That seemed to fit the facts we found, and consequently at around 30 years old they develop the symptoms of AIDS. Sometimes it was possible to trace the time of infection with great accuracy for example from rape, when the person had no further sex after that time and it was easy to verify that one decade passed before AIDS showed itself. For example in Rwanda, many people were infected by rape at the time of the genocide and ten or so years later developed AIDS without having had any other sexual activity. Often they were children when they were raped, and as they grew up there were very few men around and they were in any case too traumatized to consider sexual activity.

False positives

When it comes to the link between HIV and AIDS there is another complication. The HIV-test itself, the Elisa[28] and Western blot methods are clearly not 100% accurate and can easily lead to false positives. Especially in people with compromised immune systems that have acquired some other disease. False positives look like an AIDS patient superficially but don't have anything like the same case history.

AIDS test results

When it comes to the viral load, the HIV virus is not actually measured or seen under electron microscopes or otherwise isolated. No one is saying the test actually measures the HIV virus, only its consequences. It may be that the HIV viral load test measures things other than the effects of the HIV virus. We don't think this is disputed but it's a question of percentages. In general the argument is that the viral load test measures the effect of the HIV virus. We don't know what it measures, as it is completely outside our area of expertise. What we do know is that the person who invented the test for other reasons says it is completely inadequate to test a viral load.

28 The enzyme-linked immunosorbent assay (ELISA) is a common serological test for the presence of particular antigens or antibodies.

When it comes to the more detailed measurements of AIDS, CD4 and Viral Load in our limited experience showed that these two corresponded reasonably well. When you plot viral load on a logarithmic scale as is common practice, the virus increases over time in a linear fashion and the CD4 count plummets correspondingly.

While our experience of the tests was limited because at the time we had to pay for them and they cost something like $150 each time, the results roughly corresponded with the clinical picture of the patient. We say roughly corresponded because there were exceptions, but when we talked to the leading AIDS immunologists that we knew at the time, this was their experience too. Incidentally, what we saw was that those patients having unprotected sex with a partner at the end stage of AIDS, were compromised by that sex. This supported for us the sexual transmission route.

AIDS shows in population figures while the population still grows

When you look at the World Bank population statistics for South Africa you see clearly that there is a dip in the population growth graph from 2000 to 2008, which corresponds exactly with the highest figure of AIDS-related deaths in the country.

Nevertheless, despite AIDS the population in Africa, including sub-Saharan Africa, is increasing. The age at which many people die of AIDS may explain these apparently contradictory observations. Often the people die after they have produced their relatively large family, so that the population is increasing even while the parents are dying.

What is AIDS?

Our observation above is that AIDS has a very definite profile that corresponds to conventional medical literature. Peter found his AIDS profile by looking closely at 94 cases and by treating hundreds more. The profile he developed independently corresponded more or less exactly with the other evidence produced by a variety of medical sources and he didn't see any real conflicts in the clinical picture.

In Part II of this book we already discussed our analysis of what AIDS may really be about. What we learned from working in Africa, from meeting gay AIDS-patients, from the Shamanic Journey to HIV by Eileen Nauman (Part II), the proving of PC1 by Dr. Chetna Shukla (Part XI) and from thinking all these experiences through is that AIDS is a teacher of love. The core of AIDS, whether or not related to a virus, seems to be a lack of love, care and responsibility for oneself and others that cause the epidemic to continue. A lack of love, care and responsibility may play a role in many more diseases, but with AIDS there is a strong link with sexuality, placing the central theme within the realm of intimate relationships.

Drugs can kill

We are led to understand is that the original drug, AZT, at the recommended dosage level for AIDS, although appearing initially to mitigate the disease and bring people back to life, was sufficiently toxic to kill people and probably did help wipe out the first generation of gay men who took the drugs. Mistakenly the research into the drugs was stopped as soon as they were seen to work on humanitarian grounds. It seems to us it was fine to administer the drugs on humanitarian grounds but no reason to stop continuing the research to make sure they were in fact safe.

It was mistakenly thought that these patients died of AIDS when in fact they died of a combination of AIDS and the toxic drugs. The patients were misled by the doctors' interpretation of the drug side-effects as effects of the disease. There are many people who were also wrongly diagnosed as HIV-positive, who took the drugs and died. This is a medical catastrophe that so far is being covered up by drug companies and general medical denial as we understand it. This is typical of what happens with the drugs based medical system. There is nothing unusual about it. It's driven more by profit than it is by science or ethics.

Certainly if AZT were a hidden factor in killing off many thousands of gay men, this should be openly brought into the public domain, examined and appropriate action taken including discontinuing the distribution of it to Africans. This is nothing to do with the HIV/AIDS debate but is an important issue in its own right. What we have seen on the ground in Africa is that in a significant number of patients antiretroviral drugs including AZT are in fact causing serious side effects, for example paralysis – a complication still seen a lot in Africa (See the cases in the AIDS chapter). It's still common to confuse or attribute drug effects to disease effects when people are getting worse, and we suggest this may be the general rule, not the exception.

Alternative Opinions about the HIV-causes-AIDS-conflict

There are a number of interesting films on this aspect typically the *House of Numbers* [www.houseofnumbers.com] and many other sites for those interested in exploring this controversy further. Bad Science sites will give you the opposite opinion. We stress opinion on both sides. *Ten Lies About Aids* by Etienne De Harven, M.D., with Jean-Claude Roussez gives a serious scientific set of questions to think about.

www.thetruthbarrier.com is another source of information.

A very thorough documentation came out in 2011:
http://www.youtube.com/watch?v=PQFxratWh7E&feature=youtu.be

From our point of view all the above discussion is based upon materialistic science and conflicts within it and this is not so important. For our point of view the above discussion is about a puppet and not about who is pulling the strings.

The HIV-paradigm

From early on there have been heavy disputes in scientific circles about the hypothesis that HIV is the cause of AIDS, involving some of the world's best virologists and other experts. The critiques from the specialists opposing the HIV-paradigm (so-called AIDS-dissidents) have until today not been sufficiently answered, but nevertheless they have been heavily attacked showing that the whole discussion was moved from a scientific one to a political or commercial one. We, the authors of this book, know about the existence of alternative theories but lack the knowledge to make a proper judgment, and in the interest of AIDS-patients, have kept out of the dispute. For the selection or creation of a homeopathic remedy, or for it to act, the scientific story behind the phenomena (signs and symptoms of AIDS) is of little relevance. Homeopathy is controversial enough by itself and we felt that, provided we had sufficient knowledge to do so, by choosing sides in this discussion we might jeopardize our attempts to make PC1 available in Africa to as many patients as possible. For the remains of this chapter we will discuss AIDS as if the HIV-paradigm is valid. If at some point proven different this would change our understanding of the pandemic in several ways, but not so much the cultural change AIDS demands in Africa for the African people to survive.

AIDS-dissidents

Here is how Dr. Juliane Sacher, one of today's AIDS-dissidents, explains AIDS [www.praxis-sacher.de]:

> This is my more than 25 years of experience in treating HIV-positivity and AIDS, considering mainly the work of Dr. Heinrich Kremer ('The silent revolution of cancer and AIDS'), Prof. Alfred Haessig (the founder and former leader for 40 years of the organisation for blood donation in Switzerland and 30 years advisor of the WHO), Dr. Toni Gradl (The researcher from a German Max-Planck-institute and inventor of natural treatment for immune disbalance), Dr. Gerhard Ohlenschläger (Biochemist from the university in Frankfurt/Main - the most famous researcher about the molecule glutathion).
> By knowing and experiencing all the symptoms and blood results that occur in "HIV/AIDS"-patients nobody can simply ignore them. However a lot of things don't fit in with it being a virus disease.
> Since many years I know for sure, that nobody ever isolated a virus called HIV, so that this virus cannot be the reason for the disease "AIDS" and the next conclusion is, that the so-called antiviral medication cannot be the right treatment.
> For treating a disease one has to follow the symptoms and understand the cause – then look for non-toxic treatment to influence the body for changing and repairing malfunction.
>
> By speaking with a HIV/AIDS patient it becomes obvious that the most important thing is for him/her the T4-cell (CD4-cell) and PCR (so called "viral load") level. That's what they pursue intensively – does it increase or decrease?
>
> **But what is the reason for low T4-cells?**
>
> In the very beginning of treating HIV/AIDS patients I saw that parallel to a very low T4-cell count – sometimes zero, but fully able to work – patients had a very high amount of antibodies (gamma-globulins). However I remembered why T4-cells are called helper cells: They help the B cells changing into plasma cells to produce gamma globulins (immune globulins or immune antibodies). How could it be that just the patients who have a loss of T4 helper cells have such extremely high gamma globulins? I have never seen as high with any disease, namely more than 35-40, even 45 per cent, instead of the normal eighteen per cent.
>
> Actually they already would have had to find out, at that time, what only appeared in experiments many years later: That the T4 cells were not destroyed, but rather that they had migrated out of the blood and are therefore no longer measurable in the blood.
>
> Now we know since the beginning of the 1990´s from cellular research that there is not just one kind of T4 cells, but two different kinds, the TH1 and the TH2 cells. They also found out that HIV/AIDS patients have a shift in the balance of TH1/TH2 cells, namely in the direction of TH2 – that means they have a lack of TH1 and the TH2 even increases. However the TH2 cells migrate out of the blood, to where they can carry out their tasks, namely into the lymph vessels and into the lymph nodes for meeting the B cells assisting in production of gamma globulins.

With this knowledge the mystery is solved. There is no need for a new virus to explain the T4 cell reduction. As now noted they were not destroyed either, but rather only migrated from the blood into the lymphatic tissue.
This then also explains the lymph node swelling typical with HIV/AIDS patients, namely by knowing that the process is accompanied by histamine production and inflammation.

Now it also becomes clear why the official "Combo Therapy", which is a cytotoxic and anti-inflammatory therapy, often – not always – results that the T4 cell increase in the blood and the lymph node swellings decrease, because the T4 cells migrate back into the blood and again become measurable. Research also proved that these "increased" T4 cells are in no way a question of newly produced T4 cells, but they proved that it is a matter of old T4 cells which therefore could not have been destroyed.

Why do they nevertheless stick to the virus theory? To this day nobody can yet show how "HIV" destroys the T4 cells.

Back to the two totally different ways of immune-response: We know, that the balance of TH1 and TH2 is important for a healthy immune function. TH1 is responsible for the intracellular germs, opportunistic infections and cancer cells and TH2 for bacterial infections and parasites.

During evolution the new mechanism as immune response has to come into being. So bacteria and parasites can be destroyed by this new way of immune response, the non cell-related (humoral) immunity – the TH2-assisted response. This new way manages by inhibiting and destroying microbes without the typical side effects on the healthy body cells through the NO gas (nitrogen oxide) attack – the former only way of immune response – the TH1-response.

So in cases of frequent contact with different and strange bacteria – for example – it makes sense to switch from TH1- into TH2-immune response, because bacteria proliferate faster than opportunistic pathogens.

This corresponds to our experience in treating AIDS with PC1. Patients who were nearly dead, dying in hospices, recovered in days and weeks. It could not be that they generated new T4 cells; it has to be that somehow the cells were activated from a storage place, as recovery was so quick in such devastated people.

Conclusions about AIDS

There are many opinions and there is not enough openness and not enough research to clarify the fundamentals around AIDS. There are obvious confusions and vested interests, for example the gay press and the conventional AIDS community, the AIDS conspiracy theorists, and the pharmaceutical industry all have strong vested interests which they protect and defend strongly; these are essentially ego defences and positions, stances based on false rigid thinking.

The minorities are unfairly treated and ostracized and funds cut off so that a proper scientific debate based on different research results cannot take place.

In this situation it is very hard to come to sensible, sane conclusions. In this situation it is also difficult to propagate a new approach to AIDS.

In the case of our new approach to AIDS, PC1 it requires some exemplary research, the developments of a new concept or paradigm to put the new approach into context, and science to move into areas where it would seem unlikely to want to go in the short term.

This effectively means that new approaches to AIDS, which could save millions of lives and billions of dollars, may not be implemented on a large scale in the foreseeable future. We may have to wait until materialistic science has failed consistently for generations, as it has in cancer, before new ideas can come to the fore.

AIDS in Africa

AIDS is the fourth largest killer worldwide but especially hits sub-Saharan Africa.

If you want to have a good impression of how AIDS is tearing the heart out of Africa read the book *28 stories of AIDS in Africa* by Stephanie Nolan. Not only is it very well written and therefore a joy to read but it summarizes the whole long history of AIDS and gives you 28 intimate human stories. If your heart can bear it this is the book to read.

In sub-Saharan Africa it is estimated that 25 million people are infected with HIV (2007). Every day 14,000 new people are being infected. The total number is still increasing, although the growth rate is decreasing. The good news is that in some countries successful prevention programmes have been rolled out that slow the epidemic down. The bad news is that in some countries the percentage infected is so high, more than one third of the population, and so many have already died, that due to that, the epidemic is literally dying down.

There are many reasons why the disease has been spreading so much in Africa. A lot has to do with the position of women and promiscuity. African women often do not have the right to refuse sex. The way the disease spread over the continent also has a lot to do with the socio-economical situation. Where men are away from home for long stretches of time, sex workers swarm around them. Truckers that take goods from the few big ports on lorries with bald tyres and badly maintained engines take weeks to reach their destination over roads that are full of holes. Around the ports, the places of rest and the borders, prostitutes step up in their cabins and provide sex for less than a dollar. Men that work in mines are often away from their family for more than a year. Again prostitutes fulfil their sexual needs.

It takes typically eleven years before AIDS becomes manifest. So for many years people can be ignorant of their situation, or ignore the risk and assume they are safe or that some magic or traditional medicine will safeguard them. The typical situation is that first the man falls ill. He starts losing weight, gets pains all over the body, gets TB or other infections as well, loses his appetite, stops working and providing for the family and often, without seeing a doctor, dies. The taboo on AIDS is still very strong in most places, and people would rather die of so called TB, than investigate whether they are HIV-positive and get treatment, that is if available. Typically some years later the wife starts to develop symptoms as well, and feeling the responsibility for her children, hopefully overcomes the taboo and consults a doctor.

It's the adults, those that work and raise children, who get AIDS and die from it, leaving a huge gap between the generations of children and grandparents. There are many AIDS-orphans all over sub-Saharan Africa. By 2010 it is estimated there will be 15 million. In Swaziland, which has the highest percentage of infected people, one out of three children is an orphan. They often have to raise themselves and the oldest girl acts as the mother to the whole family. If she's lucky she still has the family home but if she's pretty the local men will start harassing her. If she's lucky she finds an aid agency to give her money for food or maybe she makes some money by braiding people's hair after school. She also needs money to educate her brothers and sisters and if she's got quite a few of them that is often impossible.

Poverty is, besides sexual behaviour, an important factor in the spreading of AIDS. People are often uneducated and are therefore prone to all kinds of beliefs and misconceptions regarding health and disease, AIDS in particular. Poverty also leads to a lack of proper nutrition. It is the reason why doctors, hospitals or medicines are often not available at all or are too expensive. In one country there are only 50 active doctors (2007) for a population of millions. Prevention is often a difficult issue. Men do not like using condoms and the Catholic churches have often preached against them. And although condoms can be provided to Africa for around three cents and are often given away free their availability is still a problem, as with many things in Africa.

The world is pumping billions of dollars into Africa for AIDS each year, but lots of it never reaches its intended goal. The implementation methods chosen are often very inept and open to corruption. Billions of dollars have been spent to develop a vaccination programme for HIV, but all attempts have failed, and the one for which researchers had the highest hopes turned out to infect people rather than prevent infection. Funds for ARVs controlled by some religious organisations are sometimes deliberately withheld from people like sex workers, who are often supporting large families, as they are viewed as evil.

Altogether this draws quite a hopeless picture, but nevertheless there is also progress being made. More and more African men and women dare to stick their neck out, to defy the taboo around AIDS. They state in public that they are HIV-positive. Positively living with HIV/AIDS is a slogan used by many. They visit schools, prostitutes and orphanages and educate their brothers and sisters about prevention. They set up hospices to provide those in end stages with the love and care they need. These are the people that will make the change. These are the people that deserve our support.

Another source of hope is that there is a treatment to complement ARVs and prevention programmes that is effective, cheap and without side-effects. This treatment with PC1 is a real ray of hope.

Children and AIDS

In 2008 it was estimated there were fifteen million children orphaned as a result of this disease and this figure is expected to rise to 45 million by 2012.

Save the Children Sweden has recently published a report T*ell Me More: Children's Rights and Sexuality in the Context of HIV/AIDS in Africa*.[29] They found that young children are rarely targeted in work on HIV/AIDS prevention and sexual and reproductive health initia-

29 Tapiwa Gomo: Regional Communications Officer, Save the Children Sweden: www.savethechildren.se

tives. The report explores children's perspectives and strategies for dealing with sexuality and relationships in the face of HIV/AIDS in sub-Saharan Africa and is based on a study of research conducted in thirteen African countries.

Children have many strategies to avoid HIV/AIDS, the most popular being involvement in school or recreational activities. Children mentioned that strict gender norms make it difficult for boys and girls to negotiate sex and not fall into society's expectations of their sexual behaviour (boys to have multiple sexual partners and girls to be uninformed about sex and sexuality). These gender norms and societal pressure also encourage transactional and cross-generational sex, which are prevalent throughout Africa.

Most children get information on sexuality from the media. They found the sexuality education provided in schools and communities to be too technical, negative and moralistic. It does not address issues that concern them such as love, body image, relationships, identity and how to negotiate safe sex. Children found the focus on ABC (abstinence, be faithful and use condoms) to be simplistic, not well explained and unrealistic for them. Because adults are often uninformed themselves, shy and have strong moral ideas about what is right and wrong within the realm of sexuality, the education children receive is not explained very well, it is judgmental and does not help children understand how to deal with difficult issues like how to negotiate sex and condom use.

One of the most important conclusions that can be drawn from this report is that it is vital to strengthen children's self-esteem, their capacity to make decisions for themselves and their ability to think critically around common misconceptions. Alongside that adults will need to change behaviour as to transactional and cross-generational sex with children.

Another key issue from this study is the need to engage boys and men in order to further the agenda of gender equity. Much of the focus tends to be on teaching girls how to 'just say no'. However, it is clear from this study that this is not enough. Girls engage in transactional relationships for reasons other than love and affection.

They also frequently do not feel that they can insist on condom use, particularly if there is some kind of power differential involved. Furthermore, boys are often caught in similarly harmful gender norms such as ideas of masculinity being related to having many sexual partners and initiation into sex when one is very young. Finally, this study was based on the premise, as embodied in the Convention on the Rights of the Child and other key U.N. documents that children have certain rights in relation to their sexual and reproductive health. Countries that have ratified the Convention have the responsibility to ensure that these rights are upheld. In looking at the results of this study through the lens of these key agreed-upon rights of children, it appears that this has not been achieved in the studied countries. Children have not been consulted on their opinions of what they need, programmes do not take their perspectives into account, and they are not receiving the information they need in order to protect themselves against HIV/AIDS. Such consultations will be necessary if countries are to effectively respond to the epidemic.

More on ARVs and AIDS

The reality is that although AIDS drugs have been around since 1996 a significant portion of people in Africa who need them are not yet getting them. In the beginning a treatment with HAART (Highly Active Antiretroviral Therapy) cost $12,000 per patient per year. After adjusting international law for patents it was possible to develop ARVs that would become affordable for Africa. The cheapest cocktail – containing stavudine, lamivudine and nevirapine – now costs less than $1 per day. This still represents a lot of money considering that in the poorest African countries many have only one dollar a day to spend for food, clothes and shelter. The treatment including stavudine has become obsolete in the west because of the severe side-effects, but because of the low costs is still used in Africa.

The effect of HIV is that the immune system gradually breaks down. Once the number of available immune cells in the blood (white blood cells) decrease below a certain level, patients become vulnerable to all kinds of infections, the so-called opportunistic infections. In Africa ARVs are prescribed when the CD4 count (number of lymphocytes or T-helper cells) get below 350 – 200 cells per square millimetre.

One of the characteristics of HIV is that the virus reproduces in a disordered way causing genetic variation. This causes relatively rapid resistance to the therapy. So a medicine that kept the virus under control, at some point might stop functioning. In 2007 there were 28 ARVs approved by the American Food and Drug Administration that all influence the reproduction of the virus at different levels. In the West there are AIDS-patients that have already, due to resistance, used a dozen different ARV combinations. For Africa the first line treatment is far from being available to all needing it. The far more expensive second line and third line treatment can usually not be obtained, let alone be afforded. But these may be needed even a year after the first use of ARVs. Typically the increased life span may not be sufficient, for example to allow the children to be educated, grow up and leave home before their parents die.

Besides the changeability of the virus drug resistance is also caused when people stop taking their medication for a period. As soon as they stop taking the ARVs the virus starts to reproduce again, and new strains may be created that do not respond to the previous medication. They may stop because they have no more drugs available, the clinic, a day or more away, is too far to walk to; because the side-effects are too hard to bear or because they feel better and think they can do without.

ARVs have lots of long-term side-effects. They are toxic to the kidneys and liver and influence processes inside the bodily cells. Metabolic side-effects are for instance lipodystrophy (destruction of fatty tissues) and diabetes mellitus. Taking pauses in the therapy (interval therapy) could prevent these side-effects, but is not optimal because it induces therapy resistance more rapidly.

For decades it has been known that suppressing infectious diseases with antibiotics in the case of bacteria, or antivirals in the case of viruses, ultimately cause the diseasing agent to become more virulent and malicious. The World Health Organisation warns against this, but the medical establishment sees no other option than killing the microbes that cause diseases. Healing systems like homeopathy that do not kill the bug but instead stimulate the immune system to control the disease by itself are a serious alternative, but the present medical paradigm that believes in suppression and is controlled by the stock market, is not inclined to investigate other options.

From thousands of cases treated in different African countries the experience is that PC1 has the same beneficial effects clinically as antiretroviral drugs. It is much easier to administer and distribute and costs a fraction of even the cheapest ARVs. People usually get well very quickly on PC1. Since PC1 has no side-effects it can be taken before the CD4 count drops below 200 and antiretroviral drugs would be indicated. Patients already on ARVs only very slowly see their immune system recover. Where ARVs reduce the amount of viruses in the blood quickly the CD4 count initially drops even further and then restores very slowly. With PC1 the immune system is restored much quicker, making a combination of ARVs plus PC1 a win-win situation.

For people using ARVs (HAART) and suffering from side-effects a special PC Resonance has been developed called PC501a.

Appendix 2: Amma Resonance Healing Foundation

Introduction

The ARHF promotes the development of healing through resonance. Healing by resonance is based on the universal law that information similar to the nature of a disease and its totality of symptoms can induce a self-healing response in the diseased individual.

Healing by resonance is considered to become increasingly important as it acknowledges and strengthens the potential for self-healing in the individual, and is based on understanding the role diseases play in the collective as well as the individual; the awareness that fighting disease, besides creating undesired side-effects, in the long run creates more serious diseases by suppressing the role and purpose of the disease, which is neither understood nor addressed.

The ARHF focuses on research into the principles underlying resonance, on developing resonances specific for all kinds of diseases, on investigating all possible means of conveying healing information, and on the application of and research into its efficacy.

The treatment of epidemics and collective trauma is one of the prime targets of the ARHF, and the focus of its activities is primarily on countries in Africa and other low-income countries. Epidemics and collective trauma in these countries still determine the lives of millions of people, while medical aid is often only scarcely available, accompanied by side-effects or complicated by increasing therapy-resistance.

The treatment of chronic diseases by resonance is a second target of the ARHF. Using the same principal as is used to create healing information for epidemics it is also possible to treat chronic diseases, using the healing resonance for the disease alongside a tailor-made individualised remedy to obtain the best possible results.

ARFH recognises that there are spiritual, mental, psychological and physical dimensions to healing diseases and embraces a holistic perspective in these matters.

The Name: Amma Resonance Healing Foundation

The **Resonance Healing Foundation** part of the name speaks for itself considering the goal of the foundation. The addition of **Amma** to the foundation was made for several reasons.

One reason is that since the history of the ARHF started with Peter Chappell's inner call to heal AIDS in Africa, an African name would be appropriate. Amma is the Sky God of the Dogon, the Creator of the Universal Egg – the unformed universe that contained all the seeds or signs of the world – as well as the Creator of Mother Earth from clay.

Amma is also Mother Divine in Hindu mythology. In the Vedic Tradition, the name Mother Divine refers to the nourishing, evolutionary power of Natural Law lively within all of creation and within the silent consciousness of everyone.

AIDS is a disease born out of a disharmonious interaction between male and female principle. In the name Amma thus the Divine Male Creative power and the Divine Female Nourishing power are joined together to heal and harmonize by resonance the relationships between humans, as it was Peter's compassion and creativity that together resulted in a new technology of creating healing resonances.

Projects

Since 2007, ARHF has been involved in several projects, mainly in Africa.

The ARHF offers free treatment to individual AIDS-patients in developing countries and free remedy packages plus instructions for doctors in developing countries to treat their patients.

Amma4Africa kits and PC Rescue kits plus manuals are offered for free or for cost price to health professionals in developing countries.

Amma4Africa Clinics that offer treatment mainly for epidemic diseases and trauma are being supported financially and in terms of training. Data-collection is organized in these clinics to build up evidence for the effects of long-term treatment.

On the ground training is provided on how to treat epidemics and trauma.

On request ARHF offers relief after catastrophes, such as the earthquake in Haiti in 2010.

Amma4Africa KIT

Amma Resonance Healing Foundation has created a special kit plus manual for Africa. This kit contains PC Resonances for the following conditions:

Epidemic diseases

- HIV/AIDS
- Malaria
- Tuberculosis
- Hepatitis
- Gonorrhoea

Trauma

- Adoption trauma
- Rape & Sexual abuse
- War and Genocide
- Injuries
- Burns

Chronic diseases

- Infertility
- Diabetes
- Hypertension

The manual includes enough information for any medically qualified person to effectively use these PC Resonances for the above conditions and can used alongside any conventional treatment programme.
The manual is available as a download at www.arhf.nl and also in print at www.homeolinks.nl

PC Rescue Kit

Amma Resonance Healing Foundation has created a special kit plus manual for the treatment of trauma. This kit contains PC Resonances for the following conditions:

- Adoption trauma
- Burns
- Injuries
- Long-term grief
- Natural catastrophes
- Rape & Sexual abuse
- Shock
- Torture
- Unburied relatives
- War and Genocide

The manual is available as a download at www.arhf.nl

Donate

This is to give an idea of what money can buy if ARHF is supported:

- For €15 one AIDS-patient can be treated and become symptom-free for the duration of one year.
- For €50 a school of 600 children can receive malaria prophylaxis for a whole year.
- For €100 per month a clinic can offer free treatment to hundreds of people for epidemics and trauma.

The Amma Resonance Healing Foundation is registered in the Netherlands. The Dutch Tax Office has accepted the ARHF as a not-for-profit organisation and allows donations to the foundation to be deducted from taxes. Several EU-member-states allow donations made to non-profit organisations in the Netherlands to be deducted from taxes as well. All donations to the ARHF will be solely used to promote its projects.

At www.arhf.nl you find several ways in which donations can be made of which you can choose the most practical for you.

Donations by Bank Transfer can be made to:

Amma Resonance Healing Foundation
ABN-AMRO Bank (Rijkstraatweg 184, 9752 BP Haren, Netherlands)
Account number: 422065234

BIC (Swift code): ABNANL2A
IBAN: NL42ABNA0422065234

APPENDIX 3: Shamanic Journeys

Introduction

Eileen Nauman is a dear friend and colleague who contributed to our work on infectious diseases in a unique and fascinating way. Being half Native American Eileen was trained as an Eastern Cherokee Metis (shamanic healer) and in that capacity is able to make shamanic journeys for a person.

This is what Viola Woolcott writes on shamanic journeys:

What is a Shamanic Journey?
By Viola Woolcott

> The Shaman is said to be walking with one foot in the everyday world and with the other in the spirit world. Different cultures may express their views on the two realities differently, but the basic idea is the same. Shamans are explorers of doorways from ordinary reality into non-ordinary (NOR) reality through portals leading him from the physical to the spirit world. They are moving between those two worlds. In order to bring about a balance between the physical and spiritual worlds the shaman uses mystical powers to journey to other worlds or realities and communicates with spirits.
> The Shamanic Journey is a way of finding answers, information, healing, wisdom and knowledge as well as guidance or help with one's personal life. During the Journey he meets with spirits who may be regarded as ancestors, elders, gods, goddesses, deceased shamans, spirit guides, power animals and angels.
> These beings are seen as beings with great wisdom, power and the ones who are willing to help with guiding the living.
> A shamanic world is made up of three parts, the lower world, the upper world and the middle world. The shamans see these three worlds as a climbing tree to the next world. The tree represents power and courage and is used in the initiation ceremony. None of these worlds are above the other. They are equally important.
> Each shaman begins his journey with a theme, if he is looking for guidance on a specific issue, the theme would be whatever the issue is. A phrase or a sentence is formed and repeated over and over again. This phrase or sentence helps to transcend him into the spirit world. The shaman also finds a place of tranquillity in his mind; there can be no other noise around him, and he must achieve a totally calm state of mind with no outside distractions.
> Shamans do rely on their instincts as well as their powers. They have no limitations, they ascend into each world and they stop in each world and get the wisdom and the power they need from each world before going to the next. Once they have achieved the last world, they are ready to descend back into the present, into reality. From each world they have received word from the spirits and the knowledge to help who have come to them in their hour of need.
>
> [www.shamanicjourney.com/article/5957/what-is-a-shamanic-journey]

From personal experience we knew that Eileen is capable of finding meaningful answers to help a person in his/her individual life. At some point we asked her whether it would also be possible to make a shamanic journey to find out the purpose of infectious diseases. As we were involved with treating AIDS in Africa and wished to have a deeper understanding of the disease we hoped she could help us with that. Would it be possible to make a shamanic journey to HIV and communicate with it to get an understanding of its evolutionary role? To Eileen this was a new kind of request, and a new kind of journey, but after consulting her spiritual guides she got permission, and made the journey to HIV. The report of that journey is fully presented in the earlier chapters of this book.

After this successful journey Eileen, at our request, made several journeys to other microorganisms. They have been mentioned in the chapters dealing with their related diseases. Here you can find the full reports and some conversations that took place after them.

If something like shamanic journeys is too far out for you we suggest you omit these pages. You do not need to read them in order to use the PC RESONANCES nor were the journeys needed to create them.

We were interested in understanding the miasms to which these microorganism and their diseases are related, and in our experience the themes coming forward in the journeys often connect in a meaningful way with what we already know about them.

What struck us in general was the notice that these microorganisms are here to serve mankind and that despite the suffering caused there was nothing personal and no bad intention involved. They are serving the bigger picture.

Shamanic Journey for Gonorrhoea bacteria

Eileen Nauman 2006

Before I journeyed, my teacher told me to wear a red transparent bubble around myself. The guide who came with me was also enclosed in this red bubble. My teacher told me it was to protect us from being infected by these bacteria.

As we travelled through the void of inner space, complete darkness, I began to see a light ahead. As we got closer I saw the bacterium looked snakelike with rectangular pastel coloured blocks made up of its undulating, sensual body. In one way, the gonorrhoea bacteria reminded me of DNA strands; the segmenting or sequencing. But this was very two-dimensional when I viewed the bacterium.

It is a female bacterium. She was friendly and had a soft, eager voice and was more than happy to engage me in conversation. The bacteria were created back in Atlantis, she told me, when the power tilted in favour of men and women began to lose their equality. The bacteria were created when women were no longer held in respect. It is an earth bacterium. This was when the bacteria were created; a reaction of the Universe to the misuse of power, lack of respect and an unnatural unbalancing taking place between man and the rest of the beings on the planet. The bacteria said she infects only the human species; that all other species have a natural balance they continue to practise to this day between themselves.

We did not get into the aspects of "love" and sex. Rather, the bacterium was matter-of-fact that humans were sexual beings just as everything else was. She was not moralistic in her approach to my questions; rather that sex is a natural part of the human experience. What this bacterium was taking umbrage with is HOW the two parties involved approached the sex act. If there was only one in consent, taking from the other, this is wrong to the bacteria. Everything must be equal. Must be approved by both parties before sex is undertaken.

She said: "I am about respect. I am here to remind you that your body is a temple. Cleanliness. Honouring yourself. Being able to say no or yes when you want to participate in the sexual act. Not being made a victim without choice or voice. I am about powerlessness and disempowerment during the act of sex. I arrive when it is about the loss of respect between the genders. It is women being used without their permission (rape/incest). Or a man being abused or disempowered, as well."

Gonorrhoea in the eyes: you do not see clearly in regards to sex and the act of sex.

Gonorrhoea of the sexual organs: anger/abuse/disrespect/humiliation among many other human emotions, were being expressed through the act of unbalanced sex.

The bacterium was very feminine, talkative and her body would undulate and her colourful rectangular body parts were like pastel billboards glowing and receding in colour. She would sparkle with silver around her and then sparkle with gold; a true show-off. She said she was about glamour. About partying, celebrating. She was very sociable, amiable, pleasant and completely non-threatening compared to the other bacteria/viruses I have journeyed into.

The colours of her blocks were pink, green, yellow and blue. I saw no red, orange, purple or white colours along her snake-line body. These colours must have some specific meaning. Her colours were clean and beautiful; she had a very charismatic nature and she liked being 'beautiful' and liked to strut her sensuality as a feminine creature. She would puff up in one rectangular section and I'd see globules; like grapes; only they were many, many breasts. And then, they'd deflate, disappear and the pastel rectangle would again assume its original shape. She liked to tease me and play with me in that regard. I saw another group of globules appear and they were the faces of many, many women and some men. All beautiful, all ages, all colours. The faces were laughing, smiling. They would appear and then deflate. And then the bubbles or ballooning would appear again with different faces. It looked like a montage of faces from around the globe. This ability to go from flat, two-dimensional to these rounded, grape-like or balloon objects which were clearly three-dimensional was rather mesmerizing for me. She enjoyed showing off in this regard because she liked attention and would do this to keep me enthralled with her.

She had a non-poisonous snakelike head, with (sometimes) big eyes with black pupils. They bulged from her head when she wanted them to and they would look huge in comparison to her head. And then they would recess or recede to a smaller size and lay flat and smooth against her skull. When she opened her mouth, it was like staring into a black void. There was this caricature nature that she had. I didn't pick up any meanness, revenge or motive from the bacterium. She understood she had a duty to perform, but she did so with lightness; this is the best way to put it.

Some of the other things she imparted to me were: Our body is a temple and it is up to us to take care of it, respect it. She is not against sex; rather, promiscuous sex and that is when she comes in to remind the person that their attitude, emotions or lack of maturity were not in place – and the person pays the price accordingly.

She said when the person thinks well of themselves, approaches sex with honour/integrity, that she will not visit them. She is not anti-sex. Rather, sex with integrity, honour, respect and a balance between the two consenting parties.

She said that when a woman gets the bacteria and her vaginal area is swollen, red, leaking with discharge and has an awful odour emanating from it, it is the anger she is expressing in a physical way over the sexual act encountered with another who was not equal or respectful.

A person contracts gonorrhoea when they have been immature, imprudent, irresponsible or failed to respect themselves or their partner.

She said she would disappear from Earth once there was equality between the genders once more; when they came back into balance and respect for one another. Her job, as she saw it, was to make a person responsible for their sexuality and their behaviour toward themselves as well as others with regard to the act of sex. There was simply no judgment from the bacterium, no moral issues, either. Just a matter-of-fact kind of statement of being.

(End of journey)

Comments on the journey

Harry: The themes seem clear and from a homeopathic point of view logical. The idea of a sexual victim (no exit, fixed) is a clearly sycotic idea, as is the idea of a helpless victim in general. (See *Miasms in Labour*, van der Zee 2000)

The bubbles are interesting. They are reminiscent of a description of headaches in *Medorrhinum.* A sensation of a contraction around the crown of the head followed by a relaxation together with a sensation of bubbles in the head. This description made me think when I read it the first time of contractions during labour. After each contraction there is relaxation and, like a diver going to the surface too quickly, the result is that bubbles appear. Also the dilatation phase of labour, where these contractions determine everything and during which all a woman can do is wait until there is full dilatation, is a sycotic situation. The mother is the victim of the baby and vice versa. A fixed situation, and as long as there is no full dilatation, one without an exit. Only once the birth canal has fully opened can mother and baby work together again as equal partners in the birth process. Polarity or antagonism is clearly connected to the sycotic phase of birth, and problems arise if the polarity means inequality. An interesting thing is that the only remedy in the rubric 'Antagonism with mother' is *Thuja.* Men and women are of course clearly two sides of a polarity, and when there is no equilibrium and equality in the relationship one (usually the woman) can experience the relationship as a prison with no exit.

Also bubbles are things that tend to expand and grow, so there is a similarity to sycosis here as well. The image that comes forward is that of yeast. Bubbling, growing, expanding. Growing cell structures give a similar image. This could mean tumours as well, another sign of sycosis. Opposite to a syphilitic structure, which is like a black hole in which everything disappears, a sycotic structure keeps throwing matter and energy out from its centre.

Eileen commented on the absence of red, orange and pink in the image of the virus:
Of course she wouldn't have *red* or *orange* colours on her body if she were trying to lift a person up into the next ascending chakra – she wants people to move *out* of the tribe (red/root chakra) and out of the navel chakra (orange) and into the "I" or yellow/solar plexus chakra.

The colour *pink* is a combination of the root chakra (red in colour) and our crown chakra (white in colour). When you are a whole being, pink would show your ability to be in balance, whole and individual. Further, *blue* is the colour of the throat chakra and one of the biggest strengths of this chakra is the ability to speak up for ourselves – to speak our truth. You cannot always do that in the tribal mindset (root chakra) nor can you do it in the navel chakra (orange) where the 'we' transcends and overrides the 'I' of the solar plexus. I believe the *yellow* colour may well symbolize our solar plexus chakra, the 'I' that we are trying to become. The *green* may symbolize the heart chakra where we would go next after becoming an individual; to put it all together of not only being unique unto ourselves (the solar plexus expression) but then to move up into our heart chakra to learn how to be compassionate beings. I believe that when we can all move to the heart chakra and stay there, these bacteria will move on and disappear from the face of the earth.

Shortly before reading the journey report Peter made the following observation:
I took a toad out of my pond as it appeared completely dead and I put it on the side of the garden to await burial. It was dead and in the process of laying its eggs, these were hanging

out. This morning it has disappeared. I cannot believe the cats that roam have taken it. Could it not have been dead and come back to life?

Eileen's response: I'm rather struck that *eggs* were hanging out of the toad – remember the 'bubbling' of the gonorrhoea? Eggs certainly look like bubbles to me. Also, the sex act includes labour and giving birth and what did you find? A toad giving birth to bubbles. Also, this bacterium is an *Earth* created one ... so the toad is a very *earth*-being – it is not water a amphibian, rather *land* amphibious or *earth* oriented. And also, doesn't the *coat* or *skin* of the toad resemble the tumours or 'bubbling' we've been talking about? I think this is a fine symbol sent by gonorrhoea to you to bless and agree with what you're doing and the journey-work I've done as a messenger from it. In my world, we call this a 'double check' and it's a 'calling card' from the being we've been working with: it's saying: well done! So, it's a good, positive sign that we're on the right track.

Peter asked Eileen whether she had an idea how the "power tilted in favour of men".

Eileen: I hesitated putting this in because it was so disgusting to me. So, I omitted it from my report to you. But I'll put it in now. The bacterium showed me Atlantean scientists in a large room. In a huge cage (metal and made of criss-cross so it looked like squares) I saw a blond haired woman, naked. And in there with her was a male Chimpanzee monkey. The monkey was copulating with her (she was down on her hands and knees). The woman seemed *forced* to be in there with this monkey and she did not have a happy look on her face; it was as if she were a prisoner of these Atlantean scientists (all men by the way – older, grey hair/beards, etc.) and couldn't get out of being part of the experiment. When I saw this picture the bacterium presented to me, I got a powerful picture of the Nazis from Germany doing similar experiments on the Jewish people – utterly disgusting, inhuman and inhumane experiments; treating them less than animals. The two scenes were like two pages from the same book. Maybe the Atlantean scientists/male were immoral (a gonorrhoea theme it seems) and violating Nature at her most basic – mating two different species with one another in hopes of creating a third, new species. And maybe these same men in those lifetimes came back and reincarnated into Germans who were Nazis who used Jewish/humans for dire experiments during WWII.

Also, I know that the Atlanteans were quite advanced scientists. They knew cloning and genetics. On numerous trips back there as a shaman, I saw centaurs (half man/half horse) and understood that they were a genetic experiment undertaken (and successful) by Atlantean scientists. And that, in part, was why Atlantis was destroyed – it had become purely male/out of balance, they were going against the strict laws of Nature and so it was destroyed and everyone started all over again with the world we now have – which is known as the fourth world, from a metaphysical perspective (Lemuria was the first world, Mu, the second world, Atlantis the third world; the world of today is the fourth world and between 2000 and 2012 we are to move into the fifth world, which is the world of the heart/compassion and a thousand years of peace – if we do it right. Otherwise, the fourth world will be destroyed and we'll start over again ... as we have done before – until we get it 'right', learn to work within the Cosmic laws and constructs that are ruled by the heart/compassion toward everything and everyone on this planet.

As I said, this was SO repugnant to me that it turned my stomach. The idea of half animal and half human was, in part, what the bacterium was showing me back in Atlantis. The bacterium said that Atlanteans had created half animal/human species and that was when it was created – to stop this, in a sense, through sex acts (or not)...

The sex act of this journey isn't really about sex as much as it is disempowerment of the person (man or woman) and that was another theme of the Gonorrhoea bacterium. Women are always at the receiving end of males who conspire/trick/manipulate a woman into having sex with them that is selfish and self-serving only to the man. In this instance, this is where the Gonorrhoea bacterium would appear to stop that by infecting either the man or woman – to make them stop, think about what they did; the choices they made and perhaps learn from this (because they caught a disease) and would think twice before entering into the same kind of circumstance to have sex again. Unless it is rape, a woman still has *choices* to make. She *can* say 'no' but the sense I got from this bacteria is that women who are used/victimized are easily manipulated and 'conned' into having sex for selfish gratification only of the male who is wanting it/something from her. She still plays a role in this and the bacterium knows this (not a judgment but a logical fact) and so the woman becomes equally 'at fault' in this 'game' that is being played but for reasons that are different from the male who is selfishly pursuing her for sexual/selfish gratification.

... she showed me men *and* women partying; showed me only women partying and only men partying – it was like flashes of movie screen frames; so the idea of homosexuality was presented here but without any judgment – that it is a *natural* part of the fabric of life.

Shamanic Journey into Chicken Flu Virus

Eileen Nauman, 2006

I was covered by my master guide in an emerald green suit that would protect me when I went in search of the chicken flu virus. My master also gave me many feathers, very colourful, from many species of birds and he told me to take this as a gift to the virus. My master had blessed these feathers and said it would act as a sacred gift that would encourage the virus to receive me and hopefully, answer my questions.

When we took off, we went into outer space. I was confused. I asked my guide where we were going. My guide said that the chicken virus, the original one, lived on a comet out in space that circled the solar system sun. Stunned, I said, 'Oh.'

We landed on a lumpy looking greyish piece of ice/comet. It was out in deep space and it was dark all around us. I could see the sun; a mere gold spot in the fabric of the night surrounding us.

My guide told me to lay out the feathers in the Vesica Pisces symbol – two circles that overlap one another in the centre. I did so, again stymied and thinking that this was really different from my other encounters with other viruses. But, I did as I was told.

When done laying out the feathers, it looked like a colourful rainbow of two circles overlapping in the centre. Then, my guide instructed me to stand in the overlap area. This, I did. At that moment, I heard a small, squeaky voice and it said that I was welcome. Looking around, all I could see was greyish, dirty ice and pebbles of all kinds stuck in the surface. Again, it spoke. And this time, I saw a small, indiscriminate pebble that was slightly hourglass shaped (greyish/blackish and nothing outstanding or spectacular about it) near one of the circles. I saw a sparkle; as if it were mica in the pebble. I realized that the stone was speaking to me.

I leaned down and introduced myself and I asked if the chicken virus was in the rock. It laughed and said yes, this was its real home. It invited me into the rock where it lived. I went in.

The virus was a shimmering, small, silver being; tiny but scintillating. It said that originally, its home, the comet, was much larger than it was today. The virus showed me that the comet had come near earth in one particular path and about half of it broke off due to gravity and showered in a show of lights through the atmosphere. Bits of the comet landed in the time when Earth was only water. The virus then made its home in the water and later, attached itself to a fish, which then became a small land dinosaur, which then became a member of the bird family that we know today.

The virus said that it has been around since Earth's creation. It lives within all birds on the planet. Over time, as a virus, it infected all species of birds on the planet. I asked what its job was. It said it was to cull the weak and sick of any bird species and return them to the light. It did not see itself as 'killing' anything; rather, performing a service to those whose time was up in a physical form and returning it back to the Source of Light to rest and enjoy themselves on another dimensional level.

I asked the virus if it had ever infected humans before and it said no. It said it had never done so but that the air was so polluted and that humans were doing so much damage to the world and all species that the order went out for it to begin to change so that it could move into human bodies and into their lungs. Air is the key to this virus. It says it rules the air and everything in it. Birds/air/lungs and breathing are all a part of this virus' motif.

I asked if it was going to make the jump to humans and it said that it would. It would cull the weak and old within the human chain of life just as it did in the realm of bird life. There was no sense of malice or revenge in the virus. It was just a matter-of-fact statement of its job in our dimension.

I asked if there was anything we could do to stop it from making the jump. It laughed and said, "Clean up my air." But the virus felt it was too late for that, and that it would move into humans sooner or later. I again asked if there was anything we could do to not be infected by this virus.

It said that people who tried to not pollute the Earth would be spared. The Vesica Pisces symbol could be put on the door of a house and the virus would honour the sacredness and not inhabit the house or the people who lived in it. I asked the virus why this symbol was important to it. It said that where the circles overlap, it looks like a fish; and it was the fish of the sea in prehistoric times, that it lived within. This brought to mind the Bible when Moses warned the Pharaoh that if he didn't let the Jews go that he'd unleash epidemics and an angel who would slay the first born son in every household. And, Moses was told by the Angel of Death that if the Jewish people would paint the blood of a newly slain lamb over their door, that the angel would pass them by and not harm them.

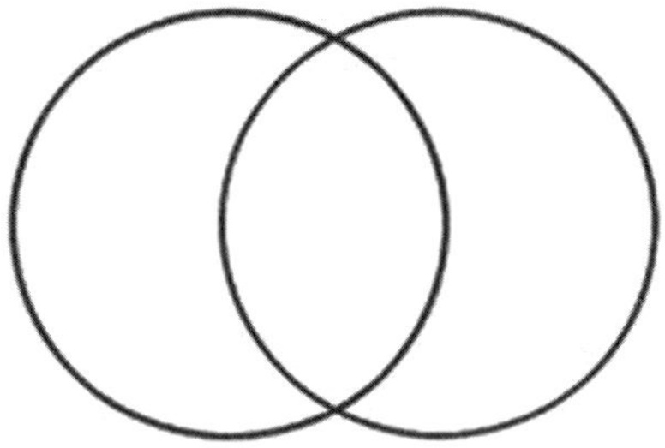

Fig. Vesica Pisces

I thought this was an interesting turn of events; since each virus seems remarkably different in pattern and personality. This virus is very proud that it lives in the bodies of all birds of the world. It loves the air and it loves to fly and the movement of flying. That would explain the movement of a comet – never still – always moving in some way, shape or form.

I thanked the virus for the audience and left. I found this virus very light, jovial, talkative and in a good mood. The other viruses I've visited were *heavy* feeling. This one was not. Perhaps, like the bird bones, which are hollow, making them lighter than air, this virus was very similar in that respect. Light. And happy. There was no sense of judgement by the virus on what was going on with humans; it simply was responding to an order to do what it does.

(End of journey)

Journey to Lyme Disease – the Spirochete in the Gut of the Tick

Eileen Nauman, 2006

I was taken on what looked like a repeat procession of Mother Earth, one after another. As we saw them, perhaps thirty or forty of them, we came to the one Earth at the end of this semicircular procession. It was the age of dinosaurs. I was taken to a small insect that lived back in that time. It was red with darker spots on a hard-shell outer body. It looked like a rhinoceros beetle in the head. It was all red. I asked it what it was. It said it was the first tick on the Earth. I thought that was pretty cool. Then, I asked about the disease that was in the gut of the tick. He said that yes, he carried it, but that I needed to speak to someone about it in our day and age.

We fast-forwarded to the USA. We came to New Hampshire. There was a beautiful forest for as far as the eye could see. We flew down into this forest. I found a tick sitting on a piece of wood on a bush. I asked if I could talk to it. It replied that I needed to talk to the Queen Deva Tick. I said, "Oh, that's great. Where is she?" At that moment, in the centre of the forest, I saw a beautiful bluish-white tick that was the Deva Tick. She was large and glistening and beautiful. She towered above the trees and was huge. I came to her, introduced myself and told her what my needs were. I asked if she could help me in my understanding of Lyme Disease. I could feel her smile. There was a kindness about her. A regal quality.

She said yes, she could answer my questions. I asked if she carried a Spirochete inside her body that would cause harm to humans. She said yes she did. I asked why this was so. What was the purpose behind this?

She said that long ago, when the forests of the Earth were pristine, whole and stable, ticks never infected two-legged ones. They were part of the ongoing natural balance of the forests/woodlands/jungles of the world. When Man began to come into the forest to take wood/trees/slash, cutting/hunting of wildlife – the 'take, take, take' that humans can do, then the ticks were asked to come forward and become a *defence* to try and maintain the balance of Nature within the forests. This is their mission: to maintain and preserve what is left of our forests and woodlands that Man continues to destroy without thought or care. The Deva Tick said man allows his dog to enter the forest without thought of others. Dogs need to learn boundaries and a respectful behaviour; but dogs, she said, mirror the human being. So, ticks will leap upon a dog, the dog carries the tick home and Man will find it and infect himself. Or, the tick will leap upon the human himself and infect him (or her).

The Deva Tick was concerned with Man's selfishness, insensitivity and inability to realize what he is doing. This 'taking' attitude, that all things belong to Man alone, is wrong, she says. She made the point that many humans lived in harmony with the forests in the other times/ages/epochs, until recently. She showed me the last three earths. She said that humans from these civilizations saw the forest as a by-product to be used, to make money, and to take from – but never give back to.

I asked Deva Tick if I could see or talk to the Spirochete directly and she said yes, enter her body. I did so at her request. When I moved into Deva Tick, it was warm, dark and humid within her. And then, I saw an orange/yellow light ahead. I saw a roundish Spirochete with lots of little yellow hairs all over its body. I saw craters and holes in the circular Spirochete. He had yellow, bulging eyes. I saw that he was mostly orange coloured, but I could see some red and some yellow come and go all over his spherical shape. I introduced myself and told him why I was there and asked if he would be willing to talk to me.

He was very friendly and said of course. I asked what his mission was: his reason for being was with regard to us human beings. He said that once on Earth was the Garden of Eden. He said he was using this concept or idea not as a religious theme, but rather one that would apply in general to all two-leggeds nowadays. He said at one time, the forest was a natural cycle in and of itself. Everything and everyone was in balance. They were, quite literally, Gardens of Eden.

And then Man decided to be supreme and thought he could go into the forest to kill a duck, a deer or other animals without first asking permission if they could enter the forest, much less take a life in the forest. The Spirochete said that hunters took without giving a gift. Without asking for the animal to give up its life so that they could eat and continue to live. The Spirochete said that Man disregarded all the respectful protocols that used to be in place. It used to be, the Spirochete told me, that when Indians went to hunt in the forest, they gave gifts of food, offered prayers and asked permission to come into it in the first place. Secondly, the Spirochete said, the Indian who was a designated hunter, went to a sweat lodge and cleansed himself body and soul before a hunt. Then, the medicine man or woman would give the hunter a special song to call a deer or whatever animal the hunter needed. This song was sung. The right animal answered the call of the song. The hunter then asked the deer for permission to take its life and the deer would give it. Afterward, the Spirochete said, the hunter offered prayers to the spirit of the deer to take it over to the Other Side, thanked it for its service and unselfishness so that the hunter's people could continue to survive.

You see, the Spirochete said, all of this give-and-take respect, is lost today. Hunters go in and take without asking. There are no prayers, no song, and no awareness about balance any longer. Man has encroached upon and is destroying the last preserves of forests around the world, so the Tick People have become the front line defence to stop these hunters, these people who go into the forest to take without giving, and drive them off – at least here in the USA.

I said I understood. I asked what the Spirochete did inside a human. It said that it basically did the same thing that a hunter did when it killed an animal without honouring it, or asking permission to take its life – it made the person feel very tired, feet very heavy, and the life energy slowly, like blood oozing from a bullet wound, flowed out of the person's aura. Over time, the Spirochete said, it would cause the person to stiffen because in death, all joints in a deer stiffened. In other words, the person began to die as if a hunter had shot a deer – the same response is reflected in the human body as it was in the deer's body: tiredness, exhaustion, physical malaise, stiffening up of joints so they could not move. And the Spirochete didn't want these people coming back into the forest; they wanted them incapacitated so they would stop defiling the forest and taking instead of reciprocating as it should be.

I asked the Spirochete about this Garden of Eden concept. It glowed a bright orange colour and seemed very happy to discuss this. The Tick Nation is part of the Garden of Eden/forests/jungles and woodlands of the world. They are a natural part of the fabric and part of the natural balance of it. When there is give-and-take, when there is honouring by the human to the spirits and guardians of the forests/woodlands, then the Tick people will leave this person alone. Why? Because this person honours and respects the forest and its natural cycle and way of being. They will not infect a person who comes into the forest/woodlands with respect, caring, offering (seeds, grain, cornmeal, tobacco), and a sense of being in a special place of healing. And, the Spirochete said, the forests and woodlands of the world are the last great preserve of natural healing energy from Mother Earth to all her relations, including humans. As more humans destroy the forests/woodlands, they destroy the balance that Mother Earth must have in order to survive.

One of her ways of surviving is asking the Tick Nation to become defenders of the forests/woodlands by infecting the humans who come to destroy it or inhabit it selfishly.

I asked about this Garden of Eden when a person was infected by the Spirochete. Was there any good outcome or reason that while infected it could in some way help the human be a better human being? The Spirochete smiled, very pleased with the question.

It said that when a person was too weak to move, that the human had time to discover his or her own Garden of Eden within. Usually, the people who come to destroy the forest/woodlands have a very low opinion of themselves, the Spirochete said. By infecting a person, they give them the opportunity to look at their own inner resources of their own Garden of Eden that everyone carries within them.

I asked symbolically what that could mean to a human. The Spirochete said that every human is endowed with creativity. It is the creativity that Great Spirit has given to all things. When, the Spirochete said, the person discovers their own inner beauty, their own uniqueness to be who they are, the creativity that is theirs alone, then the Garden of Eden springs to life within them. The Spirochete glowed. And then, he said, that as this person has the time to cultivate their own inner garden of possibilities, of respect for themselves, at some point, this is going to be reflected out into the world around them.

At that point, the Spirochete said, this person has had the time to move into themselves, to see themselves differently, to make adjustments or changes, and cultivate the garden of themselves. They will then see everything, even the forest/woodlands, differently. They will begin to respect that which they hadn't before. They will look upon the forest and understand that it is not to be continually destroyed by Man. They will take steps to save the forest instead - in large or small ways. One thing a person who survives Lyme Disease will do, is never look at the forest/woodlands the same way. And that, the Spirochete said, is the best that can be gotten out of this kind of situation.

Instead of this person being arrogant, wilful, disrespectful of others, they learn the opposite. They learn not to destroy, rather to cultivate. This Garden of Eden concept within an individual is the gift that the Spirochete gives to someone who has contracted Lyme Disease. It is the best that can be hoped for. And, perhaps these people who contract the disease have never honoured what they have or bring to the table of life; perhaps they've always deferred themselves away to stronger people who may appear more confident or in authority. The Spirochete said that with imprisonment comes reflection. If we are imprisoned in a body stiff and not moving, we have much time to think and look inward; to get in touch with our Garden that is always there - but rarely looked for. And this Garden of Eden is there in everything and everyone, the Spirochete said. As you cultivate your own, inner garden of awareness, deepening spirituality with Mother Earth and revealing of your gifts you have, you are less likely to destroy the gardens out in your world, aren't you?

I asked the Spirochete that if hunters would show respect by asking permission to go into the forest, to ask permission to hunt and kill something, if the Tick Nation would find this acceptable. He said they would. It is a start. But the Spirochete was far more adamant about the *loss* of forest/woodlands and its destruction of balance that Mother Earth needed in order to stay as a functioning being. Humans are destroying these sacred groves around the world. The Spirochete also said that in different forests/woodlands around the world, different bacteria, virus and other beings, were defending them as well. The Tick nation was not the only one doing this, on the front lines as defenders of the forest/woodlands that are left.

I also felt that perhaps people who contracted Lyme Disease had been taken *from*. That is to say: they were the person in the family who gave, gave, gave and were never regarded with respect or equality. And the family took from this individual without respect or regard for them. Perhaps a convenient whipping post for the family dynamic. Or, perhaps this person had a type of personality where they gave, gave, gave until they gave too much and didn't know when to stop and pull back. This person does not know how to say NO, to protect his or her own boundaries. Poor boundaries, in other words, because Lyme Disease, according to the Spirochete is all about strong boundaries, i.e., the boundary of the forest as an example – of stopping people who come to steal/take/disrespect or alter the fabric of the natural environment in some way. This Spirochete could be drawn to takers who are selfish and insensitive to anyone but themselves, but also, the other end of this spectrum, people who give away their life blood, their energy, literally and they don't know where to stop, where a healthy boundary exists.

I believe, from talking with the Spirochete, that these personality types can both attract the Lyme Disease.

I asked the Spirochete about two others that it worked with. He said that they were subordinate to him (the spirochete), but that they each had duties similar to what he had outlined above. And they worked with their human counterparts in all these areas of application. After all, the Spirochete said, that is the number three and that is the number of creation: the mother + father = child. And the Garden of Eden is about the innate creativity that each and everything on the face of and within Mother Earth, has.

(End of journey)

Discussion

On discussing the journey the following came up:

The ticks carrying the spirochete are parasites, as are the spirochetes themselves. They suck off others without permission. They are takers. The boundary issue is very powerful because what do parasites do? They pick on the weak and the open/vulnerable who can't say no or are not able to erect the proper boundaries to stop it from taking from them – poor immune response or perhaps a lowered immune response, too – or, breaking down the boundaries/barriers of the immune system, perhaps, is a more appropriate way to say it here concerning this character.

Eileen: As a shaman, I see these types all the time. We call them psychic vampires and parasite would be another word to describe what they do, too. Most are victims without boundaries and feel helpless and have no confidence in themselves nor do they believe they have what it takes to get out of their victim life (although all of this is mostly in an unconscious and subconscious way). Psychic vampires are different from a sorcerer ... but both do the same thing ... they 'feed' off the energy/aura of other people without their permission. The only thing that separates one from the other is that a psychic vampire/victim does it unconsciously and will suck off anyone who allows it to happen to them (again, mostly an unconscious process) whereas a sorcerer does it with knowing, conscious intent. They know how to *hook* (looks like a fishhook) into an unknowing person's chakra (usually the solar plexus, although the navel/sacral chakra is often chosen, too) and then they begin to 'suck' life energy (prana) out of the person's chakra/etheric layer of their aura on either a 24, 48 or 72 hour cycle. And when they suck, the person gets these symptoms:

- exceedingly tired, will complain of being tired, will use the word exhausted
- will want to go to sleep, to nap
- may complain of a headache, dizziness or malaise or just not 'feeling well' but there is no key acute symptom they can point too.

This vampirism by either the victim or the sorcerer yields the *same* set of symptoms. The only difference is the victim isn't aware of what he or she is doing and the sorcerer certainly is.

Now, I find with Lyme Disease (the chronic fatigue factor) exceeding exhaustion and tiredness. And this is very much like being sucked dry ... so it begs the question: does the person who has CFS/Lyme Disease have a vampire-victim relationship with their spouse/relatives/children or are they in a job that is doing it? It still comes down to a person who feels helpless to say no, helpless to defend themselves, helpless to do anything but get used and abused by another person/place/thing/situation ... therefore, they get sucked dry of their auric/pranic energy and it is no wonder they are in a cycle of terrible, ongoing exhaustion.

So, this Spirochete is about boundaries for sure – in every way. This character sees himself protecting, i.e., erecting a boundary, to save the forests to save Mother Earth. It does not see its actions as parasitical at all. I find this fascinating. But then, you know, every human being is just like this – we like to think we are heroes doing something good for whatever our reasons (justified or not, right or not ...), and we overlook or ignore our other darker, less healthy tendencies that are in the extreme other direction.

What is the other end of the heroic hero but the villain? So, when I talked to this Spirochete, it was showing me its heroic side – no less like a human ... I mean, after all, are you going to tell another person how *bad* you are? Your weaknesses? Your dark side? I think not. And I think this Spirochete, when I visited it, was showing me its 'good' side, its heroic side, and what it does to help (not harm). Fascinating to me. I did not get the sense from this Spirochete that it was necessarily a highly evolved spiritual being either ... so maybe this is why it only showed me it's good/heroic side ... So, it does attack but sees it as justified and defending (i.e. the hero saving the world) ... never mind that it's a parasite looking for hapless/helpless victims to infect.

Harry: The Borrelia spirochete causing Lyme has a bit of the same nature as the Chlamydia causing parrot's disease. Also the ticks that carry them just take. They jump on an animal or human and suck their blood. Giving nothing in return except Lyme disease if they carry the spirochete inside of them.

I have wondered what the advantage is for Borrelia to attack a human body in the way it does. Usually, not always, it will start with a rash. From there it can go to rather vital organs. Knee joints preventing walking. Nervous system. Brain. Heart. It slows down a person in many ways. This idea that it helps to find a source within is interesting. Parasites are missing a source within, so they only take.

Eileen: interesting – you know the character I was talking with looked like a rash – the changing of the colour – red with dots, I believe ... the colour of it was mainly red, which is symbolic of eruptions/skin, to me, of *anger*, vitality/energy, aggressiveness/ assertiveness. And of course, this parasite is aggressive and sucks the vitality/energy out of a person. But, moving along this line of thinking, when I see *red* things, like this Spirochete, I think of anger. And as a homeopath, I often see *anger* as a basic foundation of dis-ease. What I'm trying to say is that if we suppress/repress *anger*, it can sit and fester and cause dis-ease. High blood pressure, for example. Lung problems where we don't speak out what anger (or injustice) we have experienced ... In other words, my question to all of you is: are Lyme victims really sitting on a powder keg of unresolved/repressed/suppressed *anger* that they've never discharged or released or spoken of or given voice too?

I know many, many women who sit on their anger/rage because in our world today, women aren't allowed to express their anger – but it's okay that a man does ... and consequently, this rage builds and festers and poisons the woman from the inside out. I see a lot of anger in *depression*, but I also wonder if it isn't one of the key elements of the human that sets them up to receive Lyme disease as a way to express/discharge this rage? Better out than in, as I say. If the rage/anger is expressed, people get well.

But a victim ... and here's where I see it really being important ... a victim never is able to express this rage/anger ... and so they draw (like draws like, like cures like) a violent/angry/ aggressive being to them, to help them catalyse and get rid of their rage/anger ... in this case, the Spirochete which is a parasite, which takes ... and the victim feels taken from continually too ... like always attracts like in my world as a shaman ... I see it all the time.

If we have grown up in an abusive household what do we do as an adult? We draw an abusive spouse. We abuse our children. Like draws like. This is another example of this in action.

But, back to our Lyme Disease person. I believe that they are victims and victims do draw parasites; it's the perfect dance. Victims have no voice, no way to express their needs, much less their latent anger, so they have no boundaries, no way to say "no" to break this helpless victim cycle. The Lyme disease parasite is there to help them do that. After a while you get so tired (bad pun here) of being tired that you get taken down to your essence ... where you have a choice ... you either surrender yourself over to a higher power and therefore, get the healing you require, or you give up and die.

I have seen this scenario play out again and again.

Many of us must be brought to our knees, learn how to surrender, and keep a faith that our surrendering, when we have nowhere else to turn ... is the right and healthy thing to do.

However, we don't realize this consciously, so we must play out this dance unconsciously, but get taken down to our knees where, finally, we do surrender.

And I'm not saying all people surrender or make the correct choices here. Many do not ... and they continue in this pattern of weakness/helplessness/ and mire of human suffering. One of the things we're supposed to learn on a spiritual level is the power of faith alone. And this is a tough one for us to learn – it may take 100s of lifetimes to get this. But one way we get it is to be brought down – completely – and Lyme Disease does do this, as other chronic diseases certainly can, too. When we're in the bottom of our personal barrel, when we are in the utter Dark Night of the Soul, this is when we reach out in faith to a higher power/being for help, because we realize we cannot fight this, erect the proper barriers or pull ourselves up by our own bootstraps. This is when we realize we need another/we need help.

Part of a victim's returning to health is the ability to reach out and *ask for help*. By surrendering, it is a plea for help. And again, all of this is generally unconscious in an individual. By giving over, we open up the possibility of our healing to come to us ... reaching out, asking on whatever level we do ... and help always comes.

Harry: the image of takers and the other side, those that have been sucked out by others, seems very appropriate to me. Lyme is connected to the Ericaceae like *Ledum* and *Kalmia*. These plants usually live under hard conditions, like heather. Living on sand and trying to get enough from this poor depleted soil to be able to exist. So a kind of poverty consciousness, 'I do not have enough', is connected to them.

Following some information from Anton Kramer on Ericaceae:

> "If we collect the common symptoms of Lyme disease from reports in the conventional medical literature, we can begin to construct a group anamnesis of the disease, in order to identify the most likely remedies for the disease Genus ...
>
> We can take these common symptoms of Lyme disease, obtained from the population affected and treated as if of one person; and repertorize this list, to find:
> *Kalmia* and *Ledum* lead the analysis. Intriguingly, Kalmia latifolia (Mountain Laurel) and Ledum palustre (Labrador Tea) are closely botanically related, both belonging to the botanical family Ericaceae; the Heath family.
>
> A small-remedies weighting brings up several remedies poorly represented in our literature. Notably, *Rhododendron chrysanthum* – another Ericaceaed – moves up to fourth position.
>
> The algorithms used in the Vithoulkas Expert System bring out *Ledum* as the remedy bearing closest similitude to this group anamnesis. *Kalmia* and *Rhododendron* make good showings in this analysis as well. Leading the list of "very small remedies" here is *Gaultheria procumbens* (wintergreen, teaberry) – a fourth member of the Ericaceaed family.
>
> Whereas *Ledum* may have a slow and long-continued pace (reflected in its presence in the rubric Perspiration – long-lasting), these remedies as a group – including Ledum – are characterised by periodic and alternating symptoms. This actually is a rather interesting aspect of the general similitude of this group of remedies to the characteristic pace, or development over time, of Lyme disease."

Richard Pitt: Thanks so much for all your work and thoughts on the Lyme phenomenon. It has given me much to think about here. A few thoughts I have: The Borrelia spirochete is a bacterium – a tenacious one at that – whereas the co-infections of Babezia (another tick bite disease) are parasites. Some initial distinction is useful here as it may help in understanding the complexity of the symptom picture of this condition – from the initial inflammatory stage – perhaps more the bacteria effect – to the secondary more chronic debilitative conditions – perhaps more the parasitic effect.

I think exploring both individual and collective stories of the susceptibility to Lyme is useful. The notion of victim-hood is perhaps important. It could explain that those infected may have nothing to do directly with the exploitation and abuse of nature, the forests and all that lives in there, but still are bearing the responsibility for the collective guilt that we humans have created. Otherwise, I think that those most responsible for the abuse of the forests would be most infected whereas I don't think this is the case.

It makes sense also purely from a point of view of the natural balance of nature that through "inevitable" exploitation of natural resources, the fragile biological balance is disturbed, leading to the proliferation of viruses, bacteria and other "phenomena" that then wreak their effect on humans (and other animals). Similar ideas regarding the spread of Ebola have been put forward, and also AIDS. The man-made possibility of the spread of the virulent form of Lyme Disease is also well documented (in a book *Lab 245*), which documents that ticks were being experimented on as vectors of disease for biological warfare, and then leaked out!

This is not dissimilar to various AIDS-related theories. No doubt, any of this kind of ignorant behaviour will have consequences. With Lyme disease now, it has spread throughout the USA, Europe and many other countries. It does seem that the more virulent modern form of the disease spread originally in the USA, perhaps reflective of the prevailing dynamic of cultural antagonism with the natural world, more so than we find in Europe. Here, the earth is still something to be tamed, controlled, exploited and abused, the traditional literal Judeo-Christian relationship to the natural world. In Europe, we've done that and perhaps are beginning to think differently.

There is evidence now that the disease can also spread through sex, and the tick is no longer the only vector for the disease. From a miasmatic point of view, it looks very like a variation of the syphilitic miasm, the destructive dynamics of human consciousness finding another expression and yet further confrontation with the planet – one that is still angry with the earth for having deserted us, leaving us all alone and yet now with tools with which to really do some damage.

The question as to why some people are more likely to be chronically infected than others is interesting. In four of my cases in which there are really serious complications of the disease, the victim dynamic is strong in situations that are both acute and chronic; experiences of being on the receiving end of some abuse. However, in these people, they are not weak, they are tenacious and are fighters, resisting with a great struggle.

Shamanic Journey on Malaria

Eileen Nauman, 2006

I was told by my teacher not to go inside the Malaria. Instead, remain outside of it to speak to it; otherwise, I may become infected energetically with this being. We flew off to the jungles of Africa. There, we met a female mosquito. I asked if I could go inside her to contact the Malaria protozoon. She asked if this process would harm her and I said no, that it would not. She gave me permission.

What I saw when I entered her abdomen was a yellow-green, egg shaped protozoon with cilia or hair sticking out all over it. It reminded me of a porcupine in full quill array and in a defensive position. Or, maybe a land mine with all the spikes sticking out all over it. I have no idea of what it looks like under a microscope, but will try to find out after the journey. I was struck by the symbolic shape of it; oblong, like an egg. And the cilia or 'hair' all over it reminded me of the aggressive, restless nature that it has. I don't know if under a microscope the protozoon is like this, or its 'real' colour.

The protozoon was scrambling around, ceaselessly, restless and always moving. I asked if I could talk to it and it said yes. At no time did the protozoon remain still or quiet; always moving. Restlessness was key with this protozoon; always moving. There was a lot of aggressive feeling to it, as well, but not threatening.

I asked the protozoon what its function with human beings was. It said its job was to cull the weak and strengthen the species. The other job it had was to keep the population down by killing off those who contracted the malarial protozoon. It was very matter-of-fact about this; no judgment and no sense of anger or revenge in it.

The protozoon said it knew who to infect because he could see it (weakness) in the person's aura. It would direct the female mosquito to that person.

I asked what other things it could do for humans that was positive. It said that its cycle of symptoms and then no symptoms gave the person, when sick and hallucinating, information that they could later digest as they came up and out of the roller-coaster symptoms that are associated with it. It was a time of reflection, the protozoon said.

So it's chief reason for being was to cull the weak and reduce the population.

I asked about those who did not die, rather, they continued to have symptoms for years, on a cyclic timetable. Of what good could this be to this person?

The protozoon said that the immune system was strong enough so the person did not die, but that it gave them an opportunity to have information come up – from their past or present – to work on. When sick, the protozoon reminded me, a human has a lot of time on their hands to think and feel through things. The protozoon feels in these individuals it is an opportunity to work through blocks/wounds/suppressed or repressed energy and release it. The protozoon sees its job here as positive and healing on many levels.

(End of journey)

Discussion

Comment Peter: Yes, that makes sense, when we are weakened it is easier to touch and connect to our inner state that we suppress when strong. I was wondering about the possibility that malaria creates struggle in order to succeed as in *China* Materia Medica and if its purpose was also to wake people up from a sort of unconsciousness?

Eileen: absolutely, I guess I wasn't saying this too well. The whole idea of aggressiveness was to 'shake up' the individual. This protozoon saw it as his (and I should add here it is a *male* protozoon energy only) that when contracting malaria – it is a time to dig deep into yourself – God knows – you'll have the time to do it. But the protozoon made it clear that it was in the hallucination stage that the *unconscious* of the person could *talk* to the conscious person – hallucinations are often symbols – and we know our unconscious talks in a language of symbols to us – look at our dreams, as an example.
The malaria's job, as he sees it is to 'wake you up', shake you up – aggressively by shocking you, I suppose, with these roller coaster symptoms. And by shaking you up – you 'get out of the way' and your unconscious can then speak to you more directly. The protozoon made a point of telling me the hallucinatory stage was an entrance to getting deeper into one's self for healing purposes. Even disease serves as a teacher for us. And a door opener. And malaria's modus operandi is a big door opener.

Comment Eileen: actually none of them are yellow-green (as they looked in the journey) but for the most part they are egg-shaped. There doesn't appear to be hair or cilia all over it – but frequently I see these things because they are important to the nature of the individual, or in this case, a protozoon.
The yellow is indicative of the Solar Plexus chakra and it has rulership over a person becoming an individual and leaving their 'tribal roots' to explore the possibility of becoming unique. Most of the places where Malaria is are very nuclear family type of situations and they are about community and tribe vs. the free will of the individual. So, perhaps the people who become infected either need to develop a sense of individuality or they are having trouble detaching or disconnecting from the tribal mindset to start down that path toward Individuation?
The green is indicative of the Heart chakra and I wonder if people who become infected have suffered grievous 'heart' shock or trauma – perhaps the loss of a loved one? A parent? Been abandoned by the family of origin? Loss of a spouse? Divorce? Loss of entire family or part of it to disease or war?

Harry: what is known from research is that people get malaria more easily when leaving their home village or when returning there. So going in or out of the family/village/tribe seems to be a clear issue making the person more susceptible to falling ill with malaria. It reminds me of something we may all have observed in ourselves and others, that patterns change when leaving home and that coming back to the family home brings them all back within a split second. It's like entering a magnetic field and the compass needle can't help but turn. This change can be experienced positively or negatively of course. In tribal cultures with extended families (you'll be amazed how many friends and relatives an African meets if you travel with them) leaving the village and tribe is a much bigger thing than in Western culture.

Eileen: The protozoon's cilia or hair reminds me of someone who is very highly threatened, is very defensive and believes that a good defence means a good offence: 'attack first, ask questions later' mindset. And so, perhaps people who are infected with Malaria become more aggressive? Are more restless? Cannot sit still? And they mirror what I saw in the journey to the Malaria protozoon?

Shamanic Journey to Tuberculosis

Eileen Nauman, 2006

I received permission to journey to talk to the Tuberculosis bacteria. I was taken down into the Earth, to a secret and sacred place known only to shamans. There, I met a pterodactyl (flying reptile) name Gzork. He was reddish-brown in colour with red eyes, telling me he was one of the original creations by the Creator and was very old and wise. Gzork said he would take me to the TB and I said fine. We flew from this sacred/secret place, up a tunnel deep within Mother Earth, into the air. We went to Australia, to Uluru, the oldest area of land that is not submerged under water. (I have been to Uluru for seven days and she is a huge, oval shaped (like an egg) red sandstone mountain that rises out of the 'red centre' as it is known – the red desert of Australia.)

When Gzork landed, he called the TB. I saw this beautiful, glowing silver being who reminded me of a hairy caterpillar. He was all silver with silver hairs, millions of them, all around his worm-like body. He came up and out of one of the caves of Uluru on the east side of her.

He was wavelike and flowing in front of me – towering hundreds of feet above me. I saw the undulations of his silver/hairy body and he was beautiful and I did not feel threatened by him. I asked if he could reduce in size so I could talk to him. He immediately became miniaturized like a small silver, hairy caterpillar the size of my palm next to where I sat on Uluru.

I asked TB what he was about. He said he was born of the wind and birds when Mother Earth was one piece of land (Gondwanaland is what the Geologists call this period of time on Earth when all continents were one. And Australia is the oldest recorded land from this period that is still above water. As the continents split and started drifting away, this one area, along with Uluru, who is considered the *heart* of Mother Earth, the *centre* of her, remained above water. The aboriginal people knew this and have, for millions of years, kept Uluru and this land around her sacred as a result of this memory's being verbally passed down through them to this day).

The TB said that at one time, long ago, humans were in connection and concert with every living thing. This was when the land was *one*. When the humans, both genders, decided they would not honour and respect all living beings, the *split* between them and all others, was created. I humorously said, is this the Adam and Eve story that was concocted? That Eve took the apple from the snake and God drove them from the Garden of Eden?

The TB replied that yes, the human story was about this time and what happened, but it was not the fault only of women; men were equally at fault in this decision to disconnect from all their relations and feel they were superior to them. When this occurred, the land/continents began to split.

Out of curiosity I asked the TB if Gondwanaland was the continent known as Lemuria. (In my training and knowledge, Lemuria was when humans were here in *one* form, joined and lived in harmony with all other beings created on Mother Earth.) TB said yes, it is called many names, but what is more important is to realize that all things were in *oneness*, together and connected and respect/honouring of the entire system of being was lived.

I asked TB how he was formed. He said he was formed within the lungs of a bird. That birds and the wind are his symbols, although he can lie in dry earth/soil/sand and the wind picks him up and scatters him into the air and then he can infect a human being.

I asked TB why he would infect a human being. He said he could settle in any part of a human's body, but he preferred the lungs. I asked why?

He said that his job was to teach the person to speak the *truth*, to speak up for themselves, to say how they feel, rather than suppress/repress this cry, this anger, this disgust, humiliation, shame or whatever other unhealthy human emotions that we stuff into ourselves and allow to sit there and boil quietly on an unconscious level.

TB infects people who have not 'given voice' to their feelings, or to their truth (and they allow others to run over them, manipulate them or beat them down verbally/emotionally/spiritually/ physically so that they remain *mute* and *silent*). TB's job when it settles in the lungs of a human being is to teach this person to 'give voice' to how they really feel, or to tell what really happened to them, or to stand up for their *truth*.

I said that many people in this country (USA) who contracted TB in the East came West to a dryer climate in hopes of getting rid of it. He said yes, and when the person left the environment where he/she could not give voice, that the move was actually a physical speaking of their truth. By moving they were saying, in effect, that they were not going to stay in the unhealthy environment where they had no voice, where they could not speak and be heard. By moving, this is a catalyst act of speaking without giving voice, but serving to give voice through action, instead; and those people who did this, often improved or were healed.

Some did not, TB said, for they dove back into the same pattern of behaviour instead of allowing the move to free them, to help them start a new life. Instead they give their voice/truth to others. Those that chose to go back into the same kind of environment, with the same kind of people/situation, then die of TB.

I asked TB what kind of climate it preferred. It laughed and said, "See where I live?" Indeed, the Red Centre is hot, dry, windy, sand/desert. TB said that it lives in the soil and relies on the wind to pick up the soil so that it can fly and move into a person's lungs. He said wind is his main conveyance. And that humans breathe wind into their lungs. He is about the wind and what it symbolizes. Without wind (breath) he reminded me, all things die.

I asked about his job in regard to a human being once he was in their lungs; what was he trying to get the human to do?

TB said that it was his job to get this person to stop, have time, to do nothing else (because if you can't breathe properly, you cannot go on living your life as you did, ignoring your pain/ your suppression/ repression of your voice/ your speaking up and communicating your needs or asking for help from others), that you will sit a lot and think. And TB wants this person to have the time to think, to unplug from their hectic outer life and go inwards to discover their beautiful life within themselves. TB said that if the person responds correctly to his invasion into their lungs, they will stop, become aware that not all is well, and take time out for themselves; to take this journey into themselves to discover what they must give voice to. They must tell the truth about themselves to themselves as well as others. That is his *real* job, he said: to make people slow down, stop, think, meditate and go inward on a journey of self-discovery.

As the person goes inward, because they now have the time to do it, TB hopes that the person will also realize their connection to others; that he or she must rely on others for help, to ask for help and in doing this, realize a greater conscious connection that we are all one. We are all connected to one another, whether we like it or not. By realizing this connection, we are now on a path to inner wholeness which will translate to the person's outside world. When this occurs, either consciously or unconsciously, TB leaves the person.

TB also said that it may drive the person to be alone, like a hermit in a cave, to hear and listen to their own inner voice of truth. That they may go to the mountains to be alone, in order to hear this voice within them. This, he says, is good and he supports such a *move*. Only by becoming still and stopping our frantic outer world, will we be able to hear the voice of our *true* selves, our own *truth* that is within us and that we must pursue this. If we do, TB will leave us alone.

TB says it will infect only people who are sitting on so much repression/suppression that they have not given 'voice' to. He said they could write it out, like a novel, dance it out, sing it out, speak it out or in some creative way, *discharge* this unhealthy stuff that is deep within us. By discharging it, he says he will leave them and they will heal.

I asked about TB infecting other parts of a human's body. His answer was that their work (their inner journey) was symbolic depending upon where he infected them. If it was in a bone, then the *foundation* of the person was the wound. Foundation for him and me meant the foundation of the parents/ being born through the mother, into a specific home environment that created suppression/ repression of some sort that has continued to infect the person's ability to have a foundation (skeletal) to enable achievement of their dreams/vision of what they wanted to do in this given lifetime. If the bones are involved, then that means the foundation is 'weak' and the person cannot achieve what they want; they are 'crippled' by weak bones and that cannot carry them in any way (on any level) to their goal/dream/vision. So, the wound is located in the family dynamic and growing up in a toxic environment that has wounded the baby/child's ability to stand on their own two feet, be independent, grow up to be independent and have the courage/fortitude/endurance to achieve his/her dreams or goals. With weak bones or bone infected by TB, the TB tells the person to look at their toxic family and maturing years because that is where the wound is. If the person will work with the family wounding, then the TB will leave his/her bone(s) because they have 'voiced their truth' and not continued to live with the darkness or shadow of unhealthy energy that they carried around with them either before birth or after birth. They have finally discharged it.

TB repeated that the wind is his friend, the main element that he works with in concert to move. He said he did infect the lungs of birds a long time ago; that is where he was born. Birds and winds are his symbols, he said. These are the two parties that he works with.

While I was talking with him, I noticed TB was never still; as the tiny silver, hairy caterpillar, he was in constant, nonstop movement. Most often, he would form a circle with his head touching his tail, and he would go around and around and around in a circle. And sometimes he would look like a series of "s" and undulated around. But he never stopped moving.

TB loves the heat, the dryness and the desert. Uluru is his home. He lives there in spirit in one of the caves on the east side of Uluru where the sun rises first. The East, for us, is birth, the starting of something new (such as a new awareness, a new decision, a decision to move from one city to another or one state or country to another, as an example).

I found TB to be friendly, outgoing, but there was only him. I asked if he needed a lot of others of his bacterium type around or people around him and he said no, that even he, as a bacterium, was evolving. His journey, he said, as ours, was an inner journey of self-awareness and evolving to become whole and then *one* again. Therefore, he did not need a lot of outside friends or help. He glowed beautifully as he spoke of his inner journey within himself and I could feel his warmth, his love and sincerity as we spoke about this element about himself.

I thanked him for speaking to us. I took Gzork back to our sacred/secret place, thanked him for taking me to the TB bacteria.

(End of journey.)

Discussion

Comments Eileen: I felt that this ONENESS vs. the duality (the split that took place eons ago that made the gender male or female) is a strong theme of TB. I got the sense that TB was about working with the wounded element within ourselves. Jung said that within each man, was the feminine, and within each woman was the masculine. He said in order to be whole, you had to *integrate* these two energies that were within us. This, he called the *individuation* process that usually takes place, starting about age 40.

As an Eastern Cherokee metis (shamanic healer – the authors), I was taught that within us, our LEFT side symbolized the feminine and our RIGHT side symbolize our masculine. I was shown that the one that was wounded, where our 'work' was for a given lifetime, was the side that got the *most* injuries. For example, if you broke your left arm, leg, finger, collarbone, then you have female issues to work out; that your female energy side was your most wounded side and that was where the work was needed to heal yourself. That could mean issues with your mother, sister, female relative, your wife: your female boss would continue to bring you the lessons, to open up this wound, so that you could consciously begin to work on it. The feminine, at least for us, is about being creative and birthing things on all levels of ourselves; whether on the spiritual/mental/emotional or physical plane. It is about being receptive, learning to work with others, being a team and teammate, honouring what others say or have ideas/thought about other than your own, living in community and being responsible to the community, an awareness of more than just the "I" here, an awareness of the "we" and "us." The feminine, in its wounded extreme expression, can be a person who has the victim-mentality, poor me, lacking ability to assert herself (or himself), being weak, playing the bird with the broken wing routine, being manipulative or passive-aggressive. Why? Because the wounded feminine sees no way to confront and change his/her life, so they resort to subterfuge, to manipulate people/places/things to get what they want. Although, I must say that most people are highly unconscious of this, but progress can still be made through dreams, etcetera or meditation.

If we injure the right side of ourselves, i.e., our masculine/male side it means that we have issues with our father, our brother, another male relative, male friend, male boss or spouse. The masculine is about assertiveness, creating movement and chance to change our present third dimensional reality and manifest another reality that is our dream, vision or need. It is about being unafraid to confront another, to seize what you want, to go after what you want in some way, shape or form. At the same time, it is about learning about the 'I', the Ego, selfishness vs. unselfishness, learning to be alone, to go it alone without the help of others. And often, when moving into male energy, we all go to extremes first, before we come into the awareness and centre of this energy expression, where you learn to become a good leader and manager of not only yourself, but also others. Male energy is about holding the intent in a bowl of energy (the physical manifestation) long enough so that it can materialize and be realized in some form or format. That is the strength of the masculine energy expression. It is not only assertiveness, but intent to hold that energy so it can manifest and materialize. This is the finest expression of the masculine when done right. Otherwise, the masculine extremes become warlike, aggressive, assaultive, attacking, taking what they want, when they want, dictatorial, and all the things associated with males when they are out of balance.

Humans must come to terms with their wounded side, regardless of their gender, in my training. And they must address the wounded side, heal it and then, as Jung says, integration occurs.

TB is talking about going on the inner journey to give the person her/his 'voice' back for whatever is suppressed/repressed within them – (unhealthy human emotions/events experienced – shock/trauma/ a way of living that wounded an individual as a baby/child growing up, etcetera) – and working through it. As TB sees it, he comes along and infects the person to stop them and give them time to go inward because they have a lot of time on their hands and have little else to do. If you can't breathe well, you sit around a lot.

My analysis of this would be that TB is directly helpful to us in addressing our wounds, whether resulting in damage to our feminine energy or masculine energy within us, giving us the time to go inward to connect with these wounds, work on them, give them voice (as TB said, it could be through words like writing a book, a speech, writing a play, dancing, singing, or in some way discharging or working through the event/feeling(s), to release it from us, once and for all).

From my experience, people with lung, throat, sinus problems have what I call the "primal scream" that was never released – but should have been – but the person, for many reasons (conscious or unconscious) jammed it down into this particular part of their body where it has fermented, boiled and infected us on every level over time. When we release this 'scream' that is our right to do, we then cleanse ourselves inwardly, give voice to the pain of our experience/trauma/shock/unfairness that occurred from in utero onward to this moment in our life. By doing so, we release the deadly, unhealthy energy that has kept this wound from being healed. By 'screaming' or 'giving voice' to our *truth*, we can then begin our path to wellness with this particular wound.

If a person has throat problems or symptoms, this means that the primal scream is lodged there – it is higher up than the lungs, so this is a good sign that the person is trying to discharge it (consciously or unconsciously).

If the person has sinus problems or symptoms, this means that the primal scream is lodged there. It is higher up than the throat or lungs, so this is a good sign that the person is trying to discharge it and is much closer to doing it (consciously or unconsciously).

As a shaman, I can watch the energetic discharge of any event, trauma or shock to a person by its placement in a person's body, mental and spiritual fields. Sticking with the lungs – if it is deep within the lobes, versus higher up in the upper lobes - this shows a progression of energy movement up and out – in other words – releasing of the energy is on the *move* (another TB keyword). And this is a healthy sign that the Vital Force, the person is grappling with this issue (usually unconsciously) and it is moving towards release, i.e., up out of the lungs, through the throat, into the sinuses and finally, down into the mouth where it is "given voice."

Comment Harry: Hi Eileen, today I had the time to read the SRE on TB. Very interesting and it shows why TB is something of all times. Below I will print some comments I made on *Tuberculinum* in my book (*Miasms in Labour*). It seems to me there are certainly some parallels there with your SRE.

> "At first sight *Tuberculinum* seems hard to categorise within the concept of the theory of miasms. It seems to have traits of each miasm. As I said in my introduction, a linear model of the miasms and of the individuation process is a violation of truth, but since it is the best way for us to get some understanding of the process, it is the model we work with. Restricting ourselves to that linear reproduction my feeling is we need to anchor *Tuberculinum* in the psoric miasm first, and that the sycotic miasm is the next main station. So I place *Tuberculinum* between psora and sycosis. Why?
>
> What is striking in *Tuberculinum* is the restless impulse to change, to travel. He has a romantic, nostalgic streak, and is discontented with the place and circumstances he is in. There is a longing for a better place, which we can connect with the memory of the state of primal union. Paradise is lost, and *Tuberculinum* still has the hope to find it back. In this he reminds us of the archetype of the pure fool. Not hindered by any knowledge or any sense of danger he just walks into the wide world.
>
> - Discontented
> - Hopefulness
> - Desire to travel
> - Desire for change
> - Desire to wander from place to place
> - Sentimental
> - Audacity
>
> Instead of working on the development of skills in order to survive in this world, he wanders over the planet to re-find the gate to paradise. Hope is very strong in this remedy. He does not learn to adjust himself to his circumstances; he just leaves or behaves antisocially. This antisocial behaviour will especially be expressed when he is held back from following his nostalgic longing. He feels restricted by having to sit at the table, by having to go to school, by living always in the same house etc.
>
> - Destructiveness
> - Defiant
> - Disobedience
> - Wants to escape
>
> The psoric idea of shame we find in:
>
> - Dreams he is prude
>
> The restlessness of *Tuberculinum* can also be seen as an anticipatory fear for the next phase, sycosis, where the restrictions he is so sensitive to, will become even worse. As if as long as he is busy, runs

around and roams about he can prevent becoming fixed. The fixity comes nevertheless, as we can see expressed in the tubercles (sycotic growth); the tuberculosis that forces him to stay in bed for months or even years. Being confined to one spot, to move as little as possible, that is hell (sycosis) for *Tuberculinum*. There is nothing he can do to change this situation, but to keep quiet and endure it. (See under sycosis)

- Desire for activity
- Fear of consumption
- Fear before medical examination
- Hopelessness

Ultimately tuberculosis ends with death when the body is totally wasted. This is the reason why some say that the remedy is mainly sycotic (tubercles) and syphilitic (wasting). From the central idea of the remedy, I think the psoric root is very likely. When we discuss the syphilitic miasm later, it will become clear that this stage is not really reached by *Tuberculinum*. He does not come out of his fixed situation, with the hope that there is something worth fighting for. The wasting is more the end stage of sycosis, like when you confine a prisoner to the dungeons, and you don't feed him properly, at some point he will simply waste away. A hopeless situation in which the person has no powers whatsoever to change his situation. And the possession of one's power to fight one's condition is, in my understanding, a syphilitic element, and fixation without hope sycotic."

The process you describe of individuation starts with encountering one's shadow. Without doing this first the feminine and masculine side cannot come together to create. Speaking the truth has a lot to do with this. In the formation of the persona parts of our true nature are hidden there where we feel we cannot express these because they would not be accepted by our surroundings. Thus our shadow is formed including all kinds of hidden qualities we do not dare to express. The tubercular miasm might then indeed have to do with avoiding standing still and looking into the mirror. I like the expression of speaking one's personal truth that comes from the SRE. It is really about giving air, words, and wings, to what is experienced inside. And it is not about the truth in a metaphysical or spiritual way, but *your* truth, as you sense it inside of yourself. Great stuff Eileen. I love it.

Comment Eileen: Hi Harry, the joke here is: I've been very weak about my knowledge and understanding of miasms as individuals or as a lump sum of what they mean. So, to do SRE's on these bacteria/viruses/etc, I've really gotten a much better, more indelible understanding of them than I ever did from any book.

What I find fascinating is how they project their personality on me, as a shaman, symbolically and how it matches what you see as a miasm. So, this has certainly been a rewarding journey for me, too. I loved the info from your book – it sure matched the restlessness of the TB bacteria I talked to – always moving, never still. I didn't grasp the depth of what that meant until you sent the excerpt from your book.

The 'truth' isn't just an outer truth to TB as I spoke with it. This was about either being 'honest' deep within yourself, i.e., who are you? Where are you at? Are you happy? Are you going where you need to go? Are you reaching out for your dreams to fulfil them? Questions that require truth from within us. And of course, we all know we lie to ourselves – we aren't always truthful within ourselves for ourselves.

And this is what TB was getting at – the truth of speaking up and owning ourselves for where we were and where we saw ourselves going or what we wanted to become – and not being there – but being honest enough to admit and then making the internal changes to make it so. To pursue one's inner truth, or vision, dream, goal that one really wanted to work toward instead of lying to oneself and chasing what I call "Pie in the sky" kinds of dreams that never will come true. Another example of what I'm trying to say here and what TB meant was what I call the 'eternal dreamer' kind of person – you and I have all met this type of individual – they have all these grand dreams and ideas but they never have the elbow grease or hard work, the organization, discipline or endurance to set their dream into physical reality. You see, this is a basic *truth* of TB. TB wants the person to lie down and work for their vision. And if the person is the 'eternal dreamer' then TB can come and visit them ...

Final Notes on Shamanic Journeys

As said before, shamanic journeys may be too far out for you. If you nevertheless have read them we don't expect you to accept any of it. You can use PC Resonances without knowing or believing anything about them, and in the creation of PC Resonances the journeys were not used.

It was curiosity into the forces behind epidemic and infectious diseases that lead us to use this unorthodox approach of exploring them, and we are grateful to Eileen for her dedicated help.

We were interested in understanding the miasms to which these microorganism and their diseases are related, and in our experience the themes coming forward in the journeys often connect in a meaningful way with what we already know about them.

We have researched the topics covered in this book with an open mind. Knowledge is subject to continuous change so the truth of anything written on these pages is relative. The acid test to what is discussed though are the effects seen in cases in which PC Resonances have been used. Treating the many ways in which mankind is suffering has been and remains our driving force, so ultimately the effects in everyday practice is all that counts. This book results from the feeling that we have reached the point where we, from our experience and that of many colleagues, can conclude that the methodology we have used ever since 2002 is effective and valuable enough to recommend you to use it as well.

Appendix 4: The Inner Workings of Survival Instincts

The survival instincts are best understood by considering present day reptiles, which were around at the same time as dinosaurs. A reptile has bad eyesight, and sees movement clearest. When a reptile sees a movement, possibly a predator or prey, it first stays very still and by this strategy expects not to be seen, as that is its experience – this is the freeze response. Their next reaction is to run and get away (flight), or to attack if cornered (fight) and maybe kill and feast (eat) or subdue and have sex (sex).

There are five basic survival instincts that we have identified and call the 5Fs: Fight, Flight, Freeze, Food, F…sex/reproduction, which includes the usual three generally talked about in this context.

In play and sports the survival instincts can be observed and studied very well. Whatever can be observed there is true in other areas and concerns us all. We learnt a lot about the survival instincts by interviewing ice hockey players about what stopped them from performing well in ice hockey. So here we frequently reference what we found in ice hockey research and sports in general. We examined sports frequently during our research. Sports people, by pushing the limits of human endeavour, show all sorts of problems very clearly that are generally more hidden in the normal population.

As we can particularly observe in the animal kingdom, play is practice for the real thing. Lion cubs hunt each other; dogs run after the sticks we throw away and bring them back to us. Little boys in all cultures tend to fight in a playful way preparing them to become warriors. The other way around, play and sports has become an outlet with clearly set rules to ventilate aggression in society and avoid war. Children play hide and seek and many other games to practice survival skills.

Because the underlying phenomena of survival instincts are not recognized or understood many top athletes are still ridden with survival fears. It limits their careers. Yet it is what makes the difference between Olympic winners and losers. It is not technique, it is not stamina nor fitness; it is not nutrition, but survival instincts, which are commonly called 'nerves,' that rule the day. 'Nerves' is a dustbin term for survival instincts.

Here is an extract from a newspaper report about the recent Winter Olympics. "Our former European ice skating champion did not excel here at the Olympic Games (2010) – his unsuccessful combinations and a fall during triple axel condemned him to the 19th place. 'I do not have a good season,' he acknowledged sadly. His coach was pensive on the subject too: 'This year we trained twice as much, but *I guess it is in his head*.'"

Saying that the performer failed 'because it is in his head' is a caveman level of understanding, (sorry cavemen). You would think Freud had never lived only a few hundred kilometres from where this was said. Clearly neither the Olympic coach nor the Olympic performer understands the depth of the problem nor knows what to do about it. When we get to understand our survival instincts and how they create stress in us, it's as simple as ABC to understand.

Freeze

Hyped freeze survival instinct is about being too frightened to participate and not taking the opportunity life presents. It is about being too nervous to concentrate.

Freeze is the first survival instinct, aroused in the first ten milliseconds when danger looms. It is the idea of first seeing what is going on in an emergency, being alert, taking it all in, being quite still, and then responding appropriately. This initial response may take the form of pretending to be dead or not moving in the hope of not being noticed. Freeze also happens in the last moments of the chase, when there is literally no possibility of 'fight or flight' – the victim will experience the freeze response and will feign death by 'playing possum.'

In sport life is lived in milliseconds when swinging a bat to ball etc, and a short freeze is all it takes to miss, hit or just miss. Hesitation comes from the freeze instinct. One ice hockey player we interviewed was constantly bothered by hesitation when hitting the puck.

In life it is the situation that you miss. You freeze completely under stress and can't understand the exam question. You are silent when you need to shout "Stop!" or "No!" You go blank. You don't react quickly enough. You remain silent too long. You can't think what to say in time.

The phrases 'scared stiff,' 'frozen with fear,' '*I froze* in total *panic*,' 'rabbit caught in the headlights' are freeze instinct in action.

Many people are puzzled when they recall how they froze in the face of inescapable danger. Indeed, they are frequently filled with shame about their reaction to what happened. It happened to me (Peter) in downtown Bucharest a decade ago. My colleague had her purse strapped around her waist. As we boarded the airport bus, a gang of six big men surrounded her and took off her purse. She screamed for help; I froze and was incapacitated by it. It was over in seconds and there was practically nothing sensible I could do (as I realised later); yet I was strongly upset by my reaction.

When we are in the freeze state, research shows that our heart rate drops, we get stiffer, hold our breath, sigh a lot and breathe shallowly.
We can connect freeze to underperforming, to shrinking, a life lived in observing, being a wall flower, and becoming a victim to circumstance in the moment of action, which in turn builds into a general underperformance. In miasmatic terms we connect it to **psora**.

Honza, a former ice hockey pro and now professional coach tells this story.
When he holds a summer school of perhaps twenty potential ice hockey players, at least ten of them have natural talent. Of this naturally talented ten only three are likely to become ice hockey players because the other seven are too scared to perform in public.

Now the potential ice hockey players who come to his summer school come from very well functioning families who have paid for the best education and the summer school itself is quite expensive. Their children have had extensive sports coaching and the best that life can offer in their country. In other words these are the winners of the education system and life.

Seven out of ten of them can't achieve professional status because they're too scared. Since this is an upper echelon of society it might be that for the total population 97 people out of 100 are too scared to achieve their potential.

Let's take another example. A gymnast who trained for thirteen years to be a top-level gymnast never won any medals because she couldn't perform in public. She was too scared. And even today she is too scared of so many things that she lives in a prison of fear. Her whole career as a gymnast was stunted and unsuccessful because of her fear.

Clearly there were no tools in her training to address her fears.

One person described it this way, "a blankness, as if I were not there." "If I am criticised, or if someone is angry with me, my whole body goes numb and my mind goes blank and I can't make a decision. I am not there and I don't want to be *seen*" (a key freeze idea).

Freeze can become systemic over the generations and become a lifestyle. If you are an observer of life, or have any kind of passive job, or feel like a wallflower in any way, this may be because the stage of freeze happened at birth or soon after. Or it is a family trait you inherited, which has become deeply ingrained and you have made it into a career. We are all shaped by such inherited and early influences like it or not.

It's part of the idea behind the children's game of hide and seek and also tag. Hiding is the freeze, not wanting to be seen, and being found is about coming to terms with facing the fear. Survival instincts are a reason these games exist and endure from generation to generation.

Flight

You know the situation of a bird table filled with sunflower seeds outside the window. The birds are constantly alert to any danger and often one is on watch while the other is eating. If we move inside the room they immediately fly off. This is the flight survival instinct. It's the same with deer when they enter the garden. It's fine if we watch them without moving from inside the house. But if we move they flee immediately. With tortoises their first response when approached is to pull their head inside the shell. The snakes in the garden wriggle away as soon as they know they're spotted. These are all flight survival instinct in action.

When it comes to confronting an important official, or going for an important job interview the person in flight is unlikely to turn up to the interview. They simply run away from many opportunities in life.

A friend gave an example of a typically flighty person and told that the best time to talk with that person was driving on the motorway where the flighty other had no escape and was forced to listen and converse.

Flight is addictive and everyone's doing it.

Our modern everyday reality reflects this: Fox News is classic hyped TV. BBC TV executives have steadily hyped the programme makers over decades into speedy TV. The TV news is all hyped, rapid changing, no-depth stories, a lot of distraction in the form of adverts in between the already hurried tempo … all to get our attention. Instant TV for very hyped people constantly trying to zap away from reality. We are all living in the same goldfish bowl of speedy

addiction, thinking it's normal. What actually happens is that we run away from the deeper experience of what the news confronts us with: death, war, famine, rape etc. In fact we stay on the surface and escape from the reality of what we are seeing. We don't allow ourselves to recognize what we are seeing because it's too painful.
Sports that reflect flight are obviously sprinting and running. These are flight made into a sport.

Accumulating hyped flight survival instincts, unresolved for many generations, are now showing in the growing number of hyperactive children. In some places people call it an epidemic. These hyperactive children are now to be found globally with maybe half of them continuing into hyped adulthood.
We only have to imagine being in a chronic hyped up state to get the idea of the consequences commonly seen in children today. They ...

- are easily distracted
- miss details
- forget things
- frequently switch from one activity to another
- have difficulty focussing on one thing
- become bored easily
- have trouble sitting still
- are very impatient, can't wait

It is not just that hyperactive children are becoming common, it's that they are the worst cases of a common problem. They are the proverbial tip of the iceberg of a global agitation. In miasmatic terms we suggest flight is mostly connected with **sycosis.**

Freeze and Flight

The combination of freeze and flight survival instincts forms a prison. They are the bars of the cage that restricts our life. The bars are made of different fears. We can have a fear of snakes or spiders, the fear to perform in public, the fear to confront authority figures, the fear to say what we really think etc. These, and a thousand fears like them, condemn us to half a life. Yet the door of our self-inflicted prison is there to open: the key to the prison door is to keep focussed in the here and now, instead of allowing the survival instincts to become hyped by the traumas of the past and the fears for the future.

Freeze and flight are instincts that rule the lives of many and can also be seen in sports. How often do you hear a coach say, "His mind is not in the right place right now." "It's a mental thing," or "He's got to get his head right," or "It's between his ears?" Sometimes the coach may be right, but too often the words are just another sporting cliché to disguise the fact that the coach him/herself doesn't know what's wrong. If it is not a physical problem, it must be a mental one. Almost never considered is the possibility that it is an unconscious thing, an ancient survival instinct kicking in and causing the athlete to underperform. Although sports psychology has been introduced in practically all kinds of sports we wonder whether coach or athlete understands the real root of the problem or knows what to do about it.

"Want the ball?" yells the coach from the touchline, "Get in the box, attack it!" But his striker doesn't really want the ball and he's afraid to attack it. As the ball comes across, the striker hesitates, just a fraction, but it's enough for the defender to get across and put him off. The striker goes through the routine anyway. He jumps; the ball glances off his forehead and sails harmlessly away. It looks like a reasonable effort, but deep down the striker knows he bottled it. In great shape, there would have been no indecision. He would have lost the defender, met the ball firmly and bulleted it into the net. But that seems like a long time ago now. Of course, it's partly a mental issue. He's on a long goalless streak, so he's lost confidence. He tries to tell himself that all goal scorers experience this, that even Alan Shearer had his barren spells, but he can feel the coach and fans losing patience, and the pressure building. The greater the need to score, the greater the fear of missing. Relaxation has disappeared from his play and is replaced by fear. Unknown to the striker, his fear is trying to protect him by holding him back. There is an unconscious game being played out here: if I don't quite get there, I can make a decent effort; I won't actually miss, so it won't look so bad. Fear is pulling him back, causing him to hide and 'flee' from the very situation on the pitch that is both most stressful and productive for a striker; being one on one with the goalkeeper.

Flight and freeze are about escaping from perceived/imagined danger. They pull you back, stop you from participating, which means that you aren't ready, or relaxed enough to take the opportunity when it comes. It's about being so nervous that you can't focus clearly or react spontaneously in the moment. Thus we avoid, we hide, but all the time doing just enough to make it look as if we really are trying. And there is no easier sport to hide in than a team game, especially one played over a large area with a significant number of players. Quite often fans, coaches, and even fellow players don't notice when a particular player goes 'missing' during a game.

Fight

Competitive sports are a way of channelling the fighting instinct. International sports are a safe way of dealing with the national communal survival instincts. Fight is what you do when you are cornered and have to defend or attack to survive. There are many ways of being cornered.

A Husband and Wife Example. It's time to get ready for work, to get the kids ready for school etc. He has mislaid his toothbrush so he uses his wife's. She does not mind. He puts it down, somewhere other than where it's kept, and then knocks it on the floor. She then loses her cool; he reacts and loses his; the morning starts as a micro war. Both go into survival fight mode (attack and attack back) and both leave home before there's a chance to sort it out.

Fight is based on anger. The anger is most often turned against ourselves. We can attack ourselves for making a mistake or turn the anger apparently on others and attack them. We can blame the referee, our teammates, or our coach etc. In reality the anger always is an attack on ourselves since an attack on others is basically an inside process externalized.

Blaming ourselves is insidious. Done often enough it can turn into guilt, which is a chronic self-blame. It can turn us also into victim, where being wrong becomes a life posture and a chronic habit, leading into living half a life.

Blaming is an essential ingredient in destroying our game in sport.

Here is some of our ice hockey research.

The anger at mistakes could take many forms for example:

- venting such as swearing
- blaming the opponent or somebody else
- blaming themselves

- feeling guilty/shame – they've let the team down or feel as if committed a crime
- ruminating over the mistake while sitting on the bench
- the mistake is staying in his head and he's ruminating over it and his body cramps up and he can't be free; instead he's spastic.

The anger could last for

- seconds
- minutes
- hours
- days
- to the next game

Even if it lasts seconds it can wreck a player's next play. If it wrecks his next play it then easily builds up to destroying several plays. A whole season can be washed out this way.

In life generally anger and blame can lead to a person's losing confidence in their work or their career and failing to succeed in life. Main themes of Fight include the experience of that life is about 'us against them' and where others are viewed as 'enemies'. Hatred is a common way the fight instinct is revealed. When we use the word 'hate', whatever the context, it reveals the fight survival instinct. It's the basis of all kinds of war. If it were not already clear from the term *fight* alone, homeopathically-speaking by now it is clear that this is the terrain of the **syphilitic miasm**.

Fight is a common motivator of social affairs. There are many slogans employing the word: fighting crime, fighting oppression, fighting bureaucracy and fighting cancer. This may sound like a winning script, but in the long run it's always a loser. Crime is about long-term social exclusion. Cancer is often about internal emotional exclusion. Solving crime at the root means increasing the inclusiveness of society over generations. Fighting is about separation: them and us. Inclusion is about recognizing the similarity of us all, about unifying.

In relationship, fighting does not win long-term either; it's the route to discord, separation and divorce. Fight is linked to Type A personality and heart attacks.

When it comes to children, Fight would seem to be a factor in refusal ~ we might call them 'NO' kids, the stubborn instinct to say NO that is totally out of control in some children. That 80% of kids say No before Yes when learning to talk may indicate the prevalence of the fight instinct.

NO Kids

- lose their temper
- argue with adults
- actively defy or refuse to comply with adults' requests or rules
- deliberately annoy people
- blame others for their mistakes or misbehaviour
- are touchy or easily annoyed by others
- are angry and resentful
- are spiteful or vindictive

Fight in sports

"We had to keep fighting all the way;" "It was a real battle:" sporting clichés or sporting truths? Some team sports, like rugby or American football, reflect both the brutality and strategy of warfare. And in ice hockey, it seems that almost anything goes. Individual sports are hyped into pseudo-gladiatorial battles, in which only the strong and most skilful can survive. Federer against Nadal: winner takes all, the loser crushed. To paraphrase the revered former Liverpool manager Bill Shankly's famous quote: "Sport isn't a matter of life and death; it's more important than that." Shankly's tongue may have been lodged firmly in his cheek, but you wouldn't know it when you see what goes on the field of play. Rinus Michels, the successful Dutch soccer coach with whom Ajax won the European Cup three times in a row, said, "Soccer is war." If we see how players attack each other, often resulting in serious injuries, it seems justified to replace the term 'play' by 'war.'

From prehistoric times the fight instinct has been deeply ingrained in our psyche, particularly so in men, who are more likely to respond to emergency situations with aggressive and combative behaviour. Fight is what you do when you're in a corner, with your back against the wall, and there's nothing for it but to attack in order to survive. However, because such situations are relatively rare in modern life and sport, the fight response is generally inappropriate and only likely to undermine our ability to achieve our goals.

Unfortunately, this message is lost on many athletes, with serious consequences for both their performance and their team. Take a high-profile example from the World Cup Final of 2006. France and Italy were locked at 1 - 1 in extra time. Zinedine Zidane jogged back to position alongside the Italian defender Materazzi. They briefly exchanged words and Materazzi pulled at Zidane, who began to walk away. Materazzi continued to talk. Zidane stopped, turned back towards the Italian and head-butted him in the chest, knocking him to the ground. Zidane was sent off and France spent the rest of extra time on the defensive, before losing 5 - 3 on penalties (Zidane was a very good penalty taker). This is the modern version of the fight response, triggered not by a 'life-threatening' situation, but by an 'ego-threatening' one.

The relentlessly competitive nature of modern sport means that every challenge, every point is often seen as a mini-battle within a greater battle, and everything must be done to win. In a way individual sportsmen or teams are fighting things out for society at large. E.g. Holland against Germany is still about WWII, and it's a very healthy alternative. It allows those unresolved hurts and prejudices to be expressed in a healthy way. Consequently, there are many opportunities for a player's ego to feel threatened. Losing a vital challenge, being responsible for conceding a goal, getting a bad decision, being outplayed ... all build frustration if you let them. Sports can be a way to release the built-up tension from repressed survival instincts.

But when you give in to the fight response, you've already lost. Lost your cool and, with it, the ability to think logically and execute key skills calmly. Very few individuals are able to use anger as a galvanizing force for better performance (John McEnroe may have been one of the exceptions). The Australian cricket team led by Steve Waugh understood this and so mastered the 'art' of 'mental disintegration'; sledging the opposition batsman so that he got wound up, became angry, lost his head and, sooner rather than later, threw his wicket away.

Sex/Reproduction

The survival of the fittest, in one interpretation of Darwin, is the survival of the most reproductive. And when we watch the human race we see that reproduction is a very powerful instinct that overpowers individual preferences. Young adults are heavily involved in the mating game whether they realize it or not. Many young adults have babies before they realize the full implications of what they have done. It is done by instinct. And that instinct is the survival of the species. Typically, as in the animal world, the top sportsman gets the top fashion model so supposedly the best genes are being brought together. Einstein had another view on it. The story goes that when Marilyn Monroe suggested they should have a child that could have his brains and her looks, he replied it might not be such a good idea, as the child might also inherit his looks and her brain.

Falling in love is part of this reproduction instinct; it is a powerful force and easily addictive. Hollywood and Bollywood run on it. Falling in love blots out the reality of the other person. Love is blindingly beautifying with the survival intention of getting babies organised, before the falling in love wears out.

When sexuality gets out of control it undermines the fundamentals of life for many people and sports careers. We saw Tiger Woods struggling with this in 2010 and failing to resolve it. Meanwhile golf itself at the top level was suffering from the absence of crowds his magic brings.

The easy option appears always to be a divorce, and then to remarry the same problem. Actually divorce is very expensive and for normal earning people quite debilitating financially.

The real challenge is to solve the problem, which usually boils down to learning to relate, and there are three key points necessary – communication, communication with others, communication with self.

Fortunately this is not rocket science. Relating better produces better relationships, which increase the skill to relate better which creates even better relationships. It's the winning spiral.

When the reproduction instinct calms down, we can learn to relate better generally. We will find the ability to relate translates into better choices and less urge to rove. From this comes the ability to deepen relationships, to deepen sexuality, and to have more deeply satisfying relationships.

Soldiers in war routinely rape the population. It's a form of ethnic cleansing to intimidate the men and to impregnate all the enemy's women so that they are forced breed the enemy into their racial or social stock and so lose their culture. It's happened in Europe as recently as in the last 20 years. Rape is common in war all over the world. In Africa we have witnessed how through rape women especially bear the burden of war trauma. They lose their loved ones and on top of that are raped by those who killed their husband and kidnapped their children to become child soldiers or serve as prostitutes for the rebels.

Sex and power regularly meet. It is, after all, the alpha monkey whose semen is most wanted by the females. Politicians' sex scandals fill the tabloids and even priests and bishops abuse their power as adults to have sex with the children under their care.

Food

The survival instinct around food relates to famine and in the history of the human race there have been appalling famines. England went through 200 years of near famine in its distant history. Ireland suffered terrible famine when the potato crop failed on consecutive years. In many regions of Europe people suffered from starvation during WWII. Around the world, war and famine often go hand in hand. Whether cause by draughts, natural catastrophes or war, many families all over the world have survival memories of famine.

Feeding newborn babies by the clock is a systematic reinforcement of the food/famine instinct, as the babies are effectively starving before being fed. This really activates the survival food instinct, as do most diets.

For many people the food survival instinct is very simple to see in operation. When they feel upset, they open the fridge and stuff food in their mouths. It is thought of as normal. Very often the food survival instinct is active under the surface and driving the action.

Cigarette smoking seems to be an eating disorder: smoking is addictive, the cigarette is white with a nipple-coloured filter, is the size of a nipple, and you suck something out of it. It's so close to being on the breast that it's hard to imagine that cigarette addiction is not a feeding addiction.

Monica Seles was world number one professional tennis player and was the youngest ever champion at the French Open and went on to win nine grand slam tennis singles titles. In one game against Steffi Graf their game was called the 'greatest match of the open era'. Monica wrote an autobiography, *Getting a Grip - of my game, my body, my mind and myself*, a very good read by the way if you have a weight problem. She spends more words and pages on her concerns about food and gaining and losing weight than anything else. She mentions spiralling out of control when she makes a lot of mistakes and loses concentration and all the other things we found in our sports research. Fight, flight and fight instincts are there in the book everywhere but food is what dominates without a doubt.

Initially she was a skinny kid. But later after the terrible stabbing incident she started binge eating and gaining weight. Then food issues became a dominant part of her life, limiting and restricting and finally ending her career. She tried the harshest regimes of strictly controlled diet 24/7 with the toughest physical activity and the very top coaches and Stalinesque support. And essentially this failed. Sometimes she sabotaged it by binge eating late at night. Sometimes it didn't work and sometimes it did work but it was such hard work that she couldn't keep it up. She lost boyfriends over her weight. All she needed was one tactless remark when she was trying her hardest and the relationship was over. And invariably this happened. Her career illustrates just how important survival instincts around food are.

What is really interesting is that in the end of her career she finally gave up all attempts to forcefully control her weight and figured out how to do it all by herself in a less stressed way. She says she made *a few big changes* in her thinking, which affected some *deep-seated behaviour (i.e. food survival issues)*. So after something like a ten-year struggle she managed to get to grips in some way with her food survival issues. She stopped classifying food as allowed or forbidden. She embraced moderation and banished absolutes. She waited after she had eaten a little to see if she needed any more. It was hard for her especially in America where every portion is huge compared with other countries like Japan where virtually nobody is fat and all the portions are small. She learned to live her life more fully by choosing less. We can say that the USA in particular has huge food survival issues from its portion sizes.

If we look at food issues

- People eat too quickly and don't give the body time to send a message that they've had enough (that's hyped survival flight); eating more slowly and waiting allows for the natural feedback to occur
- People eat over large portions (although this may differ from one culture to the other)
- Any number of very tough dietary and exercise regimes are not sustainable
- Any dietary regime without a comparable exercise regime is probably doomed to fail or simply won't work
- Urban life, desk jobs and motorised transport have resulted in a huge decline in natural physical exercise
- The global food market with (for the countries battling with overweight) abundant supplies all year through has replaced the normal cycle of adding weight in summer and losing weight from natural fasting in winter.
- Overweight has entered the world agenda as a major issue. It seems like a combination of issues including the survival instincts: food/famine + flight/eat when anxious + fast foods + no exercise.

Developing effective strategies on how to deal with the survival instincts to improve the results of homeopathic treatment is one of the possible future developments we are currently working on.

The Process of Failure

We carried out research with ice hockey players about what the issues were that impeded their performance and success. We later found this confirmed in all the one hundred or so athletes we studied.

Although they all expressed it in different ways, boiled down to its essence there were three things concerning failure:

- Being angry in various ways at making mistakes
- Fear and anxiety and anticipation about the next action
- Loss of confidence as a consequence of these two

What is being described here is a vicious spiral to failure.
In the vicious cycle failure leads to self-blame which damages confidence, which leads to anxiety, which leads to failure, which leads to self-blame, which further damages confidence, which makes anxiety higher and failure more likely.

This is the cycle that affects us all and sorts out the winners from the losers in life. What is more, once you understand it, you have the possibility of breaking the cycle.

These cycles are incredibly simple to understand. Tennis players get it. Students facing exams get it. It's completely obvious. They affect us all and sort out the winners from the losers in sports and life generally.

Our conclusion is that the failure spiral *predominates everywhere*. (See Fig. 2)

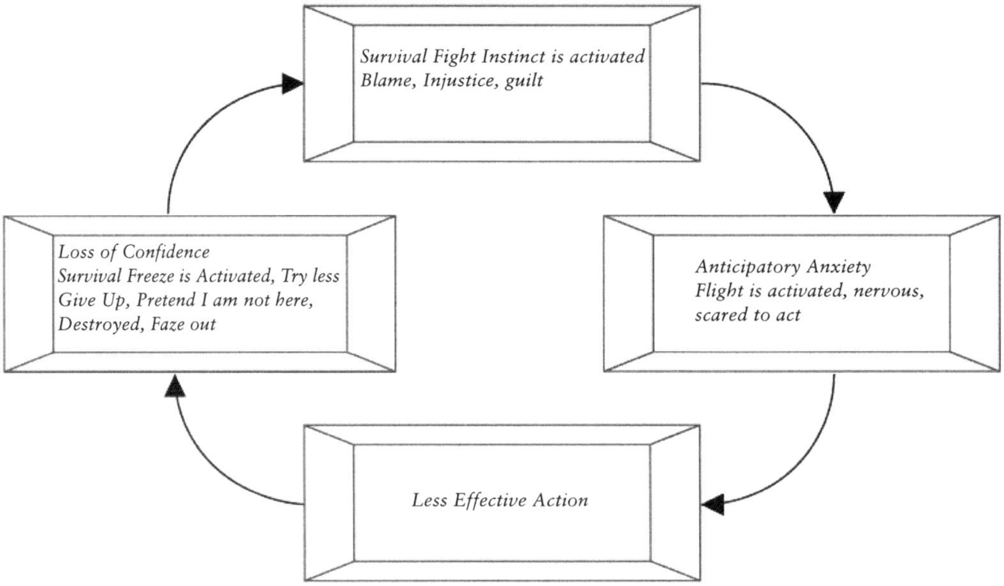

Fig. 2

This failure survival cycle is critical to understanding how human beings fail. It is critical in understanding the difference between the rich and the poor, between the relatively well-functioning members of society and the under-functioning members of society. It explains why some people underperform and get sick and live many years less than those who perform well.

Restrictive Beliefs

If we examine ourselves closely while thinking in the present, what we experience is that whenever we decide an action – to speak, to move, to run, etc. – alongside it occurs an old, limiting, restrictive thought or emotion that is inappropriate and that belongs to history.

You can try this out for yourself. You can conduct this thought experiment right now and verify exactly what is being said here.

- Think about anything that you would like to do, or could never do, or that is really challenging for you – hang gliding, hair extensions, keeping a snake, spider or rat as a pet, tattoos, taking final exams, deep sea diving, caving, confronting the boss, teacher or official, etc.
- Think about doing it and look at what the feeling or thought is that comes with it.
- Write it down.
- Now the question is, does that feeling or thought have any relevance to the action you are proposing to take?

If you look closely, you should see that the feeling is entirely irrelevant (it may feel like the truth but look harder, it's not), but at the same time our reaction is totally compulsive and beyond our ability to control.
That is the problem.

If for example, you are a sports sprinter ready to leave the starting blocks in a race but you are nervous, which you think is part of you, it's less likely you're going to win the race, than someone without this hang-up.
If again you are a sports sprinter, and you are more interested in the design on your fingernails and how you look to males, you could easily be distracted at the beginning of the race.

If you look closely:
- the feeling or thought that you experience has been handed down to you from one of your parents or someone else very close.
- it's not just the exception, it's the rule.

If you take a simple problem, such as in the thought experiment above, you quickly get back to unconscious memories belonging to a previous generation inherited down the family line.

It really is the rule and not an exception.

- If you don't believe you have inherited any one of your common restrictive thoughts, think again of a challenging situation for you.
- Now ask yourself which of your parents also has that?
- You must surely know this.
- Then ask them where they got it from if you don't know this already.
- So then go to the oldest person alive in your family and actually ask them where they got this (limiting) thought pattern?

By this method you can trace any one restrictive thought back three or four or five generations.
If you don't believe this is a general process try another common challenging thought.
You will discover that the first instance is not an isolated example.
You will discover that you are using many hand-me-down restrictive thought patterns going back into the history of your family, at least a hundred years.
You will start to wonder what is really you! You may find there is nothing you tend to identify with that given the test is really you! What freedom!

Old grandmothers have been studied who can remember the stories told by their grandmothers when they sat on their grandmothers' knees as children. By this method, they can get back 200 years, and they discovered exactly the same thing. Restrictive thoughts are being passed down ten generations.

It's not just you and me. Everybody is using a set of hand-me-down negative thought patterns in response to everyday activities. Yet we think this is our personality, who we are. We think it is normal. However, these thought patterns have little to do with us:
they are just a lot of old history lessons we are carrying around.

Obviously you've got lots of good things as hand-me-downs too, like life itself, and the problem is to sort out which ones
- you want
- you don't need
- are positive handicaps to living a successful life.

But as with the negative patterns, the positive ones also say nothing about you, and to identify with those is just as limiting.

This is a major problem of the human race right now. It does not affect solely athletes. It affects everybody and limits the ability of the human race to function well. You could say that the human race has become a mental case!

Training and coaching easily deal with the superficial effects. But gradually as we develop, we push our personal inner limits harder and run into the deeper obstacles in our minds, and these are very hard to shift. This situation is general. Automatically, by making themselves successful in sports, athletes run into their personal limiting thought-history.
Once that happens it becomes very hard work. It can limit their whole careers – the English tennis player Tim Henman was a case in point, always tensing up when it really mattered. This makes the difference between winners and losers in sport and between top sports people and the average sports person.

We suggest that all limiting beliefs are really extensions of our survival instincts. For example, if we believe winning is hopeless, behind this is a freeze or flight instinct.

Background information:
Some of the cutting edge pioneers in explaining clearly this field of human behaviour and brain science are:

- Bruce Lipton - www.brucelipton.com
- Chilton Pearce - www.conferenceworks.com/speakers/joseph_pearce_bio.html
- Caroline Myss - www.myss.com
- Byron Katie - www.thework.com
- Stephen Covey - www.franklincovey.com
- Dawson Church - www.dawsonchurch.com
- Eckhart Tolle - www.eckharttolle.com

They mostly if not all agree that limiting, restrictive thoughts that we tend to believe are true are the number one problem of the human race right now.

APPENDIX 5: List of Available PC Resonances

- Epidemic Diseases & Miasms
- First Aid
- Traumas
- Toxins
- Chronic Diseases
- Behavioural issues
- Tonics

Epidemic Diseases & Miasms

AIDS - Female Africa – PC1AF
AIDS - Male Africa – PC1AM
AIDS in the West – PC1HW
Anthrax – PC2120k
Babesiosis
(Lyme Disease Complex) – PC1024b
Barmah Forest Virus & Ross River Virus – PC1001a
Barmah Forest Virus – PC1003c
Bartonellosis (Cat-scratch Disease) – PC540s
Bilharzia – PC132d
Bird Flu – PC202k
Borreliosis (Lyme Disease) – PC232n
Borreliosis (Lyme Disease Complex) – PC1024b
Botulism – PC135g
Bubonic Plague – PC131c
Candida – PC141d
Chagas Disease – PC148k
Chlamydia – PC144g
Cholera – PC2141p
Cigoe flea Tunga Penetrans – PC512n
Coxsackie A and B – PC2142q
Dengue Fever – PC153g
Diarrhoea in infants and children in Africa – PC152f
Diphtheria – PC408h
Dys-Co - Shigella – PC155j
Epidermolysis Bullosa – PC161f
Epstein Barr (mononucleosis infectiosa) – PC2162r
Erlichiosis (Lymes Disease Complex) – PC1024b
Escherichia Coli – PC2160p
Foot and Mouth Disease Cattle – PC173j
Gaertner - Salmonella enteritidis – PC184k
Gonorrhoea – PC180g
Guinea Worm – PC183j
Hepatitis (all types) – PC191i
Hepatitis A, acute, chronic, ailments since – PC198n
Hepatitis B acute, chronic, ailments since – PC199p
Hepatitis C acute, chronic, ailments since – PC2190q
HIV/AIDS - Female Africa - PC1AF
HIV/AIDS - Male Africa - PC1AM
AIDS in the West – PC1HW
Influenzas – *see First Aid*
Jiggers/Chigoe flea/Tunga Penetrans – PC512n
Leprosy – PC230l
Lyme Disease – PC232n
Lyme Disease Complex (Borreliosis +Babesiosis+Erlichiosis) – PC1024b
Malaria falciparum – PC1019w
Malaria vivax – PC1020x
Malaria general – PC240m

Meningitis – PC249v
Morgan – PC2240w
Neisseria Mucosa -Sycotic Co – PC299b
Onchoceriasis (River Blindness) – PC253r
Pneumonia, Streptococcus – PC2292e
Poliomyelitis – PC262r
Proteus Vulgaris – PC268x
Rabies – PC282t
Reiter's Disease – PC409j
River Blindness – PC253r
Ross River Virus & Barmah Forest Virus – PC1001a
Ross River Virus – PC1002b
Scabies – PC290s
Shigella dysentreriae (Dys Co) – PC155j
Sleeping Sickness (Trypanosomiasis) – PC321g
Smallpox – PC291t
Staphylococcus aureus – PC2291d
Streptococcus pneumoniae – PC2292e
Streptococcus pyrogenes – PC410k
Sycotic Co - Neisseria Mucosa – PC299b
Syphilis – PC293v
Tetanus – PC301u
Thread Worms – PC2342w
Toxoplasmosis – PC303w
Trypanosomiasis African (sleeping sickness) – PC321g
Tuberculosis – PC300t
Tunga Penetrans/Chigoe Flea/Female Jiggers – PC512n
Typhoid – PC302v
Typhus – PC313h
Worms, guinea – PC183j
Worms, thread – PC2342w
Yellow Fever – PC350y

First Aid

Abscesses – PC401a
Adhesions, scar tissue – PC297z
Air Travel, jet lag – PC406f
Bird flu (H5N1) – PC202k
Bites, Dog (Rabies) – PC282t
Bites, Insect – PC1025c
Bites, Snake – PC295x
Boils, abscesses, carbuncles – PC401a
Broken Bones, to speed mending – PC403c
Burn from fire, hot oil, hot water, acid etc – PC10b
Carbuncles – PC401a
Caries/Cavities (Tooth Decay) – PC545x
Cat-scratch Disease Bartonellosis – PC540s
Common Cold – PC2143r
Dandruff – PC451f
Dog Bite (Rabies) – PC282t
Fungal Infections (between toes/fingers, under nails etc) – PC452g
Gingivitis – PC541t
Haemorrhoids – PC457m
Herpes from Chicken Pox – PC197k
Herpes Type 1&2 – PC192j
Human Papilloma Virus (warts) – PC193k
Chicken Pox – PC197k
Influenza All (H1N1, H2N2, H3N2, H5N1, H7N7, H1N2 – PC1023a
Influenza Bird (H5N1) – PC202k
Influenza Vaccination Toxic Effects – PC504d
Influenza Spanish (H1N1) – PC200i
Influenza Swine (H1N2) – PC579e
Injury to spinal cord – PC405e
Injury – PC201j
Insect Bite – PC1025c
Jet Lag – PC406f
Laryngitis of speakers and singers – PC453h
Measles – PC2241x
Mononucleosis infectiosa – PC2162r
Mumps – PC2242y
Periodontitis – PC542u
Piles/Haemorrhoids – PC457m
Rubella – PC284v
Scar Tissue – PC297z
Spinal Cord Injury – PC405e
Swine Flu (H1N2) – PC579e
Tooth Decay (Caries/Cavities) – PC545x
Travel Sickness - general – PC407g
Varicose veins, piles – PC457m
Varrucas – PC193k
Warts and Varrucas (HPV) – PC193k
Whooping Cough – PC341w
Worms Parasitic general – PC264t
Wounds, see Injury, Bites, Burn

Traumas

Abortion Trauma – PC524a
Abuse Trauma – PC310e
Adoption Trauma – PC309d
Birth Trauma – PC308c
Caesarean birth trauma – PC314h
Female Circumcision Trauma – PC1013n
Genocide and War Trauma (PTSD) – PC304x
Incest trauma – PC459p
Learning Trauma – PC527d
Miscarriage Trauma – PC1017t
Missing Twin Syndrome Trauma (died and maybe absorbed in pregnancy) – PC1006e
Nagasaki and Hiroshima Atomic Trauma – PC307b
Natural Catastrophe Trauma (PTSD) – PC305z
Rape and Rape Stigma Trauma – PC435p
Shock Trauma – PC11c
Unburied Relatives Trauma – PC315k
War Trauma – PC304x

Toxins

Antibiotics (streptomycetaceae) – PC2121m
ARVs/ HAART Toxins (detox) – PC501a
Chernobyl Radiation Toxicity and Illnesses – PC1012m
Cortisone toxicity and allergy – PC147j
Detox antibiotics (streptomycetaceae) – PC2121m
Detox HAART/ARVs – PC501a
Detox, Penicillin – PC261q
Detox, Vaccination (all) – PC320v
Dog Bite (Rabies) – PC282t
Environmental Toxins – PC168m
Fish Allergy – PC419v
Food poisoning – PC404d
Gluten intolerance – PC503c
HAART toxins – PC501a
Histamine – PC195m
Influenza Vaccination Toxic Effects – PC504d
Insect Bite – PC1025c
Nut Allergy – PC420w
Penicillin allergy and toxicity – PC261q
Snake bite – PC295x
Vaccination Detox – PC320v

Chronic Diseases

Acne (cystic, nodular) – PC125f
Acromegaly – PC129j
Alopecia – PC1016s
Alzheimer's disease – PC121b
Anklyosing Spondylitis – PC128i
Anorexia – PC126g
Aorta Sclerosis and Stenosis – PC1011k
Arthritis Psoriatica – PC269y
Arthritis – PC123d
Arthrosis – PC2122n
Asthma and Atopic Eczema together – PC160e
Asthma – PC447b
Astrocytomas – 511m
Bechterev Disease – PC130k
Blood Pressure High – PC423z
Blood Pressure Low – PC424a
Cancer - Cervix – PC412n
Cancer - Colon – PC2148g
Cancer - Hodgkin's – PC414q
Cancer - Kahler's – PC413p
Cancer - Larynx – PC416s
Cancer - Leukemia – PC231m
Cancer - Leukemia, Acute Lymphoblastic – PC518u
Cancer - Leukemia, Acute Myelocytic – PC519v
Cancer - Leukemia, Chronic Lymphocytic – PC520w
Cancer - Leukemia, Chronic Myelocytic – PC521x
Cancer - Lung – PC2147f
Cancer - Mamma – PC2145d
Cancer - Ovarian – PC514q
Cancer - Pancreatic – PC515r
Cancer - Papillary Thyroid Carcinoma – PC538q
Cancer - Prostate – PC2149h
Cancer - Stomach – PC2150k
Cancer - Testicular – PC522y
Cancer - Uterus – PC2146e
Cancer, general, inherited disposition – PC140c

Celiac Disease – PC417t
Cholesterol, raised levels – PC449d
Chronic Fatigue Syndrome (CFS/ME) – PC142e
Cirrhosis of the liver from alcoholism – PC2144s
Colitis ulcerosa – PC331v
Complex Regional Pain Syndrome (CRPS) – PC143f
Congenital Heart Defects – PC146i
Creutzfeldt-Jacob Disease – PC418u
Crohn's Disease – PC149m
Cystitis (Interstitial) – PC145h
Deep Vein Thrombosis – PC523z
Delayed Growth – PC1021y
Dementia (non specific) – PC156k
Diabetes Type 1 – PC157m
Diabetes Type 2 – PC158n
Diabetes Types 1&2 – PC150d
Diverticulitis – PC529f
Down Syndrome – PC151e
Duodenal Ulcer – PC411m
Eczema (Atopic) & Asthma together – PC160e
Eczema – PC448c
Emphysema – PC166k
Epilepsy in Africa – PC162g
Extra Systole – PC550c
Eye Defects in Africa in old age – PC163h
Fibromyalgia – PC172h
Gout – PC181h
Haemophilia – PC190h
Hair Loss – PC1016s
Hallervorden-Spatz Syndrome – PC570y
Hernia (all) – PC1014p
Huntington's Disease – PC502b
Hypercholesteromia – PC449d
Hypertension – PC423z
Hypotension – PC424a
Infertility – PC171g
Kyphosis – PC422y
Leukaemia – PC231m
Leukemia, Acute Lymphoblastic – PC518u
Leukemia, Acute Myelocytic – PC519v
Leukemia, Chronic Lymphocytic – PC520w
Leukemia, Chronic Myelocytic – PC521x
Low Blood Pressure – PC424a
Lupus (SLE) – PC233o
Marfan's Syndrome – PC248u
ME/CFS – PC142e
Meniere's Disease – PC247t
Menopause Problems in Africa – PC246s
Metabolic Disorder, Syndrome X – PC539r
Migraine – PC241n
Motor Neurone Disease – PC242o
Multiple Sclerosis – PC243p
Myasthenia Gravis – PC245r
Myopathies – PC244q
Nocturnal enuresis in children – PC445z
Non-Hodgkin's Lymphoma – PC516s
Noonam Syndrome – PC400n
Osteoarthritis – PC252q
Osteoporosis – PC251p
Parkinson's – PC260p
Pectus Excavatum – PC544w
Peripheral Neuropathy – PC575d
Post Vaccination Syndrome – PC320v
Postpolio Syndrom – PC517t
Psoriasis – PC263s
Psoriatic Arthritis – PC269y
Raynaud's Disease – PC454j
Rheumatoid Arthritis – PC281s
Sarcoidosis – PC546y
Sclerodrema including Crest – PC421x
Scoliosis, kyphopsis – PC422y
Schizophrenia Paranoid – PC1018v
Schizophrenia – PC294w
Sjøgren's syndrome – PC1022z
SLE – PC233o
Spina Bifida – PC292u
Stomach Ulcer – PC298a
Thrombosis Deep Vein – PC523z
Tinnitus – PC456k
Tourette Syndrom – PC525b
Ulcerative colitis – PC331v
Ulcerative Diseases (All) – PC330u
Ulcers, duodenal – PC411m
Ulcers, Stomach, gastric – PC298a
Varicocele – PC543v
Vitiligo – PC513p
Wegener's Granulomatosis – PC340v

Behavioural Issues

Alcoholism – PC120a
Anorexia – PC126g
Autism spectrum – PC124e
Bed Wetting in children – PC445z
Bulimia – PC133e
Chronic Blaming Alternating
With Hopelessness – PC533j
Depression, chronic, long lasting – PC427d
Dyslexia & Dysgraphia – PC526c
Eating Disorders (All) – PC167l
Impotency – PC437r
Obesity due to famine reflex – PC170f
Paranoid Schizophrenia – PC1018v
Schizophrenia – PC294w
Smoking, to reduce habit – PC430h

Tonics

Adrenal tonic – PC376f
Ear & Hearing Defects in Africa in old age – PC164i
Eye Defects in Africa in old age – PC163h
Kwashiorkor, Marasmus – PC220k
Loss of sense of taste and smell in old age – PC444y
Marasmus – PC220k
Ovaries Tonic – PC378h
Pancreas Tonic – PC375e
Pineal Tonic – PC372c
Pituitary/anterior Tonic – PC370a
Pituitary/posterior Tonic – PC371b
Prostate Defects in Africa in old age – PC267w
Smell sense, loss of in old age – PC444y
Taste Loss of in old age – PC444y
Testicles, tonic – PC377g
Thymus Tonic – PC374d
Thyriod Tonic – PC373d

This list will be regularly updated at www.vitalremedies.com

Index of Indications

Here we include conditions discussed in case histories or otherwise in this book. In appendix 5 many more indications for which PC Resonances are available have been listed.